KU-511-406

TELEPEN
6 00 159905 X

A. M. DALE

COLLECTED PAPERS

A. M. DALE

COLLECTED PAPERS

CAMBRIDGE
AT THE UNIVERSITY PRESS
1969

Published by the Syndics of the Cambridge University Press
Bentley House, 200 Euston Road, London N.W.1
American Branch: 32 East 57th Street, New York, N.Y.10022

Library of Congress Catalogue Card Number: 69–10574
Standard Book Number: 521 04763 3

Printed in Great Britain
at the University Printing House, Cambridge
(Brooke Crutchley, University Printer)

CONTENTS

Preface *page* vii

Miss A. M. Dale ix

PUBLISHED PAPERS

1 Lyrical Clausulae in Sophocles, from *Greek Poetry and Life* (1936), pp. 181–205 1

2 Metrical Observations on Aesch. *Pers.* 922–1001, from *C.Q.* XXXI (1937), 106–10 25

3 Stasimon and Hyporcheme, from *Eranos* XLVIII (1950), 14–20 34

4 The Metrical Units of Greek Lyric Verse, I, from *C.Q.* XLIV (1950), 138–48 41

5 The Metrical Units of Greek Lyric Verse, II, from *C.Q.* I (1951), 20–30 61

6 The Metrical Units of Greek Lyric Verse, III, from *C.Q.* I (1951), 119–29 80

7 Κισσύβιον, from *C.R.* II (1952), 129–32 98

8 An interpretation of Aristophanes, *Vesp.* 136–210 and its consequences for the stage of Aristophanes, from *J.H.S.* LXXVII (1957), 205–11 103

9 Seen and Unseen on the Greek Stage, from *W.S.* LXIX (1956), 96–106 119

10 Resolutions in the Trochaic Tetrameter, from *Glotta* XXXVII (1958), 102–5 130

11 The Hoopoe's Song, from *C.R.* IX (1959), 199–200 135

12 The Transformation of Io, Ox. Pap. XXIII, 2369, from *C.R.* X (1960), 194–5 137

13 Ethos and Dianoia: 'Character' and 'Thought' in Aristotle's *Poetics*, from *AUMLA*, XI (1959), 3–16 139

14 Words, Music and Dance, Inaugural Lecture, 1960 *page* 156

15 A Heroic End, from *B.I.C.S.* VIII (1961), 47–8 170

16 Stichos and Stanza, from *C.Q.* XIII (1963), 46–50 173

17 Note on Euripides, *Helena* 1441–50, from *Maia*, XV (1963), 310–13 180

18 Observations on Dactylic, from *W.S.* LXXVII (1964), 15–36 185

19 The Chorus in the Action of Greek Tragedy, from *Classical Drama and its Influence* (1965), pp. 17–27 210

20 The *Electra* of Sophocles, from *For Service to Classical Studies* (1966), pp. 71–7 (expanded for a lecture in Stanford) 221

UNPUBLISHED PAPERS

21 Speech-rhythm, Verse-rhythm and Song 230

22 Expressive Rhythm in the Lyrics of Greek Drama 248

23 Interior Scenes and Illusion in Greek Drama 259

24 The Creation of Dramatic Characters 272

25 Old Comedy: The *Acharnians* of Aristophanes 281

Bibliography 295

Index Locorum 297

General Index 303

PREFACE

The published papers are put first. The others are included, even where, as sometimes, they overlap the published papers, partly because they all contain something new, partly because, as lectures, they sometimes preserve the warmth and immediacy of delivery. Nos. 21 and 25 are dated to 1959. Nos. 23 and 24 are earlier versions of nos. 13 and 9 and were given to branches of the Classical Association soon after the war, and no. 22 belongs to the same period.

Acknowledgements are due to the editors of the publications from which the papers are taken. Those papers which first appeared in the *Classical Quarterly* and *Classical Review* are reproduced with the concurrence of the Classical Journals Board, The Clarendon Press, Oxford. Acknowledgement is also made to the Editor of *The Times* for permission to reproduce the obituary notice on pp. ix–x. Miss Clare Campbell assisted in the reading of the proofs and also compiled the index. We are all very grateful to the Press both for welcoming this project in the first instance, and for the care they have taken in preparing the copy for publication.

T. B. L. WEBSTER

January 1969 E. G. TURNER

MISS A. M. DALE

[Obituary notice from *The Times*, 7 February 1967]

Miss A. M. Dale (Mrs T. B. L. Webster), Professor Emeritus in Greek in the University of London since 1963, died on Saturday, February 4, 1967, at the age of 66. She was the foremost living authority on Ancient Greek metre, and a rare spirit.

Born in Sheffield in 1901, she studied at Somerville College, Oxford, and in the Universities of Vienna and of Lund, and then taught in Oxford as fellow and tutor of Lady Margaret Hall until the war in 1939 interrupted normal routines, and took her into work at the Foreign Office. As a consequence of her marriage in 1944 to Professor T. B. L. Webster, she moved after the war to Manchester, and then to London. In 1952 she became Reader in Classics in Birkbeck College, and in 1959 was made Professor, a post from which she retired in 1963.

In 1948 her book *The Lyric Metres of Greek Drama* revealed her outstanding feeling for the way poets express themselves, and their choice of rhythms to do so. She rebelled against the currently accepted analysis of ancient lyric poetry into arbitrary units labelled 'feet' by metricians, and insisted on the need to look for those groups of rhythmic units which gave life, movement, and shape to the ideas and emotions they were intended to convey. The influence of this book and of subsequent articles (especially a series in the *Classical Quarterly* during 1950 and 1951) has been enormous, and has spread widely an appreciation of the variety and effectiveness of rhythm developed by the ancient poets.

Miss Dale had a flawless sense of pulse, and a matchless sensitivity to shades of emotion and nuances of language. Her wonderfully lucid mind was at the service of colleagues troubled by a crux of interpretation, or the hunt for a parallel expression, and they rarely came away unsatisfied. A trenchant style and vigorous delivery made any paper or lecture by her an event. Her inaugural lecture at Birkbeck College in 1960 on 'Words, Music and Dance' opened deliciously with a passage from Gilbert and Sullivan, and communicated to its hearers a passionate feeling for the miraculous wholeness of the three aspects of art alluded to in its title. As an interpreter of Greek tragedy Miss Dale was no less successful, as shown in her commentaries on Euripides' 'Alcestis' (1954) and 'Helena' (which appeared only in January 1967). She had an inborn sympathy with Euripides as artist and dramatist as well as a scholar's feeling for the meaning and arrangement of words.

Her later work was completed by an heroic effort of will against the handicap of increasing ill-health stoically borne. Her friends remember a woman of lively sympathies who took pleasure in many forms of the contemporary arts, was an expert on Dorothy Sayers as well as Benjamin Britten, and especially enjoyed string quartets and 'lieder' singing. No trouble was too great for her to take on behalf of her students, and her pupils at Birkbeck College had the warmest regard for her.

Miss Dale was elected a Fellow of the British Academy in 1957 and an honorary Fellow of Somerville College, Oxford, in 1962.

E. G. T.

1

LYRICAL CLAUSULAE IN SOPHOCLES

The close of a lyric stanza, which is left echoing on the ear and so has an important part to play in keeping the impression of the rhythmical whole distinct and intelligible, is treated by the Greek dramatic poets as a problem with a great variety of solutions. A comparative study of their technique is profitable only within certain limits. Thus, for instance, the relatively high degree of uniformity in the metres of most of the choral lyrics of comedy restricts the choice of clausula and the intricacy of its relation to the rest of the stanza. Again, Aeschylus, especially in his earlier plays, composes many systems which are a series of short periods in responsion—not stanzas so much as the elements of stanzas—and some of these periods simply stop; it would be arbitrary to isolate the last colon here and call it a clausula. Nor would a formal classification of clausular rhythms in the drama be likely to lead to any very enlightening conclusions as to the practice of an individual poet; the multiplicity of phenomena is too great, especially in Sophocles and Euripides. Nevertheless, in the relation between the final clausula and those phrases earlier in the stanza where a metrical period comes to a close, it seems possible to formulate a distinctively Sophoclean technique; and the examination of this throws some light on the division into cola, and in one or two cases perhaps even on the text itself.

Here obviously great caution is necessary. Clausulae, like the rest of the metrical elements in a lyric, are often welded into preceding cola so that it is difficult to say precisely where they begin; and again division is sometimes merely an academic question, and there is nothing to be gained or inferred by adding syllables here and taking them off there. But it often happens that the clausula is easier to isolate than other phrases, and the responsion of strophe and antistrophe is here a valuable guide. It is the assumption of this article that, for all our ignorance of the sound of Greek lyric and its relation to music and dance, rhythm is more likely to have been used, at any rate by Sophocles, to bring out the meaning of a passage than as a superimposed system of scansion related perhaps to the music but overriding the natural rhetorical effect. Clearly this is not a principle of detail, such as can be applied indiscriminately to each sentence of a lyric; but if, for instance, both strophe and antistrophe show a clear grammatical pause at the same place, particularly when this cuts off one phrase at the end, a division into metrical units which coincides with this pause is *a priori* more probable than one which ignores it. Conversely, the absence of diaeresis before what is normally a separable metrical unit may mean that here the clausula proper is of greater extent, as for instance in Aesch. *Ag.* 452–5 = 471–4, where the correct formula is not 2 pherecrateans, glyconic, pherecratean, but 2 pherecrateans+priapean.[1] This may be as important a principle as the absence of regular diaeresis in the paroemiac close of anapaests. And though it is sometimes impossible to determine whether a particular phrase is trochaic or iambic, choriambic or ionic, it is still important to try to establish such distinctions by correct division wherever there appears to be reasonable ground to go upon, since there is good evidence that the rhythmical movement of these feet was in fact different.

Where textual questions are involved, metrical criteria, outside certain well-established limits, are notoriously unsafe, since the range of phenomena is often too narrow to warrant general conclusions, and the interpretation of them is controversial. Admittedly, arguments based on metrical analogy would be valueless if they conflicted with a well-authenticated text, but where counsels have been divided and certainty is unattainable it is of interest to consider the metrical argument along with the rest and see which line of emendation is supported by all parallel cases among Sophoclean clausulae.

If we consider the clausula in relation to the rest of the stanza, one characteristic that emerges as peculiar to Sophocles is his extreme care to avoid any monotony of repetitive effect. There are very few cases where the final clausula repeats an earlier period-close within

[1] Cf. Wilamowitz, *Griech. Vers.* p. 457.

the stanza, nor are final clausulae repeated from one pair of strophes to the next. This is in marked contrast to the practice of Euripides. To take first of all glyconic systems, which are among the most homogeneous in both authors and are usually restricted to the simplest kinds of catalectic clausula: in Soph. *Phil.* 169 ff. the clausula, a pherecratean, repeats the fourth phrase, and this is the only case of repetition in this metre in the extant plays. In *Phil.* 1081–1100, a passage with an unusually uniform movement, the changes are rung on all the regular glyconic clausulae, – – – ∪ ∪ – – (pher.), – – – ∪ ∪ – ∪ – – (hipponactean), ∪ – ∪ – ∪ – – (iamb. dim. cat.) and at the end – ∪ ∪ – ∪ – – (chor. dim. cat.). *O.C.* 192–206 has similar variations. A fair case for comparison would be Eur. *Phoen.* 202 ff., which has roughly the same degree of uniformity in general movement; the pherecratean clausula is a precise echo of two earlier period-closes in strophe and antistrophe and again in the epode; nine repetitions in all within the compass of forty-eight lines.[1] There are passages in Euripides where this metre is prolonged over a series of strophes and refrains of a special hieratic character; here the pherecratean returns again and again, as ordinary metrical unit, as period-close, and as final clausula. Such are the famous cult-hymn celebrating the exploits of Heracles,[2] and the hymn of the Bacchae,[3] which resembles the ἐφύμνια of the *Agamemnon*[4] and may well be a reminiscence of the Aeschylean *Lycurgeia*. This type of lyric nowhere occurs in the extant plays of Sophocles, so that there is no proper basis for comparison; but it is worth noting that of the long κομμοί in the two *Electras* the Euripidean[5] achieves its plangent effect by an extraordinary metrical monotony largely due to the continually recurring pherecratean catalexis, whereas Sophocles in a lyric[6] of very varied movement returns indeed several times to an iambic form of close, but only once repeats, in a final clausula, l. 172,

[1] Cf. in the same metre Eur. *Andr.* 501 ff., *Supp.* 990 ff., *I.A.* 164 ff.

[2] *H.F.* 348–441.

[3] *Bacch.* 862–911.

[4] In the chorus beginning l. 355, cf. Aesch. *Supp.* 625 ff.

[5] ll. 112–212.

[6] ll. 121–250.

a form of trimeter ⏑ – – – ⏑ – ⏑ – – which occurs as a mid-verse close in the previous pair of strophes, l. 127.[1]

The same difference is noticeable in their use of other common types of clausula. The ithyphallic[2] close of Eur. *Andr.* 125 is repeated from three earlier phrases in the strophe and appears again at the close of the next pair: it recurs over and over again in *Phoen.* 1018–66. It is common enough in Sophocles in simple and in elaborate systems, but nowhere does a clausula of this form repeat an earlier phrase from the stanza nor is it ever used to end successive strophes in the same chorus. The same applies to his use of the various forms of reizianum, one of which Euripides repeats twelve times, including the three clausulae, in *Ion* 453–509. Again, just as in dimeters ⏑ – ⏑ – ⏑ – – and – ⏑ ⏑ – ⏑ – – are used as minor variations on the equivalent pherecratean, so a trimetric clausula

θυμοῦ τ' Ἀτρείδαις μεγάλων τε νεικέων[3]
– – ⏑ – – ⏑ ⏑ – ⏑ – –

picks up without repeating the equivalent phalaecean five lines back

θοᾶν ὠκυάλων νεῶν, ὅτ' Αἴας
⏑ – – ⏑ ⏑ – ⏑ – ⏑ – –

There is no parallel in Sophocles to the repetitive effect of Eur. *Supp.* 1123 ff., where the similar clausula

εὐδοκίμων δήποτ' ἐν Μυκήναις
– ⏑ ⏑ – – ⏑ – ⏑ – –

has its exact counterpart in the middle of the verse and again at the close of the next pair, each time following a full iambic trimeter.

The extent of Aeschylean lyric available for comparison is

[1] ll. 249–50 should probably be taken as a tetrameter (so Bruhn and Schroeder) rather than as reiz. + trim.

[2] The name is used as a convenient label for the phrase – ⏑ – ⏑ – – without prejudice to the question whether in any particular instance it is iambic or trochaic.

[3] *Aj.* 718.

limited,[1] and the form which his repetitions more often take is that the same rhythm closes successive stanzas: in *Ag.* 681 ff. a pherecratean (or priapean) ends three pairs running and appears also in mid-verse, and *Supp.* 524 ff. has – ⏑ ⏑ – ⏑ – – at the close of four pairs besides containing several trimeters ending in the same phrase.[2] But this is rather a symptom of the more homogeneous character of many of Aeschylus' metrical systems than significant for his use of clausular rhythm in particular. The point which is noteworthy for the Sophoclean lyric is that in no stanza does the final clausula repeat more than one earlier 'close',[3] and that the repetition of even one is exceptional, while epodes and consecutive pairs of strophes within the same system always vary their clausulae.

The exceptions are worth noting. But first it should be made clear that there are a few lyrics which cannot be said to have a clausula properly speaking at all—some of those, for instance, which consist largely of dochmiacs or dochmiacs mixed with iambic trimeters. Neither the acatalectic trimeter nor the dochmiac pair which so often ends such a series is here a detachable clausular rhythm; it is significant that there is the same freedom of responsion in such final dochmiacs as in any others. Again, *O.T.* 158 is hardly so much an 'adonean' clausula as the end of a dactylic πνῖγος, just as *O.T.* 511 (not a repetition) is the end of an ionic πνῖγος.[4] Of clausulae proper the exceptions are, besides *Phil.* 179 already mentioned: *Aj.* 232, where βοτῆρας ἱππονώμας echoes the iambic dimeter 224 ἄτλατον οὐδὲ φευκτάν; two cases of a repeated iambic trimeter catalectic (*Ant.* 976 and *O.T.* 202) and one of an acatalectic trimeter (*El.* 1390); *Ant.* 614, perhaps the most striking,[5] where an ionic trimeter *a maiore* – – ⏑ ⏑ – – ⏑ ⏑ – ⏑ – – is repeated from the third phrase of the

[1] See p. 1.

[2] Instances are frequent in Eur., cf. *Hipp.* 1110 and 1130 (iamb. dim. cat.), *Suppl.* 606 and 625 (ithyph.).

[3] Unless *O.T.* 151 ff. be taken as containing a series of adoneans, but see below.

[4] The 'twin' clausulae discussed below (p. 7) are a separate phenomenon.

[5] *El.* 1069 would be no less so, if it were admitted as an alcaic decasyll. But see below, p. 17.

strophe; and *El.* 515, an interesting case, in that πολύπονος αἰκεία repeats πολύπονος ἱππεία of l. 505, the special intention being unmistakable.[1]

This limited scale of exception is so remarkable, as compared with the proportion of repeated phrases in Euripides, that it seems reasonable, where the text is disputed, to be suspicious of a conjecture which is *markedly* at variance with this characteristic technique. In *Aj.* 1199 ff. the strophe begins in LA ἐκεῖνος οὔτε στεφάνων and the antistrophe καὶ πρὶν μὲν ἐννυχίου. The Byzantine scholar's insertion of οὖν before ἐννυχίου, though in itself perfectly sound Greek, is an obvious effort to supply the missing syllable; G. Wolf substituted αἰὲν νυχίου, which has been adopted by Jebb, Pearson, and Radermacher, presumably from a conviction that the metre is choriambic, since otherwise Hermann's emendation of the strophe, οὐ for οὔτε, is simpler and more probable.[2] Now if the metre is choriambic the first period closes 1201 with the adonean τέρψιν ὁμιλεῖν, from which the next period follows on (is the awkward first syllable a sort of anacrusis?) with two more choriambic dimeters ending in τέρψιν ἰαύειν. After a connecting bacchiac (so L's κωλισμός) the rhythm continues in glyconics and choriambics to the third and final adonean μνήματα Τροίας. It looks temptingly neat, till we realise that precisely this symmetry is un-Sophoclean. For the adonean metra among choriambics are real clausular rhythms (of the so-called 'hypercatalectic' relation), not segments of dactyls as in *O.T.* 151 ff. If, on the other hand, Hermann's emendation is adopted the whole rhythmical movement is changed.[3] The first period is ionic *a minore*, starting from an iambic metrum, and ending on -ψιν ὁμιλεῖν. The second is ionic *a maiore*, ending in a common catalexis -αύειν. ἐρώτων δ' makes the transition to glyconics, which duly end

[1] The metre ⏑ ⏑ ⏑ ⏑ – – – is a resolved version of ⏑ – ⏑ – | – –, a 'brachycatalectic' iambic dimeter like ὅπου μακραίωνι *Aj.* 193. This curious epode is a series of variations on the same short theme, and in such a case of course each modification must count as a real variant.

[2] The combination οὐ...οὔτε is characteristic of Sophocles, and easily leads to corruption, cf. *O.C.* 702. See Wilamowitz, *Berl. Klass.* v. 2. v. 65 n.

[3] Cf. Wilamowitz, *G.V.* p. 511.

in the clausula μνήματα Τροίας, the first and only adonean of the stanza.

The κομμός of nurse and chorus in *Tr.* 879 ff. is not in antistrophical structure, and the metrical composition of such passages has a technique of its own. But in these too the disposition to end with a clausula which avoids repeating the effect of an earlier period-close is equally persistent. The last sentence of this passage runs in the MSS[1] ἔτεκεν ἔτεκεν μεγάλαν ἁ νέορτος ἅδε νύμφα δόμοισι τοῖσδ' Ἐρινύν, clearly three dimeters of some kind. As the double ἔτεκεν defies metrical analysis, most editors follow the *recentiores libri* which read ἔτεκε for the second. The first dimeter, the equivalent of two cretics, must then end with μεγάλαν, and we are left with a trochaic dimeter ἁ νέορτος ἅδε νύμφα followed by a clausula in which Jebb, Radermacher, and Wilamowitz[2] follow Nauck in reading δόμοις for δόμοισι solely in order to make it correspond exactly to the double bacchiacs of 890 and 892. In the first place it is now clear that this triple parallel is not in Sophocles' manner and should not be gratuitously forced upon the text. But further, a division into cola which makes an iambic metrum (whether ⏑ – ⏑ – or ⏑ – –) follow upon an acatalectic trochaic – ⏑ – –, without even a grammatical pause, is surely an intolerable violation of the 'principle of alternation'.[3] Schroeder's conjecture[4] ἔτεκ' ἔτεκε is a simple emendation, and brings ἁ into the first dimeter, so that the last two are identical forms of the iambic dimeter catalectic:

νέορτος ἅδε νύμφα
δόμοισι τοῖσδ' Ἐρινύν.

There are two other instances in Sophocles of such 'twin' clausulae: *Tr.* 223–4 again in this metre, and *Aj.* 199–200

γλώσσαις βαρυάλγητα·
ἐμοὶ δ' ἄχος ἕστακεν,

[1] Taking the universally accepted reading of the scholia ἁ νέορτος.

[2] *G.V.* p. 609.

[3] Cf. P. Maas, *Gr. Met.* p. 35.

[4] Adopted by Pearson in the Oxford text.

which might be analysed as a telesillean with spondaic close, analogous to the glyconic and asclepiad with the same peculiarity. Euripides seems hardly to have used the 'twin' form:[1] Aeschylus has one clear example, *Pers.* 556–7 = 566–7 (two pherecrateans); *Cho.* 469–70 has two hipponacteans, but the strophe is too short for this to be taken as the clausular period; it is simply part of the internal structure of the five-line stanza *abbcc.* The particular interest of the Sophoclean examples is that all three occur in non-antistrophic lyrics, as though such passages were felt to require an extra degree of internal responsion.

A further illustration of Sophocles' care to avoid too monotonous an assimilation of the clausula to the rest of the verse is his manipulation of heavy closes. Both he and Euripides have a liking for the *rallentando* of three or more consecutive long syllables at the end of a period or of the strophe. It is not always possible to analyse such a phrase with certainty: the effect appears sometimes to be achieved by adding a long syllable or a spondee to a recognised colon, sometimes by lengthening a penultimate syllable which is normally short. It is common for such a trisyllabic 'drag' to occur more than once in the context, in order to diminish the abruptness of a departure from normal rhythm:[2] thus the clausula *O.T.* 872 ends in γηράσκει after the penultimate phrase λάθα κατακοιμάσῃ, and in *Aj.* 400 the spondee added to the iambic dimeter gives the close ἀνθρώπων,[3] supported three phrases later by the heavy dochmiac ὀλέθρι' αἰκίζει.[4] But Sophocles shows characteristic scrupulousness in avoiding too much repetition of the same effect. It would be idle, of course, to look for any parallel among his lyrics to the long series of spondaic anapaests in Eur. *Tro.* or *I.T.*, but Eur. *Hipp.* 141 ff. is an ordinary choral strophe which makes play with spondaic closes, and

[1] Perhaps *Hec.* 905 ff. ends in two hipponacteans. [2] See below, p. 20.

[3] Cf. *Aj.* 596 ff. where the pauses in strophe and antistrophe indicate that 597 and 604 should be shown as identical cola, both of this type, glyc. + sp., giving εὐδαίμων and εὐνῶμαι.

[4] Dindorf's correction is much the most satisfactory here. εὔφρονες Ἀργείοις 420 is a recognised variation in dochmiac responsion, – ∪ ∪ – – – with ∪ ∪ ∪ – – –.

here the clausula is the fifth phrase of the type, while the preceding pair of strophes also ended in one. The most spondaic of Sophocles' lyrics is probably the ode to Sleep, *Phil.* 827 ff., but here the clausula breaks the series of heavy closes and the epode has none. It is again significant that the only clausulae of this type which echo more than one earlier – – – occur in epodes, *Aj.* 192 ff., *El.* 504 ff., *O.C.* 1239 ff.,[1] in all of which the degree of repetition is in marked contrast to Sophocles' antistrophic technique.

The Sophoclean clausula, so carefully differentiated from its context, is nevertheless in clearly audible relation to it, and where a sequence of quantitative syllables admits of more than one metrical interpretation the most reasonable analysis is that which sets it most clearly in such a relation. In *Ant.* 353 ff., for instance, the movement of the last four lines makes it clear that the final ξυμπέφρασται is an abbreviated variant of the lecythion 362 φεῦξιν οὐκ ἐπάξεται:[2] *O.T.* 1096–7 is a variation on the familiar 'Archilochian dicolon' (enoplius+ithyphallic) with the second member syncopated to – ᴗ – – – in order to avoid exact repetition of the ithyphallic τοῖς ἐμοῖς τυράννοις which closes the dactylo-epitrites just before: *El.* 486–7, which has just the same variant, both avoids repeating the ithyphallic εἶσιν ἁ πρόμαντις and picks up in acephalic form the rarer ᴗ – ᴗ – – – (sync. iamb. dim.) ὕπεστί μοι θάρσος 479. The same picking up of an earlier phrase in slightly modified form is seen in *O.T.* 1196, where the 'reizianum' οὐδὲν μακαρίζω is really a catalectic version of the telesillean τίς γάρ, τίς ἀνὴρ πλέον 1189, appearing instead of the expected pherecratean because that has occurred twice already as a period-close. *O.T.* 910 ἔρρει δὲ τὰ θεῖα has the same sequence of syllables, but is here in 'brachycatalectic' relation to the enoplii – – ᴗ ᴗ – ᴗ – – 900 and 902. *Aj.* 181 should be taken as an indivisible logaoedic unit – ᴗ – ᴗ – ᴗ ᴗ – – set at the end of

[1] Wilamowitz's analysis of the last four lines (*G.V.* p. 256) destroys the natural coincidence of rhythm and sense, and is much less probable than the division adopted by Radermacher, Schroeder, and Pearson. I take the final ο of ἀπό to be lengthened by the initial ρ, however, so that the clausula is not a paroemiac but – – ᴗ ᴗ – ᴗ – – –, exactly the same as *Aj.* 1191.

[2] See below, p. 20.

the smoothly running dactylo-epitrites because it combines both trochaic and dactylic elements.[1]

Wilamowitz[2] conjectures that the 'refrain' is an historical antecedent of the clausula. Whatever may be the truth of this general hypothesis, I shall endeavour to show that metrical analysis suggests the possibility of a more precise and direct connection between the refrain and one particular type of clausula, in which a metrical and rhetorical unit is detachable from the end of the verse. Sometimes, of course, such a unit is nothing more than a normal closing rhythm with a pause in the sense before it, and this may be an actual refrain: Aeschylus' αἴλινον refrain,[3] for instance, is a dactylic close following upon an iambic dimeter; so too Euripides[4] ends a little ἐφύμνιον with ὅ τι καλὸν φίλον ἀεί, a pherecratean following a choriambic dimeter. The penultimate phrase in each case required some metrical close, and the detachment of the last phrase has no particular *metrical* significance. But there are cases where the detachable phrase is appended as a kind of extra clausula to a stanza which appears, metrically speaking, to have already reached an end; and in several of these, though the actual words are not repeated, there is verbal reminiscence from strophe to antistrophe, an echo of a ritual cry of appeal or lamentation, repetition of a key-word at the same place in the line, a general similarity of meaning, or a parallelism in the form and syllabic length of the words. In Aesch. *P.V.* 588 the clausula of the strophe is a line consisting of dochmiac + two cretics:

κλύεις φθέγμα τᾶς βούκερω παρθένου;

[1] Wilamowitz, *G.V.* p. 403 takes the clausula here as a reizianum ἐτείσατο λώβαν, with μαχαναῖς ending the dactylo-epitrites, but the cretic attached without linking syllable to the last hemiepes – ∪ ∪ – ∪ ∪ – is impossibly harsh. The whole phrase is merely a variant of the 'alcaic decasyllable'; such logaoedic lengths have as a matter of fact no rigidly fixed number of short syllables: cf. another form, *Aj.* 701 – ∪ ∪ – ∪ – ∪ – – repeated *O.C.* 129 καὶ παραμειβόμεσθ' ἀδέρκτως. Soph. *Tereus*, frag. 532 ἔξοχος ἄλλος ἔβλαστεν ἄλλου has the normal form of the decasyllable, again as a clausula to dactylo-epitrites.

[2] *G.V.* p. 445.

[3] *Ag.* 121.

[4] *Bacch.* 881, cf. Aesch. *Supp.* 165.

and its counterpart in the antistrophe is

θρόει, φράζε τᾷ δυσπλάνῳ παρθένῳ.

The lines are both self-contained, and metrically form an additional clausula to a strophe of mixed dochmiacs and iambics which has already come to a natural close in the ithyphallic πημονὰς ἀλύξω. A further stage away from the refrain may be seen in *P.V.* 135, where the chorus, having closed their ionics with the choriambic dimeter catalectic τὰν θεμερῶπιν αἰδῶ,[1] add σύθην δ' ἀπέδιλος ὄχῳ πτερωτῷ, answered in the antistrophe by τὰ πρὶν δὲ πελώρια νῦν ἀιστοῖ:[2] here are the self-contained phrase and the preceding close, without the verbal reminiscence. As a final development, the principle may be applied in a purely metrical form, where the sense runs on through the two last lines without pause but the penultimate line is itself an unmistakable closing rhythm to the preceding period and appended to it is the final clausula. In *Ag.* 681 ff. a strophe of trochaics and ionics has such a double close, first a variant of the priapean tetrameter – – – ∪ ∪ – ∪ – – ∪ ∪ – ∪ – –, one of the commonest forms of clausula, and then a pherecratean δι' ἔριν αἱματόεσσαν which continues the same sentence. (There is no trace of a triadic scheme running through the stanza.) The final strophe of the same canticum is a simple iambic series ending with a catalectic trimeter of an ordinary type ∪ – ∪ – – ∪ ∪ – ∪ – – *plus* a repetition of the two last metra – ∪ ∪ – ∪ – – εἰδομέναν τοκεῦσιν: this in the antistrophe is rhetorically as well as metrically separate. *Ag.* 225–6 has a similar effect.

This appears to exhaust the certain instances of the kind in the extant plays of Aeschylus. They are enough, however, to make it probable that Sophocles adopted from him this form of clausula, in which there is a kind of *coda* to the whole stanza following the close of the last period. But Sophocles, instead of restricting it to these simple forms, elaborates the theme in a variety of formulae, with which there is nothing to compare in either of the other tragedians.

1 Or (according to the κωλισμός adopted) with the reiz. θεμερῶπιν αἰδῶ.

2 As l. 132 is an alcaic decasyll., this may be formulated as the same with an extra syllable in front.

In Euripides, in spite of the far greater extent of lyric available for comparison, there appear to be only four certain instances of the kind,[1] and one only of these is supported by a grammatical pause.

Before examining the treatment of the two consecutive clausulae in Sophocles, it should be made clear that the phenomenon is quite distinct from a mere *change* of rhythm in the penultimate phrase to prepare for the clausula, which then often swings back to the earlier metre. To take a simple instance: Aesch. *Pers.* 125 ff. is a trochaic[2] strophe with a dactylic hemiepes ἀμφοτέρας ἅλιον as a penultimate phrase leading into the final ithyphallic πρῶνα κοινὸν αἴας. But the hemiepes could not itself act as a clausula to the strophe. There are also penultimate phrases which might, considered in isolation, be used as clausular rhythms, but not in the context where they appear; thus the glyconic clausula Eur. *Hipp.* 741 gives no licence to treat the multitude of glyconics found in the penultimate position as part of a double clausula. Further, where the clausula properly speaking is a tetrameter or dicolon, and appears to be preceded by a 'penultimate close', the whole group may be merely part of the symmetrical structure of a stanza ending in the formula *aba*β,[3] as for instance Aesch. *Cho.* 639 ff. has as its last four lines iamb. dim.+lecyth., iamb. dim.+ithyph.; in such a case, though the lecythion does occur elsewhere as a clausula in Aeschylus, it would not be proper to speak of a double clausula. The 'twin' clausulae mentioned above as characteristic of Sophocles' epodes are also omitted from consideration here, though they are in fact a special form of the clausula in question.

The rhetorically self-contained clausula with an echo of the words in the antistrophe, as in Aesch. *P.V.* 588, is found in *O.C.* 1456, at the end of a stanza which, like the example from the *Prometheus*, is of mixed dochmiacs and iambics. The double dochmiac of 1455, if not strictly speaking a clausula, does end other stanzas of the type,

[1] *Alc.* 576–7, *Phoen.* 248–9 and 1294–5 (with pause), *I.A.* 799–800. Possibly also *Ion* 1059–60.

[2] With iambic admixture, or conceivably iambic throughout; the cretics and lecythia are ambiguous.

[3] Taking β as a modified (here catalectic) form of *b*.

and appended to it is the phrase – ∪ ∪ – – – – ἔκτυπεν αἰθήρ, ὦ Ζεῦ, with its echo in the antistrophe ὦ μέγας αἰθήρ, ὦ Ζεῦ. The next pair of strophes continues the *motif*, appropriate to the exalted religious excitement of the occasion; again there are two dochmiacs in the penultimate, followed in the strophe by the cry Ζεῦ ἄνα, σοὶ φωνῶ, in the antistrophe by the appeal to an earthly king, σπεῦσον ἄισσ', ὦναξ. In the opening κομμός of the *Electra* the repeated cry αἰαῖ[1] again has a suggestion of refrain, though the sentence is here continuous with the preceding lines; the dactylic series comes to a close in the iambic dimeter catalectic ἐᾶτέ μ' ὧδ' ἀλύειν, and the reizianum is added αἰαῖ, ἱκνοῦμαι, answered in the antistrophe by αἰαῖ, δακρύεις. *Ant.* 614 again has this double clausula with an echo in the second, though only in the antistrophe is there a pause in the sense between the two. 613 is a resolved ithyphallic ∪ ∪ ∪ – ∪ – –, reminiscent of the last period-close 610 – ∪ ∪ – ∪ – –, and then follows an ionic trimeter *a maiore* ending in each strophe with ἐκτὸς ἄτας.

The telesillean with heavy close ⊻ – ∪ ∪ – – –, which appears as the 'twin' clausula of the epode *Aj.* 192 ff., is the penultimate phrase of *Aj.* 693 ff., followed by a choriambic trimeter catalectic, the separation between the two being emphasised by *syllaba anceps* in the strophe

ὁ Δάλιος εὔγνωστος
ἐμοὶ ξυνείη διὰ παντὸς εὔφρων.

The same phrase *Tr.* 848 is followed by a grammatical pause in both strophes, and the final clausula is an unbroken ionic pentameter *a maiore*

849 ἁ δ' ἐρχομένα μοῖρα προφαίνει δολίαν καὶ μεγάλαν ἄταν.
860 ἁ δ' ἀμφίπολος Κύπρις ἄναυδος φανερὰ τῶνδ' ἐφάνη πράκτωρ.

Here the complete coincidence of diaeresis and the parallel openings are still a reminiscence of the refrain.

The two last examples throw some light on the κωλισμός of *O.T.* 863 ff. The last five lines of the strophe run as follows:

πατὴρ μόνος, οὐδέ νιν ⊻ – ∪ ∪ – ∪ –
θνατὰ φύσις ἀνέρων – – ∪ ∪ – ∪ –

[1] l. 135 = 152.

ἔτικτεν οὐδὲ μήποτε ⏑ – ⏑ – ⏑ – ⏑ ⏑[1]
λάθα κατακοιμάσῃ· – – ⏑ ⏑ – – –
μέγας ἐν τούτοις θεός, οὐδὲ γηράσκει. ⏑ ⏑ – – – ⏑ ⏑ – ⏑ – – –.

Two telesilleans are followed by an iambic dimeter and the period is closed by a telesillean with spondaic end. The final clausula is presumably a trimeter of some kind, perhaps a variant of the protean choriambic trimeter, again with spondaic end.[2] *O.C.* 520 shows the same clausula except that a single long syllable replaces the opening two shorts. In that context it appears to be related to the trimeters 513 and 518 – – – – ⏑ ⏑ – ⏑ – – with a long syllable added to form a heavy close. *O.T.* 872, therefore, may well be the same with a resolution of the first molossus designed to pick up the rhythm of κατακοιμάσῃ.[3] However it is analysed, the line must be left in its unity as the clausula. The grammatical pause in the antistrophe comes at the same point, and both lines form a clear rhetorical *coda* with diaereses largely coincident, while the repetition of θεός 872, θεόν 881, θεόν 882 recalls the threefold ἄτας ἄταν ἄτας in corresponding lines *Ant.* 614, 624, 625. Analogy and common sense alike suggest that the rhetorical *coda* was a metrical *coda* too, isolated by the familiar device of a period-close in the line before. The analysis of Wilamowitz,[4] giving an anapaestic dimeter in the penultimate position,

871 λάθα κατακοιμάσῃ· μέγας ἐν
881 λῦσαι θεὸν αἰτοῦμαι· θεὸν οὐ

destroys the unity of rhythm and sense, and the suddenness of the anapaest's intrusion is inadequately explained as a reminiscence of the last lyric but one,[5] where the pair of dimeters form part of a recognisable metrical structure.

[1] Syllaba anceps, cf. μήποτε in the antistrophe.
[2] See above, p. 8.
[3] Cf. Aesch. *Supp.* 165, apparently a chor. trim. with opening resolution in its first metrum χαλεποῦ γὰρ ἐκ πνεύματος εἶσι χειμών.

⏑ ⏑ – ⏑ – – ⏑ ⏑ – ⏑ – –

[4] *G.V.* p. 515.
[5] ll. 469–70. The strophe is analysed in the next paragraph.

O.T. 463 ff. is a conveniently simple illustration of Sophocles' clausular technique. The scheme is: 2 choriambic tetrameters catalectic, 2 telesilleans + telesillean catalectic, 2 anapaestic dimeters + telesillean catalectic: ithyphallic. Again the clausula of the whole stanza follows immediately upon the last period-close, here metrically though not grammatically detached.

In *O.T.* 1086 ff. and *O.C.* 1074 ff. the last period of a dactylo-epitritic series is (epitrites+) hemiepes – ∪ ∪ – ∪ ∪ – ⏑̲ + ithyphallic, exactly the same as the final clausula of Eur. *Med.* 419–20

ἔρχεται τιμὰ γυναικείῳ γένει
οὐκέτι δυσκέλαδος φά-
-μα γυναῖκας ἕξει.

But Sophocles each time uses this as a penultimate close and appends a further clausula, in *O.T.* the Archilochian dicolon in syncopated form, in *O.C.* an iambic trimeter catalectic.

In *Ant.* 857 ff. (the strophe is corrupt) an iambic tetrameter 867–8 is followed by a catalectic tetrameter with the familiar close – ∪ ∪ – ∪ – – and an iambic trimeter catalectic closes the whole.

O.C. 118 ff. is an interesting example. Each strophe is divided into two parts, of which the first is sung by the chorus, the second is an interchange between the chorus and Oedipus. The second part is in regular anapaests, but these begin, curiously enough, three lines before the end of the first part, where the mixed lyric metres lead into them in the middle of a sentence. The transition, however, is made distinct metrically by a double clausula 132–3, first the hipponactean ἰέντες· τὰ δὲ νῦν τιν' ἥκειν answering to the ennea-syllable 129 – ∪ ∪ – ∪ – ∪ – –[1] and next the reizianum λόγος οὐδὲν ἅζονθ'.

O.C. 679–80 is a curiously elaborate double clausula in which a phalaecean is followed by a hipponactean: the metrical detachment of the second, peculiar to this type of clausula, justifies the hiatus in Triclinius' correction οὐδ' αὖ | ἁ in the antistrophe, as against Elmsley's impossible emendation of the strophe, θεαῖς for θείαις.

[1] See above, p. 10, n. 1. The unity of the hippon. is seen more clearly in the antistr. 165 κλύεις, ὦ πολύμοχθ' ἀλᾶτα;

Even in the *Ichneutae* there appears to be an instance of this kind of clausula,[1] where a long cretic πνῖγος closes with the line ἀντ' ἐκείνου γύναι σάφ' ἴσθι, and is followed by an iambic tetrameter catalectic.[2]

The number of instances is large enough to justify the conclusion that Sophocles had a liking for this type of clausula and experimented with it in a variety of forms. There are a few passages where, though metrical analysis may be uncertain, the application of this formula brings the cola into better relation with the sense and natural division of the words, a conformity which is on the whole more carefully observed in the clausular period than elsewhere. Here the combined evidence of strophe and antistrophe is the surest guide. In *Ant.* 140=154, by cutting off the adonean δεξιόσειρος and Βάκχιος ἄρχοι as the most natural final clausula we are left with the preceding period as follows:

– ∪ –   – ∪ –
– ∪ ∪ – – ∪ ∪ –
– ∪ ∪ – – ∪ ∪ – –

in which the third phrase is an obvious closing rhythm, bearing the same relation to the second as hipponactean does to glyconic, or as *Ant.* 782 to 781.[3] Another form of enneasyllable may well be a penultimate close in *Ant.* 789–90:

οὔθ' ἁμερίων σέ γ' ἀνθρώπων,
ὁ δ' ἔχων μέμηνεν.

– – ∪ ∪ – ∪ – – – is used as a clausula *Aj.* 1191 and *O.C.* 1248, and in the latter stands in relation to the 'dragged' phrase αἱ δ' ἀνατέλλοντος – ∪ ∪ – – – two lines before exactly as it does in the present context to ἀγρονόμοις αὐλαῖς. The reiziana ὁ δ' ἔχων μέμηνεν and θεὸς 'Αφροδίτα are the most natural rhetorical units to split off as the final clausula.

El. 1058 ff. is usually represented[4] as a strophe with choriambic periods at beginning and end, each terminating in an alcaic deca-

[1] ll. 324 ff.

[2] Adopting Wilamowitz's conjecture μηδέ for ἐμοὶ δέ.

[3] Cf. *Aj.* 226 τὰν ὁ μέγας μῦθος ἀέξει, again an unmistakable period-close.

[4] E.g. by Schneidewin–Nauck–Bruhn, Pearson, Wilamowitz, *G.V.* p. 327.

syllable, and a middle glyconic period. If this is correct, it is a very striking exception to the general avoidance of symmetry which I have tried in the first part of this article to establish as characteristic of Sophocles. The last period is analysed as follows:

ὢ χθονία βροτοῖσι φά-
-μα, κατά μοι βόασον οἰ-
-κτρὰν ὄπα τοῖς ἔνερθ' 'Ατρεί-
-δαις, ἀχόρευτα φέρουσ' ὀνείδη.

The corresponding decasyllable in the antistrophe is

'Ερι]-νύν. τίς ἂν εὔπατρις ὧδε βλάστοι;

The coincidence of pause in the sense at once raises suspicions of this artificial division into cola.[1] There is no need to suspect the earlier caesurae (in φάμα and οἰκτράν); it is quite usual in choriambic dimeters to achieve the effect of a πνῖγος in this way.[2] But by keeping the natural clausula as an enoplius the preceding line becomes a penultimate close -κτρὰν ὄπα τοῖς ἔνερθ' 'Ατρείδαις (the enneasyllable of *Aj.* 701 and *O.C.* 129) and the final clausula is left in audible relation to the earlier decasyllable without being a repetition of it. It is analogous to the clausula *P.V.* 135 (quoted above, p. 11), where the decasyllable of 132 is modified by the addition of an extra syllable in front.

Care for variety, therefore, and reminiscence rather than repetition of earlier phrases, must be taken as the most general characteristics of Sophocles' manipulation of the clausula, together with a special handling of the internal responsion of passages not in antistrophic correspondence; but besides these, his elaboration of the *coda* type of close is sufficiently remarkable to justify us in regarding it as a distinctively Sophoclean technique, one aspect of the supple and varied polymetry of his lyrics as a whole.

1 In the earlier decasyllable 1062 = 1074 there is not the same coincidence between strophe and antistrophe.

2 Cf. *Phil.* 206–8, 687–9. In the latter passage the division of ὑπάρ-χοι in the antistrophe with nothing to correspond in the strophe shows that caesura may or may not occur, indifferently.

There remain in connection with the *coda*-clausulae two passages which I have reserved for consideration at the end, since in them the metrical interpretation is complicated by textual corruption and must be examined in greater detail.

The first of these is *Phil.* 209–18, where misunderstanding of the metrical problem has darkened counsel. διάσημα γὰρ θροεῖ at the end of the strophe is out of responsion with the antistrophe προβοᾷ γάρ τι δεινόν. Where editors have accepted one or the other of these as correct, they appear to have conceived of the choice as lying between two forms of a choriambic trimeter as clausula, the one ending in an iambic metrum -μα γὰρ θροεῖ, the other in a trochaic γάρ τι δεινόν. Others would adopt Wunder's transposition in the antistrophe τι γὰρ δεινόν and emend θροεῖ in the strophe to θρηνεῖ with Dindorf;[1] some, including Jebb and Campbell, make Wunder's transposition but retain θροεῖ as a licence of responsion.

The last can be dismissed at once; Sophocles could never have set a regular to match a 'limping' iambic at the close of a stanza.[2]

Metrical considerations apart, there would be nothing in the words themselves to arouse suspicion, though of the two the antistrophe might be thought the weaker as a form of poetic expression. If the unexceptionable strophe be taken as the model, Lachmann's αἴλινον for τι δεινόν is palaeographically ingenious though less satisfactory in terms of diction; perhaps τι δεινόν should simply be obelised. Wilamowitz,[3] however, keeping the text of the antistrophe, follows

[1] Both this correction and the transposition of αὐγάζων and ὅρμον l. 218 increase the exactness of correspondence between strophe and antistrophe; but while this is admittedly carried to an unusual length in the context it is disputable whether we are therefore justified in pushing it yet further.

[2] The nearest approach to a parallel would be Eur. *Hipp.* 741 = 751, where (if the text is sound) a glyc. ending in a spondee αὐγάς corresponds to one ending in θεοῖς. But the emendation θεοῖσιν is probable, and in any case the spondaic close to a glyc. is so ordinary a variant that responsion is not considered necessary in other places than the clausula, cf. Soph. *O.T.* 1187 = 1197. Nor is it safe to argue without more ado from the practice of Euripides to that of Sophocles.

[3] *G.V.* pp. 298, 533. The reading is adopted by Pearson in the Oxford text.

Triclinius' transposition in the strophe διάσημᾱ θροεῖ γάρ. Palaeographically this is easily accounted for, and though the lengthened final vowel may strike some ears as extremely harsh, and parallel examples in the Sophoclean lyric, except in dactylic passages, are all open to doubt, it cannot be dismissed as impossible.

The question of the metrical clausula is bound up with the division into cola. The stanza consists of an iambic trimeter followed by an ionic trimeter, then, according to one method of division, five choriambic dimeters[1] and a trimeter. If the reading of LA be retained, the clausula then takes shape as a choriambic trimeter:

αὔ]-δα̃ τρυσά-νωρ. διάση-μα γὰρ θροεῖ – – – –⏑⏑– ⏑–⏑–.[2]

Mathematical scansion could hardly be further divorced from the natural rhythmical sense of the passage. In the antistrophe the words προβοᾷ γάρ τι δεινόν follow a strong pause at the same point in the line, and with the parallelism of meaning too it is difficult to believe that in a clausula of all places rhythm could be so used to obscure the significance of the words; at least the assimilation of the first three syllables of this phrase to a choriamb beginning with the last syllable of the preceding one would be a disagreeable necessity, to be accepted only if there were no reasonable alternative. Schroeder, too, though he begins the line with τρυσάνωρ, keeps to the choriamb -νωρ· διαση- and counts τρυσα- as a separate metrum with both shorts suppressed.

Wilamowitz strains this creaking scansion yet further. He accepts the trochaic version of the last metrum (as a separate clausula -μα θροεῖ γάρ), taking the sharp twist thus given to the rhythm as a variant of the type ἀναξιφόρ-μιγγες ὕμνοι with a choriamb in place of the iambic metrum, and quotes in its support other examples, including in this play[3] the dimeter ναὸς ἵν' ἡ-μῖν τέτακται, again –⏑⏑ ––⏑––. But the objection to this interpretation of the *Philoctetes* passage lies in its complete isolation from anything in the metrical context. If Sophocles, or indeed either of the other tragedians,

[1] For the caesurae involved in this division see p. 17. Wilamowitz would assume 6 dims. + –⏑–– as clausula.

[2] So Schneidewin–Nauck–Radermacher.

[3] l. 1180.

makes a departure from normal metrical sequence, this is either at once intelligible as a mere variation on the expected phrase, or it is supported by another licence of the kind in its neighbourhood, or by a similar rhythm arising nearby in a more familiar sequence. In *Phil.* 1180, for instance, the metrum -μῖν τέτακται is an echo of 1176–7, which are anaclastic ionics of the usual type ⏑ ⏑ – ⏑ | – ⏑ – – and so end in the same phrase. Of the other dramatic parallels adduced by Wilamowitz, Aesch. *Supp.* 96 ἀφ' ὑψιπύργων πανώλεις follows ἰάπτει δ' ἐλπίδων, which has the same effect in a syncopated form and is followed again by ⏑ – ⏑ – | – ⏑ – ⏑ – –. In any case this is not a clausula nor the end of a period, and therefore no more admissible as a parallel than *O.T.* 1086, where the phrase – ⏑ ⏑ – | – ⏑ – ⏑ εἴπερ ἐγὼ μάντις εἰμί occurs as a gambit, and leads into epitrites, which secure the metrical continuity. In Soph. *Ant.* 364 the clausula ξυμπέφρασται, which might at first look like a parallel, emerges clearly from the context as a variation on the lecythion 362:

361	τὸ μέλλον· Ἅιδα μόνον	⏑ – ⏑ – – ⏑ –
	φεῦξιν οὐκ ἐπάξεται.	– ⏑ – ⏑ – ⏑ –
	νόσων δ' ἀμηχάνων φυγὰς	⏑ – ⏑ – ⏑ – ⏑ –
	ξυμπέφρασται.	– ⏑ – –.

The continuity of rhythm (*ab*αβ) is unmistakable; there is no 'Eindruck einer Umbiegung zum Schlusse'.[1] In *Phil.* 209, on the other hand, the impression would be remarkable indeed, and the combination of abnormal metre and abnormal prosody is at least suspicious. The position of γάρ as the closing word of a strophe and of a sentence three words long, neither of the preceding words being proclitic or enclitic, might be felt a still further strain on the credulity.

The analogy of other examples, as well as an unbiased reading of the passage, suggests that the two matched phrases διάσημα γὰρ θροεῖ and προβοᾷ γάρ †τι δεινόν† form a metrical as well as a rhetorical unit at the end of the stanza. They do appear, indeed, as

[1] Wilamowitz, *G.V.* p. 516. Cf. Eur. *Or.* 966 πήματ' οἴκων, a period-close which is a shortened variant of the ithyphallics 962 and 970. So Eur. *Supp.* 372–4–6, all in relation.

part of a trimeter here, but if the division between metra coincided with the diaeresis and pause the line could be treated as 1+2 metra without difficulty. The only possibility of fulfilling these conditions seems to be to treat the trimeter as ionic, keeping the strophe as the model. The first metrum would then be τρυσάνωρ, leaving the preceding line an enneasyllable -θει βαρεῖα τηλόθεν αὐδά, a penultimate close to the four choriambic dimeters, of the type of *El.* 1066–8. The clausula would be of a regular ionic type – – –. ⏑ ⏑ – ⏑ – ⏑ –, with anaclasis of the second metrum and catalexis of the last, as in Aesch. *Pers.* 107 πόλεών τ' ἀναστάσεις. This would also have the advantage of taking up the ionic trimeter of the second phrase of the stanza, and the clausula so interpreted would be a catalectic version of *Aj.* 634, where the hendecasyllable δοῦποι καὶ πολίας ἄμυγμα χαίτας, though it may be labelled phalaecean, is in obvious relation to the ionic trimeter 629 and should be analysed – – – | ⏑ ⏑ – ⏑ | – ⏑ – –. The case would, of course, be neater if αὐγάζων and ὅρμον were transposed in the antistrophe, as Dindorf first suggested, but it is hardly permissible to tidy up the text without more ground for suspicion.

Dindorf's γὰρ θρηνεῖ, with Wunder's transposition τι γὰρ δεινόν, would also make a possible ionic clausula,[1] but it involves the hypothesis of a double corruption. And though θροεῖν appears in *Aj.* 582 as a v.l. for θρηνεῖν, it does not follow that the words can be treated as interchangeable wherever they occur.[2]

The second passage which presents a difficult problem of text and metre combined is *O.C.* 703–6=716–19. The structure of the whole pair of strophes is clear and simple except for one line 704=717. It is of mixed ionic and iambic elements with a priapean as clausula, the latter a particularly appropriate rhythm for closing ionics since the pherecratean of the type – – – ⏑ ⏑ – – is identical in form with the first half of the opening ionic tetrameter.[3] The scheme is as follows: ionic tetrameter+pentameter, iambic trimeter+dimeter, then an

[1] Cf. Eur. *Bacch.* 72 Διόνυσον ὑμνήσω. [2] Cf. *El.* 853.

[3] Not to be confused with it nevertheless. The opening of the antistrophe clearly shows a continuous ionic tetrameter as the first period, while the glyc. 705 leaves no doubt as to the following pherecratean.

abab period of iambic trimeter+ionic trimeter repeated. Between this and the final priapean falls a line which in the strophe appears in L as ὁ γὰρ εἰσαιὲν ὁρῶν κύκλος and in the antistrophe as χερ]-σὶ παραπτομένα πλάτα. Both cannot be right, and editors differ as to which should be emended.[1]

Is the phrase ὁ εἰσαιὲν ὁρῶν κύκλος Διὸς λεύσσει νιν acceptable in itself? Jebb's translation 'the sleepless eye' glosses it over; it might rather be felt to make much the same impression as 'the forever-seeing eye of Zeus beholds it'. But if this be dismissed as too subjective, the metrical difficulty remains. It will not do to say with Campbell that this reading 'sustains the choriambic rhythm', since an asclepiad συνναίων...κύκλος distended to embrace four choriambs is a monster unknown to Greek metric. If the rhythm is to be sustained this phrase must continue the ionics *a minore* and the reading of L must be emended, since ⏑ ⏑ – ⏑ – is obviously inadmissible as the close of the series. The alternative is to assimilate the line ὁ γὰρ...κύκλος to the priapean following, but as what kind of unit? It must all go together in spite of the division of the word χερ-σί in the antistrophe; the *abab* sequence 700–3 is unmistakable, and Pearson's overhanging ὁ followed by a correct glyconic looks like an outlandish revival of the antispast. A glyconic, then, of the form ⏑ ⏑ – – ⏑ ⏑ – ⏑ –? Ὁρᾷς τὸν πόδα τοῦτον; Sophocles is nowhere else guilty of this solecism.[2] *On metrical grounds*, therefore, the case for taking L's reading in the strophe as correct and devising a longer substitute for †παραπτομένα† to match it seems a weak one.

Many editors therefore follow Hermann in the reverse procedure and read αἰὲν ὁρῶν. It is not easy, however, to account palaeographically for the appearance of εἰσ in L. Nor is the metrical prob-

[1] Schneidewin–Nauck–Radermacher 1909 keeps both in the text, while giving a metrical analysis which covers only the second.

[2] The correction ἐς αἰέν would give a form of glyconic possible in itself ⏑ ⏑ ⏑ – ⏑ ⏑ – ⏑ –, and Triclinius' emendation παραπεπταμένα evidently aims at this, but of course the verb πετάννυμι is out of place here. Meineke's παραϊσσομένα gives the same metrical solution and is palaeographically accountable. But a glyconic with resolved base *unrelated to anything in the metrical context* would be an erratic departure from Sophocles' normal practice, cf. above, p. 20.

lem yet solved. The assumption seems to be[1] that the phrase continues the ionics of the preceding line in a dimeter of the form ⏑ ⏑ – ⏑ ⏑ | – ⏑ – with resolution of the second long of the first metrum and catalexis of the second. Now resolved longs in general are not common in the ionics of drama, and though of course – ⏑ – – does occur after the full ⏑ ⏑ – – without anaclasis I have been unable to find any parallel in the dramatic poets for this 'irrational' long first syllable, whether in catalectic or acatalectic metrum, emphasised by such a preceding resolution,[2] and the effect is too unpleasing to be *a priori* likely. If Hermann's emendation is right, the line ὁ γὰρ αἰὲν ὁρῶν κύκλος must be taken as a telesillean with resolved base and grouped with the following priapean. The difficulty is again the absence of support from the context: the colon (an uncommon one) is found Eur. *Ion* 468–9 and *Hec.* 905, but in each case with clearly related rhythms showing the same resolution in its neighbourhood. Moreover παραπτομένα itself has raised several doubts. Is it the aorist participle of παραπέτομαι (the tense is awkward), or a syncopated form of the present participle, 'flitting along past the hand', or does it come from παράπτομαι in the sense of 'fastened at the side' and so 'fitted to the hand'? None of the possibilities commands immediate conviction.

As far as the meaning is concerned, then, the most that can be said is that neither strophe nor antistrophe as given in L is impossible (though of course the combination is so). But the palaeographical difficulties of altering either to suit the other are considerable, and the metrical *impasse* is still more serious. In the circumstances, the reading of A and other MSS in 704, εἰσορῶν, which gives an intelligible sense,[3] has received less attention than it deserves, partly

[1] So Radermacher and Schroeder.

[2] Wilamowitz (*Isyll.* p. 136, and *G.V.* p. 298) analyses Ar. *Clouds* 812 τάχεως· φιλεῖ γάρ πως τὰ τοιαῦθ' ἑτέρᾳ τρέπεσθαι in this sense: ⏑⏑–⏑ | ––– | ⏑⏑–⏑⏑ | –⏑––. But ionics are notoriously easy to discover if looked for with a will; the line is a chor. tetram. cat. of an ordinary type.

[3] Cf. l. 1536. I think it not inconceivable, however, that the text originally ran ὁ γὰρ εἰσαεὶ κύκλος, the unusual position of the adverb (for which cf. l. 1140 ἀνδρός τοι τὸ μὲν εὖ δίκαιον εἰπεῖν) having led to the insertion of the unwanted ὁρῶν.

perhaps because it has been taken for granted that εἰσορῶν has arisen by error of omission from εἰσ αἰὲν ὁρῶν, partly because the metrical difficulties of the longer reading have been underestimated. Metrically, however, the word is perfectly appropriate; ὁ γὰρ εἰσορῶν κύκλος is another anaclastic ionic dimeter catalectic of the pattern of πόλεών τ' ἀναστάσεις. The *abab* sequence of 700–3 is undisturbed, since this dimeter, while continuing the rhythm, forms a separable unit, rounding off the ionics in a phrase which in its closing rhythm anticipates the glyconic of the next line. It is another instance of the penultimate close, followed by a priapean clausula. But παραπτομένα remains stubborn, and all that can be said is that it could be obelised without a pang.

2

METRICAL OBSERVATIONS ON AESCH. *PERS.* 922–1001

Text, interpretation and metre present a tangled problem in this threnody, and the solutions of editors differ widely. The chief function of detailed metrical study in such corrupt passages of lyric is to weight the scales in favour of—or more often against—certain methods of handling the text. The positive results of this present attempt to apply metrical criteria are necessarily modest and tentative; negatively they are, I think, sometimes decisive.

The version of the text given is that which seems best supported by metrical considerations. The critical notes are confined to readings directly discussed in the commentary.

TEXT

Χο.	γᾶ δ’ αἰάζει τὰν ἐγγαίαν	922	– – – – – – – –
	ἥβαν Ξέρξᾳ κταμέναν Ἅιδου		
	σάκτορι Περσᾶν· ᾁδοβάται γὰρ		
	πολλοὶ φῶτες, χώρας ἄνθος,		– – – – – – – –
	τοξοδάμαντες, πάνυ ταρφύς τις		
	μυριὰς ἀνδρῶν, ἐξέφθινται.		
Ξε.	αἰαῖ αἰαῖ κεδνᾶς ἀλκᾶς.	928	– – – – – – – –
Χο.	Ἀσία δὲ χθὼν †βασιλεῦ γαίας†		
	αἰνῶς αἰνῶς ἐπὶ γόνυ κέκλιται.		– – – – ◡ ◡ ◡ ◡ ◡ ◡ –

928 choro continuat Meineke.
Wil. αἰαῖ ⟨βασιλεῦ⟩ κεδ. ἀλκ. deleto βασ. γαι. 929.
fort. αἰαῖ ⟨γαίας⟩ κεδνᾶς ἀλκᾶς.
Ἀσία δὲ χθὼν [βασιλεῦ γαίας].

Ξε.	ὅδ’ ἐγών, οἰοῖ, αἰακτὸς	932	paroemiac
	μέλεος γέννᾳ γᾷ τε πατρῴᾳ		anap. dim.
	κακὸν ἄρ’ ἐγενόμαν.		doch.

Χο. πρόσφθογγόν ⟨νύν⟩ σοι
νόστου [τὰν] 935 paroem.
κακοφάτιδα βοὰν κακομέλετον
ἰὰν 2 doch.
Μαριανδυνοῦ θρηνητῆρος anap. dim.
πέμψω πέμψω πολύδακρυν
ἰαχάν. 2 doch.

935 νύν conieci deleto post Wil. τάν.

Wil. 935 πέμψω πρόσφθογγόν σοι νόστου anap. dim.
938 πέμψω πολύδακρυν ἰαχάν. paroem.

Ξε. ἵετ' αἰανῆ [καὶ] πάνδυρτον 939
δύσθροον αὐδάν. δαίμων γὰρ
ὅδ' αὖ
μετάτροπος ἐπ' ἐμοί.
Χο. ἥσω τοι καὶ πάνδυρτον 943
λαοπαθέα σέβων ἁλίτυπά τε
βάρη
πόλεως γέννας πενθητῆρος
κλάγξω ⟨– –⟩ ⏑̲ ⏑ ⏑
ἀρίδακρυν.

944 λαοπαθέα Wecklein σέβων Elmsley λαοπαθῆ τε σεβίζων codd.

947 κλ. δ' αὖ (δὲ Blaydes) γόον ἀρ. codd. ⟨κλάγξω⟩ δ' ἀρίδακρυν ἰαχάν Hermann.

Wil. 943 ἥσω τοι ⟨σοι⟩ καὶ πάνδυρτον anap. dim.
σὰ πάθη τε σέβων ἁλίτυπά τε
βάρη anap. dim.
πόλεως γέννας, πενθητῆρος anap. dim.
κλάγξω δ' αὖ γόον ἀρίδακρυν. paroem.

Ξε. Ἰάνων γὰρ ἀπηύρα, 949 ion. dim.
Ἰάνων ναύφρακτος Ἄρης
ἑτεραλκής, ion. trim.
νυχίαν πλάκα κερσάμενος
δυσδαίμονά τ' ἀκτάν. anap. trim. cat.

Χο. οἰοιοῖ [βόα] καὶ πάντ'
ἐκπεύθου.– 955 ⏓ ⏓ – – – – – – paroem.
ποῦ δὲ φίλων ἄλλος ὄχλος, chor. dim.
ποῦ δέ σοι παραστάται lecyth.
οἷος ἦν Φαρανδάκης lecyth.
Σούσας Πελάγων........ anap. dim.
.........Σουσισκάνης τ' 960 anap. dim.
'Αγβάτανα λιπών; doch.

955 choro tribuit Lachmann, Xerxi codd. βόα delevi. fort. οἰοῖ vel ὀτοτοῖ. Wil. Χο. οἰοιοῖ. Ξε. βόα καὶ πάντ' ἐκπεύθου.
961 ἀγαβάτανα Weil.

Ξε. ὀλοοὺς ἀπέλειπον 962
Τυρίας ἐκ ναὸς ἔρροντας ἐπ'
ἄκραις
Σαλαμινίασι στυφελοῦ
θείνοντας ἐπ' ἀκτᾶς.
Χο. οἰοιοῖ ποῦ [δέ] σοι
Φαρνοῦχος 967
'Αριόμαρδός τ' ἀγαθός,
κτλ.
τάδε σ' ἐπανερόμαν. 973

967 οἰοιοῖ ⟨βόα⟩ deleto δέ Hermann. 968 κ' ἀριόμαρδοστ' M. κ' del. Brunck.

Ξε. ἰὼ ἰώ μοι τὰς ὠγυγίους
κατιδόντες 974 ⏑ – ⏑ – – + paroem.
στυγνὰς 'Αθάνας πάντες
ἑνὶ πιτύλῳ – – ⏑ – – + doch.
ἐὴ ἐὴ τλάμονες ἀσπαίρουσι
χέρσῳ. ⏑ – ⏑ – – + ionic dim.
Χο. ἦ καὶ κτλ. 978
ἔλιπες ἔλιπες; ὢ ὢ ὢ δᾴων 985 ⏑ ⏑ ⏑ ⏑ ⏑ ⏑ – – – – –
Πέρσαις ἀγαυοῖς κακὰ
πρόκακα λέγεις. – – ⏑ – – ⏑ ⏑ ⏑ ⏑ ⏑ ⏑ –

974 μοῖ μοῖ M Wil. κατιδόντες ⟨τὰς⟩ post Blomfield Mazon.

Ξε. ἴυγγά μοι δῆτ' ἀγαθῶν 988
ἑτάρων ⟨ἀνακινεῖς⟩
⟨ἄλαστ'⟩ ἄλαστα στυγνὰ
πρόκακα λέγων.
βοᾷ βοᾷ ⟨μοι⟩ μελέων
ἔνδοθεν ἦτορ.
Χο. καὶ μὴν κτλ.
ἔταφον ἔταφον οὐκ ἀμφὶ
σκηναῖς
τροχηλάτοισιν ὄπιθεν
ἑπομένους. ⏑ – ⏑ – ⏑ ⏑ ⏑ ⏑ ⏑ ⏑ ⏑ –

988 δῆτα Schroeder 989 ἀνακινεῖς conieci ὑπομιμνήσκεις codd. ὑπορίνεις Hermann.

990 ἄλαστ' add. Hermann. 991 ἔντοσθεν post Blomf. edd.

Wil. ⟨ἰὼ ἰὼ⟩ δῆτα,
ἴυγγ' ἀγαθῶν ἑτάρων μοι
⟨κινεῖς⟩ ἄλαστα κτλ.

COMMENTARY

928–9. Hardly enough ground, perhaps, for introducing conjectures into the text, but βασιλεῦ γαίας is certainly suspicious after Ἀσία δὲ χθών, and some of Σ make an effort to connect γαίας with ἐπὶ γόνυ κέκλιται. Wilamowitz's emendation is perhaps undesirable on formal grounds in that (1) it breaks the triadic recurrence of spondaic lines to which Schroeder calls attention (but this is not of much significance), (2) the parallel with 918 ὀτοτοῖ βασιλεῦ στρατιᾶς ἀγαθῆς, in an anapaestic series of different type, is hardly probable. I would suggest that αἰαῖ γαίας would easily account for the codd., given the predilection for filling in missing monometers in anapaests, and would give a rather better sense to κεδνᾶς ἀλκᾶς. Is there any urgent reason for following Meineke as all edd. do in taking 928 from Xerxes? 932 is not his introductory utterance in any case; he has spoken 909–17. (Wilamowitz's punctuation after αἰακτός thus seems mistaken.) Wilamowitz and Schroeder call attention to the 'separation of the last triad' by hiatus after 927, and Wilamowitz suggests that it was spoken by the coryphaeus. The hiatus could more naturally be attributed to Xerxes' intervention; but as a matter of fact the exclamation itself is quite sufficient excuse, cf. 932.

The omission of a monometer is not in itself objectionable; Schroeder's three equal triads with a paraceleusmatic in the close instead of catalexis is only one possible account of the metrical pattern. It might equally well end in a penultimate monometer+ clausula of two dochmiacs. The alternative interpretations of the last line can in the nature of things never advance beyond formal analysis; the line in any case falls into two halves and the sequence of syllables is undoubted; whether a difference would be perceptible in actual elocution we shall never know with certainty. Even the test of analogy fails, since these anapaests are in a class by themselves, more regular than 'Klaganapäste' yet with the α of song instead of the recitative η. It can only be a tentative suggestion that on general grounds an alien clausula is less startling than an anapaest of the form ⏑ ⏑ ⏑ ⏑ ⏑ ⏑ – among such well-disciplined fellows; that in fact the nearest parallel would be Sophocles' ithyphallic close to an anapaestic series *El.* 200. Whether – – – – should be regarded as actually a form of dochmiac or as a 'dochmiac equivalent' is again little more than a matter of terminology; 1075–6 show the same foot in dochmiac society again. The iambic penthemimer ⏓ – ⏑ – – 975 and 986 raises the same question.

In the following threnody however there are stronger reasons for interpreting ⏑ ⏑ ⏑ ⏑ ⏑ ⏑ – as a dochmiac throughout. It can scarcely be anything else (given the context) 987=1001 κακὰ πρόκακα λέγεις and ὄπιθεν ἑπομένους, and in 976 πάντες ἐνὶ πιτύλῳ it removes all doubt by lengthening the first anceps. As freedom of responsion in such lengthening is a prerogative of dochmiacs we are entitled to take the most obvious correction of λαοπαθῆ τε 945 and read λᾱοπαθέα without trying to explain λᾱ- as an 'intensive prefix' or conjecturing some such word as νεοπαθέα. Wilamowitz following Burney reads σὰ πάθη τε, making the line an anapaestic dimeter. Coupled with such a phrase as ἀλίτυπά τε βάρη and in responsion with κακοφάτιδα βοὰν κακομέλετον ἰὰν in a θρῆνος so formally elaborate, this is a heavy lapse into stylistic and metrical bathos. A dochmiac clausula at 934 and 973 is again more easily assumed than an anapaestic monometer. Ἀγβάτανα λιπών 961 is a more dubious case. Weil's suggestion (prompted by Ἀγαβάτας 959) is untempting, and it might be better to explain – ∪ ∪ ∪ ∪ – as a resolution of the dochmiac form – – – –, the proper name being sufficient excuse for the licence of responsion. Certainly at the close of the play it would be difficult to explain τρισκάλμοισιν 1075 as anything else, given the following βᾶρισιν ὀλομένα, which cannot be anapaestic. 985=999 thus also falls into place as a clausula of 2 doch. dims. ∪ ∪ ∪ ∪ ∪ ∪ – – – – – | ⊻ – ∪ – ⊻ ∪ ∪ ∪ ∪ ∪ ∪ –.

More important is the problem of 938=948. It happens that the prosody of both πολύδακρυν and ἰαχάν is ambiguous, and the great majority of edd. give a paroemiac clausula, deleting one πέμψω. But in cases of faulty responsion, especially in a much-corrupted text, the sound method is surely to consider first whether either strophe or antistrophe is in itself unobjectionable and can be taken as a fixed starting-point, not to force the good line into conformity with the weaker because emendation happens to look more straightforward that way, nor to make adjustments from both sides. πέμψω πέμψω πολύδακρυν ἰαχάν after the clausula 930 gives excellent style, sense and metre, and if it had not been for the antistrophe would never have roused a suspicion. κλάγξω δ' αὖ γόον ἀρίδακρυν – – – ∪ ∪ ∪ ∪ – – on the other hand is a paroemiac of a shape nowhere else found among anapaests of any kind, even the freest 'Klaganapäste' subsequently elaborated by Euripides. The rare sequence – ∪ ∪ ∪ ∪ – is except in proper names confined to the opening of the line, i.e. is comprised within the same metron.[1] If Aesch. *had* used such a form here it is almost inconceivable that he should not at least have set it in strict responsion, but πέμψω πολύδᾱκρυν ἰᾱχάν is as pedestrian a form as could be wished. Moreover (1) δ' αὖ is not easily explained so late in the sentence except by giving a forced sense to πενθητῆρος and putting a stop after it. (2) The codd. in this context are liable to break out in conjectures apparently inspired by a desire to touch up

[1] E.g. Eur. *I.A.* 1322 ὤφελεν ἐλάταν πομπαίαν. The one exception appears to be Eur. *Hec.* 97 πέμψατε δαίμονες ἱκετεύω. Nauck deletes the line; I suspect wholesale interpolations in the context. In any case the fact that the first metron is wholly dactylic mitigates the abnormality here.

the metre of odd phrases taken in isolation, such as 945 λαοπαθῆ τε σεβίζων (clearly the starting-point was the contraction λαοπαθῆ), 939 ἵετ' αἰανῆ καὶ πανόδυρτον. These are not *clever* metrical conjectures related to the context, such as the insertion of πέμψω 939 would have been (for that it arose by the accident of dittography will scarcely be claimed). The more pretentious metrical conjectures like οἶ οἶ λέγε καὶ πάντ' ἐκπεύθου 954, ποῦ δέ σοι φίλων ὄχλος 955 are found only in one or two manuscripts and are Byzantine work. (3) To return continually to the same closing formula (here ⏑̲ ⏑ ⏑ ⏑ ⏑ ⏑ –) in successive stanzas in long lyrical odes is very much in Aesch.'s manner.

Emendation of the antistrophe is not easy. Hermann's conjecture is violent palaeographically and gives too close a parallel to the strophe. κλάγξω ⟨κλάγξω⟩ δὲ γόον ἀρίδακρυν leaves πάνδυρτον without a substantive expressed and thus cuts out the most natural interpretation of γέννας πενθητῆρος = Mariandynian. Moreover both δέ and δ' αὖ (if the latter be kept as a permissible dochmiac variant) are open to the metrical objection that alone in this whole threnody they break the diaeresis in the middle of anapaestic or dochmiac dimeters. It is possible that δ' αὖ γόον conceals δύσθροον (cf. 942) and that a disyllabic substantive has dropped out after κλάγξω picking up πάνδυρτον and the genitive γέννας πενθητῆρος—some such word as φωνάν.

Wilamowitz, followed by Schroeder, complicates matters by transferring the πέμψω left on his hands to 935 and omitting τάν, thereby making this line an acatalectic dimeter. Apart from the violence of the procedure this gives a broken diaeresis and involves an awkward emendation of the blameless antistrophe. But in rejecting τάν he is surely right: as he says, 'foedum vitium admittebant qui articulum in catalexi tolerabant'. In the lyrics of tragedy the first syllable of a word, or a proclitic monosyllable, is tolerated at the end of a colon after a *long* penultimate[1] only in recognised synartete

[1] A legitimate exception to this rule occurs where the lengthened penultimate is an irregular variation on a normal short, cf. Soph. *O.T.* 1196 (corresponding to a short), *Ant.* 1132 (a chor. dim. *rallentando*). The many other violations printed in our texts are due to faulty colometry.

dicola (such as the Archilochian after Archilochus, see *Heph.* 15, 88) and in metres of the 'dactylo-epitrite' type, where the last syllable of a colon is designed to be the link with the following colon. On the same grounds Blomfield's insertion of ⟨τάς⟩ at the end of 974 in order to save ὑπομιμνήσκεις in the antistrophe should never have been adopted by modern editors. In 935 if a monosyllable such as νυν had dropped out τάν might have edged itself in from the line below, as a corrected variant on ἰάν. Once τάν is away the balance of the sentence is restored and its interpretation easier; instead of τὰν κακοφάτιδα βοὰν Μαριανδυνοῦ θρηνητῆρος (Wilamowitz points out that the article is stylistically out of place here) with πολύδακρυν ἰαχάν in apposition, it is possible to take the genitive νόστου more closely with κακοφάτιδα and κακομέλετον and the whole phrase πρόσφθογγον...ἰάν as predicative: 'Therefore to greet your ear, a cry of ill omen, a voice of ill boding for your return, will I send the Mariandynian mourner's weeping lament.'

Xerxes resumes 949 in ionic metre. 'Reiziana' are in the fashion now, but here I would suggest that (1) with such colometry the contraction ναῦφρακτος and shortened syllaba anceps in *both* strophe and antistrophe are suspicious; (2) the ionic trimeter is found in this form in hieratic song, Ar. *Ran.* 330 and cf. Anacr. frag. 51 (Bergk) γαλαθηνόν, ὅστ' ἐν ὕλης κεροέσσης; (3) trimetric construction of a studied and unusual form is characteristic of this context, cf. the next phrase, an anap. trim. cat., and in the next strophe again the trimetric combination of anapaestic and ionic elements.

955. Lachmann was the first to restore the correct assignment of speakers here, and in an ode of this formal regularity there can be no departure from strict correspondence. ἐκπεύθου is therefore self-exhortation of the Chorus, which then turns to Xerxes with the natural formula 'But where...?' If ἐκπεύθου were Xerxes' invitation, as Wilamowitz takes it, δέ would be meaningless. In the confused double corruption of 955=967 perhaps the best starting-point is the antistrophe, where Hermann's excision [δέ] 967 and Brunck's [κ'] 968 are universally accepted. The most natural explanation of the syllaba anceps in Φαρνοῦχος is catalexis, i.e. the line is a paroemiac. If it is to be a complete anap. dim. as Wilamowitz and

Schroeder take it we must add τ' to keep synaphea. But the paroemiac is supported by (1) the preceding σοι and καί in 955, both of which would break the diaeresis in a complete dimeter; (2) the excellent parallel with the other paroemiac gambits of the context, 932 and 936 (preceding strophe), 978 (following strophe). It follows that οἰοιοῖ must either be shortened to οἰοῖ with F R Tricl. 955 or emended to ὀτοτοῖ or pronounced with correption. It is possible that in 955 the corruption goes deeper, but the simplest expedient is to cut out βόα, cf. *Sept.* 89 where βοᾷ has intruded into the text, apparently in place of an actual cry of dismay.[1] Wilamowitz would have βόα spoken as a single bark, which still does not explain how in his version nine long syllables are conceived to correspond with eight.

974–8=987–91. Wilamowitz and Schroeder retain the double μοι of M, which causes difficulties in the antistrophe. Schroeder's hiatus after δῆτα has no particular metrical or rhetorical support, while Wilamowitz's disturbance of the text goes unnecessarily far and it is hard to believe that his paroemiac ἴυγγ' ἀγαθῶν ἑτάρων μοι would have satisfied Aeschylus's ear. A reconstruction in Hermann's sense is the most natural (for my suggestion ἀνακινεῖς cf. Soph. *Tr.* 1259. I take ὑπομιμνήσκεις to be a gloss on the whole phrase ἀνακ. ἴυγγα). With Dindorf's generally accepted ⟨μοι⟩ 991 this gives a series of three cola founded on the iambic penthemimer ⏑ – ⏑ – ⏓, a phrase which sometimes appears among dochmiac variants (as here 976 and 986) and more often as a constituent part of cola where it is detachable only by formal analysis: so here 977 = 990, a line essentially similar to *P.V.* 128 and 133. Anacreontics pass over easily into regular ionic dims. or ⏑ ⏑ – – – ⏑ – – (cf. *P.V.* 400 and 406), and it is just possible that we may keep ἔνδοθεν here as a licence of responsion such as occurs *P.V.* 400=408 (the text is quite sound) and several times in the hymn Ar. *Ran.* 323–50.

[1] It is tempting in *Pers.* 955 to imagine a disyllable imperative='Cry οἶ.'

3

STASIMON AND HYPORCHEME

In chapter 12 of the *Poetics*, defining the formal or quantitative divisions of tragedy, Aristotle subdivides the choral lyric into Parodos and Stasimon, which are found in every tragedy, and adds that some plays have songs from the stage and Kommoi also. Songs from the stage are lyric but not choral—the transition of thought is natural and inoffensive; Kommoi are divided between stage and orchestra. The purely orchestral lyric can always be ranged under two heads (exodic lines, where they occur, are generally few and perfunctory, and Aristotle ignores them), Parodos and Stasimon: χορικόν, τούτου δὲ τὸ μὲν πάροδος, τὸ δὲ στάσιμον. The two are mutually exclusive, and no Greek, hearing them together like this, could fail to be aware of the implied antithesis between ὁδεύειν and ἵστασθαι. In the Parodos the chorus is 'coming on', and has to move on to and across the orchestra to take its place in the middle; in all the stasima, however active and lively the dance, its evolutions are performed from that middle position (*a choro tenente stationes suas*, as Hermann said in 1844), and do not involve processional movement.

This distinction is simple and straightforward; it is also practical. Since this is the first extant use of στάσιμον as a technical term, there has been much speculation as to its origin. It is quite likely to have originated in the theatre itself; what more practical mode of designation for the χοροδιδάσκαλος calling for rehearsal? Parodos requires special grouping and position; the rest would be first Stasimon, second Stasimon, and so on. Unfortunately the amplification of these terms by Aristotle a few lines further on has led to a great deal of subtle theorising as to the origin, real meaning, and applicability of the word Stasimon, and the term itself misled later grammarians who tried to expand and interpret Aristotelian doctrine at a time when choral lyric in the classical tradition was no longer a living art.

The words are: χορικοῦ δὲ πάροδος μὲν ἡ πρώτη λέξις ὅλη [ὅλου

Ac] χοροῦ, στάσιμον δὲ μέλος χοροῦ τὸ ἄνευ ἀναπαίστου καὶ τροχαίου, κομμὸς δὲ θρῆνος κοινὸς χοροῦ καὶ ἀπὸ σκηνῆς. Here Aristotle is giving general definitions, without troubling to make the reservations and qualifications necessary for complete accuracy; thus for instance the κομμός is not always threnetic and the orchestral contributions need not be sung by the whole chorus, the Parodos may take commatic form, and so on. 'Parodos is the whole first utterance of the chorus, Stasimon is choral song proper, i.e. (τὸ) it contains no [recitative] anapaests or trochaics.' The words τὸ ἄνευ ἀναπαίστου καὶ τροχαίου are an amplification of μέλος, and ἀν. and τροχ. stand for the overwhelmingly commonest forms of these metres, the anapaestic dimeter and tetrameter and the trochaic tetrameter catalectic, which here convey the meaning 'recitative metres' in general. The words do *not* imply that there were other kinds of μέλος which did contain such metres; μέλος by definition excludes recitative. Aristotle ignores (as an exception) the substitution of anapaests for a proper stasimon, Eur. *Med.* 1081 ff., and does not count occasional introductory anapaests as part of a stasimon proper. Trochaic tetrameters delivered as choral recitative occur in the parodoi of comedy, not in any of our extant tragedies. Σ Ar. *Ach.* 204 could be taken as evidence that they were to be found in some lost tragedies, but the assumption is not absolutely necessary here. The Stasimon is sung; it therefore excludes recitative; these are the commonest kinds of recitative metre, and they can both be associated with progressive movement, anapaests with marching, trochaics (cf. Σ Ar. *Ach.* 204) with running; hence this negative formulation is appropriate to Stasimon. Parodos is differently defined; it is 'the chorus's first utterance taken as a whole', whether song or recitative or both; hence the use of the general word λέξις. Hence too ὅλη (Westphal) is a necessary emendation of ὅλου: (*a*) ὅλου is pointless; even if parts of the Parodos were occasionally given by the leader alone, or by individual choreutae, they would still belong to the Parodos, (*b*) ὅλη corresponds to all the other definitions in the context (πρόλογος μὲν μέρος ὅλον τραγῳδίας etc.), (*c*) πρώτη λέξις ὅλη, and not πρώτη καὶ ὅλη λέξις is, *pace* Gudeman, the correct Greek for what Aristotle wants to say, (*d*) the corruption is an easy one, and the fact that the text of Tzetzes' paraphrase has ἄλλου (i.e. probably ὅλου) only means that it occurred at an early date, (*e*) Plutarch's reference, *An Seni Sit Ger. Resp.* III 785 a, to Soph. *O.C.* 668 ff. as the parodos of that play (see Schmid–Stählin I 2, p. 56, n. 5) can only be a lapse of memory; no interpretation of Aristotle's words could convert this stasimon into a parodos.

Aristotle's definitions are thus in line with what we know of fifth-century tragedy. Moreover, since the term Stasimon is adequately accounted for as a simple antithesis to Parodos, it can only lead to confusion to seek to substitute or superimpose here some other possible sense of the word στάσιμον in isolation or in other contexts. Kranz in his *Stasimon* (1933) repeats the view of his earlier dissertation *De Forma Stasimi* (Berlin 1910) that the original sense of the term must have been the opposite of κινητικόν, the tragic ode being essentially a reserved, stately movement in *tempo moderato*. There is no evidence for such a use as early as this, for certainly none can be made out of Aristotle's τὸ ἄνευ ἀναπαίστου καὶ τροχαίου. These are not typically rhythms associated with rapid or wild movement (cretic-paeonic and ionic would have been a better choice); nor should we connect τροχαίου here with Aristotle's remarks elsewhere about the orchestic nature of the trochaic tetrameter as opposed to the iambic trimeter. The context here, in particular the association with ἀναπαίστου, shows that it is recitative, not wild dance, that is being excluded.

Nor are there any grounds for crediting Aristotle with the views of later grammarians—to call them Alexandrians is to be more precise than the evidence warrants—on the sense in which the Stasimon is 'stationary.' Schmid–Stählin I 2, p. 56, n. 4 deprecates accusations of 'errores grammaticorum Graecorum' in this connection, but it is possible to trace the growth of error here more clearly than usual, and error, moreover, which leads to mutually contradictory conclusions. There is one school of thought which, while adopting the threefold division of choral lyric into παροδικά, στάσιμα and κομματικά, interprets these as three successive stages in the development of the action; thus an interpolation in the Hypothesis to Aesch. *Pers.* runs: τῶν δὲ χορικῶν τὰ μέν ἐστι παροδικά, ὅτε λέγει δι' ἣν αἰτίαν πάρεστιν, ὡς τὸ 'Τύριον οἶδμα λιποῦσα' (Eur. *Phoen.* 202), τὰ δὲ στάσιμα, ὅτε ἵσταται καὶ ἄρχεται τῆς συμφορᾶς τοῦ δράματος, τὰ δὲ κομματικά, ὅτε λοιπὸν ἐν θρήνῳ γίνεται. On the other hand, the Scholiast on *Phoen.* 202 expressly claims that song as a stasimon: ὅταν γὰρ ὁ χορὸς μετὰ τὴν πάροδον λέγει τι μέλος πρὸς τὴν ὑπόθεσιν ἀνῆκον ἀκίνητος μένων, στάσιμον λέγεται τὸ ᾆσμα. πάροδος δέ ἐστιν ᾠδὴ χοροῦ βαδίζοντος ᾀδομένη ἅμα τῇ ἐξόδῳ ὡς τὸ 'σῖγα σῖγα λευκὸν ἴχνος ἀρβύλης τίθετε' (Eur. *Or.* 140). He would include, apparently, under Parodos only those instances where the words expressly indicate the Chorus's emergence and progress. It is difficult to understand why Aly (*RE*, *s.v.* Stasimon) and Schmid–Stählin assume that this is good Aristotelian doctrine. Whatever our uncertainties as to how, and where, the chorus sang and danced an ode *in responsion* on its first appearance, Aristotle explicitly reckons such odes under Parodos: ἡ πρώτη λέξις ὅλη χοροῦ, and says that every play contains both Parodos and Stasimon. The Scholiast's qualification πρὸς τὴν ὑπόθεσιν ἀνῆκον gives the show away; the words do not mean 'rein sachlichen Inhalts', but 'relevant to the plot', i.e. he is distinguishing στάσιμον from ἐμβόλιμον.

More serious, however, is ἀκίνητος μένων. It is evident that this scholiast shared the error of so many grammarians and took στάσιμον to mean an ode without dance, whose performers stood stock still. Not all betray themselves so unambiguously, however. The occurrence of the word στάντας in Ar. *Vesp.* 270 starts the Scholiast off on a muddled note about the types of choral song: πρὸ τῶν θυρῶν τοῦ Φιλοκλέωνος στάντες οἱ τοῦ χοροῦ τὸ στάσιμον ᾄδουσι μέλος κτλ., with illustrations drawn from tragedy and comedy indiscriminately. (It is doubtful whether Aristotle would have regarded the tragic terms as applicable to the much more complex forms of the chorus of Old Comedy, and the fact that later grammarians do so treat them is no reason for interpreting, with Aly and others, the phrase κοινὰ μὲν ἁπάντων ταῦτα in *Poet.* chap. 12 as 'common to all *forms of* drama', much less as 'common to all forms of choral lyric', and ἴδια δὲ as 'peculiar to tragedy'.) The words, however, do not expressly commit the Scholiast to the notion of a comic chorus rendering the following ionics as a static oratorio.

Similarly, Σ Ar. *Ran.* 1281, misinterpreting στάσιν μελῶν as στάσιμον μέλος, adds ὃ ᾄδουσιν ἱστάμενοι οἱ χορευταί, and in this non-committal but certainly misleading form the definition reaches the lexicon of Suidas. The ἀκίνητος μένων of Σ *Phoen.* 202 leaves no room for doubt.

A few modern scholars have swallowed this whole, though such a divorce of dance from song is contrary to all we know of the classical tradition of choral lyric. Others conjecture a change of habit towards the end of the fifth century, on the strength of Plato Com. Σκευαί (frag. 130 K):

> ὥστ' εἴ τις ὀρχοῖτ' εὖ, θέαμ' ἦν· νῦν δὲ δρῶσιν οὐδέν,
> ἀλλ' ὥσπερ ἀπόπληκτοι στάδην ἑστῶτες ὠρύονται.

It is not at all certain that this refers to tragic choreutae, but in any case the jibe of a comic poet is not to be taken as a piece of literal evidence. Are we to imagine a paralytic chorus of Bacchae? The remark would be much more likely to raise a laugh if, for instance, there had recently been a notorious instance of a chorus cumbersomely dressed (cf. the title Σκευαί) and unable to execute much foot-movement.

Once this false notion of στάσιμον had become fixed, the commentators found themselves in difficulties with those choruses where the words expressly refer to dancing movement; thus Σ Soph. *Tr.* 216 notes the exception: τὸ γὰρ μελιδάριον οὐκ ἔστι στάσιμον, ἀλλὰ ὑπὸ τῆς ἡδονῆς ὀρχοῦνται. And the authorities whom the Byzantine Tzetzes follows added to Parodos, Stasimon and Kommos a fourth εἶδος χορικοῦ to cover these exceptions, calling it a ὑπόρχημα, or 'song accompanied by dance'. This has led to endless confusion, since the term, used here in a general sense, has also a technical meaning, as a particular category of lyric performance. To determine accurately the special characteristics of the various lyric types is an impossible task for us, and the more our store of fragments is added to the more irretrievably mixed the categories appear. The Hyporcheme is peculiarly troublesome, since our ancient authorities give contradictory accounts of it (Lucian, *de Salt.* 16 mentions a kind where choirs of singers and dancers were separate performers,

Athenaeus I 15 regards the mimetic dance accompanying a solo-citharode as the ὑπορχηματικὸς τρόπος which flourished under Xenodamus and Pindar, whereas to Plut. *Quaest. Conviv.* IX 152 and *Etym. Mag.* it is essentially an art of simultaneous dance and song) and are always liable to pass from the technical to the general sense without warning (cf. the inextricably confused account in Ath. XIV 628–31); in this respect the word is as vague as ὕμνος and ὑμνεῖν. The Hyporcheme may have originated in Crete (cf. Pind. frag. 97), and has given its name to a cretic-paeonic type of foot ⏑ ⏑ ⏑ –, the ποῦς ὑπορχηματικός of the Scholiast to Hephaestion, though this metre is not at all prominent in our extant fragments. What seems to emerge with fair probability is that the Hyporcheme was particularly at home in Sparta, that it was characterised by dancing of especial speed, vigour and expressiveness, and that its form was non-responsive; at least our longest fragment, from the Hyporcheme of Pratinas, shows no trace of responsion in its 19 lines. In connection with this fragment counsel has been yet further darkened by all those scholars who insist that it must come from a satyr-play, though Athenaeus XIV 617 is quite explicit that it was a Hyporcheme and a protest by the author against the professionalisation of flute-playing and choral dancing. Pohlenz's account of the poem (*Gr. Tr.* pp. 21–2) as depicting a fight between choruses of two rival types followed by the rout of the one and the triumphal dance of the winner is further elaborated by Schmid–Stählin I 2, pp. 179 f. into the grandiose picture of an early type of Satyr-play anticipating the dramatic criticism of Old Comedy; but the picture is wholly imaginary, since what the fragment shows us is a chorus turning in mock anger on its own flute, i.e. flute-player (θόρυβος and χορεύματα are the horrid skirlings of the instrument), and reducing him to a properly subordinate state of mind and performance. A Hyporcheme in the technical sense cannot be contained in a satyr-play or a tragedy, any more than a Paean or a Prosodion or a Dithyramb, though a tragic ode may on occasion be reminiscent, in style or content, of any of these forms. The argument, therefore, whether a given tragic ode, such as Soph. *Aj.* 693 ff., *O.T.* 1086 ff., Eur. *El.* 859 ff., is or is not a Hyporcheme, as found in some of our critical editions, is without meaning. If we knew enough about the Hyporcheme, we might find this or that stasimon to be 'hyporchematic' in tone, but this is not what Tzetzes and the older grammarians meant by their use of the word in defining the parts of tragedy. To them it was a 'song accompanied by dancing', a necessary invention once Stasimon had come to be thought a 'motionless song'.

4

THE METRICAL UNITS OF GREEK LYRIC VERSE. I[1]

I

What kind of Theory of Music and Theory of Metric was taught to the young Pindar or the young Sophocles? So far are we from an answer to this question that we do not even know how far extra study was necessary, or usual, for the professional poet as compared with the ordinary educated Greek citizen. The interdependence of music and metric in lyric poetry gave complexity to the word-rhythms but kept the study of music, the subordinate partner, theoretically simple. Doubtless by the time the young poet had learnt by heart the words of past masters of lyric verse, sung or accompanied them on the lyre, and danced them in choir or κῶμος, he had absorbed by practice and somewhat rule-of-thumb methods of training a great deal of the τέχνη which his calling would require. He would have to learn, in common with the χοροδιδάσκαλος, how to read and write a simple score, and so he must know the symbols of pitch in such scales as were then in use. The notation of arsis and thesis may have been required too, and if we knew that this was so, and how he was taught to apply it, we might be in a much better position to assess the kind of theory he learnt. But of one thing we may be sure: genius apart, it was his practical training, as performer and spectator, rather than theoretical teaching which gave his ear its cunning and technical skill to compose new rhythms. Hence the impotence of that τέχνη to survive once the composition and performance of new songs ceased to be a vital need in Greek life. There was no systematic body of theory to preserve and explain this intricate art, and by the time theoreticians got under way and began to annotate and classify they lacked the practical understanding

[1] I am indebted to Professors Paul Maas, Donald Robertson, and Bruno Snell for their kindness in reading and criticising this article.

which could have amplified and corrected the inadequate concepts and terminology bequeathed to them.

The surviving works of grammarians and metricians, therefore, even selectively used, cannot supply us with adequate equipment for the analysis and comprehension of this difficult art of 'metric'. We are driven to supplement their doctrine from our own observations and intuitions. And here there is a risk that we may draw upon our native aesthetic prejudices, without realising where these are derived from a poetry to which 'metric' is wholly alien or a music which does indeed 'measure' its notes quantitatively but in obedience to its own autonomous laws, not within the bounds of a formalised speech-rhythm such as restricted Greek song-notes in general (at least in 'classical' lyric) to simple longs and shorts, that is, full notes and half notes.

The complexity of Greek metrical phenomena leads inevitably to a search for ordering principles on which to base analysis. This usually resolves itself into a search for rhythmical units of analysis which by combining in different ways are capable of producing all the rich variety of Greek verse. Ancient tradition found this in the various 'feet', disyllabic or trisyllabic, though these had sometimes to be taken in dipodies or 'compound feet' before they could form practicable measuring units or 'metra'. The metra have been adopted in modern theory, together with their names—iambic, choriambic, dactylic, etc., the less organic disyllabic 'feet' being generally discarded as superfluous subdivisions which cannot be inserted or subtracted singly. Here then is a satisfactory method of analysing forms of verse which have a single recurring movement κατὰ μέτρον, and the added notions of 'resolution', 'contraction', 'syncopation', and 'catalexis' bring a great many diverse rhythms into this framework. The difficulties begin with sequences of syllables which contain no smaller recurring unit. Is – ∪ ∪ – ∪ – ∪ – to be analysed as choriambic+iambic metron? Then what is – ∪ ∪ – ∪ – – – which appears in the same company? or – – – – – ∪ ∪ – or – – – ∪ ∪ – ∪ – –? And what are we to do with the common – ∪ – ∪ ∪ – ∪ –? How can we decide whether to follow the school of thought which sticks to 'quadrisyllabic scansion' (and so get involved with the 'antispast' in ⏑ – – ⏑ | – ⏑ ⏑ –) or that which revives the 'foot' and reads 'troch., troch., iamb, iamb', or a third which divides – ⏑ | – ⏑ ⏑ | – ⏑ | – and says the 'natural feeling for rhythm' demands four units each taking an equal quantity of time so that the 'dactyl' has to be hurried over—is in fact a 'cyclic dactyl', equivalent to a trochee, unlike the more leisured dactyl of the hexameter which is the equivalent of a spondee? The way out of these sterile controversies was found when it was realised that the whole 'colon' must be taken as an indivisible phrase-unit, though some cola, being 'dimeters' or 'trimeters' of recurring movement, are susceptible of analytical subdivision. There remains, however, the problem of describing the rest; can they not for convenience be analysed on a purely *de facto* basis, in which case it would not matter whether ⏑ – – ⏑ – ⏑ ⏑ – was called iamb + trochee + trochee + iamb or antispast + choriamb? But any analysis of this kind cannot avoid *implications*—the implication that disyllabic feet are real units capable of combination, or that the 'antispast' is a 'metron' on a par with other tetrasyllabic metra like the choriamb or iambic. Any analysis, in fact, which uses the names of metra leads straight into theory and must be able to take the consequences.

Analysis by metra, therefore, cannot work satisfactorily except where the movement of a colon is in fact a straightforwardly recurrent 'length' (dimeter, trimeter, etc.) of a particular movement, or where modifications can be accounted for by resolution, contraction, syncopation, or catalexis. A special case of modification can sometimes be made out for 'anaclasis', as for instance in ionics, where ⏑ ⏑ – ⏒ – ⏑ – – is clearly sometimes used as a variation on ⏑ ⏑ – – ⏑ ⏑ – – after Anacreon, and the two are even found in responsion. But outside these limits the device of 'metrising' has its dangers. Thus the notion of 'aeolic dactyls', which has held the field since the time of Hephaestion, has given rise to the false theory that a 'final anceps' (the licence to shorten a long final syllable) can equally well take the form of a lengthened final short × × – ⏑ ⏑ – ⏑ ⏑ – ⏑ ⏒. It has also obscured the relation of, for example, × × – ⏑ ⏑ – ⏑ ⏑ – ⏑ – to × × – ⏑ ⏑ – ⏑ –, or else led to the 'dactylic' scanning of the latter. Again, variations which are permissible in certain relations to a prevailing context of normal rhythm κατὰ μέτρον, such as – ⏑ – – in the anacreontic mentioned above, have been accepted outside such context with much resulting confusion of classification. For if Simonides' *Danae* be interpreted as ionics and therefore broken up into metra, then the concept 'ionic' is loosened and blurred accordingly and strange doctrines may prevail as to what is permissible elsewhere, even in responsion, in so capricious and unaccountable a metre, and the canons of textual criticism are thus also affected. Or when the licence, confined to the spoken iambics of comedy, of equating ⏖̆ – ⏖̆ – to ⏓ – ⏑ –, is made to lead to the discovery of loose and irregular 'iambics' in the highly formalised song-technique of Pindar, the proprieties of Greek metric—its nice distinction of styles—are thereby offended.

The metron, then, tetrasyllabic or other, is to be rejected as an analytic unit except in cases of recurring movement, and the names associated with metra must be similarly restricted. We come next to the cola. The disadvantage of the colon as the lowest unit is its size, which gives room for much diversity and makes theoretical grouping more difficult. Here association in contexts, the characteristics of the various types of poetry, and the favourite modifications of particular poets, have all to be taken into account in deciding how to reduce the number of categories, which can be taken as norms and which as variants, and (a common and significant phenomenon) where categories overlap. The traditional terminology has bequeathed a number of names (as distinct from 'metrising' descriptions) for whole cola, or dicola, names sometimes, like 'glyconic', derived from poets who made particular use of them, sometimes measuring by syllables (the 'Sapphic hendecasyllable', etc.), sometimes referring to occasions of use ('priapean', 'prosodiac'). This variety represents a natural, empirical process of nomenclature, though it adds to the difficulties of the subject for the modern beginner, and obscures some of the cross-relations. It also leaves a number of types unnamed, and others obscurely or contradictorily defined; and modern scholarship suffers in general from having inherited no agreed, automatic system of definition or description which shows the relation of cola to one another.

With all the defects of the received terminology, it is both practicable and desirable to use it for the analysis of most solo-lyric and the choral lyrics of drama. Its real inadequacy begins to be felt in the most difficult branch of Greek versification, the choral lyric outside drama, and here its effect has been positively and seriously misleading for a workable theory of metric. Ancient theorists had a very imperfect comprehension of this lyric, and the root of the trouble was their inorganic line-division, through which they tried to wrest it to the more familiar shapes of a different and simpler style of composition. Boeckh's edition of Pindar, with its stanzas divided into *periods* instead of cola, the end of a period coinciding with the end of a word and often supported by the occurrence of hiatus and brevis in longo, at last provided the basis for a sounder theoretical study. The repeating triads, in all but the shortest poems, give a much needed check for the determination of period-end; no calculation, no schematic patterns, and no appeal to rhythmical sense on our part could without this check give any assurance that we had found the right shape for a single stanza of this arbitrary, deliberately unsymmetrical, constantly inventive poetic technique, which gives to each ode its unique, νεοσίγαλον τρόπον. This is true especially of Pindar, who appears to have had a much greater metrical range, and greater daring, than any other lyric poet, but it applies also in varying degree to Stesichorus, Simonides, Bacchylides (perhaps least), Ariphron, the Pseudo-Arion's *Hymn to Poseidon*, Aristotle's *Hymn to Virtue*. It is true that in drama, too, each choral ode is metrically a new creation, and the degree of *unaccountability*, of irregular shape not reducible to any predictable formula, in the composition of tragic odes is much greater than in comedy, but the great difference remains that in drama the all-important structural element is the colon, whereas in other choral lyric it is the period.[1] Now cola tend constantly to repeat, to pair, to give balanced groupings, to echo back from a later to an earlier part of the stanza, to round off a full with a catalectic rhythm, a rising or 'blunt' with

[1] This statement (see below, p. 59) has to be modified to some extent for dactylo-epitrite, which, as will be seen, is the nearest point of approach between the two kinds of technique.

a falling or 'pendant' close. Many of different type are of roughly equivalent length, and each is a phrase short enough, or homogeneous enough, for the ear to carry it as a single entity. Sometimes the association of two, three, or four cola into a larger grouping or period is discernible; more often, since the stanzas usually repeat only in pairs if at all, such periods are not traceable and we can only note where the rhythm changes or where catalexis or hiatus leaves room for a pause. In either case the structural elements that carry the rhythm and are heard as separate phrases building it up are the cola; we can be fairly confident that these are the units with which the poet himself composed, and that we have some idea of the shape he intended to convey even when we are uncertain about the periods. But now consider such a stanza as this:

> ὁδῶν ὁδοὶ περαίτεραι, μία δ' οὐχ ἅπαντας ἄμμε θρέψει
> μελέτα· σοφίαι μὲν αἰπειναί· τοῦτο δὲ προσφέρων ἄεθλον,
> ὄρθιον ὤρυσαι θαρσέων,
> τόνδ' ἀνέρα δαιμονίᾳ γεγάμεν
> εὔχειρα, δεξιόγυιον, ὁρῶντ' ἀλκάν,
> Αἶαν, τεόν τ' ἐν δαιτί, Ἰλιάδα, νικῶν ἐπεστεφάνωσε βωμόν.

(Pind. *Ol.* 9. 105 ff.)[1] The period-ends are not at all certain, so that different versions are given by different scholars. As to how the periods should be analysed into smaller units, and still more over the interpretation of these, no two metricians can agree. There is little obvious repetition or rhythmical 'pick-up' to assist our untrained modern ear; the phrases do not fall apart of themselves. Word-end will not help, since Pindar often (though not consistently) makes a practice of bridging over the junctions of his phrase-units in order to carry the rhythm on to the end of the period. We are driven to theoretical study, and our theories are fallible.

One reason for their fallibility is the persistent search for cola of the same kind as in dramatic choruses, with their comfortingly familiar labels. If we set down a period in longs and shorts and succeed in dividing these up into 'anapaest + dochmiac + reizianum',

[1] Analysed in the second instalment of this article. [Pp. 72 f. in this collection.]

this is worth no more as an elucidation than to call – ᴗ – ᴗ ᴗ – ᴗ – 'trochaic+iambic metron'. A specious plausibility may be given to such analysis by sorting out several of these same elements in the rest of the stanza, but so long as 'anapaest' is used to cover both – – ᴗ ᴗ – and ᴗ ᴗ – ᴗ ᴗ –, 'dochmiac' any of the numerous varieties attested in their proper context in tragedy, and 'reizianum' such fictions as ᴗ ᴗ – ᴗ – – as well as – – ᴗ ᴗ – –, the gain is illusory. There is more justification for labelling

Ἄριστον μὲν ὕδωρ, ὁ δὲ χρυσὸς αἰθόμενον πῦρ

'priapean', i.e. 'glyconic+pherecratean', but here too there are reservations. The 'glyconic' has in every stanza an initial ᴗ –, whereas the 'pherecratean' starts – ᴗ; thus the latter is not simply a catalectic version of the former. It may prove fruitful to consider these openings in relation to other metrical units, and also to reflect upon the meaning of the difference between Pindar's 'glyconic' and the Sophoclean

τὸν σὸν δαίμονα, τὸν σόν, ὦ — – – – ᴗ ᴗ – ᴗ –
  τλᾶμον Οἰδιπόδα, βροτῶν... — – ᴗ – ᴗ ᴗ – ᴗ –

which is in responsion with

ἐμὸς καὶ τὰ μέγιστ' ἐτι- — ᴗ – – ᴗ ᴗ – ᴗ –
  -μάθης ταῖς μεγάλαισιν ἐν... — – – – ᴗ ᴗ – ᴗ –

Nor is such a combination as the priapean a metrical cliché in Pindar; its rarity in fact should again make us think twice. But the main problem is to know on what *principles* the longer periods can be split up. If Pind. *Nem.* 7. 13

σκότον πολὺν ὕμνων ἔχοντι δεόμεναι

is analysed by one scholar as an 'iambic' trimeter

ᴗ – ᴗ ᴗ – | – ᴗ – | ᴗ ᴗᴗ ᴗ –,

by another as two reiziana

ᴗ – ᴗ ᴗ – – | ᴗ – ᴗ ᴗ ᴗᴗ –

is one result preferable to the other, or are both wrong, or is it a matter of indifference? Can we hope to arrive at any notion of the kind of units the poet himself recognised? It can, I think, be accepted as certain that these periods *are* composite; all except the shortest are too long and too incredibly diverse to have been conceived as single wholes. The purpose of the present essay is to try to disengage by observation some principles of composition which appear to be discernible in all the varieties of choral lyric outside drama, and to show what this metrical art has in common with other forms of lyric and where its technique is different. It will be concerned chiefly with Pindar, as the most difficult of composers and the one who has suffered most from attempts to force his metric into conformity with better understood types of composition and to use the same terminology for all alike.

2

The rhythm of Greek verse is produced by collocations of long and short syllables punctuated by pause. Lyric verse, though sung, is based upon the natural prosody of speech-rhythm for its quantities but has sacrificed pitch-accent in favour of the principle of responsion. Since it has no returning dynamic stress such as can impose rhythm upon a lengthy sequence of notes of equal quantity, it can only use such sequences where the phrasing, the arrangement of pauses, or the prevailing rhythm of the context can keep them clear. Thus in Soph. *El.* 233–5 twenty-one long syllables are kept in a perfectly clear paroemiac rhythm:

ἀλλ' οὖν εὐοίᾳ γ' αὐδῶ
μάτηρ ὡσεί τις πιστά,
μὴ τίκτειν σ' ἄταν ἄταις

and thirty-two short syllables are achieved (as something of a *tour de force*) in Eur. *Or.* 149–50 with the help of the dochmiac echo of the whole context, into which they sink back in the next line:

κάταγε, κάταγε, πρόσιθ' ἀτρέμας, ἀτρέμας ἴθι·
λόγον ἀπόδος ἐφ' ὅ τι χρέος ἐμόλετέ ποτε.
χρόνια γὰρ πεσὼν ὅδ' εὐνάζεται. ⏑ ⏑ ⏑ – ⏑ – ⏑ – – ⏑ –

Uncontracted paroemiacs and unresolved dochmiacs are rhythms so familar that the ear takes these exaggerated variants without difficulty. But it is clear that such an effect is only possible where the movement is built up of cola, of repetitive phrase-units. Where there is no fairly simple, fairly symmetrical framework of this kind, longs and shorts must be constantly intermingled or the result will be shapeless. And such intermingling is the normal and fundamental habit of quantitative metric; the unmixed sequences are later, derivative variants.

The long syllables are, of course, the stronger of the two ingredients—in the metaphorical Greek expression of rhythm in terms of dance-movement they were the θέσις and the short syllables the unsteadier ἄρσις—and the primary formula for a rhythmic sequence is the enclosure of either one or two shorts between two longs, – ⏑ – or – ⏑ ⏑ –. Each of these can be set in movement in two ways: by repetition or by prolongation.

Repetition gives a series:

– ⏑ – – ⏑ – – ⏑ –...

– ⏑ ⏑ – – ⏑ ⏑ – – ⏑ ⏑ –...

and by the process known as ἐπιπλοκή the series may begin from the second (short) syllable, the first long being transferred to the end:

⏑ – – ⏑ – – ⏑ – –...

⏑ ⏑ – – ⏑ ⏑ – – ⏑ ⏑ – –...

Prolongation may be single or double: thus – ⏑ – is lengthened to – ⏑ – ⏑ – or – ⏑ – ⏑ – ⏑ –, and – ⏑ ⏑ – to – ⏑ ⏑ – ⏑ ⏑ – or – ⏑ ⏑ – ⏑ ⏑ – ⏑ ⏑ –. Or it may be of mixed type: thus – ⏑ – may increase to – ⏑ – ⏑ ⏑ – and – ⏑ ⏑ – to – ⏑ ⏑ – ⏑ –. Either of these hexasyllables may again add ⏑ – or ⏑ ⏑ –, forming – ⏑ – ⏑ ⏑ – ⏑ –, – ⏑ ⏑ – ⏑ – ⏑ –, etc.; or again the forms – ⏑ – ⏑ – and – ⏑ ⏑ – ⏑ ⏑ – may append ⏑ ⏑ – and ⏑ – respectively, making – ⏑ – ⏑ – ⏑ ⏑ – and – ⏑ ⏑ – ⏑ ⏑ – ⏑ –. Longer forms are found, though more rarely, as – ⏑ – ⏑ – ⏑ ⏑ – ⏑ – or – ⏑ ⏑ – ⏑ ⏑ – ⏑ – ⏑ – or – ⏑ ⏑ – ⏑ ⏑ – ⏑ ⏑ – ⏑ –; no exact limit can be given because of the ambiguity of light anceps as explained below. These units all begin and end with longs. Any of them may form a complete period by itself and in that case may prefix or append (or both) elementum anceps × – ⏑ – ×, × – ⏑ ⏑ – ⏑ ⏑ –, – ⏑ ⏑ – ⏑ – ×, etc. When two or more join to form a composite period, the whole period may prefix or append (or both) elementum anceps. The units forming the period may either be simply juxtaposed as in × – ⏑ – | – ⏑ – × – ⏑ – ⏑ ⏑ – ⏑ – | – ⏑ –, or they may be linked together by elementum anceps: × – ⏑ – × – ⏑ – ×, – ⏑ – ⏑ ⏑ – ⏑ – × – ⏑ –. Where the link anceps takes the short form it is not always possible to distinguish a composite from a prolonged form: thus – ⏑ – ⏑ – ⏑ – may represent a doubly prolonged – ⏑ – or – ⏑ – × – ⏑ –.

The single-short – ⏑ – may form a series with initial and link anceps × – ⏑ – × – ⏑ – × – ⏑ – . . . or (by ἐπιπλοκή of this) with link and final anceps – ⏑ – × – ⏑ – × – ⏑ – × . . . The double-short – ⏑ ⏑ – cannot be so treated, but in compensation may form a series by prolongation – ⏑ ⏑ – ⏑ ⏑ – ⏑ ⏑ – ⏑ ⏑. . . (this – ⏑ – cannot do); since, however, no period can end on a true short it must always run out in a blunt ⏑ ⏑ – or add final anceps ⏑ ⏑ – ×. This series may also by ἐπιπλοκή run ⏑ ⏑ – ⏑ ⏑ – ⏑ ⏑ – ⏑ ⏑ –. . . – (×).

The initial long of any unit may be omitted at the opening of a period;[1] thus – ⏑ – may take the form ⏑ – (and the combination – ⏑ – | – ⏑ –, therefore, ⏑ – | – ⏑ –) and – ⏑ ⏑ – ⏑ ⏑ – may become ⏑ ⏑ – ⏑ ⏑ –, or – ⏑ ⏑ – ⏑ – appear as ⏑ ⏑ – ⏑ –.

A period may be formed by one unit, by a series, or by the juxtaposition (with or without link) of units. Only the series is analytically divisible into metra; the regularity of such movement may be slightly obscured by resolution, by the device of syncopation (i.e. the omission of short or anceps) in the series (×) – ⏑ – × – ⏑ – × . . ., by contraction in the series (–) ⏑ ⏑ – ⏑ ⏑ – ⏑ ⏑ –. . ., and by contraction or anaclasis in the series ⏑ ⏑ – – ⏑ ⏑ – – ⏑ ⏑ – –. . . A period formed by juxtaposition of units can be analysed only into its component units. The junctions are betrayed either by the occurrence of two consecutive long syllables (the final long of one element and the initial long of the next) or by the sequence long–anceps–long, though as we saw above a short anceps may some-

[1] In the dochmiacs of drama, which appear (see below) to be a late creation of a special character, this licence is extended to the middle of a period also.

times be indistinguishable from a true short. Resolution of a long may occasionally also produce some ambiguity of division. It should be noted that the occurrence of three or more consecutive shorts always implies resolution, that except in a series two consecutive longs means the junction of two units, and that (except in a contracted series) in an apparent sequence of three longs the middle one is always anceps. In no circumstances can anceps follow anceps, nor can it follow or precede a short (except a short by resolution), in the middle of a period.[1] Anceps in the middle of a period is generally a link anceps, but in some cases is to be accounted a 'drag', i.e. the optional substitution of a long for a single-short within a unit. (This phenomenon will be examined later.)

3

The above is a brief systematisation of the *facts* of metric in Greek lyric verse; that is to say, in all verse that was sung, excluding verse spoken or given in recitative—roughly speaking, 'stichic' verse. It makes no attempt to consider the phenomena historically or (so far) to distinguish between one kind of lyric and another. The historical approach is a dangerous one; we do indeed know the relative dates of most of the poets whose works are extant, but of anything which could be described as reliable evidence of developments or influences there is little trace.[2] Each kind of lyric, solo, choral, dramatic, dawns upon us in perfected metrical technique; of its origins we know nothing, and of its development only the differences of style between its different practitioners. To attempt to trace influences from one kind to another is even more speculative; apart from an occasional

[1] The one exception to this rule is that in dramatic lyric (particularly in Sophocles) a dactylic tetrameter can be followed by a colon starting with anceps, e.g. – ᴗ ᴗ – ᴗ ᴗ – ᴗ ᴗ – ᴗ ᴗ | × – ᴗ – ᴗ – –. These must of course fall within the same period, since no period can end – ᴗ ᴗ. This exception indicates that colon-end, even where it cannot be followed by a full pause in the technical sense, has more separating effect than the end of a phrase-unit in the 'periodic' style.

[2] Only the process of decay of metrical vitality in Greek lyric can to some extent be followed.

guess we can only note what they have in common and where they differ. Theories of evolution from some imagined 'Urvers' or various types of Urvers are purely fanciful constructions; and in particular the doctrine of a more primitive and popular type of versification which at first kept a constant number of longs while putting in single or double shorts indifferently, and only later (and with occasional backsliding) tightened up its regulations, destroys the whole structure and principle of quantitative rhythm, which is based upon the absolute distinction of – ∪ – and – ∪ ∪ –.[1]

The account here given, however, remains artificial and schematic until supplemented by an examination of its relevance to the different kinds of lyric. Here it must be admitted that 'different kinds of lyric' does in the end, given the relatively small amount of material available outside Pindar and the dramatic poets, resolve itself into 'different poets', or at least groups of poets. Textual uncertainties, especially where we have to rely upon a single source of quotation and responding lines are lacking or scantily available, often make close metrical analysis or argument a rash undertaking. But some general distinctions of style emerge. Pindar, Simonides, and Bacchylides are recognisably of one group, the tragedians and comedians another, the Lesbians a third. Scolia approximate most closely to the Lesbian style. The fragments of Stesichorus appear to hover somewhere between the first two groups; Alcman, Ibycus, Corinna, and Anacreon have most in common with the dramatic poets. Thus monody, dramatic choruses, and non-dramatic choral lyric do not separate neatly. It is true that in strophic responsion the general rule is that solo-lyric is monostrophic, the choruses of drama repeat *aabb*..., and at least the more elaborate kinds of other choral lyric are composed in triads. But this inquiry is concerned with the inner composition of the strophe, which is not affected by such 'outer responsion' except in so far as period-end is more difficult to determine with limited responsion. The highest degrees of complexity in metrical construction are limited to choral lyric; the simplest forms

[1] For the apparent contradiction in the comic trimeter see my *Lyric Metres of Greek Drama*, Cambridge University Press, [second edition, 1968,] pp. 77–8.

are found in comedy because some of its lyric is least removed from stichic verse. A further complication is the spread-over of dactylo-epitrite, which to judge by its great preponderance in choral lyric must have originated as a metre for formal song and dance; it is taken over in tragedy and comedy and in some cases half-assimilated to the more familiar dramatic technique, and in his lampoon of Themistocles Timocreon of Rhodes uses it for what must have been a solo-rendering. Dactylo-epitrite might be described as the simplest type of the complex periodic style of composition, and it will be convenient to start the investigation from this metre.

Not the least of Maas's services to classical scholarship is his invention of a system of notation for regular dactylo-epitrites which cuts straight through the tangle of unreal perplexities about 'mixed scansion' or 'quadrisyllabic scansion' and the exact difference between epitrite and trochaic. It also, by discarding the received terminology, exonerates us from deciding whether, for instance, – – ⌣ ⌣ – ⌣ ⌣ – – – – ⌣ – should be divided 'prosodiac+iambic' or 'paroemiac+cretic'. The 'dactylic' or double-short unit – ⌣ ⌣ – ⌣ ⌣ – is symbolised by D, and the 'epitrite' – ⌣ – by e.[1] Initial, link, and final anceps is written in, the line quoted above, for example, appearing as – D – e. This method of presentation is more than a mere convenience; it exemplifies what I believe to be the true theory of all metrical composition in the 'periodic' style.[2]

Dactylo-epitrite is the easiest starting-point here because it is mostly limited to two units, the simple – ⌣ – and the 'prolonged' double-short – ⌣ ⌣ – ⌣ ⌣ –, and because the anceps mostly takes the long form. The varying combinations of these, with or without initial, link, and final anceps and in a variety of lengths, produce a supple, stately, yet changeable rhythm, quite easy to grasp. Its

[1] I omit Maas's double epitrite E (– ⌣ – ⏓ – ⌣ –), finding it sometimes rather unhelpful, e.g. should the fairly common 'stesichorean' be E ⏓ e (⏓) or e ⏓ E (⏓)? Neither is so satisfactory as e ⏓ e ⏓ e (⏓). My reason for not using d for the occasional – ⌣ ⌣ – is simply to keep clear of my own symbols **d** and **s** introduced later.

[2] I should here make it clear that Professor Maas himself disclaims and deprecates all extension of his principles of notation beyond the sphere of practical convenience.

flowing motion is due to the very frequent use of link anceps, so that the harder impact of blunt against blunt at a junction of units (⏑ ⏑ – | – ⏑, etc.) is not too often heard. The effectiveness of the rhythm depends upon its deployment over the space of the whole period, and is diminished if the period is chopped up into cola.[1] Bacchylides, it is true, tends to use his units, at least D and e – e (e by itself is too short for this purpose) more nearly as cola, by a moderately regular diaeresis immediately before or after link anceps, but Pindar is at some trouble to avoid this break. *Pyth.* 12, a monostrophic ode, is simple and regular, even repetitive, in its periods to a degree altogether unusual in Pindar, but the tendency to manipulate word-end so as to keep the period from splitting into balancing segments is unmistakable.

Αἰτέω σε, φιλάγλαε, καλλίστα βροτεᾶν πολίων,	– D – D
Φερσεφόνας ἕδος, ἅ τ' ὄχθαις ἔπι μηλοβότου	D – D
ναίεις 'Ακράγαντος ἐΰδματον κολώναν, ὦ ἄνα,	– D – e – e
ἵλαος ἀθανάτων ἀνδρῶν τε σὺν εὐμενίᾳ	D – D
δέξαι στεφάνωμα τόδ' ἐκ Πυθῶνος εὐδόξῳ Μίδᾳ,	– D – e – e
αὐτόν τέ νιν 'Ελλάδα νικάσαντα τέχνᾳ τάν ποτε	– D – e – e
Παλλὰς ἐφεῦρε θρασεῖαν Γοργόνων	D – e
οὔλιον θρῆνον διαπλέξαισ' 'Αθάνα·	e – e – e –

The metrical scholiast gives this verse fourteen cola, by splitting each of the first six periods into two; for the last two lines, which resist such even division, he has labels ready as they stand, the 'encomiologus short of one syllable', and the 'stesichorean' (trochaic trimeter). The rest runs in monotonously even short cola:

– – ⏑ ⏑ – ⏑ ⏑ –

– – ⏑ ⏑ – ⏑ ⏑ –

[1] I use the word *colon* in this essay in a sense quite different from that of metrical unit; the unit is simply an analytical division, the colon a self-sufficient rhythmical phrase. A unit of the longer sort, such as – ⏑ ⏑ – ⏑ ⏑ – or – ⏑ – ⏑ ⏑ – ⏑ –, *may* of course be a colon just as a unit or a colon *may* be a period. But in the 'periodic' style of composition there is nothing between the unit and the period, and the attempt to find segments recognisable—and nameable—as cola quite often makes the cut in the middle of a unit.

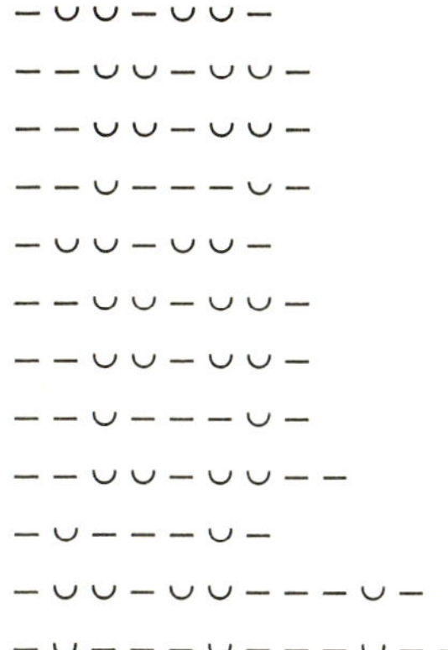

There is no obvious reason for the variation by which the penultimate pair is divided paroemiac + troch. dim. cat. rather than – – ⏑ ⏑ – ⏑ ⏑ – + iamb. dim. like the rest, nor for the curious divergence in the descriptions of – – ⏑ ⏑ – ⏑ ⏑ –: the first is 'spondee + pyrrhic + trochee + iamb' and the second, fourth, fifth, and ninth are all said to be the same as the first, but the eighth is 'major ionic + choriamb', and the eleventh is 'prosodiac with an added syllable'.

In so regular an ode as this, however, apart from the check on the flowing line of the rhythm, no great violence is done by the division into cola. Where the periods are of more irregular length, or where other units appear among the normal – ⏑ – and – ⏑ ⏑ – ⏑ ⏑ –, the division may be more destructive. In the epode of *Nem.* 1, both the simple – ⏑ ⏑ – and the triple – ⏑ ⏑ – ⏑ ⏑ – ⏑ ⏑ – occur, and the periods are uneven to a degree incomprehensible to an eye trying to normalise them into cola:

ταχὺ δὲ Καδμείων ἀγοὶ χαλκέοις σὺν
    ὅπλοις ἔδραμον   ⏑ ⏑ ⏑ – ⏓ e – D[1]
ἀθρόοι,   e

[1] This resolution of – ⏑ – is fairly common in dact.-epit. and is usually carried through all the strophic repetitions. Contraction of the double-short is much rarer, and there is no certain instance in Pindar; for *Nem.* 8. 1 see the second instalment of this article.

ἐν χερὶ δ' Ἀμφιτρύων κολεοῦ γυμνὸν
 τινάσσων φάσγανον D ⏑ ⏑ – – e – e
ἵκετ', ὀξείαις ἀνίαισι τυπείς. τὸ γὰρ
 οἰκεῖον πιέζει πάνθ' ὁμῶς· e – D ⏑ ⏑ – – e – e
εὐθὺς δ' ἀπήμων κραδία κᾶδος ἀμφ'
 ἀλλότριον. – e – ⏑ ⏑ – e – e

The scholiast's version of this is

⏑ ⏑ ⏑ – ⏓ – ⏑ – –
– ⏑ ⏑ – ⏑ ⏑ – ⏑ ⏑ –
– ⏑ ⏑ – ⏑ ⏑ –
⏑ ⏑ – – – ⏑ – – – ⏑ –
– ⏑ – – – ⏑ ⏑ – ⏑ ⏑ –
⏑ ⏑ – – – ⏑ – –
– ⏑ – – – ⏑ – – ⏑ ⏑ –
– ⏑ – – – ⏑ –

The minimum period – ⏑ – is so unexpected that he has ignored the final brevis in longo in ἔδραμον ⏑ ⏑ ⏑ (admittedly this occurs only in the third epode) and added ἀθρόοι as ⏑ ⏑ – to make a 'dactylic hephthemimer' of the second colon. Yet he has broken up the two authentic instances of – ⏑ ⏑ – ⏑ ⏑ – ⏑ ⏑ – and produced 'ionic trim. cat.' and 'ionic dim.' for the fourth and sixth cola, while for the penultimate he has an even more inappropriate 'metrising' description, 'troch. trim. brachycatalectic' (– ⏑ – – | – ⏑ – – | ⏑ ⏑ – ∧ ∧), in order to keep it in tune with the final 'troch. dim. cat.'

A period of dactylo-epitrite may genuinely open with ⏑ ⏑ – –, as in the first line of *Ol.* 7 φιάλαν ὡς εἴ τις ἀφνειᾶς ἀπὸ χειρὸς ἑλὼν ⏑ ⏑ – – – ⏑ – – – ⏑ ⏑ – ⏑ ⏑ –, but this does not of course mean the intrusion of an 'ionic dim.' (anacreontic) on foreign ground; it occurs on the principle stated in §2 that the *initial* unit of any period may open headless. ⏑ ⏑ – is a headless – ⏑ ⏑ –, just as in *Pyth.* 3 the final period of the epode μεταμώνια θηρεύων ἀκράντοις ἐλπίσιν opens with a headless (–) ⏑ ⏑ – ⏑ ⏑ – (*not* with an anapaestic metron), and *Ol.* 6. 6 begins ⏑ – – e – . . . instead of e – e – . . .

It is not surprising that the ancient metricians, working with this miscellaneous collection of cola—iambic, trochaic, dactylic, ionic, choriambic, iambelegus, etc.—failed to recognise the unity of this large dactylo-epitrite class of metres, and have nowhere recorded that more than half of the epinicians, together with a large but now unspecifiable proportion of the rest of choral lyric (e.g. all surviving fragments of Pindar's hymns, prosodia, and threnoi, most of his encomia and many dithyrambs, with about the same proportion of extant Bacchylides and a good deal of Simonides) are all written in the same type of metre.

The combined straightforwardness and flexibility of dactylo-epitrite doubtless encouraged its widespread use. It could carry words of any prosodic form, it was easily grasped, and its rhythm was utterly distinct from the metrising technique of stichic verse. Its origins are of course untraceable; the earliest certainly known to us is found in Stesichorus. Some of his scanty fragments (those from his *Oresteia*, for instance, parodied by Aristophanes in the *Peace*) seem to have been already of completely orthodox form; others which appear to contain some unusual elements (e.g. καὶ τριγάμους τίθησιν – ∪ ∪ – ∪ – – frag. 17 D²) *may* be evidence for an early, less regularised manner of composition, but it would be unwise to build too much theory on so unverifiable a text. No fragments are long enough to show with any certainty whether Stesichorus' long dactylic and dactylo-anapaestic series were mingled with single-short periods or units and if so whether the result bore any resemblance to dactylo-epitrite with longer runs of each kind. Certainly some lines that can be made into extracts of dactylo-epitrite appear to have a higher proportion of double-short than most later verse of this kind; so frag. 10 D from the *Helen*

πολλὰ μὲν Κυδώνια μᾶλα ποτερρίπτευν ποτὶ δίφρον
  ἄνακτι, e ∪ D – D ∪
πολλὰ δὲ μύρσινα φύλλα καὶ ῥοδίνους στεφάνους D ∪ D
ἴων τε κορωνίδας οὔλας ∪ D –

and possibly frag. 22

παιγμοσύνας ⟨τε⟩ φιλεῖ μολπάς τ' Ἀπόλλων. D – e –
κάδεα δὲ στοναχάς τ' Ἀΐδας ἔλαχεν. D ∪ ∪ – ∪ ∪ –

This last line, if it is really dactylo-epitrite, has one parallel in Pindar:

Οὐρανίδα γόνον εὐρυμέδοντα Κρόνου – ∪ ∪ – ∪ ∪ – ∪ ∪ – ∪ ∪ –

(*Pyth.* 3. 4). This should, I think, be interpreted as the maximum prolongation of – ∪ ∪ –. Pindar nowhere exceeds this double-short length in any kind of metre; that is to say, he makes no use of the dactylo-anapaestic 'series' described in §2. Stesichorus and Simonides (e.g. frag. 40 D and probably frag. 28) both use the dactylo-anapaestic series; Bacchylides (frag. 21) has unbroken trochaics with light anceps. With these exceptions I can find no use of composition in series in these poets, and thus descriptions in terms of 'metra' are strictly speaking inapplicable to the general run of periodic composition.

When Bacchylides addresses an encomion to Alexander son of Amyntas (frag. 20*b* Snell) in dactylo-epitrite quatrains of this form

ὦ βάρβιτε, μηκέτι πάσσαλον φυλάσσων	– D ⊻ e –
ἑπτάτονον λιγυρὰν κάππαυε γᾶρυν·	D ⊻ e –
δεῦρ' ἐς ἐμὰς χέρας· ὁρμαίνω τι πέμπειν	D ⊻ e –
χρύσεον Μουσᾶν 'Αλεξάνδρῳ πτερόν...	e – e – e

the distinction between the style of choral lyric and Lesbian monody is at vanishing point. Each of the first three lines is a combination of two units and the fourth of three 'epitrites', but the effect is of a simple repetitive arrangement of periods only distinguishable from cola by their composite nature and somewhat greater average length. Anceps at the end of a period is never followed by anceps at the beginning of the next, so that the carry-over is perfectly smooth. The middle two lines are metrically exactly similar to the two encomiologi of Alcaeus (frag. 40 D²) quoted by Hephaestion as the first two lines of a poem:

῏Ηρ' ἔτι Διννομένῃ τῷ τ' 'Υρρακήῳ
τἄρμενα λάμπρα κέοντ' ἐν Μυρσινήῳ;

This welding of two units into a whole which by balanced repetition becomes so familiar that it has the effect of a single phrase is characteristic of Lesbian monody, though, as we shall see, its favourite combination is not the dactylo-epitrite pair – ∪ – and – ∪ ∪ – ∪ ∪ –, but – ∪ – and – ∪ ∪ – ∪ –.

In the dramatic poets dactylo-epitrite gives the nearest approach to the periodic style of composition, and is sometimes indeed (e.g. *P.V.* 526–44, *Med.* 410–30) hardly distinguishable in technique from the more regular of the Pindaric stanzas. But in general it is much more apt to combine the units in pairs after the manner of the Bacchylides quoted above; further, it allows an occasional admixture of alien cola, particularly as clausulae. Thus the effect is to approximate these stanzas after all to the prevailing dramatic manner of composition by cola. *Med.* 824 ff. is typical:

Ἐρεχθεΐδαι τὸ παλαιὸν ὄλβιοι	⊻ D ⊻ e
καὶ θεῶν παῖδες μακάρων, ἱερᾶς	e – D
χώρας ἀπορθήτου τ' ἄπο, φερβόμενοι	– e – D
κλεινοτάταν σοφίαν, αἰεὶ διὰ λαμπροτάτου	D – D
βαίνοντες ἁβρῶς αἰθέρος, ἔνθα ποθ' ἁγνάς	– e – D –
ἐννέα Πιερίδας Μούσας λέγουσι	D – e –
ξανθὰν Ἁρμονίαν φυτεῦσαι.	hipponactean

Neither in strophe nor in antistrophe is there any formal clue to period-end—hiatus or brevis in longo or final followed by initial anceps. Yet there is no ambiguity; the balance of the lines imposes the divisions unequivocally upon our ear. The modification of the prevailing rhythm in the final clausula is a technique very common in dramatic choruses; in dactylo-epitrite this often takes the form of prolonging the last – ∪ – (–) unit into the ithyphallic – ∪ – ∪ – –. This prolongation is not used by Pindar in pendant form, and not as a clausula (since such closing modification is not a very common characteristic of the 'periodic' manner), but the blunt – ∪ – ∪ – occurs in *Nem.* 8. 14 ἀστῶν θ' ὑπὲρ τῶν δ' ἅπτομαι φέρων – e – – ∪ – ∪ –, and the – ∪ – – – of *Pyth.* 9. 2 σὺν βαθυζώνοισιν ἀγγέλλων is a 'dragged' version of the same unit (cf. *Pyth.* 1. 3 πείθονται δ' ἀοιδοὶ σάμασιν – – – ∪ – – e). Ariphron in his fourth-century hymn to Hygieia uses – ∪ – ∪ – both pendant and prosyllabic,[1] and

[1] Wilamowitz, *G.V.* p. 495, makes much to-do over the 'schwieriger Vers' ∪ | – ∪ – ∪ – | – D (with prosyllabic – ∪ – ∪ –). I do not know why.

this variant on e is of course of analogous form to – ◡ ◡ – ◡ ◡ – ◡ ◡ – as a variant on D.

Soph. *Aj.* 172 ff. is a more subtle study of the modification of dactylo-epitrite to suit dramatic technique:

ἦ ῥά σε Ταυροπόλα Διὸς Ἄρτεμις,	
ὦ μεγάλα φάτις, ὦ μᾶτερ αἰσχύνας ἐμᾶς,	dact. tetram. D e – e
ὥρμασε πανδάμους ἐπὶ βοῦς ἀγελαίας,	– e – D –
ἦ πού τινος νίκας ἀκάρπωτον χάριν,	– e – e – e
ἤ ῥα κλυτῶν ἐνάρων	D
ψευσθεῖσ', ἀδώροις εἴτ' ἐλαφαβολίαις;	– e – D
ἦ χαλκοθώραξ εἴ τιν' Ἐνυάλιος	– e – D
μομφὰν ἔχων ξυνοῦ δορὸς ἐννυχίοις	– e – D
μαχαναῖς ἐτείσατο λώβαν;	– ◡ – ◡ – ◡ ◡ – –

The thrice-recurring iambelegus is a familiar colon in dramatic lyric outside dactylo-epitrite; the opening rhythm is a dactylic 'series', and – e – e – e has the form of a lyric iambic trimeter; the clausula is an aeolic enneasyllable like the hipponactean. The whole effect, though most of it can be expressed in dactylo-epitrite symbols, is singularly different from dactylo-epitrite written in the periodic style.

5

THE METRICAL UNITS OF GREEK LYRIC VERSE. II

4

Dactylo-epitrite has established itself in a privileged position among choral lyric metres, since the greater volume of material and the greater regularity of its component units have encouraged a more careful study, and closely reasoned controversies have arisen and been resolved over its structure. Other kinds of Pindaric metre have for the most part been analysed in a hit-or-miss spirit, and arbitrary schemes have been produced of which rarely are two alike for the same poem, yet little attempt has been made to base any preference upon a theory. Few scholars nowadays are prepared to take – – ◡ ◡ – ◡ ◡ – – – ◡ – as – – ◡ ◡ | – ◡ ◡ – | – – ◡ – major ionic+choriamb+iambic, since the notion that there was a free responsion which worked by groups of four syllables has been disproved by Maas; the fallacy of dividing (–) – ◡ ◡ – ◡ ◡ – (–) either – – ◡ ◡ | – ◡ ◡ – or – ◡ ◡ – | ◡ ◡ – – is generally recognised. And the iambo-trochaic series is so familiar that in (–) – ◡ – – – ◡ – (–) no one thinks of splitting before or after the short syllable. These restraints, however, are taken to apply only to the particular units in question; outside dactylo-epitrite such cuts as – – ◡ – | ◡ ◡ – ◡ ◡ –... or ◡ – ◡ ◡ – – | ◡ – ◡ ◡ – – | ◡ – ◡ – or ◡ – – | ◡ – ◡ – ◡ ◡ – | ◡ – – are accepted without question so long as the bits can wear familiar labels—iambic, bacchiac, anapaest, reizianum, choriambic dimeter, etc. Two bacchiacs or two reiziana in the same period, or a cluster of reiziana or dochmiacs within the same stanza are generally felt to be one up on an analysis which strays into more categories, even though the 'dochmiacs' may run ◡ – – ◡ – | – ◡ ◡ – ◡ –...– ◡ – ◡ – or the 'reizianum' in one line take the form – – ◡ ◡ – – and in the next ◡ – ◡ – –. But on the whole analysis of such periods is very much an affair *ad lib.*, which nobody takes very seriously.

So far as I know, the idea has never been worked out that dactylo-epitrite, though a special stereotyped form of periodic composition, can provide a clue to the sort of metrical units Pindar used in his other poems—'aeolic' or whatever one chooses to call them—and the way he put them together to form composite periods. I am aware of the danger of allowing oneself to be mesmerised by schematic patterns of longs and shorts; the worst difficulty of Greek metric is the docility with which its simple ὕλη accepts such εἴδη and even permits them to work out an elaborate set of relations. Nevertheless the only way to test each attempt at systematisation is to try its capacity to bring the phenomena into an ordered whole and occasionally to give a better explanation than hitherto of puzzling factors by setting them in a new relation to others.

One important task is to keep a sharp eye upon terminology and see that it does not lull us into a false sense of security; another is to be aware of what we are doing when transferring concepts familiar from one kind of lyric to a different kind. In what sense can an 'iambic' be followed by a 'trochaic' in ἀναξιφόρμιγγες ὕμνοι, or an 'anapaest' by an 'adonean' in ὑψηλοτάτων μάρτυρ' ἀέθλων? The answer is that these names and concepts belong to a different manner of composition, in which they could never be found in this close association. If we apply to these two lines the principles deduced from dactylo-epitrite construction, we find that the sequence of two longs in the middle of each means a junction of two units ⏑ – ⏑ – | – ⏑ – – and – – ⏑ ⏑ – | – ⏑ ⏑ – –. Each ends with a final anceps, and the second has initial anceps also; the case of the first is less certain, since the first syllable may be short anceps or the whole unit may be a headless form of – ⏑ – ⏑ –. Examination of the whole stanza and its various responsions may give the answer, or the question may have to be left open.

It is clear that by proceeding in this fashion we shall find ourselves with some units that have ready-made names and others that have not; thus there is no particular harm in calling – ⏑ ⏑ – – 'adonean', but the partly similar – – ⏑ ⏑ – is nameless, to say nothing of ‸ ⏑ – ⏑ –. The only way to deal with this problem is either to avoid naming altogether or to invent for the sake of convenience a set of formal symbols to express these diverse units, like the Maasian D and e for dactylo-epitrite. Since lyric of the periodic style taken as a whole needs more elastic symbols than dactylo-epitrite alone, adaptable to the different forms of 'prolongation' in single- or double-short, I suggest the following:

– ⏑ – = s, – ⏑ ⏑ – = d. Prolongation is indicated by the mere addition of s or d: thus – ⏑ – ⏑ – = ss, – ⏑ ⏑ – ⏑ ⏑ – = dd, – ⏑ – ⏑ ⏑ – ⏑ – = sds. Anceps is written in; a blunt junction of units is indicated by a short vertical line: thus ὑψηλοτάτων μάρτυρ' ἀέθλων would be rendered – d | d –. A headless initial element is shown by ‸, so that ἀναξιφόρμιγγες ὕμνοι might be ‸ ss | s ⏓. Resolution in the form ⏑ ⏑ ⏑ – = ^{r}s, – ⏑ ⏑ ⏑ = s^{r}, ⏑ ⏑ ⏑ ⏑ ⏑ = ^{r}s^{r}. Drag is shown s̄, the σὺν βαθυζώνοισιν ἀγγέλλων of *Pyth.* 9. 2 becoming s – ss̄.

There is no inherent improbability in the notion that dactylo-epitrite is merely a special kind of periodic composition which works on fundamentally the same principles as all the rest. While it is true that nearly all dactylo-epitrite odes are unadulterated, Bacchylides writes his third Epinician with the strophe in 'aeolic' and the epode in dactylo-epitrite; and in *Ol.* 13 (analysed below) Pindar actually mixes the two styles to a considerable extent. Moreover, such lines as *Nem.* 11. 5 οἵ σε γεραίροντες ὀρθὰν φυλάσσοισιν Τένεδον, d | s | s – d, though technically within the limits of dactylo-epitrite variation, would be indistinguishable in isolation from any other kind of periodic metre. Even the most striking difference between dactylo-epitrite and the rest—its avoidance of mixed single- and double-short units—is occasionally overruled, as in *Nem.* 10. 79 καμάτου μεταλαμβάνειν. ὣς ἔννεπε· Ζεὺς δ' ἀντίος ἤλυθέ οἱ ‸ dds ⏓ s – dd, and probably also in the much vexed epode of *Ol.* 7, where I believe the true period division and analysis to be (ll. 14–15)

ὑμνέων, παῖδ' Ἀφροδίτας Ἀελίοιό τε νύμφαν, s – s – dd –
Ῥόδον, εὐθυμάχαν ὄφρα πελώριον ἄνδρα παρ'
  Ἀλφεῷ στεφανωσάμενον. ‸ dd | ^{r}sdd ⏓ dd

The strophe of *Ol.* 13 melts into orthodox dactylo-epitrite in the middle of the sixth period:

Τρισολυμπιονίκαν ‸dd ⏓
ἐπαινέων οἶκον ἥμερον ἀστοῖς, ⏓ s ǀ sd ⏓
ξένοισι δὲ θεράποντα, γνώσομαι ‸ss^{r}s – s
τὰν ὀλβίαν Κόρινθον, Ἰσθμίου – s$^{(r)}$s ⏓ s[1]
πρόθυρον Ποτειδᾶνος, ἀγλαόκουρον· ‸ds ǀ sd ⏓
ἐν τᾷ γὰρ Εὐνομία ναίει, κασιγνή-
  τα τε, βάθρον πολίων ἀσφαλές, ⏓ sd – s – dd ǀ s
Δίκα καὶ ὁμότροφος Εἰρήνα, ταμίαι‿ἄνδράσι
  πλούτου, ⏓ dd – dd ⏓
χρύσεαι παῖδες εὐβούλου Θέμιτος. s ǀ s – d

The epode is in dactylo-epitrite throughout, with the licensed variants – ⏑ ⏑ – and initial ‸ ⏑ ⏑ –. It seems highly improbable that such a transition could be made if the principles of synthesis into periods were not the same for all kinds of metrical units.

5

The implications of this method will probably become clearer if a few Pindaric stanzas are now analysed in detail. *Ol.* 1 is as good a starting-point as any. Strophe and antistrophe contain eleven periods:

Ἄριστον μὲν ὕδωρ, ὁ δὲ χρυσὸς αἰθόμενον πῦρ ‸s ǀ ds ǀ sd ⏓
ἅτε διαπρέπει νυκτὶ μεγάνορος ἔξοχα πλούτου· ‸(s̄)^{r} ǀ s ǀ ddd ⏓
εἰ δ' ἄεθλα γαρύεν sss
ἔλδεαι, φίλον ἦτορ, sd ⏓
μηκέθ' ἁλίου σκόπει sss
ἄλλο θαλπνότερον ἐν ἁμέρᾳ φαεννὸν ἄστρον
  ἐρήμας δι' αἰθέρος, ss^{r}s ⏑ ssd ǀ ss
μηδ' Ὀλυμπίας ἀγῶνα φέρτερον αὐδάσομεν· sss ⏑ d ǀ s
ὅθεν ὁ πολύφατος ὕμνος ἀμφιβάλλεται ‸s^{r}s^{r} ⏑ sss
σοφῶν μητίεσσι κελαδεῖν ‸s$^{(r)}$ ǀ s ǀ ^{r}s
Κρόνου παῖδ' ἐς ἀφνεὰν ἱκομένους ‸s ǀ ss ǀ ^{r}s
μάκαιραν Ἱέρωνος ἑστίαν. ⏓ s^{r} ǀ ss

1 $^{(r)}$ indicates that at least one of the responding stanzas has resolution, (s̄) that at least one has drag.

Period-end in the epode is not always certain; I give the following version with eight periods:

Συρακόσιον ἱπποχάρμαν βασιλῆα, λάμπει δέ οἱ κλέος	‸ ss^r ǀ s ǀ ds ǀ ss
ἐν εὐάνορι Λυδοῦ Πέλοπος ἀποικίᾳ·	‸ s ǀ d ǀ s^{r}ss
τοῦ μεγασθενὴς ἐράσσατο Γαιάοχος	sssd ǀ s
Ποσειδάν, ἐπεί νιν καθαροῦ λέβητος ἔξελε Κλωθώ,	‸ s ǀ s ǀ d ⏑ sd –
ἐλέφαντι φαίδιμον ὦμον κεκαδμένον.	‸ d ⏑ d ǀ ss
ἦ θαυματὰ πολλά, καί πού τι καὶ βροτῶν	– ds ǀ ss
φάτις ὑπὲρ τὸν ἀλαθῆ λόγον	^{r}sd ǀ s
δεδαιδαλμένον ψεύδεσι ποικίλοις ἐξαπατῶντι μῦθοι.	‸ s ǀ s ǀ ds ǀ ds –

The main differences between this style of composition and dactylo-epitrite are its frequent mixture of **s** and **d** in the same unit, the great frequency of blunt junction without link anceps, and the strong preference for light anceps. The last of these makes analysis much harder, or, to put the matter differently, Pindar deliberately obscures the junction of metrical units; the audible effect is of long unbroken sequences in such lines as the sixth, seventh, and eighth of the strophe. In these circumstances analysis remains somewhat theoretical; there is no real difference between that given above for ὅθεν ὁ πολύφατος ὕμνος ἀμφιβάλλεται (⏑ ⏑ ⏑ ⏑ ⏑ ⏑ : ⏑ : – ⏑ – ⏑ – ⏑ –) and ⏑ ⏑ ⏑ ⏑ ⏑ ⏑ ⏑ – : ⏑ : – ⏑ – ⏑ – or ⏑ ⏑ ⏑ ⏑ ⏑ ⏑ : ⏑ : – ⏑ – : ⏑ : – ⏑ –. The principle I have with some hesitation assumed is that since the maximum prolongation of **d** that Pindar uses is **ddd**, i.e. – ⏑ ⏑ – ⏑ ⏑ – ⏑ ⏑ –, so probably his maximum prolongation of pure single-short is – ⏑ – ⏑ – ⏑ –. It is not quite certain whether we should assume as a principle that a unit which has once moved out of double-short should not return to it: whether, that is to say, – ⏑ ⏑ – ⏑ – ⏑ ⏑ – (dsd) should always be reckoned – ⏑ ⏑ – : ⏑ : – ⏑ ⏑ –, and a possible dssd– in the fourth period above either – ⏑ ⏑ – ⏑ – : ⏑ : – ⏑ ⏑ – – or – ⏑ ⏑ – : ⏑ : – ⏑ – ⏑ ⏑ – –, but this is most probable.

The question of initial ⏑ – is a difficult one, extending to problems beyond the compass of this ode. The normal explanation, that

⏑ – – ⏑ ⏑ – ⏑ – (str. 1) is a 'glyconic' with the freedom of base inherited from Lesbian lyric and found also in drama, that ⏑ – – ⏑ – (str. 9) is an ordinary 'dochmiac' and ⏑ – – ⏑ – ⏑ – (str. 10) 'bacchiac+iambic metron', etc., does not seem to me satisfactory. Apart from the inapplicability of 'metra' to units in this style of lyric (and ⏑ – – ⏑ – ⏑ – has in Pindar as much right to be called 'lecythion' as ⏑ – – ⏑ ⏑ – ⏑ – glyconic), I regard 'dochmiac' as a misleading notion in Pindar. In the drama there are so many instances of purely dochmiac passages in which ⏓ – – ⏑ –, ⏓ ⏑ ⏑ – ⏑ –, ⏓ – – – – and many other variations occur consecutively, often paired in cola and often in free responsion to each other, that the whole movement clearly indicates a unity of concept, 'dochmiac', beneath these variations, and when some of these dochmiacs appear mixed with other metrical groups such as cretic-paeonic or iambic we can accept the notion of a compound movement, such as the 'iambo-dochmiacs' of Aeschylus.[1] But in Pindar there is no more reason for equating ⏑ – – ⏑ – with – ⏑ ⏑ – ⏑ – or – ⏑ – ⏑ – than there is for giving a common name to – ⏑ – and – ⏑ ⏑ – or – ⏑ – ⏑ ⏑ – ⏑ – and – ⏑ – ⏑ – ⏑ –. Thus ⏑ – – ⏑ – can be represented, on the same principles as I have applied to all other periodic units, as ⏑ – ǀ – ⏑ –, and similarly we have ⏑ – ǀ ss, ⏑ – ǀ d, ⏑ – ǀ ds, or ⏑ – ǀ dd as in *Ol.* 10 epode μέλει τέ σφισι Καλλιόπα ⏑ – ǀ – ⏑ ⏑ – ⏑ ⏑ – for which no one has found a very happy colon label, or again ⏑ – ǀ sds τεᾷ τοῦτο μειγνύμενον φρενί *Pyth.* 5. 19; ⏑ – on this showing is parallel to initial ⏑ ⏑ – or ⏑ ⏑ – ⏑ ⏑ – in dactylo-epitrite, a headless unit such as can only occur at the opening of a period. The fifth line of the epode ἐλέφαντι φαίδιμον ὦμον κεκαδμένον opens similarly with ‸ d.

The question of initial anceps is as hard to resolve as the incidence of short anceps later in the Pindaric period. There appear to be three different ways in which the length of a syllable can be 'ambiguous' in Greek metric. A final syllable may be anceps in the sense of brevis

[1] The dochmiac appears, at least on negative evidence, to be a creation of dramatic lyric, perhaps of Aeschylus. Whether he got the idea from choral lyric is impossible to say, but if so he moulded it into something quite new by adapting it to the technique of composition by cola.

in longo, i.e. a naturally long element has licence to be filled by a prosodically short syllable if it comes last in a period, as when final – ⏑ ⏑ – ⏑ ⏑ – changes to – ⏑ ⏑ – ⏑ ⏑ ‿. Or an element may be true anceps (i.e. either long or short), as in the iambo-trochaic series, and in all cases where it falls outside a metrical unit in a period (i.e. in initial, link, or final position); in dactylo-epitrite, where its occurrence is easiest to control, this true anceps is given long quantity in the great majority of cases, with occasional shortening in one or another of the responding stanzas, but here and there Pindar chooses to use the short form all through, as, in *Ol.* 7, the first link anceps in the fifth period of the epode, which is short in all five repetitions of the verse. In other styles, as we have seen, he makes frequent use of short anceps to gloss over the junction of metrical units in all responding stanzas, so that often we have no means of knowing whether a syllable is true short or link anceps. In these circumstances it seems most practical to register prolongation except where the length of single-short appears excessive or in those few instances where the surrounding units give a strong lead. Sometimes an isolated instance of lengthening enables us to correct this, as in *Nem.* 3, where the sixth period of the strophe appears in seven of the eight repetitions to be a single prolonged unit – ssd ⏓ but in l. 46 corrects itself to – s ⏓ d ⏓ Κένταυρον ἀσθμαίνοντα κόμιζεν. In other cases anceps is long throughout (as in the first syllable of the line just quoted), while in others again it is more evenly shared between long and short.

The third kind of elementum anceps is a short between two longs which has occasional licence to lengthen, a phenomenon which I have called 'drag'.[1] The commonest place for this to occur is the first short in a prolonged unit, less frequently the last short is lengthened, and there are a few instances of two consecutive lengthenings of the kind: so, for instance, we get | – ⏓ – ⏑ – |, | – ⏓ – ⏑ ⏑ – ⏑ – |, | – ⏑ – ⏓ – |, | ⏑ – ⏑ – ⏑ ⏑ – ⏓ – |, | – ⏓ – ⏓ – ⏑ ⏑ – |, | – ⏑ ⏑ – ⏓ – ⏓ – |. Whether the drag is descended from the 'aeolic base' of the Lesbians is a matter of speculation; if so, it is

[1] Maas suggests 'cholosis' (cf. χωλίαμβος) as an international technical term for 'drag'.

certainly applied quite differently by Pindar and differently again by the dramatists. There are hardly enough instances for the principles of its use to be securely formulated; I believe, however, that the apparent occurrence of 'spondee', in Pindar at least, can be best accounted for in this way, with one or two exceptions which may be due to contraction of double-short ⏕. In some of Pindar's odes the drag is a conspicuous motif, and one or two of these are analysed below.

To return to *Ol.* 1 and initial anceps, such an opening short syllable as in ὅ-θεν ὁ πολύφατος κτλ., Συ-ρακόσιον κτλ. may be accounted for in one of two ways; either it is short anceps and can therefore be represented ⏑ $^{r}s^{r}$ . . . and ⏑ s^{r} . . ., or it starts a headless unit like the instances of initial ⏑ – | – already discussed. As there is no means of distinguishing between these alternatives where responsion gives no instance of initial long, their notation is a matter of indifference. It is tempting to suppose that, as I have heard Professor Gilbert Murray suggest in a different connection, the dancers set down a foot to a silent long element before these headless initial units and thus gave point to the distinction.[1] In the last period of the strophe l. 80 gives μναστῆρας ἀναβάλλεται γάμον, so that here initial anceps is indicated.

There remains the problem of the second period, where the manuscripts at l. 89 give ἃ τέκε λαγέτας, – ⏑ ⏑ – ⏑ – for ⏑ ⏑ ⏑ – ⏑ – of the other seven verses. If we are not to follow the Byzantine scholars in emending here, this opening must of course be taken as a resolution of ⏓ – | – ⏑ –, not, as one might have been tempted to read it, of – ⏑ – ⏑ –. (Cf. l. 20 ὅτε παρ' Ἀλφεῷ in the ninth period of the strophe, corresponding to σοφῶν μητίεσ-σι ⏑ ⏔ – ⏑ –.) Even so, the admission of anceps in ‸ ⏓ – | is unexpected, and is indeed very rare in Pindar, but not unparalleled; there are two instances in the strophe of *Ol.* 10, the fifth period ⏓ – – ⏑ ⏑ ⏑ – – ⏑ –, which might be either ⏓ – : – : ^{r}s | s or ⏓ – | s^{r} – s (the resolu-

[1] I have sometimes wondered whether such a supposition would account for the unidentified symbol ι̇ (with its superimposed dot indicating thesis) in the middle of the dochmiac cola of the *Orestes* musical fragment (see the text in Powell and Barber, *New Chapters*, ii. 148).

tion is, as so often, ambiguous), and the seventh period ⏓ – ǀ ds. I can find no other in choral lyric. This is not the ordinary initial anceps before the beginning of a metrical unit, the true anceps of the second category mentioned above, but the third kind of anceps which lengthens a normally short element. It seems then to be occasionally admitted thus at the beginning of a line, probably by analogy with ordinary initial anceps. But in ἃ τέκε λαγέτας Pindar has taken this a step farther, by allowing it even when the following long is resolved. The only parallel to this in choral lyric is the doubtful one in the first period of Bacchylides' Ἠΐθεοι (Snell 17) where ⏑ ⏑ ⏑ – ⏑ – ǀ – ⏑ – ⏑ – ǀ – ⏑ ⏑ ⏑ ǀ – ⏑ – ⏑ – opens in l. 90 with ἵετο δ' ὠκύπομπον δόρυ. The most likely scansion of ἵετο is – ⏑ ⏑, but it cannot be taken as certain that Bacchylides did not here scan it ⏑ ⏑ ⏑. I am inclined to believe that the Byzantines may have been right in emending *Ol.* 1. 89.

Pindar's earliest epinician, *Pyth.* 10, gives a fairly simple demonstration of some of the points raised in this essay:

Ὀλβία Λακεδαίμων,	(s̄)d ⏓
μάκαιρα Θεσσαλία· πατρὸς δ' ἀμφοτέραις ἐξ ἑνός	∧ s ⏓ ds ǀ d ǀ s
ἀριστομάχου γένος Ἡρακλέος βασιλεύει.	∧ sdd ⏓ d ⏓
τί κομπέω παρὰ καιρόν; ἀλλά με Πυ-θώ τε καὶ τὸ Πελινναῖον ἀπύει	∧ s ǀ d ⏓ d ǀ sd ǀ ss
Ἀλεύα τε παῖδες, Ἱπποκλέᾳ θέλοντες	∧ s ǀ ssds ⏓
ἀγαγεῖν ἐπικωμίαν ἀνδρῶν κλυτὰν ὄπα.	∧ dds ⏓ (s̄)s
Ὀλυμπιονίκα δὶς ἐν πολεμαδόκοις	⏓ d ǀ (s̄)ds
Ἄρεος ὅπλοις·	d ⏓
ἔθηκε καὶ βαθυλείμων ὑπὸ Κίρρας ἀγών	⏓ sd ǀ d ǀ s
πετρᾶν κρατησίποδα Φρικίαν.	⏓ sd ǀ s
ἕποιτο μοῖρα καὶ ὑστέραισιν	⏓ sds ⏓
ἐν ἁμέραις ἀγάνορα πλοῦτον ἀνθεῖν σφίσιν.	⏓ ssds ǀ s

In this poem the distinction between the headless initial units of the strophe and initial anceps in the epode is notably clear. (In this first epode the openings are as it happens all short anceps, but all are lengthened in one or another of the corresponding stanzas.) There are three cases of drag, all in the first short of a unit. The first of these, in the opening period (25 καὶ ζώων ἔτι νεαρόν – – – ⏑ ⏑ – –), has been cordially received, since a 'pherecratean with aeolic base' is a familiar concept, but the other two have caused confusion. The first period of the epode has in l. 49 θεῶν τελεσάντων οὐδέν ποτε φαίνεται ⏑ – ⏑ ⏑ – ꜝ – – – ⏑ ⏑ – ⏑ –. The 'glyconic with aeolic base' is indeed another familiar concept, but the cut before its first syllable leaves an initial unit ⏓ – ⏑ ⏑ – which is not among the 'recognised'. It cannot be thrust on to 'anapaest' because of the initial anceps. Wilamowitz (*G.V.* 321) divides correctly by dint of calling this a free iambic metron; Schroeder and Turyn commit the solecism of leaving two adjacent ancipitia in the middle of a period ⏓ – ⏑ ⏑ – – ꜝ ⏓ – ⏑ ⏑ – ⏑ – 'reizianum+telesillean', though the latter notes this *commissura thesium* as something of a curiosity, comparing *Nem.* 7. 5 where he introduces a similar division. The remaining drag is at the end of the strophe ⏑ ⏑ – ⏑ ⏑ – ⏑ – : ⏓ : – ⏓ – ⏑ –. This form is found again in the epode of *Pyth.* 8 (analysed below), in *Paean* 2 (strophe, second period), and in Bacchylides' Ἠΐθεοι (strophe, eighth period, ⏑ – ⏑ – ꜝ – ⏓ – ⏑ – : ⏑ : – ⏑ ⏑⏑ . . . where θίγεν δὲ λευκᾶν παρηΐδων responds in l. 102 to ἰδὼν ἔδεισεν Νηρῆος ὀλ-βίου κτλ., and there is no need either to emend or to juggle with the natural division of the periods; a proper name is precisely the place where an isolated instance of drag might be expected). There is thus no need to shy at θαυμαστὰν ὁδόν in l. 30 here, and Mair's emendation at l. 60 ἔρωτες ἔκνιξαν φρένας gains in probability.

The penultimate period of the strophe and the last of the epode could of course be represented alternatively as ⏑ – ꜝ – ⏑ – : ⏑ : – ⏑ ⏑ – ⏑ – : ⏓ and ⏓ : – ⏑ – : ⏑ : – ⏑ ⏑ – ⏑ – : – ⏑ – respectively, but the decasyllable given as a single unit in **ssds** is of a type (containing one **d**) which does undoubtedly exist in Pindar.[1] Apart from many instances like this which *could* be decasyllabic units (for instance *Nem.* 3, strophe period 7: ἀεθλονικία δὲ μάλιστ' ἀοιδὰν φιλεῖ – ⏑ – ⏑ – ⏑ ⏑ – ⏑ – ꜝ – ⏑ –), there is the decisive evidence

[1] It also existed in Lesbian lyric, cf. Alc. frag. 14 D² and see below, Part III. [Chapter 6 of this collection.]

of the drag in *Pyth.* 8, strophe period 5 – ⏑ ⏑ – | – ⏓ – ⏑ – ⏑ ⏑ – ⏑ –, where the position of the anceps precludes any other division. The usual explanation of this as – ⏑ ⏑ – – ⏓ | – ⏑ – ⏑ ⏑ – ⏑ –, a sort of 'cholo-dochmius+glyconic', is inadmissible, since if – ⏑ ⏑ – – – is a single unit it can only be a dragged form of – ⏑ ⏑ – ⏑ –. The last element is in fact a true long, and short anceps in such a position would therefore be brevis in longo, which can in no circumstances occur in the middle of a period. Bacchylides 18 begins with a period containing a similar unit: βασιλεῦ τᾶν ἱερᾶν 'Αθανᾶν, τῶν ἁβροβίων ἄναξ 'Ιώνων ⏑ ⏑ – | – ⏑ ⏑ – ⏑ – | – ⏓ – ⏑ ⏑ – ⏑ – ⏑ – : –, here with a pendant close; since, however, this has the label 'phalaecean' to hand, it causes no trouble. Cf. also 19. 18 'Ινάχου ῥοδοδάκτυλος κόρα – ⏑ – ⏑ ⏑ – ⏑ – ⏑ –. It is possible that two similar decasyllables are to be found in the strophe of *Nem.* 7, second and fourth periods: – ⏑ ⏑ – ⏑ ⏑⏑ ⏑ – ⏑ – | – ⏑ ⏑ – ⏑ – | – ⏑ – ⏑ – and ⏑ – ⏑ – | – ⏑ ⏑⏑ ⏑ – ⏑ ⏑ – ⏑ – : ⏓.

The most interesting exploitation of the drag motif is in *Pyth.* 8, which contains units with this anceps in the first short, in the last short, and doubled.

8 τὺ δ' ὁπόταν τις ἀμείλιχον	ʳsds
καρδίᾳ κότον ἐνελάσῃ	sdʳs
τραχεῖα δυσμενέων	– sd
ὑπαντιάξαισα κράτει τιθεῖς	∧ ss | ds
ὕβριν ἐν ἄντλῳ. τὰν οὐδὲ Πορφυρίων μάθεν	d |(s̄)sds
παρ' αἶσαν ἐξερεθίζων. κέρδος δὲ φίλτατον,	⏓ sd | (s̄)ss
ἑκόντος εἴ τις ἐκ δόμων φέροι.	⏓ s ⏓ (s̄)s

Ep. 57 Ἄβαντος εὐρυχόρους ἀγυιάς. τοιαῦτα μέν	∧ ssd(s̄) | (s̄)s
ἐφθέγξατ' 'Αμφιάρηος. χαίρων δὲ καὶ αὐτός	⏓ sd | (s̄) d ⏓
'Αλκμᾶνα στεφάνοισι βάλλω. ῥαίνω δὲ καὶ ὕμνῳ,	(s̄)ds | s̄d ⏓
γείτων ὅτι μοι καὶ κτεάνων φύλαξ ἐμῶν	– d | dss
ὑπάντασεν ἰόντι γᾶς ὀμφαλὸν παρ' ἀοίδιμον,	∧ s | ds | sds
μαντευμάτων τ' ἐφάψατο συγγόνοισι τέχναις.	– (s̄)(s̄)dss –

Of these drags only that in the third period of the epode – – – ⏑ ⏑ – – is carried through all the verses, and it is as a matter of fact a doubtful case, since the line may quite possibly contain two periods

– ⏓ – ⏑ ⏑ – ⏑ – – and – – ⏑ ⏑ – –; it shows this diaeresis throughout though with no hiatus or anceps. The remainder have led to a variety of inadmissible analyses. The units with dragged first short are: – ⏓ – ⏑ ⏑ – – ep. 2, – ⏓ – ⏑ ⏑ – ⏑ – (or – ⏓ – ⏑ ⏑ – ⏑ – – with the alternative period-division) ep. 3, – ⏓ – ⏑ – ⏑ ⏑ – ⏑ – (the decasyllable above referred to) str. 5, – ⏓ – ⏑ – str. 7, – ⏓ – ⏑ – ⏑ – str. 6. Ep. 1 shows drag in the last short ⏑ – ⏑ – ⏑ ⏑ – ⏓ –, and ep. 6 (l. 42 υἱοὺς Θήβαις αἰνίξατο παρμένοντας αἰχμᾷ) has the double drag – – ⏓ – ⏓ – ⏑ ⏑ – ⏑ – ⏑ – –. The unusual – ⏓ – ⏑ – ⏑ – of str. 6 has probably an echo in Bacchylides 18, third period (the whole dithyramb is full of drags) Σίνιν, ὃς ἰσχύϊ φέρτατος θνατῶν ἦν, Κρονίδα Λυταίου σεισίχθονος τέκος ⏖ ⏓ – ⏑ ⏑ – ⏑ – | – ⏓ – ⏑ ⏑ – ⏑ – | – ⏓ – ⏑ – ⏑ –, though the period division is not quite certain. Bacchylides also uses tail-drag for a proper name in 16, fourth period, ἔνθ' ἀπὸ λαΐδος εὐρυνεφεῖ Κηναίῳ – ⏑ ⏑ – ⏑ ⏑ – ⏑ ⏑ – ⏓ – : –. I am inclined to believe that the same phenomenon accounts best for the complex difficulties of the first period of *Isth.* 8, where the break after ἀλλά l. 11 in order to emend to ἐμὲ δεῖμα μέν is improbable; Pindar nowhere ends a period with ἀλλά.[1] If ἀλλ' ἐμοί or Bergk's ἀλλ' ἔμ' οὐ is accepted, ἐνεγκὼν κοιμᾶτο is perfectly possible as a drag ⏑ – | – ⏑ – ⏑ ⏑ – ⏑ – ⏓ – | – ⏑ – ⏑ – ⏑ ⏑ –. The resolution in the proper name Ἑλέναν l. 52 ⏑ – | – ⏑ – ⏑ ⏑ – ⏑ – ⏑ ⏑ ⏑ | – ⏑ – ⏑ – ⏑ ⏑ – has a similar echo in the sixth period – ⏑ – ⏑ ⏑ – ⏑ ⏖ | – ⏑ – ⏓. In the epode of *Ol.* 9 the principle of drag and double drag accounts satisfactorily for the repeated accumulation of longs without the assumption of strange iambics and cholanapaests and spondees. The strophe contains four instances of ordinary first-short drag, and the epode continues:

ἐγὼ δέ τοι φίλαν πόλιν μαλεραῖς ἐπιφλέγων
  ἀοιδαῖς, ⏑ s ⏑ sd ⏑ ss ⏓
καὶ ἀγάνορος ἵππου θᾶσσον καὶ ναὸς
  ὑποπτέρου παντᾷ ‸ dd⁽s̄⁾s̄ | dss̄

[1] For *Ol.* 9. 55 see analysis below, where the running of what are commonly given as periods 2 and 3 into one line gives a more intelligible explanation of the long syllables.

ἀγγελίαν πέμψω ταύταν, ds̄(s̄)
εἰ σύν τινι μοιριδίῳ παλαμᾷ – ddd
ἐξαίρετον Χαρίτων νέμομαι κᾶπον· ⏓ sdds̄
κεῖναι γὰρ ὤπασαν τὰ τέρπν'· ἀγαθοὶ δὲ
καὶ σοφοὶ κατὰ δαίμον' ἄνδρες ⏓ s ⏓ sd ⏓ sds ⏓

(I have assumed the first period to resemble the last, but it is of course impossible to be sure which syllables are short anceps.) Here there are two single tail-drags and two doubles. In the last stanza, however, the second period normalises the first of the doubles: μελέτα· σοφίαι μὲν αἰπειναί ⏑ ⏑ – ⏑ ⏑ – ⏑ – – –, and in l. 57 the third period normalises the second of them: ἄντλον ἑλεῖν. κείνῳ δ' ἔσαν – ⏑ ⏑ – – – ⏑ –. The proper Pindaric form ἔσαν need not be emended to the dubious ἔσσαν or ἦσαν, nor need we resort to Schroeder's expedient of deleting δ' and transferring ἔσαν to the following line. A similar fluctuation in double drag can be seen in *Nem.* 4, strophe, sixth period. In *Ol.* 4 the lack of responding triads makes it impossible to be sure of the analysis of the string of long syllables in strophe, period 6, or of the period-division; possibly it should be s̄s̄ ׀ sssd. Drag in dactylo-epitrite is very rare, but I have already called attention to – ⏑ – – – in *Pyth.* 9; *Nem.* 8 begins with one in ὥρα πότνια, κᾶρυξ Ἀφροδίτας which responds in l. 39 to αὔξεται δ' ἀρετά, χλωραῖς ἐέρσαις (s̄)d – s –.

Of resolution and contraction there is little to say except that the former is very common and the latter extremely rare. The great majority of resolutions are carried through all responding verses, and among those that are not, proper names account for most of the divergences. Ambiguities of analysis (⏑⏑ ⏑ or ⏑ ⏑⏑) are inevitable in most cases where three consecutive shorts appear. Where there are four or more they are to be kept in **s** movement rather than in **d** wherever possible, e.g. *Ol.* 1, ep. 2 is ⏑ – ׀ – ⏑ ⏑ – ׀ – ⏑ ⏑⏑ ⏑ – ⏑ – rather than... : – : ⏑⏑ ⏑ ⏑ – ⏑ – or ... ׀ – ⏑ ⏑ ⏑⏑ ׀ – ⏑ –, since the ascertainable instances of resolution in double-short are very rare. *Nem.* 7, str. 7 – ׀ – ⏑ ⏑ – ⏑ – ׀ ⏑ ⏑ ⏑ – ⏑ – has in l. 70 Εὐξένιδα πάτραθε Σώγενες, ἀπομνύω – ׀ ⏑⏑ ⏑ ⏑ – ⏑ – ׀ ⏑ ⏑ ⏑ – ⏑ –, and the last line of *Ol.* 10 also shows the opening

⏑ – ⏑ ⏑ ⏑⏑; most striking of all is *Isth.* 3–4. 63 ἔρνεϊ Τελεσιάδα – ⏑ ⏑ ⏑⏑ ⏑ ⏑ – in dactylo-epitrite. All these occur in proper names, but in *Pyth.* 8, str. 2 (quoted above) the sequence – ⏑ – ⏑ ⏑ ⏑⏑ ⏑ – sd^{r}s in all verses is preferable to s | ^{r}s^{r} – with resolution of the last long before a final anceps. Some poems, such as *Pyth.* 2 and *Pyth.* 5, play conspicuously on the resolution motif. I quote the latter, since its sequences of shorts are unusually well controlled by sporadic long syllables in one or another of the verses, and by the surrounding rhythms.

	ὁ πλοῦτος εὐρυσθενής,	‸ ss | s
	ὅταν τις ἀρετᾷ κεκραμένον καθαρᾷ	‸ ss$^{(r)}$ | ssd
	βροτήσιος ἀνὴρ πότμου παραδόντος αὐτὸν ἀνάγῃ	‸ ss^{r} | sds | ^{r}s
	πολύφιλον ἑπέταν.	‸ s^{r} | ^{r}s
	ὦ θεόμορ᾽ Ἀρκεσίλα,	s$^{(r)}$ | d
	σύ τοί νιν κλυτᾶς	‸ s | s
	αἰῶνος ἀκρᾶν βαθμίδων ἄπο	– s | ds
	σὺν εὐδοξίᾳ μετανίσεαι	‸ s | sds
	ἕκατι χρυσαρμάτου Κάστορος·	‸ ss | s | s
	εὐδίαν ὃς μετὰ χειμέριον ὄμβρον τεάν	s | d | ^{r}s | s
	καταιθύσσει μάκαιραν ἑστίαν.	‸ s – $^{(r)}$sss
23	Ἀπολλώνιον ἄθυρμα. τῶ σε μὴ λαθέτω	‸ s | s^{r} | ssd
	Κυράνᾳ γλυκὺν ἀμφὶ κᾶπον Ἀφροδίτας ἀειδόμενον,	‸ s | dsss | sd
	παντὶ μὲν θεὸν αἴτιον ὑπερτιθέμεν,	sd | ^{r}sd
	φιλεῖν δὲ Κάρρωτον ἔξοχ᾽ ἑταίρων·	‸ ss | sd –
	ὃς οὐ τὰν Ἐπιμαθέος ἄγων	‸ s | d | ^{r}s
	ὀψινόου θυγατέρα πρόφασιν Βαττιδᾶν	d | ^{r}sd | s
	ἀφίκετο δόμους θεμισκρεόντων·	‸ s | $^{(r)}$ss$^{(r)}$s –
	ἀλλ᾽ ἀρισθάρματον	s | s
	ὕδατι Κασταλίας ξενω-	
	θεὶς γέρας ἀμφέβαλε τεαῖσιν κόμαις.	$^{(r)}$(s̄)ds | ds$^{(r)}$s | s

αἰῶνος in the seventh period of the strophe is sometimes (for instance by Schroeder and Turyn) given a period to itself. A slight modification of the received text is required in one verse or another for either rendering. But on metrical grounds I have no doubt that the single period is better. Appeal is made to ἀθρόοι in *Nem.* 1 (see pp. 55 f.) and to ἕν' ἀνδρῶν in *Nem.* 6. The former is checked by preceding brevis in longo and following hiatus; the latter only by diaeresis; – ⏑ – is a whole unit; ‸ ⏑ – ˡ – is just possible. But what is – – ⏓? Turyn says 'palimbacchius', but even in 'metrising' contexts the palimbacchiac – – ⏑ is not in isolation a self-supporting metron, any more than the dactyl – ⏑ ⏑ or the so-called 'major ionic' – – ⏑ ⏑. A final short lengthened to final anceps is a fiction.

Contraction is an elusive phenomenon, since unless the double-short is left intact in response it is impossible to be certain that a long syllable represents a contracted double-short. It is conceivable, for instance, that the series of longs quoted above in *Ol.* 4. 6 conceal contraction rather than drag. Ascertainable contraction is extremely rare. A possible instance is in *Ol.* 14. 7, where σεῦ ἕκατι μελαν-τειχέα... corresponds to οὐδὲ γὰρ θεοὶ σεμ-νάν ...– ⏑ – ⏖ –, but μειλαντειχέα (Maas) would give – ⏑ – ⏑ – : – : – ⏑ ⏑... in both and should perhaps be adopted. The only certain case[1] is in a proper name in the fourth period of the epode of *Ol.* 10. This period is so remarkable that it needs further consideration:

15 καὶ χάλκεος Ἄρης. τράπε δὲ Κύκνεια μάχα καὶ ὑπέρβιον
59 ἀκρόθινα διελὼν ἔθυε, καὶ πενταετηρίδ' ὅπως ἄρα
103 εὐάνορα πόλιν καταβρέχων· παῖδ' ἐρατὸν δ' Ἀρχεστράτου

These three versions give ⏖ – ˡ ⏑ ⏑ ⏑ – ˡ ⏑ ⏑ ⏑ – ˡ – ⏑ ⏑ – ⏕ – ⏑ ⏓, or with alternative treatment of the resolutions ⏖ – ⏑ ⏑ ⏑ ˡ – ⏑ ⏑ ⏑ : – : – ⏑ ⏑ – ⏕ – ⏑ ⏓. The contraction in Ἀρχεστράτου (one verse out of five) is clearly genuine. The initial syllable is more surprising. Four verses give a long syllable, of which ἀκρόθινα in the fifth appears to be a resolution. Resolution of initial anceps, though rare, is occasionally found in other kinds of lyric, but Pindar's practice seems to be strict. The only possible parallels occur in a corrupt passage of *Nem.* 6, where the two penultimate periods run:

[1] Possibly also in *Paean* 6. 117 -μεν βίου ἀμφιπόλοις – ⏑ ⏑ – ⏑ ⏑ – ~ πατρὶ Μναμοσύνα – – – ⏑ ⏑ –.

21 Νεμέᾳ δὲ τρεῖς, ἔπαυσε λάθαν ⏕ – ⏑ – ⏑ – ⏑ – –
44 βοτάνα τέ νίν ποθ' ἁ λέοντος
67 δελφῖνί κε τάχος δι' ἅλμας

22 Σωκλείδα', ὃς ὑπέρτατος
45 νικάσαντ' ἔρεψε δασκίοις
68 ἶσον εἴποιμι Μελησίαν

If the agreement of ll. 22 and 68 is taken as establishing – ⏑ ⏑ – ⏑ – for the end of the second of these periods, Hermann's ἤρεφε is an easy way of bringing l. 45 into conformity. Are there two syllables or three preceding this? The only way of giving three syllables to Σωκλεί-δα' is to read (with Wilamowitz) Σαοκλεί-δα', but this gives ⏑ – –, which might correspond to νικάσαντ' – – – but hardly to ἶσον εἴ-ποιμι – ⏑ –. ἴσον ϝεῖ-ποιμι ⏑ – – (see Schroeder, proleg. ii. 5) is dubious; Wilamowitz has ἴσον κ' εἴποιμι, emending κε in l. 67 to καί. But if two of the three lines are to be emended, it seems easier to require the already corrupt l. 45 to conform to Σωκλείδα' and read νικῶντ' ἤρεφε with Hermann. If then the pattern is to be – – – ⏑ ⏑ – ⏑ – the simplest course is to take ἴσον εἴποιμι as its equivalent ⏑ ⏑ – – ⏑ ⏑ – ⏑ –. This sends us back to the preceding line (κεν in l. 67 is easy). If βοτάνα is accepted in l. 44, then Νεμέᾳ is also to be read as a trisyllable. Hermann proposed ποία (with Νεμέ͜ᾳ). But surely the case for an opening ⏕ is much strengthened by its appearance in two consecutive lines. There is no force in the special objection to ἴσον εἴποιμι on the ground that particular odium attaches to a glyconic of this form (remembering the ὁρᾷς τὸν πόδα τοῦτον; of the *Frogs*), since those sequences of syllables which in other kinds of lyric can be grouped together as 'glyconics' have no special community of habits or taboos in the periodic kind. No one, as far as I know, has attempted to emend the opening of Bacch. 18 βασιλεῦ τᾶν ἱερᾶν 'Αθανᾶν, τῶν ἁβροβίων ἄναξ 'Ιώνων ⏑ ⏑ – – ⏑ ⏑ – ⏑ – – ⏓ – ⏑ ⏑ – ⏑ – ⏑ – –.

Are we then to say that in these three cases (two in *Nem.* 6 and one in *Ol.* 10) we find initial anceps resolved into double-short? If so, we must at least stipulate that the anceps must take the long form, so that no equation of ⏑ to ⏑⏑ is licensed. But it is possible that this can be formulated better by taking the cue from Ἀρχεστράτου in the last metrical unit of the period in *Ol.* 10. Since that is a contraction, the initial ⏕ may also be a contraction; and it should be noted that in the first of the two periods in *Nem.* 6 Νεμέᾳ and βοτάνα set the measure first, before δελφῖνι. I think it quite possible that there are three kinds of initial syllable in Pindar: true short, as indicated in the headless units, true anceps, and true long, which is occasionally capable of appearing as two shorts, like the headless ‸ d of, for example, the ἐλέφαντι φαίδιμον ὦμον of *Ol.* 1. Thus an initial true long would be a contraction of a 'headless' opening. The distinction may seem academic on paper, when so often there is no means of distinguishing true anceps from either of the other two, but there is every reason to believe that in the actual tempo of performance each of these three was allotted a different time-quantity. If, further, a headless element really was preceded by a silent dance-step, the distinction would be perfectly clear.

I have already called attention to the prevalence in certain odes of some particular metrical feature—resolution, drag, unusually regular or irregular length of periods, and so on. Dactylo-epitrite is of course another particularity of rhythm. One ode, *Ol.* 2, is unique in being composed, except for one **sd** at the close of the strophe, entirely in single-short, the nearest parallel being, as the detailed study of Maas[1] has shown, the Ἠΐθεοι of Bacchylides, which admits the double-short in one period, the seventh of the strophe (dss ⏑ dd ⏑ ss). There is, however, one notable difference between the two poems; the Ἠΐθεοι contains many more prolonged single-short units, especially – ⏑ – ⏑ – ⏑ –, and even longer sequences where it is impossible to determine which syllable is anceps. *Ol.* 2 is much less

[1] *Die neuen Responsionsfreiheiten b. B. u. P.*, pt. 2. I am in entire agreement with Maas as to the necessity of assuming corruption in the anomalous responsions of unequal length (such as ⏑ – ⏑ – to ⏑ ⏑ ⏑ –), though I see no need to suspect – ⏑ ⏕ or ⏕ ⏑ – or – ⏓ – ⏑ – (drag in a proper name, as indicated above); possibly also – ⏓ – ⏑ – ⏑ – (l. 83). My analysis does not, of course, correspond altogether to his, since the principles I have suggested do not admit 'bacchiacs' or 'dochmiacs' which involve the cut – | ⏑ in the middle of a period.

ambiguous, and the following analysis shows the remarkable extent to which it is dominated by the movement s | s | s . . .

Ἀναξιφόρμιγγες ὕμνοι,   ‸ ss | s ⏓
τίνα θεόν, τίν' ἥρωα, τίνα δ' ἄνδρα
  κελαδήσομεν; $^{(r)}$ss | s^{r} | s^{r} | s
ἤτοι Πίσα μὲν Διός· Ὀλυμπιάδα δ' ἔστασεν
  Ἡρακλέης   – s | s^{r} | s$^{(r)}$ – s | $^{(r)}$s
ἀκρόθινα πολέμου·   s | ^{r}s
Θήρωνα δὲ τετραορίας ἕνεκα νικαφόρου   ⏓ s^{r} | s | ^{r}s | s
γεγωνητέον, ὄπιν δικαίων ξένων, ἔρεισμ'
  Ἀκράγαντος,   ‸ s | s^{r} | s$^{(r)}$ | ss | s ⏓
εὐωνύμων τε πατέρων ἄωτον ὀρθόπολιν·   – s | ^{r}s ⏑ sd
17 λοιπῷ γένει. τῶν δὲ πεπραγμένων   – s | s$^{(r)}$ | s
ἐν δίκᾳ τε καὶ παρὰ δίκαν ἀποίητον οὐδ' ἂν   ss | ^{r}ss | s ⏓
Χρόνος ὁ πάντων πατὴρ δύναιτο θέμεν
  ἔργων τέλος· ^{r}s | ss | ^{r}s | s
λάθα δὲ πότμῳ σὺν εὐδαίμονι γένοιτ' ἄν.   – s | s$^{(r)}$ – ^{r}s ⏓
ἐσλῶν γὰρ ὑπὸ χαρμάτων πῆμα θνᾴσκει   ⏓ s^{r} | s | s –
παλίγκοτον δαμασθέν.   ‸ sss –

The separation of the last two periods is not quite certain, since it rests on unsupported diaeresis, but as there are five verses it is probably correct. The structural units are – ⏑ – and – ⏑ – ⏑ –, with resolutions thirteen times carried through, five times with one or two exceptions, and once with the resolution itself the exception. A proper name is only three times the excepted instance, so that emendation in any of the others simply for the sake of uniformity has a weak case. The opening of the second period is a little uncertain, since the manuscripts at l. 46 read πέφνεν οἱ (this should of course be πέφνε, since οἱ is regularly preceded by hiatus), and at l. 62 ἴσαις δ' ἐν ἁμέραις, which is unmetrical. If the Byzantine ἴσα δ' ἐν ἁμέραις is accepted for this, then πέφνε οἱ can stand, and the notation is ⏑̲⏑̲ ⏑ – ⏑ –, $^{(r)}$ss. If Mommsen's ἴσαις δ' ἁμέραις is read, the Byzantine ἔπεφνέ οἱ must be taken, giving ⏑ ⏑̲⏑̲ | – ⏑ –, ‸ s$^{(r)}$ | s. It is of course quite illegitimate to leave (with some texts) ⏑̄⏑̲⏑̲ – ⏑ –, which gives different elements in different verses. The third period (ἤτοι Πίσα κτλ.) could alternatively be analysed – s – ʳs ˡ ʳs ˡ s ˡ s; in any case the line contains one link anceps, as again in the fourth of the epode. The short anceps of the last period of the strophe is as usual uncertain; the line from τε to the end might be a single unit **sssd.** It is noteworthy that in both strophe and epode here Pindar has so marked a clausular rhythm, which departs from the movement of the rest.

6

THE METRICAL UNITS OF GREEK LYRIC VERSE. III

6

I am not proposing in this essay to treat at length and in detail of the metric of other lyric poets. In most cases questions of metre are intimately involved with questions of text, into which so many other considerations enter that in dealing with them proportion would be lost, while metrical analysis of such material would still remain largely speculative. What follows is therefore little more than a general account of the principles of composition which these poets appear to me to follow; I have, however, indicated a few passages where emendations made purely on metrical grounds and widely accepted seem to me, in the absence of responsion, based on too ready a desire to reduce all poems to the best-known formulas of versification.

Of the great names, only Simonides and Bacchylides seem to compose habitually in the free periodic style like Pindar. The longest fragments of the former, the Ἄνδρ' ἀγαθὸν μέν and the *Danae*, however reconstructed (and I regard the attempt to find responsion in the latter as to say the least unconvincing), are undoubtedly of this type. It is interesting to find him writing, besides regular dactylo-epitrite (as in frags. 23, 57 D^2), a sort of near dactylo-epitrite, using all the rarer variants, so that, at least in the small fragments we possess, the borderline between this metre and others is very indistinct. Thus frag. 48 D^2 is very nearly regular:

τίς κεν αἰνήσειε νόῳ πίσυνος Λίνδου ναέταν
  Κλεόβουλον   s – dd – dd –
ἀενάοις ποταμοῖς[1] ἄνθεσί τ' εἰαρινοῖς   dd ǀ dd
ἀελίου τε φλογὶ χρυσέας τε σελάνας   dd – d –
καὶ θαλασσαίαισι δίναις ἀντιθέντα μένος στάλας;   s – s – sds̄

[1] Possibly we should read ποταμοῖσιν, dd ⏑ dd.

ἅπαντα γάρ ἐστι θεῶν ἧσσω· λίθον δέ	⏑ dd – s ⏑
καὶ βρότεοι παλάμαι θραύοντι, μωροῦ φωτὸς	
ἅδε βουλά.	dd – s – ss –

The encomium on the dead at Thermopylae (frag. 5 D²) is slightly more irregular in type; none of the emendations required to convert it to strictness (see Wilamowitz, *Sappho u. Simonides*, p. 140, n. 3) is very difficult, but none is necessary, except for the deletion of the οὔτε, which as Wilamowitz justly says is a matter of style as well as metre:

τῶν ἐν Θερμοπύλαις θανόντων	s̄ds –
εὐκλεὴς μὲν ἁ τύχα, καλὸς δ' ὁ πότμος,	s ⏑ s ⏑ s –
βωμὸς δ' ὁ τάφος, πρὸ γόων δὲ μνᾶστις, ὁ δ'	
οἶκτος ἔπαινος.	– dd – dd ⏑
ἐντάφιον δὲ τοιοῦτον εὐρὼς	dds –
οὔθ' ὁ πανδαμάτωρ ἀμαυρώσει χρόνος	sds – s
ἀνδρῶν ἀγαθῶν, ὁ δὲ σηκὸς οἰκέταν εὐδοξίαν	– dd ⏑ s – s
Ἑλλάδος εἵλετο· μαρτυρεῖ δὲ Λεωνίδας	dd ⏑ ds
ὁ Σπάρτας βασιλεύς, ἀρετᾶς μέγαν λελοιπὼς	s̄dd ⏑ s –
κόσμον ἀέναόν τε κλέος.	sdd

The defence of the unusual rhythms is their echo, **sds** and **s̄ds, sdd** and **s̄dd, ds** and **dds.** It is generally assumed that the first line begins in the middle of a period, but it stands perfectly well by itself, answered by οὔθ' ὁ πανδαμάτωρ ἀμαυρώ-σει χρόνος four lines later. εὐρὼς stands badly at the beginning of the following line; it is claimed as a parallel to στάλας in the fragment quoted above, but the parallel only works of course on the usual assumption that each is a 'spondee', i.e. – ‸ – ‸. If my interpretation of these as 'drag' is correct, εὐρὼς οὔθ' ὁ π. ἀ. χ. would give a drag in a single **s** unit (– ⏓ –) and I know of no parallel to this. Simonides uses drag very frequently in the surviving fragments.

A further stage away from dactylo-epitrite is seen in such fragments as 30:

δίδωτι δ' εὖχος Ἑρμᾶς ἐναγώνιος	⏑ ss ǀ ds
Μαιάδος οὐρείας ἑλικοβλεφάρου παῖς·	
ἔτικτε δ' Ἄτλας	d – dd ǀ ss –

ἑπτὰ ἰοπλοκάμων φιλᾶν θυγατρῶν τάν γ'
ἔξοχον εἶδος, dd ⏑ d – d –
ταὶ καλέονται Πελειάδες οὐράνιαι. d ᑊ sdd

Here only the relative frequency of **dd** and link anceps survive. The latter persists to a degree quite unfamiliar in the 'aeolic' of Pindar, even in fragments like 32 and 37 which have severed all other connection with dactylo-epitrite:

32 ὃς δουρὶ πάντας – s –
νίκασε νέους δινάεντα βαλών – d – d
Ἄναυρον ὑπὲρ πολυβότρυος ἐξ Ἰωλκοῦ· ⏑ ddds –
οὕτω γὰρ Ὅμηρος ἠδὲ Στησίχορος ἄεισε
λαοῖς. – ds – s^{r} ⏑ s –

Thus it appears that in Simonides the distinction of metrical types is less clear-cut than in Pindar. Bacchylides also softens the transition, though differently, by way of his 'dactylo-iambics', as they are often called: that is to say, a rhythm which combines **dd** units with single-short of various lengths (not reducible to metra) and also with mixed **d** and **s**, using only short anceps for link-syllable, so that analysis is slightly uncertain. The only poem of any length that survives in this type is the dithyramb 19 Sn., which contains a single triad, the second half being mutilated. Where the evidence of responsion reaches, Bacchylides seems to have followed his usual practice (noted in Part I, p. 54) of making his diaereses either just before or just after link anceps; at least they either coincide in strophe and antistrophe or fall within one short syllable of each other, so that there is some justification for looking for link anceps at this point.

1 πάρεστι μυρία κέλευθος | ἀμβροσίων μελέων ⏑ sss ⏑ dd
19 ὅτ' Ἄργον ὄμμασι βλέποντα | πάντοθεν
ἀκαμάτοις

ὃς ἂν παρὰ Πιερίδων | λάχησι δῶρα
Μουσᾶν, ⏑ dd ⏑ ss –
μεγιστοάνασσα κέλευσε | χρυσόπεπλος Ἥρα

ἰοβλέφαροί τε θεαὶ[1] | φερεστέφανοι Χάριτες | ∪ dd ∪ dd ∪ ss –
ἄκοιτον ἄυπνον ἐόντα | καλλικέραν δάμαλιν |

βάλωσιν ἀμφὶ τιμάν
φύλασσεν οὐδὲ Μαίας

ὕμνοισιν· ὕφαινέ νυν ἐν τοῖς πολυηράτοις
τι καινὸν | – dd ꞁ dss ∪ ss –
υἱὸς δύνατ' οὔτε κατ' εὐφεγγέας ἁμέρας
λαθεῖν νιν |

ὀλβίαις 'Αθάναις,
οὔτε νύκτας ἁγνάς.

εὐαίνετε Κηΐα μέριμνα – dss ∪
εἴτ' οὖν γένετ' - - - - -

πρέπει σε φερτάταν ἴμεν ∪ sss
ποδαρκέ' ἄγγελον Διός

ὁδὸν παρὰ Καλλιόπας | λαχοῖσαν ἔξοχον
γέρας ∪ dd ∪ sss
κτανεῖν τότε Γᾶς - - - - | ὀβριμοσπόρου λίθῳ

†τί ἦν,† Ἄργος ὅθ' ἵππιον λιποῦσα | φεῦγε
χρυσέα βοῦς sdss ∪ ss –
Ἄργον· ἦ ῥα καὶ - - - - - - -· | ἄσπετοι
μέριμναι·

εὐρυσθενέος φραδαῖσι | φερτάτου Διός – ds ∪ ss
ἦ Πιερίδες φύτευσαν | - - - - - - - - -

'Ινάχου ῥοδοδάκτυλος κόρα; sdss
καδέων ἀνάπαυσιν - - - - -.

It should be noted that the fifth and sixth periods cannot be run into one, except by scanning μέριμνᾱ πρέπει, which gives units unlike those of the context.

Bacchylides' encomium in the Lesbian style (frag. 20 b Sn.) has already been quoted; his third epinician, though triadic in form, has its 3-period stanzas composed in much the same manner. Frag. 6 D² of Simonides, a θρῆνος of which 4 lines are quoted by Favorinus *ap.*

[1] So Maas for καί.

Stob., again recalls the Lesbians, though we cannot tell whether this is a complete stanza:

ἄνθρωπος ἐὼν μή ποτε φάσῃς, ὅ τι γίνεται αὔριον,	– d ꞁ d ꞁ dds
μηδ' ἄνδρα ἰδὼν ὄλβιον, ὅσσον χρόνον ἔσσεται·	– d ꞁ d ꞁ ds
ὠκεῖα γὰρ οὐδὲ τανυπτερύγου μυίας	– dddš
οὕτως ἁ μετάστασις.	šss

Nothing is here in need of emendation, for either sense or metre. The similarity of the first two lines to the 'asclepiad' metres of Alcaeus and Sappho is obvious, though instead of the disyllabic 'basis' there is here a single anceps. Drag is introduced into the last two lines.

Periodic composition is of all kinds the most difficult to attribute with certainty to a fragmentary text, and caution is particularly necessary when the less mutilated relics of a lyric poet's text belong to a different type. It is very doubtful whether any of Alcman or Ibycus can properly be called periodic; the text and prosody of the former's εὕδουσιν δ' ὀρέων are so uncertain that I can come to no conclusion about it, and although his frag. 43 D² might be dactylo-epitrite it is too short for argument. Certainly where enough survives for diagnosis their poems are clearly composed in cola, like the choruses of drama. The famous Partheneion of Alcman is written in stanzas of three sections *abc*, *a* being 8 lines of alternate trochaic dimeters catalectic and enoplians of the form ⏓ – ⏑ ⏑ – ⏑ – –, *b* all trochaic (2 trims. + 2 dims.), *c* dactylic (tetram. + tetram. cat.). Its most extraordinary feature is the free responsion in the clausula, the last line being either – ⏑⏑ – ⏑ ⏑ – ⏑ ⏑ – or – ⏑⏑ – ⏑ ⏑ – ⏑ – –.[1] Alcman, in fact, applies here a principle of responsion by syllable-counting (the number of syllables corresponds though the quantities change), traces of which are to be seen in drama, especially comedy,[2]

[1] In the second line the short second syllable of Ἐνετικός l. 51 can, as Maas points out, be accounted simply a special licence in an unhellenic proper name.

[2] See my *Lyric Metres of Greek Drama*, chapter iv.

though never as here in a clausula. The cola of section *a* are each separate periods, admitting brevis in longo and hiatus at line-end; in *b* the trimeters are periods but the dimeters uncertain (they may in fact be a single tetrameter); the dactyls in *c* run on in synaphea:

Δαμαρέτα τ' ἐρατά τε Ἰανθεμίς, – ∪ ∪ – ∪ ∪ – ∪ ∪ – ∪ ∪
ἀλλ' Ἁγησιχόρα με τηρεῖ. – ⏖ – ∪∪ – ∪ ⏑̲ –

This dactylic tetrameter is a favourite of Alcman; there are several fragments entirely composed in it, though unfortunately the evidence is nowhere really decisive as to the extent of synaphea (where the close is spondaic; final – ∪ ∪ is of course in obligatory synaphea). It seems to me on the whole most likely that Alcman composed his dactyls in 'systems', that is to say with regular diaeresis but in synaphea, like the anapaestic systems of drama. We do not know how he let them run out—what sort of colon, that is, corresponded to the paroemiac of anapaests. It is tempting to suppose that the curious clausula of the Partheneion, – ∪ ∪ – ∪ ∪ – ∪ ⏑̲ –, was his normal way of closing a system; possibly the last line of frag. 37 gives a longer version of this, but the text is uncertain.

Ibycus' manner of composition is somewhat similar, so far as we can judge. Of his most famous song (frag. 6 D²) from which the 'ibycean' – ∪ ∪ – ∪ ∪ – ∪ – takes its name only the first few lines provide a reasonably safe basis for analysis:

ἦρι μὲν αἵ τε Κυδώνιαι
μαλίδες ἀρδόμεναι ῥοᾶν
ἐκ ποταμῶν, ἵνα Παρθένων
κᾶπος ἀκήρατος, αἵ τ' οἰνανθίδες
αὐξόμεναι σκιεροῖσιν ὑφ' ἕρνεσιν
οἰναρέοις θαλέθοισιν. ἐμοὶ δ' ἔρος
οὐδεμίαν κατάκοιτος ὥραν.

Three ibyceans are followed by three dactylic tetrameters which run out in an 'alcaic decasyllable' – ∪ ∪ – ∪ ∪ – ∪ – –, in effect a pendant form of ibycean. Probably all these seven lines are in synaphea; the last four at least are. The song addressed to Polycrates is in stanzas composed in *aabc*.

a – ⏖ – ⏖ – ⏑ ⏑ – ⏑ ⏑
– ⏖ – ⏑ ⏑ – ⏑ ⏑ – ⏑ ⏑
– ⏖ – ⏖ – ⏖ – ⏑ ⏑ – ⏑ – –

The dactyls in synaphea again run out in single-short, as in one version of the clausula of Alcman's Partheneion. *b* has three paroemiacs ⏖ – ⏖ – ⏑ ⏑ – –, the last ending in anceps, and *c* two unusual lines

Πέργαμον δ' ἀνέβα ταλαπείριον ἄτα – ⏑ – ⏑ ⏑ – ⏑ ⏑ – ⏑ ⏑ – –
χρυσοέθειραν διὰ Κύπριδα – ⏑ ⏑ – – ⏑ ⏑ – ⏑ –

which are reminiscent of Lesbian rhythms. Here is a technique familiar from many odes in drama: little groups of similar cola in synaphea, forming, not a single 'Vers' or what I have in this essay called 'period',[1] but a section of a whole stanza, a 'major period', as I have elsewhere called it; where the rhythm changes synaphea is broken.

Metre is a very unreliable clue for determining whether a poem was written for solo or choral performance. In general it seems to be the case that verse composed in a metron-series κατὰ στίχον (i.e. in unvarying lengths, with pause at the end of each line) was declaimed or given in solo-recitative, with the possible exception of ionics, since Hephaestion 12 refers to ὅλα ᾄσματα ἰωνικά by Alcman, Sappho, and Alcaeus, some of which may have been of such regular form; we do not, however, know enough about the distinction between ᾠδή and παρακαταλογή (nor even whether recitative was all of one kind) to be sure of this. Other rhythms repeating κατὰ στίχον but not in metron-series hover a little uncertainly between recitative and monody, and probably varied as between one poet or group of poets and another; the dicola and tricola of Archilochus, for instance, may have been given in recitative and the Lesbian stichic rhythms sung in just the same manner as the non-stichic, but there is really no evidence as to whether the use of voice and lyre was the same or different in Sappho's hexameters, her ἠράμαν μὲν ἔγω..., and her φαίνεταί μοι..., and it is very doubtful whether Hephaestion or his sources knew either. At least it seems to be true

[1] 'Minor period' in my *Lyric Metres of Greek Drama.*

that rhythms κατὰ στίχον were never sung in chorus, though in drama they could be given in choral recitative. Triadic composition, of course, implies a chorus, and the full periodic style of composition, whether triadic or monostrophic, was almost always choral, though the bizarre exception of Timocreon's lampoon on Themistocles reminds us that dactylo-epitrite, at least, could go into circulation in a sort of scolion form. But it is the large intermediate class of poems constructed, so to speak, κατὰ κῶλον, shading off on the one side into periodic, on the other into stichic, that prevents any categorical division by metrical form into choral lyric and monody; moreover, some lines of Lesbian monody, or of Anacreon, are in isolation so like periodic as to warn us against making deductions from fragments. Most poets were composers of either monody or choral lyric, not of both, but where tradition is not clear on this point we have to rely for the distinction on considerations of subject-matter and style; where these are not decisive, as in the case of all the extant Ibycus and some of Alcman, metrical structure is no guide. Metrically, as we have seen, these two are much nearer to the choruses of drama than to any other choral lyric; but like the dramatic poets they sometimes show affinities with Lesbian monody and Anacreon.

Anacreon, in fact, in his use of aeolo-choriambic often anticipates the simpler stanzas of drama, especially of comedy. His first book consists of poems written in short glyconic 'systems' of two, three, or four cola running out in a catalectic colon (pherecratean). He also has systems, of varied length, of iono-anacreontic dimeters, trimeters, and tetrameters which sometimes at least have no special clausula. He seems to have used a variety of dicola, sometimes a full + a catalectic form, sometimes two dissimilar cola like Archilochus, κατὰ στίχον. The lines of mixed double- and single-short reminiscent of Lesbian rhythms, though rarely quite the same in detail, and others very like the rhythm of scolia, may also have been composed κατὰ στίχον, but the disjointed fragments give us no direct evidence. Once, in 54 D², he arranges tricola (iambo-choriambic tetrameter ending in anceps, iambo-choriambic tetram. + iamb. dim.) in a string of little stanzas. This is the nearest approach in the extant fragments to strophic responsion, except in the sense that a short poem such as 5 D[2] which is probably complete may consist of two little systems of equal length—here 3 full cola + 1 catalectic. Within the systems one colon may stand in anaclastic responsion to another: thus ⏑ ⏑ – x̄ x̆ ⏑ – – is treated as the equivalent of ⏑ ⏑ – x̆ x̄ ⏑ – –, and in 39 (whether these 'trimeters' are in a system or κατὰ στίχον) we get

⏑ ⏑ – – ⏑ ⏑ – – ⏑ ⏑ – –
⏑ ⏑ – ⏑ – ⏑ – – ⏑ ⏑ – –
⏑ ⏑ – – ⏑ ⏑ – ⏑ – ⏑ – –

Similarly in the iambo-choriambics of 54 x̄ x̆ ⏑ – is several times treated as interchangeable with x̆ x̄ ⏑ –.

Short systems of five or six cola, the clausula being modified to give some contrasting rhythm, are all we can deduce with certainty from the fragments of Corinna. These are either ionic dimeters, often with colon-caesura, running out in a curiously prolonged clausula, as in the Strife of Cithaeron and Helicon:

μεγάλαν τ' ἀθανάτων ἔξ- ⏑ ⏑ – – ⏑ ⏑ – –
-ελε τιμάν.' τάδ' ἔμελψεμ.
μάκαρας δ' αὐτίκα Μώση
φερέμεν ψᾶφον ἔταττον
κρουφίαν κάλπιδας ἐν χρου-
-σοφαῖς. τὺ δ' ἅμα πάντες ὦρθεν ⏑ ⏑ – – ⏑⏑ – ⏑ – –

or, in the Asopides, 'choriambic dimeters' of the form ⏓ ⏓ – ⏓ – ⏑ ⏑ – (with occasional resolution of one of the first two syllables) mixed with glyconics and running out in a pherecratean:

τόδε γέρας κατῖσχον ἰὼν ⏑ ⏑ ⏑ – ⏑ – ⏑ ⏑ –
ἐς πεντείκοντα κρατερῶν – – – – – ⏑ ⏑ –
ὁμήμων, πέδοχος προφά- ⏑ – – ⏑ ⏑ – ⏑ –
-τας σεμνῶν ἀδούτων λαχὼν – – – ⏑ ⏑ – ⏑ –
ἀψεύδιαν 'Ακρηφείν. – – – ⏑ ⏑ – –

Corinna, it appears from this, allows an ordinary glyconic to respond with a choriambic dimeter by the same sort of anaclasis (– ⏓ – ⏑ x̄ x̆ ⏑ – = – ⏓ – ⏑ x̆ x̄ ⏑ –) as Anacreon's in his iono-anacreontics; and the tragedians occasionally adopt both these irregularities.

7

The lyric so far discussed has fallen into one or the other of two classes with a fairly clear line of demarcation: that constructed in periods, consisting of units juxtaposed or linked by anceps, and that constructed by cola (some of them analysable into metra) whether in homogeneous systems in synaphea or forming heterogeneous stanzas with frequent pause and change of rhythm. Pindar, Simonides, and Bacchylides are representative of the former, while dactylo-epitrite brings in a few other poems by little-known authors, and some of the odes of drama, though these tend to develop some of the balance and repetitive symmetry of colon-lyric. The second category includes the greater part of dramatic lyric, and the most intelligible of the fragments of Alcman, Ibycus, Anacreon, and Corinna. Stesichorus cannot be grouped with any certainty, and possibly his manner does not fully coincide with either of these two. There remain Alcaeus and Sappho and the scolia, and I have spoken of an occasional approximation to the Lesbian manner in fragments of some of the poets already mentioned. I have left this group to the last in defiance of chronology because it mixes some of the attributes of both periodic and colon-composition.

The types of metrical structure used by Sappho and Alcaeus (apart from dactylic hexameters or iambic tetrameters κατὰ στίχον with which I am not here concerned) are in general reducible to two: rhythms that extend by prolongation, and rhythms that extend by the addition of whole units with or without link anceps. Extension can be measured by the number of syllables, since resolution is unknown in Lesbian lyric. Lines of either the prolonged or the compound type can repeat κατὰ στίχον or be combined (either type singly or mixed) into heterogeneous repeating stanzas of two, three, or four lines.

These two types are easily distinguishable; the prolonged rhythm has no juxtaposed longs or anceps in mid-line, whereas the compound rhythm has always one or both of these. Initial or final anceps or both may be added to either type. The *prolonged* may run wholly in double-short, or in mixed double and single, never wholly in single-short. It may change from single to double and back again, but once it has moved out of double-short it never changes back. The *compound* rhythm may contain either simple units – ⏑ – and – ⏑ ⏑ –, or prolonged units of the kind already described in §2 and used in the Pindaric period. Either prolonged or compound rhythms may start with an 'aeolic base' of two syllables *ad lib.* ⏒ ⏒, this base being unique in allowing ⏑ ⏑ to correspond to – –. Such initial freedom is found only in Lesbian verse and one or two scolia.

The shortest lines are octosyllabic.[1] The 'glyconic', i.e. – ⏑ ⏑ – ⏑ – **ds** upon an aeolic base ⏒ ⏒ is not used κατὰ στίχον but only combines with other rhythms into stanzas. The line formed by transferring the first syllable of a glyconic to the end ⏒ ds ⏒ is found only in pseudo-Sappho 94 D² δέδυκε μὲν ἁ σελάννα κτλ., four lines repeating the rhythm κατὰ στίχον. It is quoted without author by Hephaestion as an illustration of his conception of a 'major ionic dimeter', and aeolicised by editors who accept Stephanus' attribution to Sappho. Sappho 88

πλήρης μὲν ἐφαίνετ' ἁ σελάννα·
αἰ δ' ὡς περὶ βῶμον ἐστάθησαν

is a longer version of a similar rhythm, **dss** with anceps fore and aft, again used κατὰ στίχον.

Alcaeus 34 ἐκ δὲ ποτήριον πώνης Διννομένη παρίσδων must be interpreted as containing a glyconic with final anceps added (hipponactean):

ἐκ δὲ ποτήριον ˡ πώνης Διννομένη παρίσδων – – – ⏑ ⏑ – ⏑ – –

The first words, – ⏑ ⏑ – ⏑ –, probably belong to the previous line, though this might conceivably be a long compound, of the type found in Sappho 97 and 98, a stanza beginning with

– ⏑ – ˡ ⏒ ⏓ – ⏑ ⏑ – ⏑ –

[1] I regard Sappho 135–6 D² as incapable of metrical arrangement as it stands; probably some words have been omitted. The worst of all shifts is to make a single line of κῆ δ' ἀμβροσίας μὲν κράτηρ ἐκέ̄κρατο. Apart from the dubious quantity such a conjunction of two adoneans – – ⏑ ⏑ – – | – – ⏑ ⏑ – – is a metrical impossibility in any kind of verse at any time.

The aeolic base is left on the glyconic even in mid-verse, except that the double-short is not allowed, since here in mid-verse it would transform the metrical type.[1] Alcaeus 34 should in no case be interpreted (as in Diehl) – ⏑ ⏑ – ⏑ – – – | – – – ⏑ ⏑ – –. Such a dicolon formed by full+catalectic colon (as in Archilochus, Anacreon, or the dramatists) is not in the Lesbian manner, nor is tail-drag found elsewhere in Sappho or Alcaeus.

In 14 D[2] Alcaeus sets a complete glyconic **sds** on an aeolic base, thus making a decasyllable:

'Αχίλλευς, ὃ τᾶς Σκυθίκας μέδεις.

I see no reason to regard this as starting in the middle of a line or as a fragment of two glyconics with colon-caesura ⏓ ⏓ – ⏑ ⏑ –] ⏑ – – ⏑ – ⏑ ⏑ – ⏑ –. Such a decasyllable, as we have seen,[2] is found in Pindar and Bacchylides; doubtless Alcaeus' version was elsewhere capable of the variation – ⏑ – ⏑ – ⏑ ⏑ – ⏑ – also. The hendecasyllable which forms the last line of the stanza in Sappho 97 and 98 ⏓ ⏓ : – ⏑ ⏑ – ⏑ – ⏑ – : – ('phalaecean') is of similar form with the **d** shifted up and final anceps added, and Sappho 144*a* and *b* adds initial anceps to the phalaecean to make a dodecasyllable ⏓ : – ⏑ – ⏑ ⏑ – ⏑ – ⏑ – : – Ψαπφοῖ, τί τὰν πολύολβον 'Αφροδίταν; Alcaeus 93

τριβώλετερ· οὐ γὰρ 'Αρκάδεσσι λώβα ⏑ : – ⏑ ⏑ – ⏑ – ⏑ – ⏑ – : –

is another dodecasyllable with the choriamb shifted up yet again. The root form in each of these cases is the decasyllable with one **d.**

Other rhythms of the prolonged types extend **d** to **dd**, **ddd**, or **dddd.** These all begin with the aeolic base and either end with a simple anceps or prolong the last **d** into **ds.** Thus if we take the glyconic ⏓ ⏓ : – ⏑ ⏑ – ⏑ – as the shortest length of this rhythm, the next is the hendecasyllable of Sappho 137,

[1] There are two apparent exceptions to this rule, Sapph. 98, l. 4 and Alc. 54, l. 5, but I doubt if either is admissible. The former is in any case slightly corrupt and the letters not quite certainly decipherable; in the latter, if some such form as Bergk's κοίιλαι is not adopted, we should perhaps emend to ποίκιλαι with Kaibel.

[2] Above, Part II, p. 70, n.

Ἔρος δηὖτέ μ᾿ ὀ λυσιμέλης δόνει ∪ – : – ∪ ∪ – ∪ ∪ – ∪ –
γλυκύπικρον ἀμάχανον ὄρπετον ∪ ∪ : – ∪ ∪ – ∪ ∪ – ∪ –

Sappho 124 θυρώρῳ πόδες ἐπτορόγυιοι has the simple final anceps ⏑̲ ⏑̲ dd ⏑̲. The second book of her collected works is written in similar lines of fourteen syllables:

ἠράμαν μὲν ἔγω σέθεν Ἄτθι πάλαι ποτά ⏑̲ ⏑̲ ddds

of which 121

ἦρος ἄγγελος ἰμερόφωνος ἀήδων

is the shorter form with final anceps ⏑̲ ⏑̲ ddd ⏑̲. Alcaeus 99 has sixteen syllables:

κέλομαί τινα τὸν χαρίεντα Μένωνα κάλεσσαι, ⏑̲ ⏑̲ dddd –
αἰ χρῆ συμποσίας ἐπ᾿ ὄνασιν ἔμοι γε γένεσθαι

and this is the longest extant.

Of these two types of rhythm, the compound and the prolonged, the compound are the more frequent in Lesbian poetry. One common kind is formed by the juxtaposition of choriambs, which like the prolonged **dd**... rhythms just described usually start from an aeolic base and end either in **ds** or final anceps. These 'asclepiad' rhythms again start from the glyconic ⏑̲ ⏑̲ ds and mount up by choriambs, that is to say by the insertion of complete units instead of by prolongation:

Alc. 43 (end of stanza) Φιττάκω δὲ δίδοις κῦδος ἐπήρατον ⏑̲ ⏑̲ d ׀ ds
Sapph. 106 ὀφθάλμοις δὲ μέλαις νύκτος ἄωρος ⏑̲ ⏑̲ d ׀ d ⏑̲
Sapph. 57 βροδοπάχεες ἄγναι Χάριτες, δεῦτε Δίος κόραι ⏑̲ ⏑̲ d ׀ d ׀ ds

(The whole of Sappho's Bk. III was written in these κατὰ στίχον.)

Sapph. 107 κατθνᾴσκει, Κυθέρη᾿, ἄβρος Ἄδωνις· τί κε θεῖμεν; ⏑̲ ⏑̲ d ׀ d ׀ d ⏑̲
Alc. 15 Κρονίδα βασίληος γένος Αἴαν τὸν ἄριστον πεδ᾿ Ἀχιλλέα ⏑̲ ⏑̲ d ׀ d ׀ d ׀ ds

Pseudo-Sappho 93 Κρῆσσαί νύ ποτ᾿ ὦδ᾿ ἐμμελέως πόδεσσιν ⏑̲ d ׀ ds ⏑̲ begins with anceps instead of aeolic base and adds final anceps; the papyrus fragments of Bk. IV show the same rhythm with an extra choriamb (Hephaestion's 'major ionics'):

σὺ δὲ στεφάνοις, ὦ Δίκα, πάρθεσθ' ἐράτοις φόβαισιν ⏓ d ˡ d ˡ ds ⏑ used κατὰ στίχον.

Sappho 90 drops both base and initial anceps and starts from **d**:

δηὖτέ νυν ἄβραι Χάριτες καλλίκομοί τε Μοῖσαι d ˡ d ˡ ds –

If the text of Sappho 126 D² is to be trusted, the choriamb is there used not in juxtaposition but with link and final anceps:

σκιδναμένας ἐν στήθεσιν ὀργᾶς d – d –
μαψυλάκαν γλῶσσαν πεφύλαχθαι

(The second line has been considerably doctored to bring it into conformity with the first.)

Much the most common single-short unit found in compound rhythms is the simple s – ⏑ –. This is repeated in the 'alcaic enneasyllable': λαῖφος δὲ πὰν ȝάδηλον ἤδη ⏓ s ⏓ s ⏓. It is rarely combined with **dd** as in dactylo-epitrite; the iambelegus (156 D²) attributed to Sappho is as Lobel points out probably not aeolic at all, and we are left with the two encomiologi dd – s – Alc. 40, either κατὰ στίχον or paired in a stanza. Most characteristic is the combination with **ds**; so, for instance, in the first two lines of the best-known sapphic and alcaic stanzas:

ποικιλόθρον' ἀθάνατ' 'Αφρόδιτα s ⏓ ds ⏓
ἀσυννέτημμι τῶν ἀνέμων στάσιν ⏓ s ⏓ ds

in Alc. 63

ἰόπλοκ' ἄγνα μελλιχόμειδε Σάπφοι ⏓ s ⏓ ds ⏓

and in Sappho 148 D² (if it is Sappho)

Μᾶλις μὲν ἔννη λέπτον ἔχοισ' ἐπ' ἀτράκτω λίνον ⏓ s ⏓ ds ⏓ s

Similarly **s** is found in combination with the complete glyconic, the whole being sometimes part of a larger compound: thus Alcaeus 54 has two glyconics linked to **s**, in seven lines repeating κατὰ στίχον

νεύοισιν, κεφάλαισιν ἄνδρων ἀγάλματα·
χάλκιαι δὲ πασσάλοις – ⏓ ds | – ⏓ ds ⏓ s

Alcaeus 43 has stanzas of which the first and third lines give ⏓ s ⏓ ⏑⏑ ds, alternating with asclepiads. The first line of Sappho's stanzas in 97 and 98 is similar, but drops the initial anceps.

Sappho 85 and 130 substitute **s** for initial anceps or aeolic base before juxtaposed choriambs:

ἀμφὶ δ' ἄβροις λασίοις εὖ ἑ πύκασσε s ꞁ d ꞁ d ⏓

The relation of this to the regular ionic trimeters (cf. Sapph. 86, Alc. 68, 123) which Hephaestion says was the metre of whole songs of both poets is uncertain, but I should be inclined to regard the two as arrived at by different processes. The trimeters are a 'series', like the dactylic hexameters and iambic tetrameters, and it seems to me likely that such a modification as an opening metron – ⏑ – – (a phenomenon quite different from initial anceps) is a later, post-anacreontic refinement.

Longer segments of single-short[1] are much rarer, but Sapph. 114 gives – ⏑ – ⏑ – with initial anceps, juxtaposed with a prolonged unit:

γλύκηα μᾶτερ, οὔ τοι δύναμαι κρέκην τὸν ἴστον ⏓ ss ꞁ dss ⏓

the whole being apparently repeated κατὰ στίχον. The same element **ss** is paired in 154 and given link and final anceps

δεῦρο δηὖτε Μοῖσαι χρύσιον λίποισαι ss ⏓ ss ⏓

It is possible that such pairing is a characteristic form of Lesbian composition, though little has survived. Reference has already been made to Sapph. 126 d – d –, and 128 repeats κατὰ στίχον ds ⏓ ds ⏓.

This brief account attempts to show how the separate lines of Lesbian poetry are formed and extended. I use the untechnical word 'lines' advisedly, since these segments, though sometimes used like cola and sometimes like periods, are not as a whole identifiable with either. When they repeat κατὰ στίχον, then like all other rhythms

[1] Sappho 152 D[2] is so full of uncertainties that I hesitate to formulate it. If it is to be tidied up (by unparalleled synizeses) into lecythion + ithyphallic I should be very doubtful of the attribution to Sappho of such a dicolon; the full + catalectic, typical of Archilochus and Anacreon, is as indicated above un-Lesbian so far as our evidence reaches.

built 'line upon line' they have pause, and admit hiatus and brevis in longo at the end of each line, i.e. each line is a period. Such lines may of course have both initial and final anceps, since there is pause between the end of one and the beginning of the next. Where they are built up into stanzas they behave very like the cola of drama, but as we shall see with certain characteristic modifications. It may be noted that the separate lines themselves, even when they are multiple compounds of units, can sometimes be expressed in relation to each other like the simpler dramatic cola. Thus θυρώρῳ πόδες ἐπτορόγυιοι might be represented as a catalectic form of Ἔρος δηὖτέ μ' ὁ λυσιμέλης δόνει, or ἦρος ἄγγελος ἰμερόφωνος ἀήδων of ἠράμαν μὲν ἔγω σέθεν Ἄτθι πάλαι ποτά, or ὀφθάλμοις δὲ μέλαις νύκτος ἄωρος of Φιττάκω δὲ δίδοις κῦδος ἐπήρατον, etc. In Lesbian poetry, however, the catalectic does not follow the full version within a stanza; the relation is merely traceable in the construction of the lines. Further, there is a relation of ἐπιπλοκή which appears to operate in these heterogeneous lines in just the same way as between iambic and trochaic series, or cretic and bacchiac series: a new set of lines is formed by transferring an initial syllable to final place. Thus, for instance, the alcaic to the sapphic hendecasyllable:

⏑̲ s ⏑̲ ds
s ⏑̲ ds ⏑̲

Sapph. 93 ⏑̲ d ˈ ds ⏑̲ to the asclepiad, and Sapph. 63 ⏑̲ d ˈ d ˈ ds ⏑̲ to the major asclepiad.

Stanzas always respond monostrophically and are of very simple construction. Here it is almost permissible to speak of cola, even where these are already composite. Thus, for instance, the most familiar alcaic stanza is usually given four lines, but while the first two admit hiatus and final brevis in longo the third and fourth (cf. 46 B) are linked without pause, i.e. with the effect of cola. The scheme, in fact, is really *aab*; whereas in *a* the units are – ⏑ – and – ⏑ ⏑ – ⏑ –, in *b* each of these lengthens, – ⏑ – being paired and – ⏑ ⏑ – ⏑ – prolonged to – ⏑ ⏑ – ⏑ ⏑ – ⏑ –.

The same formula *aab* applies also to the Sapphic stanza, where – ⏑ ⏑ – ⏑̲ is added as a short colon to the third hendecasyllable, starting sometimes in the middle of a word. Sapph. 96 (glyc.+glyc. +⏓⏒: – ⏑ ⏑ – ⏑ ⏑ – ⏑ –) has three separable lines, but 97 and 98 give three linked cola, cf.

ἀ δ' ἐέρσα κάλα κέχυται, τεθά- s ǀ ⏓ ⏒ ds
-λαισι δὲ βρόδα κἄπαλ' ἄν- ⏓ ⏒ ds
-θρυσκα καὶ μελίλωτος ἀνθεμώδης ⏓ ⏒ dss ⏓

Alc. 118 is apparently three asclepiads+glyconic, but there is no evidence as to whether any of these are linked.

A notable point in all Lesbian stanzas is that even where there is hiatus or brevis in longo at the end of some or all of the lines, they keep a smooth carry-over by avoiding anceps at the end of one line followed by anceps at the beginning of the next. The new Alcaeus fragment 24 C in *Ox. Pap.* xviii. 2166 may, however, prove to be the first exception to this rule.

The anonymous scolia call for little metrical comment. The units of which they are composed are those familiar already from Pindaric verse; the simple stanza-structure recalls the Lesbian, though without any of the latter's special peculiarities. The major asclepiads of 14 and 19–22 D[2] are of normal alcaic type with aeolic base, and 9 has the familiar *aab* type of stanza:

ὁ καρκίνος ὧδ' ἔφα[1] ⏓ ds
χαλᾷ τὸν ὄφιν λαβών· ⏓ ds
εὐθὺν χρὴ τὸν ἑταῖρον ἔμ- glyc.
-μεν καὶ μὴ σκολιὰ φρονεῖν +glyc.

The commonest form of Attic scolion (cf. 1–7 D[2]) appears to run *aabc*; there are no instances of linked *b*+*c*. The first two lines are probably both phalaeceans with aeolic base; the one exception in 7 which begins ὑγιαίνειν μὲν ἄριστον ἀνδρὶ θνατῷ is probably an *ad hoc* variant designed to accommodate the word ὑγιαίνειν, or indeed this may have been pronounced in three syllables ⏑ – –. Similarly the anceps in the middle of the second line appears only in order to accommodate the names Ἁρμόδιος καὶ Ἀριστογείτων in the series celebrating the tyrannicides: so in 10 D[2]

[1] This is more probable than the form in which it is quoted, ὁ δὲ καρκίνος ὧδ' ἔφα, on both metrical and stylistic grounds.

ἐν μύρτου κλαδὶ τὸ ξίφος φορήσω,
ὥσπερ ʽΑρμόδιος κἀριστογείτων, — ⏑ — ⏑ ⏑ — ⏒ — ⏑ — —
ὅτε τὸν τύραννον κτανέτην
ἰσονόμους τ᾽ ᾽Αθήνας ἐποιησάτην.

It is a milder version of the *tour de force* by which Simonides achieves the name ᾽Αριστογείτων within an elegiac couplet (76 D²). The third line begins with what is probably a headless unit (‸ ds ˡ d) of the Pindaric type, possibly with a wordless twang on the lyre; the fourth is a paired **ds** juxtaposed without link anceps.

The scolia attributed to the Seven Sages (31 ff.) are mostly composed in a kind of free dactylo-epitrite, all of individual pattern but built up from the ordinary units. I quote 35 D² *exempli gratia*:

ἀστοῖσιν ἄρεσκε πᾶσιν, ἐμ πόλει αἴ κε μένῃς· — ds ⏑ dd
πλείσταν γὰρ ἔχει χάριν. αὐθάδης δὲ τρόπος — dd — d
πολλάκις βλαβερὰν ἐξέλαμψεν ἄταν. sd ˡ ss —

7

ΚΙΣΣΥΒΙΟΝ

In his great 1950 edition of Theocritus A. S. F. Gow reaffirms the theory he put forward in *J.H.S.* xxxiii, 1913, 207, that the goatherd's κισσύβιον (i. 27) was a shallow cup with the triple scenic decoration in its interior. The advantages of this interpretation are two: (1) ἔντοσθεν (32) has its easiest and most obvious meaning, (2) the three scenes depicted can be symmetrically arranged. As against this, κατ' αὐτόν (30) is left almost meaningless, whereas on the assumption that the scenes are on the exterior we have a band of ornament above and below—flowered ivy ὑψόθι, and ἕλιξ (whether fruited ivy or another plant) 'opposite it'—with the pictures 'in between' (ἔντοσθεν: cf. ἐντός in Hdt. vii. 100), and an acanthus-motif encircling the base (55). Moreover, the words describing the relative position of the three scenes—τοῖς δὲ μέτα (39) and τυτθὸν δ' ὅσσον ἄπωθεν (45)—though vague, are not very appropriate for indicating a centre-piece with a surrounding ring divided into two fields; they would on the face of it be more natural for scenes which the eye found in loose juxtaposition on the exterior as the vessel was turned in the hand. Admittedly the difficulties of arranging the three scenes on a two-handled (28) cup are considerable; it all depends how seriously you take Theocritus' description as that of a precisely visualised work of art and how far you are prepared to let this outweigh linguistic propriety.

But it seems to me that the really decisive consideration is the description βαθὺ κισσύβιον (27). Clearly, if the vessel is really 'deep' it *cannot* have the carvings on the inside. Mr Gow argues that from the scholia here and the remarks of Athenaeus (xi. 476) it appears that κισσύβιον can be used for any shape of cup; therefore, since the pictures are inside, βαθύ must here mean 'relatively deep'—deep for a saucer-shaped κισσύβιον, as it were, though not for a beaker-shaped one. But if it can be shown, as I think it can with some certainty, that κισσύβιον was normally used only of a deep shape, while there is no evidence whatever—the present passage apart—to connect it with a shallow one, then surely βαθὺ κισσύβιον can only mean either 'deep, as κισσύβια are' or 'a particularly deep κισσύβιον'.

Theocritus himself in this idyll uses the alternative terms δέπας (55 and 149) and σκύφος (143). δέπας is certainly quite neutral; not so σκύφος, which as we shall see is the most generally accepted equivalent of κισσύβιον. For the modern archaeologist σκύφος defines a stemless deep-shaped vessel which could not possibly be carved on the inside. Admittedly archaeology has to be strict in the application of technical terms where ancient usage may have been wider and looser. But there is no doubt that σκύφος, to a Greek, normally meant a deep cup; the *locus classicus* for its proportions is Eur. *Cyc.* 390 f., where Polyphemus' monster σκύφος is 3 cubits wide and 4 deep. I can find no evidence to suggest that σκύφος could be used of a shallow cup, though of course the negative argument cannot be pressed too hard.

The word κισσύβιον itself (κισσύφιον in *I.G.* ii. 1424[a]25) is an ancient one, generally believed by philologists to be non-Greek. Fritzsche on Theocr. i says that κισσοῦβι is still used in the Ionian islands for a *milking-pail*. I have not been able to confirm this, but in Chatzidakis's *Lexicon of Mediaeval and Modern Greek*, vol. ii, p. 296, there is the identification κισσύβιον· κισσοῦβι without a definition. In view of this it is interesting to find that one of the scholia to Theocr. says it could be a γαλακτοδόχον ἀγγεῖον. It was properly a rustic vessel, very likely aways of wood, though this might possibly be a literary deduction from the supposed connection with κισσός (see below). Scholiasts and grammarians have sometimes an unfortunate tendency to define things not so much from actual knowledge of the object as in terms of some (often imaginary) etymological derivation; thus one scholion on Theocr. i. 27 (repeated in almost the same words on Lucian, *Pseudol.* p. 210. 6 Rabe), after defining κισσύβιον as τὸ ἀγροικικὸν ποτήριον, ἴσως ἀπὸ τοῦ κισσοῦ, says it could be used more generally for any wooden cup παρὰ τὸ κεχύσθαι εἰς αὐτὸ τὸν οἶνον, οἷον χέω, χύσω, χυσσίβιον καὶ κισσύβιον. It is impossible in such statements to say where inference begins—whether it is simply the explanation that is invented, or whether the 'facts' are themselves deduced from the explanation. The association with country life is clear in Homer, where we meet two of these vessels: Eumaeus (*Od.* xvi. 52) *mixes* wine in one for himself and Odysseus (nothing is said of their jointly drinking from it), and Odysseus (*Od.* ix. 346) offers one full of wine to the Cyclops, presumably from the monstrous shepherd's own household equipment. The κισσύβιον in Homer, in fact, appears to be a sizeable vessel, no mere cup in the ordinary sense, even though it could be used for deep drinking. Size and rusticity are its certain characteristics, and it is at least not impossible that to Homer it meant something that could be used as a small milking-pail. (N.B. Thyrsis milks the goat into his κισσύβιον 143.)

Most scholiasts and grammarians, however, define it simply as a ποτήριον. It is identified or compared with the σκύφος (the Aeolians are said to call this a κισσύβιον, and cf. Epicharmus, *Cyclops* frag. 83 Kaibel and the Eur. passages quoted below) or the κύπελλον, itself described by Silenus as similar to the σκύφος, Ath. xi. 482. Dionysius of Samos substituted the word κυμβίον for κισσύβιον in describing Odysseus' encounter with the Cyclops, but this Athenaeus (xi. 481) deprecates; the κυμβίον, he says, is a *small* deep vessel, and even three κυμβία-full could not have made a Cyclops drunk; Philemon (Ath. xi. 476) declares roundly that the κισσύβιον has only one handle, and so we find the cup pictured, curiously enough, in at least two illustrations of the Polyphemus scene: the south Italian calyx-crater B.M. 1947, 7–14–18 (Trendall, *Frühit. Vm.*, pl. 12*b*) and the Laconian cup Paris, Bib. Nat. 190 (*C.V.A.* i, pl. 23). In Theocritus, however, it has two handles, and as the σκύφος also seems more often to have been two-handled, Philemon has been over-precise, at least where literary allusions are concerned. The only use of the word which does not seem quite to fit this general picture is in Callim. *Aet.*, inc. lib. frag. 178 Pf.:

καὶ γὰρ ὁ Θρηϊκίην μὲν ἀπέστυγε χανδὸν ἄμυστιν
  οἰνοποτεῖν, ὀλίγῳ δ' ἥδετο κισσυβίῳ.
τῷ μὲν ἐγὼ τάδ' ἔλεξα περιστείχοντος ἀλείσου
  τὸ τρίτον,

which Ath. (l.c.) quotes with the remark that Callim. uses the word wrongly in identifying it with ἄλεισον. The latter, as Mr Gow points out, is in Ath. xi. 783 described as φιαλῶδες (at last we have a shallow shape). Editors of Callim. have, however, pointed out that Ath. has misunderstood the passage, and that there is no question of the two words referring to the same vessel. The most natural interpretation of the context is to take ἀπέστυγε and ἥδετο as referring to the guest's general habits, but even if they refer to this particular occasion the κισσύβιον must be his private cup and the ἄλεισον the circulating one. What *is* unexpected is the adjective ὀλίγῳ; but it is clear, I think, that Callim. is using both these names untechnically, simply as rare and decorative (epic) words for 'cup'. We ought not to argue from a passing allusion such as this to the poem of Theocr. where the vessel is a central object in its proper rustic setting (cf. also Longus, *Daph. and Ch.* i. 15. 3, where a κισσύβιον διάχρυσον 'picked out with gilt', is a rustic gift, and Lucian, *D.D.: Zeus and Ganymede*, §4).

Size and rusticity are accepted in the fifth century as characteristics of this vessel. The word itself does not occur in extant tragedy, but κισσοῦ σκύφος, or κίσσινον σκύφος, κίσσινος ποτήρ can always be taken as a periphrasis for κισσύβιον, as we see from the contexts where they occur. In Eur. *Cyc.* 388 ff. Odysseus describes how the Cyclops milked his flock and filled a huge κρατήρ with milk, setting beside it a σκύφος κισσοῦ (see above), evidently to ladle out great draughts from the κρατήρ. (Is this why the late-fifth-century B.M. vase referred to above, which is inspired by a satyr-play, shows a single-handled vessel?) So, too, Timotheus in his *Cyclops* (frag. 2 D) speaks of a κίσσινον δέπας. In the *Andromeda* (frag. 146 N^2) Eur. describes rustics flocking together with offerings of milk and wine:

πᾶς δὲ ποιμένων ἔρρει λεώς,
ὁ μὲν γάλακτος κίσσινον φέρων σκύφος
πόνων ἀναψυκτῆρ', ὁ δ' ἀμπέλων γάνος.

(Milk is not transported in a shallow bowl.) Neoptolemus of Parium (Ath. xi. 477) called attention to this as a periphrasis for κισσύβιον. In the *Alcestis* (756) Heracles takes a κίσσινον ποτῆρα and drinks deep; the word ποτήρ only occurs elsewhere in Eur. *Cyc.* 151, and seems to have been coined by Eur. to express a particularly large ποτήριον. The palace of Admetus is not exactly a rustic setting, but the use of a κισσύβιον (associated as a drinking-cup only with the Cyclops) is evidently meant to suggest a boorish swilling. The mention of 'ivy' can have no other meaning than this identification. Editors continue to repeat that ivy-wood seems to have been a favourite material for drinking-cups, but when we find that in each case an outsize cup is in question, the statement looks odder than ever. When the stem of ivy grows to any bulk at all it is far too soft and crumbly for anything whatever to be carved from it. Cato, *R.R.* 111 is sometimes quoted as illustrating the permeability of ivy-wood vessels (hence, it is suggested, the waxing of the goatherd's κισσύβιον Theocr. i. 27), since he asserts that to test whether wine has been adulterated you should pour it into ivy-wood, which will let the wine through and retain the water. (Pliny, *N.H.* xvi. 155 echoes this remarkable bit of practical chemistry.) But he does not say 'take a vessel of ivy-wood'; he says '*make* a small container'—*vasculum facito de materia hederacea*. Euripides, and Timotheus after him, writing as town poets, not country craftsmen, assumed the derivation 'vessel of ivy-wood' for κισσύβιον, and used the (more conveniently iambic) periphrases in place of this perhaps slightly outlandish-sounding name. Some grammarians (see Ath. xi. 477, Macr. *Sat.* v. 21. 13) accepted the etymology, though with some doubts ('originally, perhaps'—ἴσως κατ' ἀρχὰς ἐκ κισσίνου κατασκευασθὲν ξύλου); Nicander of Colophon tries a different line (Ath., *loc. cit.*), citing an old custom of using ivy-leaves in making libation to Zeus of Didyma; Theocr. transfers the ivy to a decorative motif, while the Homeric scholia even toy with the idea of such ornamentation on Polyphemus' κισσύβιον. The later association of ivy with Bacchus naturally lent colour to this supposed connection.

I cannot see, then, that there are any grounds for supposing that Theocritus could have described a shallow cup as βαθὺ κισσύβιον, an interpretation which would surely require the *normal* κισσύβιον to be saucer-shaped; or that the words should be taken in any other than their obvious sense of a capacious rustic wooden 'ivy-vessel' proportioned something like the σκύφος of Euripides' Cyclops—decorated, therefore, on the exterior.

8

AN INTERPRETATION OF AR. *VESP.* 136–210 AND ITS CONSEQUENCES FOR THE STAGE OF ARISTOPHANES

Vesp. 136–210

In front of the house are two slaves, one of whom, the company's chief actor, has been commending the play to the public and explaining the situation. Bdelycleon, who has been asleep on the flat roof, wakes up and calls to the slaves: 'One of you run round here quick; my father has got into the kitchen and he is scuttering around like a mouse inside; mind he doesn't get out through the waste-hole. And *you*, up against the door with you!' Slave A, the chief actor, disappears round the side of the house, to take up position as Philocleon inside. A rapid change of mask would enable him to poke a head up through the chimney—144 οὗτος, τίς εἶ σύ;—καπνὸς ἔγωγ' ἐξέρχομαι—only to be extinguished by the bread-trough and log which his watchful son claps on. (How the chimney was represented, if at all, is anybody's guess.) Now comes a diversion from the ground floor, the exact form of which is unfortunately uncertain. RV give the unmetrical τὴν θύραν ὤθει (imperative): whether this is to be emended as Hermann ⟨ὅδε⟩ τὴν θύραν ὠθεῖ, or whether it is a gloss on the following πίεζέ νυν σφόδρα which has displaced the original text, it is clear that after being warned of the new situation Bdelycleon tells Slave B to press well and truly against the door—which implies that Philocleon is pushing from the inside. 'I'll be down there in a minute myself,' he goes on; 'look out for the bolt, and keep an eye on the bar to see he doesn't gnaw out the pin.' (βάλανος was edible as 'date', 'acorn'.) Bdelycleon thereupon disappears down the back of the roof [there was of course a staircase or ladder giving access to the roof out of sight of the spectators, as required on occasion by tragedy too (*Ag.*, *P.V.*, *Psychostasia*, *H.F.*, *Or.*, *Phoen.*)] and comes round on to the stage presumably by the same way as Slave A left it. This would take one or two minutes, and of course the next few remarks in the dialogue with Philocleon are made by Slave B, not by Bdelycleon as in the Oxford Text; he would in any case not address his father as Philocleon (163). The 'net' which Philocleon threatens to gnaw through (164) cannot be stretched across the door, which has to open unimpeded the next minute; it is over the upper part of the house only, covering the window or windows, as we learn from 367 ff., having been put up to prevent him from hopping over the courtyard wall behind (130 ff.). 164 suggests that Philocleon is talking through a window during this exchange, which would make him more easily audible. In the following episode the bolts are temporarily ignored to let out the donkey and Odysseus; at 198 both are shut in again and orders are given for a barricade: 'Push a lot of the stones up against the door, put the pin back in the bar, and get the big mortar against the beam; be quick, roll it up.' But before Slave B has time to do this, his (and our) attention is distracted by a clod of dirt falling on his head; 'Perhaps a mouse up there', says Bdelycleon unfeelingly, but it turns out to be a heliast scrabbling beneath the tiling. Philocleon is shooed back like a troublesome sparrow.

This scene has long been a crucial argument in the controversy over the stage-door in the Greek theatre: did it open outwards or inwards? The evidence for comedy in general is well presented by Professor W. Beare in an appendix to his *Roman Stage*, pp. 277 ff.; his conclusion is that like ordinary house-doors the door in the skene opened inwards. Common sense is so overwhelmingly on his side that it seems at first surprising that the matter should have been so hotly contested. How else could the constant opening and shutting of this double-door (no swing-door, but a stiffly moved contrivance) be controlled on the stage without intolerable fuss and distraction? There are, moreover, two passages in tragedy which are decisive: Eurydice's use of the words κλῇθρ' ἀνασπαστοῦ πύλης, *Ant.* 1186 (where see Jebb's note), and *Or.* 1561–2, where the angry Menelaus, arriving from elsewhere, orders his servants to *push in* the doors of the palace, προσπόλοις λέγω ὠθεῖν πύλας τάσδ'.

The only serious argument on the other side is precisely this scene in the *Wasps*. How are we to answer it? I shall not here discuss the view that different scenery (of a surprisingly solid kind) was somehow erected for comedy, since one of the main contentions of this article is to be that the basic essentials of the scene of fifth-century tragedy and comedy were the same, though for any given play—*Philoctetes*, for instance, or *Aves*—they could be modified by the addition of some details of scene-painting, whose nature we can only guess. In any case, the hypothesis of a false front, so to speak, for the house in the *Wasps*, with a door opening outwards, not only seems pointless; it resolves none of the puzzling contradictions of this scene. Slave B is told (154) to keep an eye on the bolt and bar and pin, and again (200) to put the pin back in the bolt—but bolts and bars are not fixed on the *outside* of doors, whichever way they open. Beare suggests that Bdelycleon is giving orders to someone inside, but that is against the plain sense of the passage (note σύ 199; it would need a τοῖς ἔνδον λέγω, or at least a τις). And what of the barricade? The pin and the mortar one expects to be inside, but πολλοὺς τῶν λίθων is surely the stones lying about on the ground outside. Which side of the door *are* we? At least the pushing from both sides seems clear: Beare indeed argues that the effect of pushing from the outside against an inward-opening door is to force it against its bolts and thus make it difficult for anyone inside to draw them. This is no doubt true, but as an explanation of this scene surely over-ingenious. Would the audience have been able to think it out when they saw Slave B pressing hard and heard that Philocleon was pushing from inside? As slapstick it seems less than funny.

This consideration, I think, gives a clue to the dilemma. Philocleon is trying to get out through a door and the others are trying to keep him in. The simple, farcical way to represent such a situation to the public is surely to push from both sides. Pulling is less effective, quite apart from our uncertainty whether the stage-door had in fact anything to pull by; ordinary houses doubtless had a ῥόπτρον, but grander ones, with a porter in attendance, perhaps not.[1] In any case,

[1] We might assume from 1482 that Philocleon's house had a regular porter in attendance, but the line has an unmistakable paratragic ring, and is probably not to be taken literally. Van Leeuwen's suggestion that this line is a parody of Eur. *Cycl.* 222 (but why parody a satyr-play?)

the possibilities of precaution would be exhausted by the simple pull, whereas pushing can be reinforced from the outside by further emergency measures—talk of bolts and bars and pins, and finally of a barricade, all to keep in a single, frantic heliast. It is all talk and scurrying around; there are no bolts and no mortar, and as we saw the barricading is interrupted by the next diversion. This is indicated all the more clearly by the ἀντιλαβή in 202. The stage-directions in some of our editions (Van Leeuwen's, for instance) make Slave B heave up a beam and a mortar and assemble a heap of stones against the door, all at the caesura of a trimeter. Whatever the relative freedom of metrical delivery in comedy as compared with tragedy, this seems too much to believe, to say nothing of the awkwardness of removing all this paraphernalia before the next opening of the door.

This scene lets in a flood of light upon the technique of Aristophanes. Since Philocleon never does succeed in bursting open the door, the whole normal lay-out of the inside and outside of a house and the mechanism of the door's opening and shutting can be mixed up and turned topsy-turvy for the comic effect of a single scene. Play at a rattling speed and introduce diversions at the right moment, and the audience will take it in its stride. How does this square with the laborious attempts of scholars to provide scenery in advance for all the successive requirements of an Old Comedy? Fashions in stage-directions have changed a good deal: the older commentators indulged in wonderful transformation-scenes, some of them with elaborate stage-machinery of which a whole new set would certainly be required for each play, or else they talked lightly of scene-shifters running about while the audience, far too high-minded to let their attention be distracted, concentrated on the parabasis or some choral song in progress meanwhile. One feels that

ἔα· τίν' ὄχλον τόνδ' ὁρῶ πρὸς αὐλίοις; is typical of the weakness of that whole case, and it is a pity that the Budé editors should have adopted it. All their translation and stage-directions are wrong for this passage; 1482 and 1484 are obviously spoken from indoors and are our earliest instance of that summons from within to open the door which becomes so common in later comedy (cf. πέπληχε τὴν θύραν, etc.).

Aristophanes' chorus-leader would certainly have had a word for it. Moreover, it does seem improbable that it should have been Comedy that called for all this expensive elaboration, while her more highly regarded sister-art was content with the most modest makeshifts and a permanent 'set' with one door which is the basis of every play. In the present century (disregarding such rococo fantasies as those of Bulle) there has been a welcome simplification; the general principle, with much variation of detail between play and play and scholar and scholar, is that strange and even fantastic juxtapositions did not worry poet or audience, so that for instance in *Ran.* there is a background of three houses (or possibly of one house and two paraskenia), respectively the house of Heracles, the palace of Pluto, and the inn—or perhaps only two, omitting the inn; in *Ach.* the houses of Euripides, Dicaeopolis and Lamachus, with some argument over whether what the audience is being asked to swallow is a gnat or a camel—is it the closeness of Lamachus and Euripides whom they knew, in fact, not to be neighbours, or the admission of Dicaeopolis' *country*-house between two town-houses? Pickard-Cambridge decides that in announcing his celebration of the Rural Dionysia Dicaeopolis is only pretending to be at his country-house; rather a difficult distinction for the audience to appreciate, one would have thought. Also the prologue represents the Pnyx, but scene-shifters can emerge and carry off the benches, and all will be well. In *Lys.* the central door is the Propylaea, and the side ones the houses of Lysistrata and Kalonike; thus topography is still elastic. Other plays again, as *Nub.* and *Eccl.*, only need two houses, *Vesp.* and *Plut.* not more than one. In fact the scene is reassuringly like that we are so familiar with from New Comedy, where also there is a certain incongruity, in that rich and poor live at improbably close quarters.

But have reform and simplification gone far enough? In the first place there is still the uncomfortable reflection that fifth-century tragedy never needs more than one door; why was comedy encouraged to be so prodigal of state or choregic resources? Are we to assume a number of comic 'sets', erected afresh between each play, or was there as in New Comedy a single comic set with three doors, of which any number could be used or ignored? Or was there after all a single more or less permanent background for tragedy *and* comedy, a sort of open rectangle formed of skene with paraskenia, of which it was for some reason the convention that comic poets could use the whole while tragedians confined themselves to the middle bit? In that case the simplicity of the scene in *Vesp.* where Slave A and Bdelycleon run round the side of the house must be sacrificed; they must use a door (the next-door house?) which is not accessible to poor Philocleon. Or perhaps the side-doors were hidden behind some rustic boskage or neighbouring architecture (more scenery?) or was the petit-bourgeois house a grand affair with paraskenia round which they galloped for dear life, by way of one of the parodoi?

Before deciding between these not very attractive alternatives we might remember that honest archaeologists admit that there are very few certain traces of fifth-century lay-out in the Theatre of Dionysus, and that virtually our only evidence is the plays themselves. In later centuries, for which archaeological evidence is much fuller, the action of the comedies of Menander and Plautus and Terence would be clear enough evidence in itself, apart from disputed details, of a permanent stereotyped background of the kind normally postulated. The constant interaction of two or more households is integral to these comedies, and this is naturally reflected in the juxtaposition of the houses. But what, in the name of naturalism or illusion or convenience, is to be gained by the juxtaposition of the house of Heracles, the inn, and the palace of Pluto in *Ran.*? These are not interacting, but *successive*, moments. All Aristophanes wants is a door, and since the same stage is at need the earth, the Styx, the Elysian fields, so the same door disgorges Heracles, a landlady, Pluto's porter, Aeschylus and Euripides. So in *Lys.* the door is Kalonike's house, then the Propylaea. So the *Ach.* starts on the Pnyx, i.e. on the one or two long steps in front of the skene where characters or Chorus, in tragedy or comedy, normally do sit when the action requires it; then Dicaeopolis enters his country-house (of course he celebrates the Rural Dionysia there; has he not made peace with the Lacedaemonians?); after his colloquy with the Acharnians he knocks at the same door, now the house of Euripides. This cannot be a flanking house, since the eccyclema has to bring the poet out, and one of the few fixed points in fifth-century archaeology on the site is the reinforced area in the centre of the flooring (marked T in Pickard-Cambridge's diagrams) where this frequently used contrivance slid in and out. After a long interlude as Dicaeopolis' house again it passes to Lamachus whom a Messenger summons out to fight (1070). From 1096 the fun becomes fast and furious, with Dicaeopolis and Lamachus standing one on each side of the stage and alternate slaves dashing in and out with the various objects called for. These are simply brought out 'from within'—παῖ παῖ φέρ' ἔξω δεῦρο: there are no 'houses' at this point. The audience expected no 'scene', properly speaking, in its Old Comedies; it was ready to jump with the poet from one happy improvisation to the next.

Naturally, the total disregard of 'Unity of Space' in Old Comedy has been emphasised often enough, and the number of plays for which only one door has on occasion been postulated is timidly growing, but the full consequences for the staging have not been explicitly drawn. Wilamowitz, in his edition of *Lys.* and in 'Über die Wespen des Ar.' (*Kl. Schr.* i, p. 308) seems half ready to do so, but then he stops short or eludes the question. *Ach.*, he says in the latter, begins on the Pnyx; the Chorus pursuing Amphitheos come upon Dicaeopolis in his deme of Cholleidae; when the latter needs Euripidean stage-properties the poet's house 'is there' (where?) but the Chorus 'must be supposed absent during all this scene'—presumably because the Chorus must be imagined as waiting in Cholleidae while Dicaeopolis visits Athens! After the parabasis he puts Dicaeopolis and Lamachus as neighbours in Athens without being more explicit about their houses, while the end sees Dicaeopolis and his train 'apparently leaving his house'. 'Wie der Regisseur sich geholfen hat, können wir nicht wissen, sollen wir nicht wissen wollen.' The implications of this are not very clear; in fact, of course, the producer had not to do anything about it at all.

It will be objected: 'Yes, that is all very well for comedies where these different phases of the action really are successive, but are there not Aristophanean plays where there *is* cross-reference from one house or building to another? That last scene in *Ach.* is getting perilously near it, and how is it possible to treat a play like *Nub.*, and still more *Eccl.*, in this cavalier fashion?' Let us then attack the prevailing theory at its strongest point, and consider *Eccl.*, not from the standpoint of modern preconceived notions of what constitutes a 'scene', but from the text itself.

The number of houses in the background is sometimes given as two, sometimes as three, in order to accommodate Chremes as well. I cannot here discuss the part assigned to this character by some editors, but if the much stronger and better presented case for two houses can be demolished, the house of Chremes collapses with it. The best and most detailed exposition is the essay of Eduard Fraenkel, 'Dramaturgical Problems in the *Ecclesiazusae*' in *Greek Poetry and Life*, Essays Presented to Gilbert Murray, 1936. He regards this play as an intermediate stage between Old and New Comedy. It has two houses, he says, like *Nub.* and probably other lost plays, but whereas in *Nub.* the identity of the houses remains the same throughout, in *Eccl.* the owners change: down to 729 they are Blepyrus and his neighbour, in the next scene Man A (some say Chremes) and Man B, and in the next the two courtesans (the Girl and the Hag). Nothing here seems to suggest a shift towards New Comedy; the technique seems to be the same as, for instance, that of *Ran.* or *Ach.*, only applied to two houses instead of one. But Fraenkel sees a subtle difference: 'Generally speaking', he says admirably, 'in early comedy the background does not exist for the audience, unless there is a special reference to it in the dialogue. This is not the case in *Eccl.* There the two houses and the street before them are never negligible, but are always of importance both for the conception of the poet and for the imagination of the audience.' The only concrete evidence he advances for this rather nebulous impression is that the assembly on the stage, unlike those of *Ach.* or *Thesm.*, is not an actual assembly but a rehearsal; the chief motive for this, he says, is the impossibility of holding the ecclesia in the street before the two houses. Who can say what a poet's 'chief motive' is in constructing a play one way rather than another? The rehearsal is an integral part of the prologue-exposition; it is much funnier than a real meeting because the performers' lapses can be corrected; and the stage can be cleared when they go off to the real meeting, to make room for the worried and abandoned husbands. It is, of course, true that *Eccl.*, like *Plut.*, is in some respects intermediate between Old and New Comedy; there is no parabasis, for instance, and the characters are all private citizens; the fact that the scene, throughout its imaginary changes, represents the houses of private citizens is a consequence of the whole character of the plot. But the background is no more and no less important and all-pervasive than in any other play; it behaves in the usual intermittent and improvisatory way.

Of the triple series of owners for the two houses postulated by Fraenkel we can omit the middle one; Man A brings his effects out of the house, but Man B simply walks on from the side. There is no mention of his house or his coming out or going in. The others are (1) Blepyrus and his wife Praxagora, and their neighbours (cf. τὴν γείτονα 33, ὁ γειτνιῶν 327); (2) from 877 on, the two courtesans. Now it is clear that the play opens, not with Praxagora coming stealthily out of her door, but with her presence on the stage—probably just in front of the steps, addressing her lamp which she has just placed on them. (The assembling women, who later form the Chorus, doubtless gathered in the orchestra, some of them sitting on the steps.) Praxagora *is there*, just like Lysistrata in a similar opening; and just as Lysistrata presently says of her friend Kalonike that she ἐξέρχεται, though later (199) we might suppose the house to belong to Lysistrata herself,[1] so Praxagora (34) speaks of scratching on the door to summon out her neighbour, though the door later belongs to Blepyrus, the husband of Praxagora. This is the usual technique of 'successive' moments. Where then does Blepyrus' neighbour appear in 327? τίς ἐστιν; οὐ δήπου Βλέπυρος ὁ γειτνιῶν; Before considering this question let us look at the later scene (877 ff.). Here at last, it will be said, we have quite inescapably the simultaneous occupation of two houses, with the Girl and the Hag defying each other from window to window. So we have—and there is *only one door*.

[1] The demand for objects to be 'brought out' ἔνδοθεν, however, implies very little as to ownership of a house, cf. above on *Ach.* and below on *Nub.*

Let us consider the text. The generally accepted view that the women look out of windows is clearly right, and Fraenkel's odd notion that they both stand in the open on adjacent roofs has no substance. His objection to ἕστηκα (879) as an unsuitable word for a figure seen by the audience as leaning from a window (cf. παρακύψασα 884 and παράκυφθ' 924, as in *Thesm.* 797) is unintelligible to me. Since Aristophanes knew that his actors would in fact be standing on ladders, that would in itself be enough to suggest the word to him. In real life such windows were sometimes in the upper story; exactly where or how they were represented in the skene is uncertain. Since the flat roof is often needed for action in both tragedy and comedy, any projecting pieces of upper story big enough to contain windows (and Philocleon actually gets out, or half out, of his) would have to be temporarily erected for certain comedies. The expedient seems clumsy and improbable. Conceivably the skene in its normal guise of palace or temple front had a kind of metopic band below the flat roof which had gaps big enough to use as windows for comedy.[1] A skene so built would make it easier for the voices of actors speaking 'from within' (Medea's anapaests 96 ff., for instance) to float audibly out into the great theatre.

In *Eccl.* 877 ff. at any rate we have the two courtesans making angry exchanges from two windows, which are obviously to be understood as belonging to neighbouring houses. At 934 the Youth is seen approaching in the street below, 936 the Girl withdraws, 946 the Hag follows suit, while announcing her intention of keeping an eye on events; 949 the Girl reappears, saying she has tricked the Hag into thinking she would keep inside. She invites the Youth to join her for the night; the Youth replies with a serenade begging her to come down and open the door. At the third impassioned ἄνοιξον (974), the Girl having withdrawn, he knocks urgently on the door. It opens—and the Hag appears (976). The text is unmistakable. Had there been two houses, each with a separate door, the dialogue could not possibly proceed as it does:

[1] Dicaeopolis' wife from such a position might perhaps be said to 'watch from the roof', *Ach.* 262. And the prologue of Eur. *I.T.* (113) would in that case refer to an actual feature of the scene. But this is guesswork.

οὗτος, τί κόπτεις; μῶν ἐμὲ ζητεῖς;—πόθεν;

'Why the knocking? Looking for me?' 'Is it likely?' asks the furiously disappointed Youth.

καὶ τὴν θύραν γ' ἤραττες.—ἀποθάνοιμ' ἄρα.

'Fairly battering at the door, you were.' 'I'm damned if I was.' This exchange would be singularly inappropriate if he were knocking at one door and she opened another; the episode turns on the confrontation παρὰ προσδοκίαν at the (only) door. To object that if the windows belong to separate houses the dialogue ought not to proceed to call attention to the anomaly of the single door is to misunderstand comic technique, which jumps from one assumption to the other according to its immediate requirements. Even in tragedy there is something analogous in the scenes presented on the eccyclema,[1] where the dialogue often vacillates between the imagined interior and the actual stage-front. *Eccl.* 989–90 are, as L and S indicate, a metaphor, sens. obsc.

To return to the earlier scene, it is now clear that at 327 Blepyrus' neighbour is watching him from a window in the skene, and talks to him through it (so Van Leeuwen and the Budé editors); thus he can ask Blepyrus why he is so oddly dressed without himself being committed to appearing either undressed or in his wife's clothes. Having hit on this scenic expedient Aristophanes employs it twice in the play. The words ὁ γειτνιῶν (327) carefully make the situation clear to the audience.

Having reduced *Eccl.* to a single house, or rather a skene with a single door, we are in a stronger position for the earlier plays. Of these, only *Nub.* and *Pax* present any difficulty. In general the solution is the same for both: the skene begins with one owner, passes to another, and then reverts to the former. But the details are a little more complicated than in other plays. The assumption of two houses in *Nub.* seems to be universal, because with our preconception of stability as a normal quality in a stage-scene, the knowledge of later developments in comedy, and the comfortable conviction in

[1] See my article 'Seen and Unseen on the Greek Stage', *Wiener Studien*, lxix, 1956. [Reprinted as chapter 9 of this collection, pp. 119 ff.]

the background that at least one other Old Comedy (*Eccl.*) had two houses, that is the natural picture for us to read into the play. Even so, the exact lay-out of the stage has been the subject of some uneasy speculation. Did the two houses balance each other symmetrically, so that the action was always lop-sided, grouped on one side of the stage or the other? Or was the Phrontisterion centre-stage, so that we merely have a *very* lopsided opening (1–132) and close (1212–1485), the last few lines returning to centre? For, of course, this kind of 'two-house' stage-setting is very different from that of New Comedy, where the action continually shifts from one side to the other, and where the characters can walk out into the street and meet in the middle, or stand in rival groups by each door. The choice between these two views is easy, except for those who try, at the expense of Aristophanes' wit, to manage without the eccyclema (183 ff.). The Phrontisterion must be in the centre-background. But as long ago as 1858 Schoenborn declared that Strepsiades' bedroom must be shown by means of the eccyclema, and it is hard to see what other supposition is as simple or as natural, not only because this was the accepted theatrical convention for the representation of an interior scene, but also in order to bring on the beds with their sleepers and to remove the former without those bustling but discreet scene-shifters. (Or are the beds, forlorn and unmade, to remain *in situ* throughout the play?) So we are left with the same situation as in *Thesm.*, where first Agathon's house disgorges the poet on his sofa, surrounded by the appurtenances of his craft, and later (at 276, where the old stage-direction has survived) some part of the shrine of the Two Goddesses is thrust forward on the same eccyclema from the same door. In *Thesm.* the signal for the change of scene is given by the appearance of the eccyclema, in *Nub.* by its withdrawal. First Strepsiades gets up, possibly at 75, then Pheidippides at 82. Strepsiades draws his son to one side to make his earnest appeal; exeunt beds. At 91 he points to the now closed door: ὁρᾷς τὸ θύριον τοῦτο καὶ τῳκίδιον; identifying it as the Reflectory. If Pheidippides at 125 says ἀλλ' εἴσειμι we must suppose that the change of scene is momentarily ignored even now, but the awkwardness of this is a strong additional reason for accepting Cobet's ἄνιππον ὄντ'· ἀλλ' εἶμι (cf. *Eq*. 488, *Pax* 232) which he adopted from an Oxford MS in order to avoid the harsh omission of the participle. 132 Strepsiades knocks at the Reflectory door, and already his own house is banished so far from the scene that he can excuse his clumsiness (138) by explaining that he lives in the depths of the country. The Disciple comes and talks outside, so that at 183 the door has to be opened again, and the eccyclema appears, with two or three crouching pupils and other objects of which we hear presently. The pupils obediently run within, on their own feet, at the bidding of the prefect-disciple (195); the eccyclema remains with Astronomy and Geometry (whatever they may have been) and perhaps a περίοδος γῆς. At 218 Socrates is swung into view, somewhere and somehow (I confess I have no satisfactory explanation to offer of the swinging mechanism in this play or any other), and at 237 he is dropped to earth. At 254 we find there is a ἱερὸν σκίμποδα, a mystic camp-bed, there, with a wreath (255); of course all this scene is to be imagined inside the Phrontisterion. Thus when the first part of the play ends, at the parabasis, Socrates and Strepsiades have to *step down* off the back of the eccyclema to go inside εἴσω καταβαίνων ὥσπερ εἰς Τροφωνίου (508), the eccyclema is withdrawn, the doors shut and the parabasis begins.

After the parabasis Socrates walks out in the ordinary way and calls to Strepsiades to carry out his camp-bed; the poet is simply accepting the conditions of the theatre and placing the further lesson outside the door. At 801 when Strepsiades declares his intention of substituting his son he sends Socrates inside ἀλλ' ἐπανάμεινόν μ' ὀλίγον εἰσελθὼν χρόνον (803), and himself simply 'goes to fetch' Pheidippides ἀτὰρ μέτειμί γ' αὐτόν, with no mention of going *in*. We are not meant to think of any particular locality from which Pheidippides is fetched; he is simply off-stage somewhere; and this is a further reason for accepting Cobet's emendation (125), since it is a general rule, even with all the reckless changes of scene in Old Comedy, that any character who has to return to the stage does so from the direction he went off. The mixture of strict consistency in stage-convention with the wildest disregard of unity of space is entirely typical.

A short choral song fills in the time until father and son return, talking as they come. At 843 Strepsiades fetches the cock and hen from indoors simply; we do not ask whom they belong to, since as we saw in the last scene of *Ach.* all such 'properties' are of course kept ready in the skene and they can be 'brought out' ἔξω δεῦρο or ἔνδοθεν without more ado. Socrates, who is called out (866), announces his intention of absenting himself (887) from the debate of the two Arguments, which looks very like a somewhat transparent excuse for getting him off the stage to dress up as one of the Arguments. The MSS show that a chorus is missing before 889, which gives him time to do so.[1] If ΣR is right in saying that the two Λόγοι were brought on in wicker cages like fighting-cocks (a startling piece of information, perhaps unlikely to have been invented), then they must have appeared on the eccyclema, like all heavy objects needing transport. At 1114 the Chorus dismisses everybody for the supplementary parabasis; Strepsiades goes off separately from the rest, who enter the house. He returns (1131) and knocks at the door (1145); Socrates hands over his son and re-enters (1169). At the end of the next scene (1212) εἰσάγων σε shows that we are back at Strepsiades' house, and there we remain until the last few lines. 1485 Strepsiades calls to a slave to come out with ladder and mattock and smash up the roof of the Phrontisterion, and himself runs up there with a lighted torch. The strangeness of attacking the *roof*—surely not the most obvious place to set fire to a building—has not been sufficiently emphasised, but the reason is now clear: the top part of the house is now doing duty for the Phrontisterion; the slave must have somewhere to transfer himself to, since he can hardly come out and immediately start hacking at the door from which he has emerged. Socrates and the disciples poke their heads in protest through the windows. The improvisation is not unlike that in *Eccl.*, but with the top half of the skene, for this short scene, even more completely detached from the bottom.

The chief difficulty in *Pax* is our total uncertainty as to the μηχανή, but the main scenic structure is no longer a problem; most

[1] If Socrates, as seems likely, speaks 1105 f., there is a further lacuna or dislocation at that point.

scholars have long recognised that the participation of the Chorus in the liberation of Peace inevitably places Heaven on the ground floor. But also the staging must make do with the ordinary skene. The Budé editors place the whole in the orchestra, so as to bring it within the compass of the Chorus; they have Trygaeus' farmhouse on the right; centre, a cavern blocked with stones, and left the palace of Zeus; in addition, there is in front of Trygaeus' house a stable with a practicable door. When and how was such a scene set, and removed?

It all becomes so much simpler, and no whit more fantastic, if the same door is the door of the beetle-house, of Trygaeus' house, and of Zeus' house, and at the appropriate time opens to reveal (on the eccyclema platform left inside) the pile of stones which cover the pit where Peace has been cast. The transitions seem most easily managed if the μηχανή can be assumed to pick up its load behind the skene, swing it over the roof and deposit it on the stage in front of the door; this assumption is not, so far as I can see, inconsistent with the requirements of any other play. Perhaps there was a pause on or over the roof during the pieces of iambic dialogue, first with the servant, then with one of the daughters who run out of the house (110), returning 149; the anapaests (82–101 and 154–72) would then accompany the swinging, with the nervous appeal to the mechanic as the thing settles in front of the door. Since the beetle has disappeared by 720 it was presumably swung off by the same route, probably soon after Trygaeus dismounted, so as to get it out of the way before the Chorus start operations on the cave.

Since there is no place on the stage other than the skene which could possibly represent an ἄντρον βαθύ, the doors must open to reveal it when Trygaeus asks Hermes (223) 'What sort of a cave?' Hermes' reply, Εἰς τουτὶ τὸ κάτω indicates that Peace is to be imagined *under* the stones. The obvious, and indeed the only feasible, way to haul her out is on the eccyclema, just as once long ago the Dictyulci must have hauled out Danae's chest. (This means that War and Riot must be able to walk out over the eccyclema and retire the same way.) Hence the Chorus have to *enter* to remove the stones (427) εἰσιόντες ὡς τάχιστα τοὺς λίθους ἀφέλκετε (the word is on no account to be emended). If the Scholiast on Plato's *Apology* knew what he was talking about in saying that Peace was a colossal statue, then she can only have been a bust, as it were emerging from underground, since only so could she be supposed to whisper in Hermes' ear (663). The rest is straightforward: 'How do I get down?' asks Trygaeus when he finds the beetle missing. τηδὶ παρ' αὐτὴν τὴν θεόν, answers Hermes, and Trygaeus with the two girls steps down inside off the back of the eccyclema,[1] Peace and Hermes are withdrawn, the doors close and the Chorus strikes up the parabasis, after which we are on earth once more.

[1] Or possibly even straight down the step or steps into the orchestra, and off by a parodos.

9

SEEN AND UNSEEN ON THE GREEK STAGE: A STUDY IN SCENIC CONVENTIONS

Our only reliable evidence, in detail, for the staging of fifth-century tragedy is the text of the plays themselves. But since those texts were written for performance, not with the idea of helping a reading public to visualise the scene, or even of helping a subsequent producer to stage a correct revival, the most precise indications often concern, somewhat paradoxically, what was invisible to the audience, or visible in so rudimentary a form that they needed help in interpreting what they saw. Here the text elucidates and supplements the spectacle.

Of growth or change of scenic convention in these matters we can gather only a few hints from our extant plays. Thus, for instance, only Aeschylus seems to change his scene, or at least refocus it, by the simple expedient of informing the audience what the background is at different points in the action. In the *Persae* the Chorus of councillors hold their brief token debate (140–9, interrupted by the entry of the Queen) τόδ' ἐνεζόμενοι στέγος ἀρχαῖον. This implies, of course, that they sat down, and the only place available for sitting was the long steps[1] of the nondescript σκηνή or booth which was always there in some form at the back of the stage. They sit on the steps, and the audience knows that here is an 'ancient building', a council chamber of sorts, *in* which the Chorus is supposed to be sitting; later, however, this same central[2] building becomes the tomb of Darius. Such an expedient is disarmingly simple, as befits our oldest extant play; but even in the *Choephoroe* the palace-doors upon which Orestes knocks at 653 are outer gates, the ἑρκεῖαι θύραι,

[1] This scene in the *Persae*, together with *Sept.* 185 and 265 and *Supp.* 189, is incontrovertible evidence for the existence of a step or steps even at this period, giving room to seat 12 robed choreuts with dignity.

[2] I take for granted that anything but central grouping for this climax is inconceivable.

whereas when (875) the Servant rushes on (from the side?) and clamours for the unbarring of the γυναικεῖοι πύλαι he thereby conveys to the audience that the scene has changed to the inner courtyard (though the Chorus is still able to watch). The words are inserted in each case for this specific purpose. The indication has to be kept to a minimum, since to enlarge upon it would only be to emphasise improbabilities. So too in the trial-scene of the *Eumenides* (cf. 685 ff.) we find the scene fluctuating at will between Acropolis and nearby Areopagus. To insist on one site or the other all through is to involve ourselves in difficulties of our own creating. We expect stability in a 'scene'; to the Athenian of the fifth century—especially the earlier fifth century—space as well as time had in the theatre a certain elasticity. This phenomenon is quite apart from changes of scene so drastic and so fundamental to the action (as in *Eumenides* and *Ajax*) that the Chorus has to be sent off and the stage 'set' modified by the addition of a statue or a bush.[1]

Commentators who find the daring simplicity of this manoeuvre too much for them usually explain the staging of the *Choephoroe* by supposing a palace-front with three doors, the middle one being the outer courtyard gates, and on one side the doors to the men's quarters where Orestes and Pylades are admitted (712), on the other the women's rooms from which Clytaemnestra emerges. But surely such an extraordinary lay-out would be far more puzzling to the spectators; how should they be expected to grasp that the two side doors, visible in the same plane, were supposed to be inside the wall in which the middle door opened? Such an attempt to rationalise the staging only produces much worse confusion, and the appeal to other tragedies which are claimed to need more than one door can be shown to be ill-founded in each case (see below). The fluid or adjustable scene, on the other hand, with nothing more than a word or two to indicate the change of background, may well have been a fairly familiar technique (since it occurs in three of our seven early plays); perhaps it was dropped later because it was felt to be too reminiscent of comedy, where—in a much more reckless form—it long remained at home.

[1] By means of the eccyclema; see below.

A convention which Aeschylus (by use, whether or not he actually invented it) succeeded in establishing more firmly was that of the exposure of an indoor scene by means of the eccyclema or exostra. Whatever name this movable platform was known by,[1] its use from Aeschylean times should never have been called in question. Its simplest (and indispensable) function was to extrude or withdraw heavy or immobile objects—couches or chairs with recumbent figures, Danae's chest, Prometheus' rock, the bush behind which Ajax commits suicide, etc.—through the door of the σκηνή, and its appearance did not automatically cause the spectators to register 'indoor scene'; the clue to interpretation was given in the context. Aristophanes of Byzantium took exception to the sleight of hand by which Euripides represents the sick Phaedra as brought out of the house by the nurse while actually using the eccyclema for the purpose (Σ *Hipp.* 170–1): ἀλλ' ἥδε τροφὸς γεραιὰ πρὸ θυρῶν | τήνδε κομίζουσ' ἔξω μελάθρων. It seems a harmless enough piece of stage-illusion—καίτοι τῷ ἐγκυκλήματι χρώμενος τὸ ἐκκομίζουσα [for κομίζουσ' ἔξω] προσέθηκε περισσῶς.[2] Equally 'superfluous', presumably, was the illusion of net-dragging in the Δικτυουλκοί, where the chest containing Danae and Perseus must actually have been thrust out of its 'hollow' (the σκηνή) by means of the eccyclema. But besides such instances of transport where physical movement of heavy objects was required by the stage-illusion, the eccyclema was frequently used to bring out into the sight of the audience—and of the Chorus—people and objects which clearly belong to an indoor scene.

Here the words of our texts vacillate with a curious ambiguity between the imagined scene and the actual mechanism visibly used to present it. There are, to begin with, several cases where in real life a person would naturally enter a house to see for himself what

[1] The use of the verb ἐκκυκλέω at least is attested by 425 B.C., the date of Ar. *Ach.* I assume that no such elaborate machinery as that of a turning or pivoting platform was in use in the fifth century.

[2] The explanation in the second scholion, that the eccyclema was designed to show what was happening indoors, whereas Eur. uses it to bring Phaedra actually into the open air, seems to be a confusing and mistaken addition to Aristophanes' own criticism.

was happening within, but on the stage must wait outside for the event to be brought out to him, so that the audience can witness his reaction and the Chorus on occasion share it. Here the poet's words frankly accept the situation, as for instance in *Hipp.* 808: the discovery of Phaedra's suicide and the cutting down of her body have been made known by cries for help within the house, and Theseus, returning at that moment and learning from the Chorus what has just happened, calls for the doors to be opened so that he may see the bitter sight. It is often claimed that all that is necessary then is for the doors to open and the body to be carried by attendants to the threshold, the usual place for the prothesis of the dead. But it is more likely that this scene conformed to the general pattern of such situations on the stage: that is to say, the eccyclema platform extruded the body far enough for all (including Hippolytus returning at 905) to see it comfortably. To call all such scenes 'exposure of a threshold-tableau' is to stand the problem on its head. Even if the body of Phaedra and the body of Eurydice (*Ant.* 1293) might be supposed to lie on the threshold, and might actually be placed there by attendants, and the inadequate view of some of the spectators might not matter very much (since the corpses have not to speak), there are many superficially similar scenes where no such explanation applies. Ajax among the slaughtered cattle might perhaps be supposed to be sitting immediately on the threshold, but since the doors have to open it is difficult to see how he can be got there. There is no reason to believe that the doors of the σκηνή operated on any different principle from normal doors in everyday life;[1] that is to say, they were double doors opening inwards, and given the size of some of the tableaux to be exposed their leaves must have been of considerable width. An Ajax speaking and singing through a long scene from the doorway is one thing, but an Ajax doing so from a distance of some feet inside the building is obviously nonsense. It is clear, moreover, that in many scenes there is no question of a threshold being the imagined place of action; Agamemnon would not have been taking his bath there, and Clytaemnestra makes

[1] See the discussion of this subject in W. Beare, *The Roman Stage*, Appendix G, pp. 275 ff.

the presuppositions explicit in the simple and tremendous line ἕστηκα δ' ἔνθ' ἔπαισ' ἐπ' ἐξειργασμένοις. The accepted convention, in fact, was that when an interior scene was exposed it was imagined as simply within the building, with no more precise specification. To bring it just outside on the eccyclema was only to stretch the convention one degree further, and the Chorus, which made no pretence of being inside, accepted the *fait accompli* without self-consciousness. Sometimes the necessary opening of the door is commanded by a speaker, as in Eur. *Hipp.* above; in Soph. *Aj.* 344 ff. there is similarly a reference to opening the door and seeing within, though earlier (329) Tecmessa had indicated the more natural behaviour by asking the Chorus to 'come in and help', ἀρήξατ' εἰσελθόντες. Sometimes the door is simply said to 'open', without further explanation: thus at *H.F.* 1029 ἴδεσθε, διάνδιχα κλῇθρα κλίνεται ὑψιπύλων δόμων the Chorus proceed to describe the scene (for which we have been prepared earlier by the Messenger's speech), and time is given for them and the audience to take in what the emerging eccyclema presents, before the weeping Amphitryon, who might more naturally have opened the door himself, comes slowly out. It is noteworthy that Aeschylus, who uses the eccyclema for interior scenes in each play of the trilogy, nowhere refers to the opening of the door, and indeed such references scarcely add to the verisimilitude of the convention.

Some useful indication of the size of the eccyclema platform, and therefore of the width of the doors of the σκηνή and the depth from front to back of the top step, is provided by the largest load it has to carry: a bath with two corpses and the figure of Clytaemnestra (*Ag.*), Heracles tied to a broken pillar and three corpses (*H.F.*), Orestes clasping the omphalos and three sleeping Furies (*Eum.* 140) perhaps seated (cf. 47) on the front edge of the platform; Apollo, Hermes and Clytaemnestra step on from the back as required (or did Clytaemnestra stand behind as though half emerging from the underworld, like so many figures in the vase-painter's convention?). There could not, of course, have been 12 seated Furies crammed on to the platform; the Priestess has described the whole θαυμαστὸς λόχος so that the audience know how to interpret the limited spectacle they actually see. When these leaders have waked and staggered to their feet (140 ff.) the platform can be withdrawn and the remainder assemble gradually from the temple, with Apollo chasing out the last of them at 179.

The spatial ambiguity of the eccyclema-produced interior is thus another illustration of that fluidity of stage-scene which is so alien to our convention. Aristophanes, who uses the device when he needs it, extracts an agreeable joke from this ambiguity (*Ach.* 407 ff.) when Euripides, composing with his feet up and 'too busy' to come out and talk to Dicaeopolis, is persuaded to 'eccycle' and so be outside and conversable while remaining indoors undisturbed.[1] (Opponents of the eccyclema ruthlessly sacrifice this nice point.)

The broken pillar to which Heracles is bound, visible to the spectators in front of the still standing façade of the building whose ruins it indicates, may be taken as a measure of the difference between Greek standards of stage-realism and our own. Though in its way a daringly original touch of realism, it is an illustration *post factum* of a catastrophe which in progress was conveyed only by the spoken word, in defiance of the unmoved stage-architecture. 'Look' (ἰδοὺ ἰδού), cries the Chorus[2] (*H.F.* 905), 'a whirlwind shakes the palace, its halls collapse.' This appeal to the invisible is recalled by *Bacch.* 591 εἴδετε λάινα κίοσιν ἔμβολα διάδρομα τάδε; and anticipated by Aeschylus frag. 58 ἐνθουσιᾷ δὴ δῶμα, βακχεύει στέγη, where the δή performs the same function. It would seem in fact to be a kind of stage cliché, easily ignored in the sequel when the need

[1] So too in *Nub.* 181–99 the pupils in the Reflectory are exposed at their normal tasks indoors, yet are forbidden to stay longer 'in the open air'. Agathon in *Thesm.* 96 ff. is of course using the eccyclema differently, being wheeled out for his health, like Phaedra.

[2] Not, as Wilamowitz, Amphitryon within. He is engrossed in particulars, the murder of the children, the maniac violence of Heracles (cf. 998–1000), and it would be quite out of key for him to make this wondering comment, which sums up the effect for the watcher outside. Whether Amphitryon or the Chorus speaks 906–9 is not quite certain, though it would seem more natural for the Chorus to close the interlude. In any case ὦ Διὸς παῖ is addressed to Heracles, not Pallas.

for quaking or falling masonry has passed.[1] Whether such occasions called for 'noises off' as an aid to illusion may well be doubted; when visual accompaniments were lacking it may have seemed more natural to omit aural ones too. The same may be said of various minor details of scenery alluded to by speakers: in the prologue of Eur. *I.T.* we need not suppose a splash of red on the altar or 'Greek spoils' hung beneath the coping of the temple, and the façade with 'empty spaces between the triglyphs' presented the same non-committal aspect to the spectators as that of the *Ion* with its mythological scenes that so elaborately delighted the women of Creusa's retinue.

The curious precision of Sophocles' language in *O.C.* in the description of the seating in the grove of the Eumenides is probably an indication of the sparing use of scenic camouflage, the audience being thus helped to adapt the familiar landmarks of the stage before their eyes to the rustic setting required. The σκηνή must have been partly hidden by the boskage of the grove, perhaps represented on canvas screens. The stage door is not required for this play; when Oedipus and Antigone withdraw temporarily out of sight before the entry of the Chorus (117), this probably indicates a solid bush as part of the scenery (perhaps like the one behind which Ajax fell and crawled off to return as Teucer; if so it could be placed on the half-projecting eccyclema). If τόνδ' ἱππότην Κολωνὸν (59) required a visible hero, the pediment of the σκηνή, left visible, would make an appropriate crown to a heroon, perhaps with a painted horseman beneath it. It becomes clear from the action of the play that the two areas which the audience are to recognise as separate (9–10 ἀλλ' ὦ τέκνον θάκησιν εἴ τινα βλέπεις | ἢ πρὸς βεβήλοις ἢ πρὸς ἄλσεσιν θεῶν) are demarcated by the step or steps referred to at the beginning of this article. Oedipus is a frail, blind old man, and nearly all of his lengthy role is spoken from a sitting position, until his final miraculous certitude of movement. He sits at first in the sacred grove

[1] This convenient practice prevents the 'palace-miracle' scene in the *Bacchae* from making a premature climax. See, on this subject, the Appendix to R. P. Winnington-Ingram's *Euripides and Dionysus* (Cambridge University Press, 1948).

itself, where the edge of the eccyclema would provide a ready-made 'unhewn rock' (19, 101); here, in the centre of the stage, he makes his prayer to the Eumenides 84–110. The Chorus induce him to move forward from this to the limit of the sacred area; he need not go beyond the αὐτόπετρον βῆμα (192 ff.). 'I may sit down?' 'Yes, crouch low sideways to sit upon the stone ledge.' Here is a precious indication of the lay-out of the stage: Oedipus is clearly to sit on the front corner of the steps, lowering himself over the side where they turn at a right angle. Thus he is placed to one side of the stage and his successive interlocutors will confront him from the opposite side. All movement for the rest of the play is on the lower ground level, including the final departure of Oedipus, his daughters, Theseus and attendants.

A special class of spoken allusion with no visual counterpart is formed by those passages which refer to the imagined lay-out of the interior of the building behind the σκηνή. Here there has been much misunderstanding because commentators have referred these to the visible exterior. Thus for instance Eur. *Alc.* 546 ff. (Admetus' directions for the entertainment of Heracles) is quoted as proof of the existence of more than one door in the fifth-century palace-front. But Admetus is not pointing to a side-door and saying to the servant 'Open this and put him in the guests' wing'—no Greek house was so constructed—but giving directions, explicit so that the audience can follow them, for the segregation of Heracles when he has passed into the inner courtyard: 'Take him along and open up the guest-chambers away from the main building—and see that they close the doors between the courts.' Similarly in *Hel.* 1180 χαλᾶτε κλῇθρα the king means the ordinary outer doors, and the horse-chariot which he orders out is to come from stables somewhere within the courtyard; when however the open doors immediately reveal Helen, who has not escaped as he supposed, he cancels the order. The 'neighbouring stables' (*Bacch.* 509) where Pentheus orders Dionysus to be shut up are likewise inside the palace-precinct.

The same technique is responsible for a ludicrous and widespread misunderstanding of the scene in Eur. *Or.* (1366 ff.) where the

Phrygian eunuch, describing how he has escaped in his barbarian slippers over the balconies and Dorian triglyphs of the pillared halls, is of course explaining the imagined interior scene, when he scrambled out of the women's quarters before reaching the visible outer doors through which he has just walked in the ordinary way. The Chorus had greeted his emergence in a normal 'heralding' speech: 'Hush, the door is rattling—here is one of the Phrygians coming out; we shall soon know what has happened.' Unfortunately one of the scholiasts, making a false inference from the text before him, declared that these three lines could hardly be accepted as Euripides' own; they must have been inserted by actors who did not want to risk their necks in the acrobatics described. It is quite clear from his language that he is merely drawing his own misguided conclusions from the text; there is no suggestion of the lines being missing from any MS, or called in question by an earlier tradition. Yet our texts obediently bracket the lines, which are linguistically blameless, and if deleted leave a preposterous gap in which the Chorus apparently gaze in stupefied silence—as well they might—at this acrobatic display and leave the Eunuch to introduce himself (very inadequately) and to sing them a description of what they have just seen him do.

The cave of Philoctetes is another illustration of the dramatist's explanatory technique. It is described with much insistence as a δίστομος πέτρα, as an οἶκος ἀμφίθυρος with entrances facing different ways so that a cool wind blows in summer δι' ἀμφιτρῆτος αὐλίου, through a chamber tunnelled from both ends. Our commentaries therefore often give the scene as 'a cave with two openings'—wrongly. There is only one cave-mouth on the stage—the normal door-opening (of course specially made up in the guise of a rocky cave[1]) in the centre of the σκηνή. The seaward entrance faces the spectators, while the landward entrance from behind is left to their

[1] The half-projecting eccyclema would be a simple and obvious way of adding to the height which Neoptolemus has to climb from the seashore (and cf. 814) and giving Philoctetes a 'sun-terrace' (ἡλίου ἐνθάκησις) on which he can appear, and lie asleep, and (1000) from which he can threaten to fling himself headlong.

imagination. The whole point is to make it possible for Philoctetes to emerge from the cave-mouth without being seen to go into it; he is absent when his visitors arrive, wandering off to shoot birds for his food, and he returns by the landward entrance. Thus at his first appearance he dominates the stage, aloft centre, against his proper background of rugged cave, not (as Jebb ruinously imagines it) along the shore to the spectators' right. The Chorus, as their habit is, give warning of his approach, but as something *heard*, not seen along the parodos after the usual pattern; hence too the choice of words 211 οὐκ ἔξεδρος ἀλλ' ἔντοπος ἀνήρ—he is *there inside*, about to appear at the spot to which all eyes are directed. With this in mind we can restore the natural interpretation to 145 ff.:

νῦν μέν, ἴσως γὰρ τόπον ἐσχατιᾶς
προσιδεῖν ἐθέλεις ὅντινα κεῖται,
δέρκου θαρσῶν· ὁπόταν δὲ μόλῃ
δεινὸς ὁδίτης τῶνδ' ἐκ μελάθρων,
πρὸς ἐμὴν αἰεὶ χεῖρα προχωρῶν
πειρῶ τὸ παρὸν θεραπεύειν.

The Chorus have asked Neoptolemus what he would have them do to help. For the present, he replies, you can observe the scene at leisure, 'but when the dread wayfarer comes, on his return, forth from this dwelling', be ready to come to my help as the occasion may require (πρὸς ἐμὴν χεῖρα προχωρῶν is metaphorical). The Scholiast was first responsible for connecting τῶνδ' ἐκ μελάθρων with the following line: ἐπὰν δὲ ἔλθῃ τότε σὺ τῶν μελάθρων ἀποστὰς ὑπηρέτει μοι πρὸς τὴν παροῦσαν χρείαν, following which our texts usually put the comma after ὁδίτης. But (*a*) the Chorus is in the orchestra, not in the cave, (*b*) as Jebb points out, τῶνδ' ἐκ μελάθρων in the sense of 'having quitted the cave' is not Greek, and taken with προχωρῶν makes αἰεὶ meaningless. Jebb's own emendation δεινὸς ὁδίτης τῶνδ' οὐκ μελάθρων, 'the dread wayfarer from this dwelling', is neither attractive nor necessary. He asks how Neoptolemus could know that Philoctetes would return from the landward side and emerge from the other. The answer is that the Greek sailors are spread over the seaward side and one does not ask unnecessary questions. Sophocles has in the interests of stage-realism provided for the possibility of this appearance and seen to it that the audience shall take the point. Further than that neither he nor his audience felt obliged to go.

It may be noted that this point of staging throws some light on the end of the *Cyclops* of Euripides. Odysseus (701 ff.) goes off triumphantly with his companions to sail for home. 'Not so', says the Cyclops, 'I will break off a rock and smash your ship':

> ἄνω δ' ἐπ' ὄχθον εἶμι, καίπερ ὢν τυφλός,
> δι' ἀμφιτρῆτος τῆσδε προσβαίνων ποδί.

It is a hurried ending, getting the actors off the stage and bringing in by allusion the familiar final episode of the story in Homer. The Cyclops is making for the cliff-top to get a better aim; blind as he is, he will grope his way up by the shortest route, through the back opening of the cave. It is the first we hear of this second opening, which is clearly invented *ad hoc*. (It may be objected that the nightmare of the Cyclops' closed cave is thereby spoilt; not more, however, than by the earlier necessity of letting Odysseus out on to the stage (426–7) to give his narrative speech and lay the plot with the satyrs.) The curtness of the allusion and the strangely elliptical phrase δι' ἀμφιτρῆτος τῆσδε (*sc.* πέτρας?) would be more intelligible if the *Cyclops* could be dated 408, the year after the memorable performance of the *Philoctetes*. There is nothing, so far as I can see, in the play's technique and versification to make so late a date impossible or unlikely.

10

RESOLUTIONS IN THE TROCHAIC TETRAMETER

Loose terminology, used in the name of convenience, can be a hindrance for the understanding of Greek metric. Our mechanical analyses of iambic trimeters in terms of six 'feet', with resolutions tabled under 'third-foot dactyl', 'fourth-foot tribrach', 'first-foot anapaest' etc. are apt to obscure rhythmical and quantitative realities, such as the relation of resolution to caesura,[1] to the metron, and to the quantitative shapes of words. Nor has the 'dactyl' or 'anapaest' of an iambic trimeter anything to do with the metres properly called by those names; and to use the same terms again for analysing trochaic tetrameters adds to the confusion. The 'anapaest' in iambics is produced by the substitution of two shorts for one short or for anceps, an irregularity excluded from serious poetry except at the beginning of the line or in intractable proper names; the 'anapaest' of trochaics is caused by the resolution of a long before long anceps – ⏑ ⏕ –. To isolate both these on paper as ⏑ ⏑ – and call them both 'anapaest' must not obscure their total difference in essence and in rhythmical effect.

It is perhaps some echo of this confusion that has led K. Rupprecht in the third edition of his *Einführung in die griechische Metrik*, to formulate as he does the rule for 'anapaests' in the trochaic tetrameter. On p. 32 he says of the iambic trimeter: 'In der Regel wird der Anap. von *einem* Wort gebildet[2] ('*within* a single word' would be more accurate), and on p. 40 of the trochaic tetrameter 'Die

[1] The opening syllable of phrases in falling metre, such as – ⏑ – ⏓ – ⏑ – or – ⏑ – ⏑ – was clearly felt by Greek poets as the easiest to resolve without impairing the smooth flow of the line. Most of our analytic tables do not even make any distinction between word-beginning and word-middle.

[2] For a careful analysis of exceptions to this rule in comedy see W. G. Arnott in *Classical Quarterly*, 7, 1957, 188.

Anap. werden im allgemeinen von *einem* Wort gebildet. Ausnahmen finden sich nur bei dem Anap. des 1. m.' This could easily suggest that some inhibition peculiar to 'anapaests' as such was making itself felt in both these metres. In fact, of course, the 'dactyl' is to the tetrameter what the 'anapaest' is to the trimeter, and so we find Ἰφιγένειαν – ∪ ∪ – ∪ as a trochaic metron in tragedy and πορνίδιον τρισάθλιον – ∪ ∪ – ∪, – ∪ – in Menander (*Peric.* l. 50); the irregularity is more smoothly disposed of within the single word. But there seems on the face of it no particular reason why – ∪ ∪ ∪ ⏓ should behave differently according to whether the anceps is long or short—nor in fact does it.[1] The correct formula is: 'Where the second long of a trochaic metron is resolved, the three syllables forming the second half of the metron are contained within the same word. Exceptions are confined to the first metron of the line.'

A few examples may make this clearer:

In the first metron:

I.A. 394 οὐ γὰρ ἀσύνετον τὸ θεῖον, ἀλλ' ἔχει συνιέναι
– ∪ ∪ ∪ ∪, – ∪ – ∪, – ∪ – ∪, – ∪ –

Or. 797 ὥς νιν ἱκετεύσω με σῶσαι. τό γε δίκαιον οὐκ ἔχει
– ∪ ∪ ∪ –, – ∪ – –, ∪ ∪ ∪ – ∪, – ∪ –

In the second metron:

Or. 1524 εὖ λέγεις· σῴζει σε σύνεσις· ἀλλὰ βαῖν' ἔσω δόμων
– ∪ – –, – ∪ ∪ ∪ ∪, – ∪ – ∪, – ∪ –

Phoen. 607 ἐξελαυνόμεσθα πατρίδος. καὶ γὰρ ἦλθες ἐξελῶν
– ∪ – ∪, – ∪ ∪ ∪ –, – ∪ – ∪, – ∪ –

I.T. 1232 εὐτυχεῖς δ' ἡμεῖς ἐσόμεθα. τἄλλα δ' οὐ λέγουσ' ὅμως
– ∪ – –, – ∪ ∪ ∪ ∪, – ∪ – ∪, – ∪ –

I.A. 911 οὐκ ἔχω βωμὸν καταφυγεῖν ἄλλον ἢ τὸ σὸν γόνυ
– ∪ – –, – ∪ ∪ ∪ –, – ∪ – ∪, – ∪ –

[1] Except of course where the unresolved – ∪ – ⏓ also differs, to keep the law of the final and initial cretic (the avoidance of word-end after long anceps except at the median caesura). Resolution of itself has no effect.

In the third metron:

Bacch. 613 ἀλλὰ πῶς ἠλευθερώθης ἀνδρὸς ἀνοσίου τυχών;
– ᴗ – –, – ᴗ – –, – ᴗ ᴗ ᴗ ᴗ, – ᴗ –

Or. 738 ὥσπερ οὐκ ἐλθὼν ἔμοιγε ταὐτὸν ἀπέδωκεν μολών
– ᴗ – –, – ᴗ – ᴗ, – ᴗ ᴗ ᴗ –, – ᴗ –

In the second and third metra:

I.A. 884 ὁ δὲ γάμος τίν' εἶχε πρόφασιν, ᾧ μ' ἐκόμισεν ἐκ δόμων;
ᴗ ᴗ ᴗ – ᴗ, – ᴗ ᴗ ᴗ ᴗ, – ᴗ ᴗ ᴗ ᴗ, – ᴗ –

I.A. 1354 οἵ με τὸν γάμων ἀπεκάλουν ἧσσον'. ἀπεκρίνω δὲ τί;
– ᴗ – ᴗ, – ᴗ ᴗ ᴗ –, – ᴗ ᴗ ᴗ –, – ᴗ –

Exceptions in the first metron:

I.A. 1349 ἐς θόρυβον ἐγὼ τι καὐτὸς ἤλυθον. τίν', ὦ ξένε;
– ᴗ ᴗ ᴗ | ᴗ, – ᴗ – ᴗ, – ᴗ – ᴗ, – ᴗ –

I.A. 886 ὦ θύγατερ, ἥκεις ἐπ' ὀλέθρῳ καὶ σὺ καὶ μήτηρ σέθεν
– ᴗ ᴗ ᴗ | –, – ᴗ ᴗ ᴗ –, – ᴗ – –, – ᴗ –

Out of 46 examples in Euripides of resolution of the second long of a trochaic metron 17 have short anceps and 29 long anceps. The latter naturally preponderates, since words of the shape ᴗ ᴗ – and ᴗ ᴗ – – cannot begin a metron, whereas such words as πρόφασιν ᴗ ᴗ ᴗ, ἀνοσίου are much more adaptable and tend to gravitate toward the easiest positions for resolution, at the beginning of each dimeter. But clearly the presence of resolution introduces no new distinction into the behaviour of short and long anceps; the essential is that the three syllables must be kept closely together, with occasional licence to detach anceps in the first metron. Contrast the freedom of the first half of the metron:

I.A. 859 τίνος; ἐμὸς μὲν οὐχί· χωρὶς τἀμὰ κἀγαμέμνονος
ᴗ ᴗ | ᴗ – ᴗ, – ᴗ – –, – ᴗ – ᴗ, – ᴗ –

H.F. 863 οἵ' ἐγὼ στάδια[1] δραμοῦμαι στέρνον εἰς Ἡρακλέους
– ᴗ – ᴗ, ᴗ ᴗ | ᴗ – –, – ᴗ – –, – ᴗ –

[1] This is the only position in the line where resolution ends a word overlapping from the previous metron. Cf. Archil. 74. 2 οὐδὲ θαυμάσιον, ἐπειδὴ – ᴗ – ᴗ, ᴗ ᴗ | ᴗ – –. In the fourth metron resolution is rare (in tragedy only *Ion* 1254 πολεμίους) and always at the beginning of a word

Or. 740 χρόνιος· ἀλλ' ὅμως τάχιστα κακὸς ἐφωράθη φίλοις

⏑ ⏑ ⏑ – ⏑, – ⏑ – ⏑, ⏑ ⏑ | ⏑ – –, – ⏑ –

Even the resolution itself may be divided, if it is the first long of a metron: *I.T.* 1205 ἴτ' ἐπὶ δεσμά ⏑ | ⏑ ⏑ – ⏑, *Hel.* 1635 ὃς ἔλαβεν πατρὸς πάρα, *Or.* 790 τί τόδε καινόν. Naturally this does not often happen, since the number of short monosyllables which do not form part of the next 'word' (like articles and prepositions) is very limited; but the correct formulation of the law against a divided resolution is that 'no resolution may be so divided that the first short is the final syllable of a preceding word': thus Eur. frag. incert. 909. 2 πᾶσα γὰρ ἀγαθὴ γυνὴ – ⏑ ⏑ | ⏑ ⏑ is certainly corrupt (Nauck κεδνή).

Euripides, with his large number of trochaic scenes and increasingly large number of resolutions, offers the clearest conspectus of permissible rhythms, but the older tragedians within their limited material show the same pattern. In Aesch. *Pers.* 171 γηραλέα πιστώματα there is synizesis. *Pers.* 720 ἀμφότερα· διπλοῦν μέτωπον ἦν δυοῖν στρατευμάτοιν – ⏑ ⏑ ⏑ | ⏑ in the first metron. Soph. *Phil.* 1405 gives τί γὰρ ἐὰν πορθῶσι χώραν ⏑ ⏑ | ⏑ – –, and *O.C.* 888 βουθυτοῦντά μ' ἀμφὶ βωμὸν ἔσχετ' ἐναλίῳ θεῷ shows a normal – ⏑ ⏑ ⏑ ⏑ in the third metron. There are no deviations in tragedy, and therefore in *I.A.* 356 κἀμὲ παρεκάλεις· τί δράσω; τίνα πόρον εὕρω ποθέν the faulty third metron of LP should not be corrected as the second hand in the manuscript did: τίνα δὲ πόρον εὕρω ποθέν ⏑ ⏑ ⏑ ⏑ ⏑ | –, – ⏑ –. A double resolution within one metron is elsewhere found only with proper names (*Phoen.* 636, *I.A.* 869), but also the word-division is unparalleled. Matthiae's τίνα πόρον δ' is probably all that is needed.

Comedy of all periods, though more restrained in resolution than the later plays of Euripides, disregards these restrictions in word-

which covers the whole cretic. Attic comedy, Old, Middle and New, observes the same rule; only Epicharmus disregards it. Thus, since new words must begin the first, third and fourth metra, the *potential* varieties of break in the first half of the metron would seem to be more limited than in the second half, and it is the more striking that break is nevertheless excluded from the latter.

division (as it also disregards the law of final and initial cretic and even the median diaeresis). Thus for instance Ar. *Eq.* 565 εὐλογῆσαι βουλόμεσθα τοὺς πατέρας ἡμῶν and Men. *Peric.* 148 μανθάνεις ἐξ ἐπιδρομῆς ταῦθ', ὡς ἔτυχεν, ἀλλ' ἀξιοῖ both have a third metron of the form – ⏑ ⏑ ⏑ | –. The early iambographers, within their scanty material, observe the same laws as tragedy, cf. Archil. 60, 64, 74. 2. Hipponax (70) and Ananius (5. 1) in their 'limping' tetrameters also show the same pattern. Later practice may have become less strict, since the comic poet Hermippus is quoted by Athenaeus as saying ἐν τοῖς Ἰάμβοις (*sic*):

ἐς τὸ Κυλικράνων βαδίζων σπληνόπεδον ἀφικόμην
– ⏑ ⏑ ⏑ –, – ⏑ – –, – ⏑ ⏑ ⏑ | ⏑, – ⏑ –

Whatever word σπληνόπεδον is corrupted from (σφηνόπεδον is plausibly suggested), the shape appears to break the metron in a form which Hermippus evidently transferred from his comic technique. Evidence is too scanty and uncertain to show whether such a tendency became general.

11

THE HOOPOE'S SONG

(Aristophanes, *Av.* 227 ff.)

In the course of his illuminating Notes on the Hoopoe's Song (*Eranos*, xlviii, 1950) Eduard Fraenkel shows how closely *Av.* 229–59 follow the pattern of a κλητικὸς ὕμνος with its repeated τε connecting the different sections. The birds 'are arranged in groups according to their habitat and food', and he shows conclusively that l. 240 must be taken as a single group, birds of the hills who feed on the hill-shrubs oleaster and arbutus. τὰ κοτινοτράγα and τὰ κομαροφάγα are thus in effect in apposition to τὰ κατ' ὄρεα, as indeed many translators have taken them—but without altering the text. His objections to this are cogent: (1) the hearer would inevitably take the second and third τε as connective like the first, instead of subordinated to τὰ κατ' ὄρεα; (2) metrically, the analysis into iambo-dochmiac, as in Schroeder

τά τε κατ' ὄρεα τά τε κοτινοτρά-	iamb. dim.
-γα τά τε κομαροφάγα	doch.

is ineffective because of the muddle of short syllables undefined by word-end (unlike the preceding dochmiacs which detach themselves neatly from their surroundings). His remedy is to excise the second τε ('as soon as we expel it, everything runs smoothly') and scan as a period of 6 iambic metra, ending with catalexis:

τά τε κατ' ὄρεα τὰ κοτινοτράγα	⏑ ⏑ ⏑ ⏑ ⏑ ⏑	⏑ ⏑ ⏑ ⏑ ⏑ ⏑
τά τε κομαροφάγ' ἀνύσατε πετό-	⏑ ⏑ ⏑ ⏑ ⏑ ⏑	⏑ ⏑ ⏑ ⏑ ⏑ ⏑
μενα πρὸς ἐμὰν ἀοιδάν.	⏑ ⏑ ⏑ ⏑ –	⏑ – –

But the trouble is that everything does not yet run smoothly enough. Aristophanes has a habit of keeping his metrical fantastications exquisitely clear by means of word-end, whereas in this version the last 4 metra are an untidy jumble. The charming rhyme κοτινοτράγα...κομαροφάγα is destroyed, and the calling effect of ἀνύσατε which gathers up *all* the groups from 230 onwards—ὅσοι τ'..., ὅσα τ'..., ὅσα θ'..., τά τε... is swallowed in the preceding elision; the received text which gives hiatus and period-end, followed by change of rhythm at ἀνύσατε, is clearly right. Manuscript authority is divided between αὐδάν and ἀοιδάν: by choosing the latter Schroeder and Fraenkel achieve not only some awkwardly resolved iambics but a catalexis which is alien in style to the metrical character of the whole piece, whereas with αὐδάν the line scans itself:

ἀνύσατε | πετόμενα | πρὸς ἐμὰν |
αὐδάν ◡◡◡◡ ◡◡◡◡ ◡◡– ––

Anapaests of this type recur at 328, again with the clearly defined syllable-groups: προδεδόμεθ' ἀνόσιά τ' ἐπάθομεν. Thus not only the second τε but the third also needs to be deleted in 240:

τά τε κατ' ὄρεα | τὰ κοτινοτράγα | τὰ κομαροφάγα,

leaving iambic groups which sing themselves. (Nor does one really want the hill-birds divided into those that eat oleaster *and* those that eat arbutus; a mixed diet would be more natural.) Euripides in the previous year had resorted to the same device to set a sung trimeter of solo-lyric at the farthest possible distance from a spoken one (*Tro.* 1312):

Πρίαμε Πρίαμε | σὺ μὲν ὀλόμενος | ἄταφος ἄφιλος

So too in 233 trochaic resolution is defined by word-end:

ταχὺ πετόμενα | μαλθακὴν ἱέντα γῆρυν·

and each of the rarer metres (for comedy) is similarly demarcated:

230 ὅσοι τ' εὐσπόρους | ἀγροίκων γύας dochmiac
231 νέμεσθε φῦλα | μυρία κριθοτράγων iambelegus
238 ὅσα θ' ὑμῶν | κατὰ κήπους | ἐπὶ κισσοῦ ionics

Characteristic of the song, and highly unusual in general, are the acatalectic rhythms ending in a short syllable and followed by pause and change of metre: thus 233–4 and 235–6 trochaic ‖ dochmiac, 240–1 resolved iambic ‖ anapaests, 253–4 open dactyl ‖ paroemiac, 259–60 trochaic ‖ bird-noises. The music (and solo-dance?) must have been punctuated by the oddest pauses and unexpected turns.

12

THE TRANSFORMATION OF IO, *OX. PAP.* XXIII. 2369

Why, when Io is changed into a heifer, should a γυνὴ λέαινα be found sitting 'working flax' (ἧσται λινεργ[ός or -[οῦσ' Lobel) or 'worked in flax' (λινεργ[ής Pfeiffer, 'Ein neues Inachos-Fragment des Soph.', *Sitz. Ber. Bay. Ak.* 1958, p. 24)? Commenting that a 'lion-woman' can hardly be anything other than a Sphinx (cf. Lloyd-Jones, *C.R.* lxxii (1958), 20), Pfeiffer calls for an Oedipus to solve the riddle and so perhaps dismiss the whole monster.

I would not claim to be an Oedipus, but the Sphinx must surely go. The whole metamorphosis is being directly and forcefully described by Inachus in eight lines of indignant pity, leading up to τοιαῦτα, and comparison with other compound monsters or description of embroidered cloths or carpets would tail off with debilitating effect. The seated woman can only be Io, and therefore λινεργ- must refer to her activities—or just conceivably to those of her companions; she was sitting spinning[1] when misfortune overtook her. It follows that her transformation is not total, and she is not clambering over the furniture. Her cow-muzzle, head, neck, shoulders, and hooves are mentioned, and the hooves 'clatter on' θράν-. The meaning and construction of this word are uncertain: if θράνους in the sense of 'benches' or 'footstools', the plural is slightly unnatural, but the architectural term 'joists' (beams supporting the floor) seems a most unlikely turn of expression for 'floor' or 'ground'. κροτοῦσι may be the clatter as the hands, turned to helpless hooves, seek to manoeuvre the thread or drop to the wooden bench, or as the feet rattle uncomfortably upon the stool; or the word may be θράνου in the genitive, in some phrase now irrecoverable. At any rate it seems clear that *if* Io needed to come on the stage afterwards (see Pfeiffer's

[1] Not weaving, since the upright loom of ancient Greece kept the weaver standing; see G. M. Crowfoot, 'Of the Warp-weighted Loom', *B.S.A.* xxxvii (1936), 36 ff.

arguments, *loc. cit.* p. 40), scenic conventions would after this description be satisfied by her appearance as a γυνὴ βοῦς, that is with her upper part transformed by head-mask and hoof-gauntlets (the same kind of stage-properties as in Ar. *Ach.* 740–5 the Megarian gave to his piglets before popping them in the sack). She is described not as a total heifer but as a seated 'beast-woman'.

That λέαινα could be used in this generalized sense is a bold assumption, but I can see no alternative. The word is similarly involved in a mixture of animals in Eur. *Hel.* 375–80, a passage where the grammatical construction is unfortunately obscure, but the main juxtaposition must stand:

ἅ μορφᾷ θηρῶν λαχνογυίων
ὄμματι λάβρῳ σχῆμα λεαίνης
ἐξαλλάξασ' ἄχθεα λύπης.

Callisto was traditionally transformed into a bear, and the epithet 'shaggy-limbed' shows unmistakably that Euripides follows the tradition, yet she is the next moment a σχῆμα λεαίνης: 'You who in the form of one of the shaggy wild creatures, a beast-shape in your savage aspect, put off your burden of sorrow.' The words have often been unsuccessfully emended, or deleted, but the two instances now support each other.

13

ETHOS AND DIANOIA: 'CHARACTER' AND 'THOUGHT' IN ARISTOTLE'S *POETICS*[1]

Among the most exciting of philosophical discoveries is that of a fundamental unity in apparently diverse phenomena, and Greek philosophy, which here made so great a contribution, was always susceptible of a slight intoxication at the idea. If all fields of human thought and the metaphysical scheme of the universe could be shown to be aspects of the same underlying reality, then it seemed that the same concepts should be transferable from one sphere of knowledge to another and illuminate each in turn. Under the heady influence of this notion, Plato, to his pupils' consternation, had run the philosophy of poetry into a cul-de-sac. Aristotle, scientist as well as philosopher, often uses the biologist's habits of observation, induction and classification to supplement the deductive approach, so that his conclusions usually end somewhere nearer than Plato's to what was commonly accepted as empirical reality. But the unity required by metaphysical thinking had to be satisfied too, and indeed it is the common experience of scholars that no one branch of Aristotle's multifarious activity is properly intelligible without some knowledge of the whole. Aristotelian ethics, politics, rhetoric, logic, metaphysic and natural science all make their contribution to Aristotle's theory of poetry; and it is perhaps not fanciful to detect in him some peculiar satisfaction in making the same terms do duty in different contexts. To us, with the lapse of 23 centuries and all the riches of comparative literature to draw upon, it has gradually become clear that the philosophy of poetry, as a branch of aesthetic, must work out its own principles of analysis and cannot get very far so long as it keeps to concepts which illustrate the unity of all human

[1] Based on a lecture delivered during the visit [in 1959] of Professor and Mrs Webster [A. M. Dale] to Dunedin under the terms of the De Carle Lectureship, University of Otago.

thought. However appropriate and even profound some of Aristotle's overlapping terms of analysis may seem at first to be, however skilfully he modifies and adapts them to the realities of contemporary poetry as he saw it, they sometimes prove on closer examination imperfectly assimilated to this new context, and bear the faint, ineradicable traces of the different branch of inquiry for which they were originally devised. Yet we can often see how the peculiar characteristics of Greek poetry in Aristotle's own day gave these terms a contingent plausibility, and even propriety, which as universal currency they hardly possess. Thus for instance the new version of the metaphysical 'mimesis' theory, which Aristotle uses in order to reinstate poetry high in the scale of human activities after Plato's attacks, leads to an almost exclusive attention to the least subjective aspects of poetry: the most obviously mimetic form, the drama, gets fullest discussion and highest marks, epic comes second, with dithyramb a bad third and lyric either nowhere or subsumed vaguely under music. Now this *a priori* deduction from metaphysical principles is supported by the empirical facts of the contemporary scene, since the growing-point of new poetic life was to be found in the theatre, and Homer still remained an inexhaustible fount of inspiration, while *personal* lyric had not yet found its new Hellenistic forms, and, to judge by the trends evident at the turn of the fifth/fourth century, the intellectual content of *choral* lyric (including the choral lyric of drama) had become subordinate to the new music. Thus the theory appears as the product of a fusion of two methods of approach, the deductive and the empirical, and this fusion constitutes the essential character of the *Poetics*. To disentangle these two threads is a difficult and delicate operation, but in the process of trying we sometimes find clues to the understanding of Greek poetry and to the way it was understood by its own public.

The lines on which a subject such as poetry is to be discussed are in the Aristotelian method firmly laid down by analytic definition. Poetry has an essential nature—'mimesis', it can be classified into a limited number of 'kinds' or broad *genres* (epic, dramatic, etc.), each of which has its characteristic effect or function, and each of which can by scientific classification be subdivided into a certain number of 'parts', components, or one could say that poetry itself has a certain number of parts, which are found in varying numbers and assortments in its several kinds: thus epic has four parts, mythos, ethos, dianoia, lexis, or Plot, Character, Thought, Diction, while tragedy has these four, plus Spectacle (opsis) and Music. Now clearly this analysis into component parts is of cardinal importance, since a major part of the discussion is to be carried on in terms of these components. What is involved in the notion of such 'parts', and how do we determine what they are? In the order of material objects the problem is relatively simple; we can analyse the human body, for instance, structurally into head, body and limbs, or physiologically into bone, blood, skin, muscle, etc., or again chemically, and so on. In each case the analysis if properly done is exhaustive and the whole is the sum of the parts. But what do we mean by the 'parts' of tragedy? Chapter 12 of our text of the *Poetics* shoots off into a sudden digression on the 'quantitative parts' of tragedy—prologue, episodes, choral odes, etc.; and here is firm ground: these sections will add up to the whole of tragedy quantitatively considered. But the analysis which shapes Aristotle's theory of tragedy is a qualitative one; it divides poetry into its 'formative constituents', or again (50a8) into the parts which 'give a tragedy its quality'. And these parts we find are precisely six in number, no more and no less—'every tragedy therefore must have six parts... and no more'. How are they found, and how do we know them to be exhaustive? They are somewhat schematically arranged as given, one (Spectacle) by the manner of the mimesis, two (Diction and Music) by its means, and three (Plot, Character and Thought) by its objects, but this of course does not answer the question. Aristotle expresses the result as a logical deduction—'every tragedy *therefore* must have six parts', but the premises when examined resolve themselves into a series of statements, which are clearly meant to be self-evident, except that ethos and dianoia are rather perfunctorily derived from the fact that a tragedy represents human beings in action, and the springs of human action are two, ethos and dianoia—again a statement which can be taken to command immediate assent, at least from the good Aristotelian pupil who knows his *Ethics*.

How far can we agree that these six 'parts' are objectively present and are the whole of tragedy's constituents? In the first place they are not all ingredients in the same sense. Aristotle himself drops Music and Spectacle as in some way less essential; they are present in a performed tragedy but not in a read one. A read tragedy then is left with the same 'parts' as an epic poem: if the two are nevertheless not to be understood as identical forms of poetry, the reason is that Aristotle subsequently adds to his definition of tragedy the qualification 'acted, not narrated'. It is at once clear that the sum of the qualitative parts will not add up to the whole quality of a poetic form, and therefore 'part' is not altogether a good word, and 'exhaustive' is not to be too hard pressed. Of the remaining four, Diction, which together with Music is the *means* of mimesis, stands apart from the other three, which are bracketed together as the *object*. But even these three, Plot (or Story), Character, and Thought are not quite on the same plane; we find that Plot, which alone is a direct reflection of the 'universal', is all-pervasive, while Character and Thought seem to appear only in patches up and down the play; yet surely if they are merely logical and qualitative, not quantitative, 'parts', they ought not to be spatially determinable in this way. Further, Aristotle says the modern tragedians tend to produce plays which are 'characterless'. His editors are quick in his defence: 'Only relatively, of course', or 'Of course this only means, in Aristotle's own words, "without speeches expressive of character".' But the all-important question how ethos is present in a drama except in 'speeches expressive of character' is nowhere very clearly answered; and is it altogether satisfactory to have as an essential, major constituent of tragedy something which is liable to dwindle almost to vanishing point? The awkwardness is the less present to us in that thinking in English we are apt to let 'Character' melt imperceptibly into 'the characters', forgetting that our habit of referring to the people in a drama as 'the characters' itself originates in the *Poetics*, in that Aristotle speaks of τὰ ἤθη, 'the Characters', as well as of ethos, 'Character', though his definitions make it quite clear that he means something less by either than we mean by our terms. Still, let us keep clear of the *dramatis personae* and try what is usually called 'character-drawing', which is generally understood to be required to some minimum extent in every play and may be said to be more explicitly present in some parts than in others. But even this seems to be too wide for ethos in Aristotle's sense. His prescription for the ideal tragic hero is given under the heading of Plot, not of ethos. He restricts the word ethos to the moral as distinct from the intellectual characteristics of a person, the latter being constituted in the individual by dianoia. This however is apt to be a difficult distinction to draw. We have already seen that it belongs originally to an ethical context and its applicability to drama is not immediately obvious. Why just Character and Thought in particular? Why not reason and passion? or the material and the spiritual, or a dozen other arbitrary divisions of the human personality? For these two 'springs of human action' which 'determine the quality of a man and his success or failure' are hard enough to seize separately even in the ethical sphere, and the action that springs from them is usually one and indivisible; why then should we expect them to manifest themselves in human speech in separable quanta? If the answer is given that it is the dramatist's business to show how action is generated from these two sets of individual qualities, we might retort that what is of primary interest to the student of the ethics of individual conduct is not necessarily a paramount claim upon the dramatist, who is representing the *interplay* of human wills, a composite action, not a series of individual actions. In fact here Aristotle seems to have been carried away by the identity of the term 'action', πρᾶξις, for the action of a play, and for individual 'actions' or conduct in the ethical sense. One is tempted to picture Aristotle's Tragedy as a biological entity erupting into giant 'action' as a product of its autonomous ethos and dianoia. But even if we acquit Aristotle of such fantasies, at least we can say that the dramatist need feel no obligation to answer for his quotas of explicit 'character' and 'thought', since these are only arbitrarily selected abstractions from the whole compound of personality in action which he portrays.

If however we reunite ethos and dianoia into the single concept 'character' in the English sense of personality, we get a list of three constituents—Plot, Character, Diction—which does carry some sort of objective compulsion, in that their presence is implied in the definition of drama. Words, people to speak them, and something happening to those people; these are the irreducible minimum of which a drama is composed. But to accept them as components is not to say that they are necessarily the most satisfactory terms in which to analyse drama or to determine what makes a good drama. For one thing, it is only as abstractions that they are properly separable; as soon as we begin to give them a positive content they at once become intricately involved with each other. The Plot is what happens to these particular characters, including what they say to each other; the characters have no existence except as working out this particular plot, and they are revealed, at least in read drama, solely by their words. The same applies to the dramatist's processes; he has not finished 'creating' his characters until he has put them through the whole of the action and selected every word they are to utter. And it may often happen that when we have discussed a particular drama in terms of its plot, its characters and its diction we are far from having exhausted its significance; for the *Agamemnon*, for instance, or any of Ibsen's plays of social criticism we should have to begin again from a different point of view.

These component parts, then, may enter into a general definition of drama, but for a discussion of what constitutes a good drama, or for rules of literary criticism by which to measure the achievement of a given drama or to attempt the writing of one, they are simply abstractions from which it is *possible* to set our angle in discussing the concrete whole. Other angles or starting-points may be equally or more profitable; we might for instance decide that the essence of drama is best given in terms of a relation between these components, that it shows 'character in action', or 'conflict'. But at least the meaning of these three terms, Plot, Character and Diction, is immediately obvious to us, and if Aristotle had in fact divided tragedy into these three components we should have recognised the obvious. Actually he produces four, with ethos and dianoia substituted for Character. So long as we leave these in a vague translation 'Character' and 'Thought' they may seem ordinary and relevant enough in a discussion of a drama, but the more we pursue them, the more elusive and lacking in self-consistency they seem to become; and the chief reason is, I think, that they are concepts taken over partly from the sphere of Ethics and partly from that of Rhetoric, and never wholly brought into line with each other or with the rest of the *Poetics*. Considered under Ethics, ethos and dianoia are both part of the individual make-up as, roughly, moral and intellectual qualities: they issue in action and determine a person's quality. But in fact only ethos is in the *Poetics* treated from this point of view. Psychologically, ethos is a more fundamental and abiding aspect of the personality than dianoia, which may indeed often be directed to giving others, by means of the spoken word, a misleading impression of the speaker's personality. Hence there are τὰ ἤθη, 'The Characters', related to individual persons, but never 'The Thoughts'. But also ethos, in the singular, is defined as a declaration of προαίρεσις, 'will', 'purpose', or moral choice on a given occasion 'when it is not obvious' (50b8), where the mere course of the action is not enough for our understanding, and explicitness (in words) is required. In the *Poetics* the distinction between implicit and explicit ethos, though never clearly explained, is implied in those words 'where it is not obvious' and 54a18 'if *the words or the action* reveal some moral purpose'. There is no corresponding distinction between implicit and explicit dianoia because as we shall see dianoia is peculiarly the province of the spoken word, of Rhetoric, so explicitness is its nature. No obligation is laid on the poet to make his dianoia characteristic of the person uttering it, because by definition what is characteristic belongs to ethos. It is not appropriate, says Aristotle, for a woman to be clever, and he says it in his prescriptions for τὰ ἤθη. The dianoia in the mouth of Oedipus must spring from Oedipus' situation; it is not required to be expressive of Oedipus' nature. Such is the awkward and indeed indefensible product of this dichotomy.

A divorce between Characters (in the English sense) and Plot has put many difficulties in the way of critical analysis; the divorce between ethos and dianoia, with some of the words spoken to be allotted to the one, some to the other, and some to neither, is still further from our notion of characters-in-action. Yet these distinctions are some sort of reflection of actual differences between Greek and more modern tragedy, and indeed between Greek tragedy and the New Comedy. In Menander every speaking part is 'a character' and made to speak characteristically. In tragedy this kind of 'realistic' characterisation is slightly foreshadowed in the style of speech occasionally given to anonymous humbler persons like the Nurse in the *Choephoroe* or the Watchman in the *Antigone*, who are thereby typified to some extent; on the other hand, some anonymous figures, especially those Messengers called ἐξάγγελοι, may be left deliberately blank of feature, uncharacterised; what they say simply helps to explain or push on the story. So Aristotle's τὰ ἤθη do not include every spoken part, but only those whose inner nature and moral choices have some effect on the action. In the good tragedy, he says in effect, there must be among the *dramatis personae* some who have ethos, in whose qualities and impulses we are interested, and who must therefore satisfy us by some degree of explicit self-declaration. Moreover, even these central figures do not always speak strictly 'in character'. Much confusion has been caused by modern critics who insist on taking every utterance of an Oedipus or Ajax or Medea as a bit of self-revelation. When it is essential for the audience to understand the full magnitude of Alcestis' sacrifice for Admetus Euripides commits the demonstration to Alcestis herself, without thereby seeking to characterise her as rapt in the contemplation of her own nobility—as a woman who would say that sort of thing, nor Admetus as a husband who needed that sort of thing pointed out to him. Von Blumenthal, in *Die Erscheinung der Götter bei Sophokles*, is assuredly astray in seeing in Tecmessa's description of Ajax's behaviour during his madness a female *penchant* for horrid details. Nor is there in Greek tragedy much analysis of motive for its own intrinsic interest, or for the sake of the completeness of a character in the round. Alcestis' self-immolation for her husband's sake is so essential to her traditional ethos, and so abundantly implicit in the action of the play, that Euripides has seen fit, in the interests of his conception of the whole shape of the play, to suppress in her speech all eloquence in the expression of loving devotion. Explicit ethos is required 'where it is *not* obvious'. Aristotle's isolation of ethos as something intermittent which should not be left out of a play but must be kept in its proper place does correspond to an actual and at times slightly bewildering feature of Greek tragedy.

To modern ears, however, the most unfamiliar and the most puzzling of these concepts is certainly dianoia. The 'Thought' of a play might perhaps suggest to us its underlying theme, where there is one, as distinct from its outer plot, or at least what the author himself is seeking to convey as the inner *meaning* of the action represented on the stage. Such 'Thought' is most easily detachable, perhaps, where the poet has invented characters and situations to illustrate or to symbolise what is in his mind, as Ibsen in *The Master Builder*, or Shaw in *Major Barbara*, but it may also be conveyed in the new interpretation of a given story, as in *Man and Superman*, or as the story of Antigone is adapted by Jean Anouilh to demonstrate Existentialist philosophy. Some such expression of the dramatist's 'Thought' can be disengaged from each successive new form given by the Greek tragedians to the heroic myths, and is seen at its most explicit, perhaps, in the choruses of the *Agamemnon*. But Aristotle certainly means nothing of this kind; dianoia is given its position among the essential parts of tragedy, not as a commentary on the meaning of life, but as an essential function of the human mind issuing in action. Yet as we have seen it does not emanate from the nature of the speakers in the way that ethos does. What then are we to look for?

The word is used in a wide variety of senses in Greek—in almost every sense of our word 'thought', and with 'meaning' and 'intention' added. Its everyday, untechnical use appears for instance when Aeschylus in the *Frogs* (1058–9) claims that 'great thoughts must breed great words'; this is our ordinary notion of 'expressing thoughts in words'. In the *Sophist* (263 c 2) Plato defines it as a process of thinking, a voiceless dialogue of the mind within itself, and such a dialogue issues in δόξα, an expressed opinion. Aristotle uses it in the general sense of 'intelligence' as a faculty in *Met.* 1025 b 25, and in one passage of the *Politics* (1337 b 9) it is 'mind' as opposed to 'body'. But there are one or two passages where Aristotle is using the word in a fairly general and untechnical sense which brings it nearer to the dianoia of the *Poetics*. In *Pol.* 1337a38 he says of education that it is not clear whether it should be directed chiefly to the intellect (dianoia) or the character (ethos), and in *Rhet.* III 16. 9 he contrasts dianoia with proairesis, advising the orator to let his words appear to come from the latter rather than the former, i.e. seek to appear good rather than clever. This is the same distinction as in the *Poetics*, between dianoia and the ethos which is shown in moral choices. How does this apply in the philosophy of poetry?

Dianoia (50b4) apparently comes third in order of importance of the six component 'parts'. There are three definitions:

(1) (50a7) Proofs and aphorisms are its manifestations.
(2) (50b11) It is used in proofs, refutations and generalisations.
(3) (50b4) It is a capacity for making all the relevant *points*, which in speeches is the function of the political art and of rhetoric.

The third of these is less different from the first two than might appear. In *Rhet.* 1355b rhetoric is defined as the power to survey the whole range of apposite arguments to prove your point and convince your hearers. The generalisation is a very important type of argument, and it is from this point of view, as a means of Persuasion (πειθώ), not as a bit of distilled wisdom, that Aristotle thinks of the maxim or generalisation.

In Chapter 19, 56a33, there is a somewhat longer restatement which adds little to these definitions. [It remains to speak of Diction and Thought.] 'For Thought take what I have said in my *Rhetoric*; it belongs more strictly to that subject. To the sphere of Thought belong all the effects which have to be produced by means of the words. These effects consist of proving and confuting, rousing emotions—pity, fear, indignation and the like—and also exaggerating and minimising. Obviously the play's action has also to be compiled from the same ingredients when it has to give an impression of pity or fear or importance or probability, only here the effect has to be obvious without explanation [is this the play as a Biological Entity again?], whereas in the words it is the speaker who has to produce it, from what he says. After all, why have a speaker if the required effect is obvious without the words?'

The reason given for this perfunctory treatment of dianoia as compared with Plot, Character and Diction is that the subject has been dealt with at length in the *Rhetoric*. Although the actual word dianoia is not much used in the *Rhetoric* in any technical sense, we find (III I. 7) that the art of rhetoric consists of dianoia *plus* diction in the sense of subject-matter and style, so that dianoia is in effect the whole content of rhetoric itself, and the aspects of it here summarised (in Chapter 19) are in fact a summary of that content (with one notable exception, to be discussed presently). This fact is of cardinal importance in Aristotle's interpretation of tragedy.

The insistence on the spoken word as the peculiar province of dianoia is noteworthy. The imperfect appropriateness of these concepts which Aristotle is using for the analysis of tragedy is nowhere more apparent than in the relation of the various 'parts' to the Word. Dramatic form implies that *everything* has to be conveyed by the spoken word—everything at least that Aristotle is concerned with in Plot, ethos, dianoia and Diction. But ethos (by Aristotelian definition, especially in the *Ethics*) is primarily something which a man *is*, rather than what he says or does, though both his words and his actions may be manifestations of it. Hence our uncertainties arising from the awkward distinction between τὰ ἤθη, The Characters, what the dramatic characters are, and their expressed ethos 'where it is not clear already'. With dianoia we come to something which is (again by Aristotelian definition, this time from the *Rhetoric*) precisely the province of Eloquence, of the art of rhetoric. So the appeal here is not to the intellectual make-up of the personages as part of their nature, whether or not they come out with it in speech. The dianoia in a play *is* the eloquence of the personages, employed in putting their case on any occasion which requires it with all possible clarity and force. Their dianoia is the means by which an attitude of belief is produced in their hearers: they prove and disprove, exaggerate or gloss over, stir up emotions of pity, terror, indignation, calculated to influence belief. These phrases, 'an effect of plausibility', 'pity and terror', we have heard before in connection with the Plot, the chain of probable or necessary incidents generating pity and terror; yes, Aristotle seems to say, but that is not what I mean by dianoia, which is concerned only with the kind of persuasion that induces belief by means of *words* calculated for that end.

I come now to the one omission of which I spoke in the list of dianoia's functions in the *Poetics* as compared with the *Rhetoric*. In the *Rhetoric* eloquence is said to have three tasks: 'putting across', so to speak, your own ethos, rousing the desired emotions among your audience, and, its chief business, proving your case. In the *Poetics* the first of these is deliberately omitted, though in the *Rhetoric* the well-timed bit of self-revelation is recognised as an influential weapon of persuasion. (How many gifted speakers from Socrates downwards have opened their case with 'I am no orator as Brutus is'.) And in *Rhetoric* 1395 b 13 general maxims, aphorisms, are shown to be particularly good examples of an argument which reveals the proairesis, the moral will, of the speaker, since they epitomise his attitude on the subject of the desirable; so if the maxims are morally edifying they make him appear χρηστοήθης, a good man. In the *Poetics* the aphorism is expressly kept aloof from the moral personality and brought under dianoia. In fact, of course, what we have called 'explicit ethos', the ethos 'where it is not obvious', ought to be *in the province* of dianoia, and it is only in that province that ethos can give the illusion of separability from the rest of the personality; but it cannot be put there because of the terms of Aristotle's definitions, so the issue has to be evaded or glossed over. If it be objected that we must here distinguish between a calculated piece of self-revelation introduced for a particular end by a speaker in an agonistic scene and the ordinary ethos appearing spontaneously as it were up and down the play, the answer is that Aristotle does not in fact make this distinction, and this brings us to a central difficulty in his whole treatment of dianoia.

At whom is the dianoia of a play directed? The other characters in a given scene? or the spectators? or both? Aristotle nowhere gives an answer or suggests that the question need arise. The whole subject is taken straight over from the province of Rhetoric and applied to tragedy without adaptation. In both, speeches are made, therefore the same rules of eloquence apply. The *Poetics* gives rules for good plot-construction, good character-drawing and good diction, but for good dianoia—'see my *Rhetoric*'. The summary of what dianoia sets out to achieve applies most obviously to scenes where there is a set debate, an agon, but not all rhetoric was agonistic. A lament, an appeal, even the careful portrayal of a situation, all require a capacity to find 'every possible persuasive point', and there is no suggestion of a difference between the reactions of the other dramatic characters and those of the theatre audience, or, what comes to the same thing, between what the poet wants to make *us* think and what the speaking character wants to make *his* hearers believe.

That such a difference is fundamental seems to us so obvious as to need no argument or illustration. But there is every reason why it should not have appeared so obvious to a Greek of the fourth century B.C. Greek tragedy is a highly rhetorical form of art, much more so in the hands of Euripides than of his predecessors, and as far as we can judge the intensifying process continued with increased momentum in the fourth century. After a plunge into the turgid flood of Senecan drama we may indeed cool our heads with relief in the poetical sanity of Greek rhetorical tragedy, but rhetoric can be good as well as clever; it can present 'all the possible points' in so far as they are 'relevant and appropriate'. Apart from the large number of scenes in the extant plays which develop into a more or less formalised agon, there are still more which are half-agonistic, monologues addressed to the chorus, speeches in self-justification even though no opponent replies, carefully reasoned expositions of a point of view, all presented as if the speaker were out to convince an unwilling or sceptical listener who might otherwise have tended to believe the opposite. The Athenian theatre-audience was the same as that which listened in the Assembly or in the law-courts whether as judges or as spectators, and it would be only natural if their receptive attitude were the same in each context, when the rhetorical technique used by the speakers was so similar. It is obvious enough that such scenes as the dispute in the *Hercules Furens* between Lycus and Amphitryon as to the relative merits of bow and spear were written for an audience that loved a good debate for its own sake; but the manner extends to less obviously rhetorical subjects, as when in the *Trojan Women* Cassandra to comfort her mother 'proves' that fallen Troy is happier than the victorious Greeks:

> πόλιν δὲ δείξω τήνδε μακαριωτέραν
> ἢ τοὺς Ἀχαιούς...

She is god-possessed, she says, but for so long she will hold the frenzy at bay and produce all the arguments. Or Hecuba, again, says 'Let me lie where I have fallen', and then goes on to show in detail that her sufferings are indeed 'fall-worthy', πτωμάτων ἄξια, ending with the rhetorical question 'Why then do you try to raise me up?' The controversy, the appeal, and the lament have their obvious counterparts in the context of Athenian public life; perhaps not only education and force of habit but the manner of the play's performance, as a competition before judges, and as an actors' as well as a poets' competition, and the great open-air theatre-scene itself, had their part in attracting so much of the play into the same sphere, in making the characteristic utterance of the main figures this argumentative presentment of a thesis. The temptation to listen to the dialogue of Greek tragedy as to a series of set pieces with a few looser interludes must have been strong, and the temptation to write it as such was clearly growing. Small wonder then that Aristotle referred the budding dramatist to his *Rhetoric* to learn how to write tragic speeches.

A great deal of Aristotle's analysis of tragedy, in spite of his obvious preference for Sophocles, is more appropriate to a form of drama nearer to that of Euripides but still further advanced in the same line of development. It is interesting to see how far his concept of dianoia helps us to understand Sophocles and how far it is misleading. The great agones are there, of course, though fewer than in Euripides and more carefully built into the structure of the plot: the decks, we might say, are less ostentatiously cleared for this type of display. There are also many non-agonistic speeches thrown into the characteristic rhetorical form, where the speaker is intent on making out a case; the audience to be convinced, or emotionally influenced, may be the other stage-figures, the spectators, or his own conscience, or all three; there is no cross-purpose here, and Aristotle's equation of the poet with the professional rhetorician who wrote speeches for his clients, and of the auditorium with the stage, can do no particular harm. The Greek tragic character often asks and answers his own questions, anticipates an imaginary opponent's objections, where in later Greek comedy or modern drama some minor, 'protreptic' figure would be put up to elicit replies. Self-justification is peculiarly apt to take this form, as for instance in the speech of Ajax (*Aj.* 457 ff.), beginning 'And now what must I do?' He examines the alternatives: 'Go home? Fall in battle under Troy?' He gives reasons for finding each of these inadequate. No, he says, 'I must attempt a deed which shall show me worthy of my birth and name', and ends with four maxims or generalisations which sum up his attitude to the moral decision he is making—to take his own life. Such dianoia is of course inextricably involved with ethos, and it is significant that the most perfect examples of this compound in English literature are to be found, not in drama, but in the dramatic monologues of Browning—for instance in that work of agonistic form, *The Ring and the Book*.

Self-justification again is the note of Antigone's famous, or notorious, explanation, in the course of her last lament, of her motives in burying Polynices (*Ant.* 904 ff.). Aristotle cites this in *Rhet.* 1417a29 when he is giving precepts for the handling of narrative in forensic oratory. Your version of events must be full of ethos; glimpses of your opponent's bad morals (proairesis) and your own good morals must constantly shine through. Don't let it appear that your statements are prompted by dianoia; keep them on the lines of moral choice. But if one of them sounds incredible, *then* add the reason. Sophocles provides an illustration in the passage from his *Antigone* 'that she cared more for her brother than for husband or children (proairesis); *for* these could be replaced if lost, whereas once father and mother were dead there was no hope of another brother (dianoia)'.

This is of course no use to us as a comment on this strange passage, adapted from an anecdote in Herodotus. What we find incredible is not that Antigone should have felt a duty to a brother more important than a duty to husband or children, but that she should at this point (just before her death) have chosen to justify her act on the grounds of such a preference—a purely hypothetical and gratuituous one, since she had no husband or children, and the only point of preferring a brother on the strength of his irreplaceability would be if it were a question of keeping him *alive* (as in the Herodotean version). It is the misapplied dianoia of the poet *behind* Antigone's ethic declaration and dianoetic explanation of it to which we object. It is true that Aristotle chooses his illustrations at their face value from the poets because the stories were universally known, and he is not here concerned with poetic propriety or an interpretation of Sophocles but with advice on rhetorical technique. Yet this is the treatise to which he refers the student of drama for the handling of dramatic speeches, and there is no suggestion that the objects and criteria of the one kind of eloquence are any different from those of the other. One might almost feel that this passage of the *Antigone* is an excellent illustration of the sort of passage a tragedian might write if he had followed Aristotle's teaching. At least the failure to keep these two spheres more clearly distinct might easily become a besetting weakness in Greek tragedy—probably did so become in the fourth century B.C.

The chief inadequacy of Aristotle's formula, however, is that it takes no account of the Sophoclean irony. In how many scenes does the whole conception rest upon the sharp distinction between the two audiences, the stage and the auditorium, instead of upon their equation! When Ajax deliberately sets out to deceive the Chorus as to his intentions in retiring with his sword to a lonely part of the beach, it is to this distinction that the gorgeous rhetoric of his great speech (*Aj.* 646 ff.) should be referred, not to the character of the hero. Ajax's moral will has been indicated clearly enough in the earlier speech already quoted (457 ff.), and that he should now falter in that grim resolution would be far more disturbing to our sense of the unity of his character than that he should act a whole-hearted deception. Yet he has to convince his stage-audience that he has so weakened, and all the resources of persuasive eloquence are deployed to this end, the majestic comparisons (no lesser parallels could serve for Ajax), the touch of shame, the suggestion of a solemn rite to be performed upon this malignant sword. 'Pray that my heart's desire may be fulfilled, bid Teucer look after my interests and yours, for I am going whither I must go, and perhaps you will learn that I have after all found salvation.' Every word is double-edged, and only once (667), in 'we will learn to revere the Atridae', does the mockery threaten to overreach itself. Magnificent poetry for an unworthy end? No, because every word spoken of the courses of Nature can be understood by us, the spectators, as by Ajax himself in his own heart, as true and applicable in a sense other, and more profound, than the obvious meaning they bear to his duped audience. This exploitation of 'the persuasive' on a double plane is Sophocles' method of adapting the dianoia of public life to the eloquence of tragedy.

14

WORDS, MUSIC AND DANCE[1]

Χρυσέα φόρμιγξ—'O lyre of gold, joint treasure of Apollo and the violet-haired Muses, hearing you, the foot steps out in the beginning of splendour (βάσις ἀγλαΐας ἀρχά) and the singers obey your notes when to guide the chorus your quivering strings sound their prelude.' So began the ode in which Pindar commemorated Hieron's victory in the chariot-race at Delphi in the year 470 B.C. Apollo and the Muses are its joint inspiration, for the words took shape in the poet's mind as the words of a song and dance, which he must afterwards teach to the performers and their musician.

In modern times for a union of these arts we need a collaboration: 'Lyrics by A, music by B, dances by C'; indeed we can go on, 'costumes by D, décor by E, cigarettes by F'. Let us take a famous collaboration of A and B, with C anonymous:

Bow, bow, ye lower middle classes,
Bow, bow, ye tradesmen, bow ye masses,
Blow the trumpets, bang the brasses,
Tantantara! Tzing! Boom!

The 'dance' is a march, but the Greeks would have recognised it as a dance, for it is expressive of the meaning and mood of the words. Witty and satirical verses are at home in this kind of performance; or the words may be gay, comic, sentimental. If there is spectacle, the choreographer may also be famous, but spectacle tends to drive out wit. One presence is forbidden—poetry; hers is a different world. It is dance that bars the door. With music poetry may sometimes collaborate, in a shy and modest way, but dance allied with sung words has lost caste these many centuries. In Opera, serious or comic, there is dance only when the scene represented demands it: Masetto and Zerlina may enter with a little band of villagers merrymaking and sing and dance a short rustic ballad. But if dance is to be

[1] An inaugural lecture delivered at Birkbeck College, 20 May 1960.

taken seriously it must be silent, mime or ballet, and if song is to be taken seriously the singer must be still; let dancers open their mouths, or singers start swaying or stepping out, and the performance becomes a 'musical' or a 'number'. Our serious dancing and singing have each become a highly professional matter, needing breath-control and concentration; in alliance they are either a vehicle of glamour or prettiness, or, in different circumstances, a manifestation of 'folk-art'.

In parts of the world where country-life has kept its isolation from urban and cosmopolitan pressures there may survive a union of these three arts. Morris-dancing in England had for centuries a number of short songs, like this (modernised) old one from Cheshire, in which clearly the singers are themselves performing the dance:

> Morris-dance is a very pretty tune;
> I can dance it in my new shoon.
> My new shoon they are so good
> I could dance it if I would.
> This is it and that is it,
> And this is Morris-dancing.
> My poor father broke his leg.
> And so it was a-chancing.

This is just light-hearted nonsense, but the combination can be taken more seriously. Spain, for instance, has in its flamenco and cante jondo a variety of sung dances whose words are those of folk-ballads, usually anonymous, simple, gay or melancholy. This country-art has been studied and reproduced in stylised form by specially trained troupes performing in towns, or more often in foreign countries. The main appeal here lies in the exotic charm of the dances with their accompaniment of guitars or hand-clapping; the singing is as it were an alternative form of accompaniment, and singers and dancers are usually separate performers.

Folk-art existed in ancient Greece too, of course, in all periods; but in a society where music, song and dance are all-pervasive, at all public and private occasions, in all cults and festivals, folk-art and high art blend and pass into each other with no sharp dividing line. Of the former, naturally little survives directly in verbal form. There are fragments of something like our Wassail-songs, sung mostly perhaps by children from door to door, which may have had some sort of processional dance-movement; and in a long and confused list of dances with names suggestive of miming Athenaeus (629e) has preserved the words of a dance called *Flowers* (ἄνθεμα):

> ποῦ μοι τὰ ῥόδα, ποῦ μοι τὰ ἴα, ποῦ μοι τὰ καλὰ σέλινα;
> ταδὶ τὰ ῥόδα, ταδὶ τὰ ἴα, ταδὶ τὰ καλὰ σέλινα.

> Where are my roses, where my violets, where my lovely parsley?
> These are your roses, these your violets, these your lovely parsley.

This has proved too much for commentators, who declare that it must have been a children's game. But Athenaeus is quite explicit: it was sung 'among the ordinary people' (ἰδιώταις)—folk-art, not professional—and it was an imitative dance, called *Flowers*. This is no Nuts-in-May kindergarten action-song, but a sung dance rendering in posture and movement three different kinds of flowers.

It is noteworthy that in Homer, our oldest literary authority, though we hear much of song and lyre-playing and dancing, there is no precise description of singing-and-dancing choruses. There are two words used in this connection: μολπή, with its verb μέλπομαι, which has a significantly indeterminate meaning, singing to the lyre (of the minstrel), or song with dance, or choral dance; and ὀρχηστύς, with ὀρχέομαι, the kind of dance which was a show-piece for its own sake, a performance of professional skill. Such was the dance-turn of the two Phaeacian youths put on to impress Odysseus (*Od.* viii. 378–82), where the pace grew too hot for the lyre and the timing was taken over by the young men standing round, hand-clapping or thigh-slapping,[1] amid a cheerful roar of encouragement. On the Shield of Achilles Hephaestus wrought in the City at Peace both a rustic vintage-dance (μολπή), in which the choral contribution to the words was responsive shouts (ἰυγμός), and an accomplished and intricate chorus of noble youths and maidens, who danced (ὠρχοῦντο)

[1] Like the companions of the προχορεύων on the Corinthian aryballos *Hesperia* 24, 2, p. 158 (Roebuck); cf. T. B. L. Webster, *From Mycenae to Homer*, pl. 24*b*.

'with their hands upon one another's wrists; the girls wore fine linen robes and the young men well-spun tunics faintly gleaming with oil; the ones had fair garlands and the others daggers of gold set in silver baldrics; now they circled with skilful feet, so lightly, as when a seated potter tries the wheel that is shaped to his hand, to see if it will run, and then again they ran in lines to meet each other; and a great crowd stood around enjoying the lovely dance, and the wondrous musician sang among them to the lyre, and as he led[1] the measure two tumblers spun around in the midst of them'. Such, we are told, was the dance which once in Crete Daedalus had invented for Ariadne—Daedalus who stands for all elaborately beautiful arts in a traditionally remembered Mycenaean culture—and it is a perpetual difficulty of the Homeric style of composition that there is so often no guarantee that *this* particular assemblage of lines originally belonged together. Here the last three lines, with the rather late and perfunctorily remembered musician and the two tumblers or acrobats, occur as a group elsewhere, and the latter seem an intrusion in the aristocratic picture. Music, perhaps of the flute,[2] there must of course have been in the original Cretan dance, but if there were words it is possible that the dancing chorus sang them, even though what the crowd stood around enjoying was the convolution of the dance itself.

However that may be, the author of the Hymn to Apollo in the next century seems to remember the composite picture, since on Olympus when Apollo plays the lyre and the Muses sing, and the Graces and the Hours with Harmonia and Hebe and Aphrodite and Artemis dance, their hands upon one another's wrists, Ares and Hermes, two irrepressible and mischievous gods, 'sport among them', a boisterous episode in the prevailing eurhythmy. The division of functions in the company of heaven is not so much a reflection of terrestrial performances as a consequence of mythological symbolism; Apollo's lyre stands for all music and poetry, but the direct instructors of the poet, who give him his words, are

[1] ἐξάρχοντος, cf. Athenaeus 180d. Aristarchus excised the line about the musician, in which case ἐξάρχοντες must be read, of the δοιὼ κυβιστητῆρε.

[2] As on the Hagia Triada sarcophagus.

the Muses. Apollo is never a singer, because that is what the Muses are for, and Apollo and the Muses are inseparably allied in inspiration; the 'lyre of gold' is for Pindar the 'joint treasure of Apollo and the violet-haired Muses'. Only for Hesiod are the Muses a self-sufficient choir, who dance and sing round the fountain of Hippocrene and seem to need no accompanist, for Hesiod has no concern with *literal* dance and song; he knows himself a receiver of the true word from the Muses (a didactic poet), no mere entertainer.

Memorable poetry, meant for transmission to posterity, was being composed for singing-and-dancing chorus by the seventh century B.C. Our earliest fragmentary texts and names come from the Peloponnese; later there was a school in the Far West, and in the sixth and fifth centuries we find a bewilderingly rich variety of forms for various occasions, religious and secular, and finally the choral odes of Attic drama. Any attempt on our part to classify and distinguish the different kinds under traditional generic names—paean, dithyramb, nomos, hymn, etc.—on internal or external evidence quickly lands in contradiction or uncertainty. One thing we can say: that choral lyric contains some of the most difficult Greek poetry we have—difficult not only in the interpretation of the words but often in its form and reference, in its strange and abrupt transitions of thought, and above all in its metre.

This was poetry not for reading, but essentially for performance, and not repertory performance either. We do not know what it looked like nor how it sounded; we can only read the words in their metrical patterns—time-patterns of long and short syllables. Some of these patterns are relatively simple, and agreement has by now been reached as to their shape; others are exceedingly elaborate, and hardly any two scholars can wholly agree on their interpretation. We have to read them, aloud or in our heads, bare of music, in a curious amalgam of our own, made up of our fumbling reconstruction of the sound of ancient Greek words held to a time-pattern which is determined partly by the spelling of the words and partly by the metrical scheme, and reinforced—or deformed—by our own English (German, or whatever) rhythmical habits and hungers. That through this unpromising medium somewhere in the silence of the mind's ear we feel we do catch some echo of ordered and beautiful sound is either an illusion or a measure of the vitality of Greek poetry.

Is it only an illusion? If music and dance mattered so much to Greek lyric poetry, and the music and dance are irretrievably lost, how can we claim to know anything at all about the ordering of the rhythm?

> When Britain first at Heaven's command
> Arose from out the azure main

Dance is no longer relevant, but how much should we deduce of 'Rule, Britannia' from reading the verse without music?

There are two reasons why in Greek we are not left so helpless. First, every Greek poet was his own composer, and no poet would write words in elaborate metrical schemes merely to annihilate and overlay these by a different musical rhythm. We have learnt to work out a great variety of metrical forms, with all the permitted modifications of each and their intricate cross-relations to each other, and we can study the special habits of each metrical stylist. The whole builds up into a reasonably coherent system, the very elaboration of which is to some degree a guarantee of its objective reality in the ancient performance. To take a simple analogy: if a musician chooses to set to music a poem like Masefield's 'Cargoes', where the words are cleverly made to sound their own time-relations:

> With a cargo of ivory,
> And apes and peacocks,
> Sandalwood, cedarwood, and sweet, white wine.
>
> Dirty British coaster with a salt-caked smoke-stack,
> Butting through the Channel in the mad March days

—he *cannot* destroy that rhythm and build up a new one in music; he can only follow the one that is there, made the more impregnable by its repetition from stanza to stanza, by its 'responsion'.

Secondly, in Greek poetry the relation of words to music is unique, because the word-rhythm of verse is itself quantitative. What music does to words, in any language, is to define the length of each syllable, to impose a precise quantitative scheme.

Now O now I needs must part,
Parting though I absent mourn,
Absence can no joy impart,
Joy once fled can ne'er return.

The stanza with its four seven-syllabled lines, each with four stresses, could scarcely be simpler rhythmically, but an equally simple musical setting has two alternatives at its disposal (actually Dowland switched from the one to the other): either the note-values could be equal for each syllable, letting the musical beat render the word-stress (say 2/4 time), or the stressed could be double the length of the unstressed syllables (3/4 time). The words by themselves impose no decision. English is embarrassingly full of even monosyllables, and of strings of unvoiced, indeterminate syllables in longer words—miserable, carpenter, temperament—which give the musical note little positive lead. (Perhaps in its fourteenth-century stage of development the language was kinder:

Sumer is icumen in, lude sing cucu

with its full vowels and pendant endings to what later became monosyllables.) But in classical Greek the syllables were self-determining: χρυσέα φόρμιγξ is long, short, long, long, long. This sequence could be used in different metrical schemes with slight adjustment of delivery (in Pindar's ode the first syllable of φόρμιγξ would have a little less than the length of the syllables on each side of it), but the music cannot transmute it; it can only steady and define the quantities inherent in the bare words. And these quantities will not be properly audible *except* when sung; even in Greek, by nature a far more quantitative language than English, a rhythm that has an elaborate quantitative scheme needs the assistance of singing tone to make itself heard with enough accuracy to be intelligible. In English, even so simple a rhythm as 'Now O now I needs must part' in 3/4 time becomes absurd if spoken.

An important and I think inescapable conclusion from this is that all Greek poetry must have originated as sung rhythm; only so could its metric have developed on a quantitative basis, ignoring both the pronounced pitch-accent and the slight stress which must often have accompanied a rise in pitch, and in many kinds departing from syllabism (a regular number of syllables in each equivalent line of verse). For some of its earliest forms adopted the musical principle of 'resolution' and 'contraction'—the substitution of two shorts for one long, or *vice versa*, just as one crotchet is interchangeable with two quavers; so that the heroic hexameter, for instance, the oldest surviving metre, can vary from 12 or 13 to 17 syllables. We are accustomed in English to the slipping in of an extra syllable between two stresses:

> My coúrsers are féd with the líghtning,
> They drínk of the whírlwind's stream——

But anything corresponding to resolution is rare in our spoken verse:

> ——opening on the foam
> Of *peri*lous seas, in faery lands forlorn.

though significantly in verse written for singing it is much commoner:

> He led his *regi*ment from behind.

In the course of time two of the commonest metres, used for the longest stretches line upon line, the heroic hexameter and the iambic trimeter of dramatic dialogue, had emancipated themselves from music and continued a quantitative life as spoken verse; their time-relations had become as it were second nature to Greek poets, performers and audiences.[1] Certain other regular metres seem to have been chanted in a sort of recitative to the flute, but anything more elaborate had to be sung, and if choral had to be danced. Sappho and Alcaeus, who wrote solo-lyrics, simply sang them to the lyre, and any poem which was to be sung on convivial occasions

[1] For the development of the spoken trimeter, there is a distinction to be drawn between the increasing use of resolution, which is simply carrying further an essentially musical modification, and the 'anapaestic' substitution, in comedy, of two shorts for one or for anceps, which is not a musical principle at all but a loosening of *spoken* rhythm, analogous to our extra syllable between two stresses. This is what makes such analyses as, for example, ⏓ – ⏑ ⏑ – in Pindar or tragic choruses as 'iambic metron' a regrettable solecism.

round a table was of course independent of dance. But it is probable that even the solo-lyrics of actors on the Greek stage were delivered with the help of a kind of movement which perhaps fell short of what we mean by the term 'dance' but was to a Greek an almost inevitable concomitant of sung rhythmical utterance. When Apollo played his lyre for the Olympians (in the hymn mentioned above) he paced out his music in their midst, high-stepping, with flashing feet and swinging tunic. And in choral lyric, where the rhythm could change from phrase to phrase, creating a new and individual pattern for each poem, the dance, especially when it repeated from stanza to stanza in responsion, was both an aid to the performers and a pictorial clarification for the spectators.

But that is a function of dance which has passed for ever from the world; music and words have perennially posed their problems of adjustment. For Milton there was a blest pair of sirens, Voice and Verse, which united to form Song. Having provided only one of that pair, leaving Henry Lawes to produce the other, Milton naturally saw the union of words and music in those terms. The instrumental accompaniment went along with Voice. There are various ways in which the pair can come together. The commonest is for a musician to be inspired by a poem and 'set' it to music; that is to say, he takes the rhythm to pieces and puts it together in a new way. As the Greek poet composed in music this situation never arose. Or words can be written to a traditional tune, as Thomas Moore wrote 'The Last Rose of Summer' to an old Irish melody. In the past some old tunes were used over and over again, being taken up for carols and then reverting once more to ballads, like 'Fill Ev'ry Glass' in *The Beggar's Opera*. Perhaps the simplest kind of σκόλια, the Greek drinking-songs sung at banquets, give some sort of parallel, since here the framework of syllables, the style of music and probably the tune were traditional, and the words sometimes new. And indeed in all lyric composed 'in responsion' the poet's task in the antistrophes was to some extent one of fitting words to music, to a given musical-metrical pattern. Or the poet may write for the musician, as James Thomson wrote for Thomas Arne in the masque *Alfred*

When Britain first at Heaven's command
Arose from out the azure main,
This was the charter of her land,
And guardian angels sang the strain:
Rule, Britannia, rule the waves,
Britons never shall be slaves.

It is neutral stuff waiting for the breath of music to ignite and transform it, give it pomp and brilliance. Or again, verse and music can be brought together by a careful collaboration, as by Gilbert and Sullivan, with mutual adjustments as required. Doubtless many of the best operatic librettos were worked up in this way, though rarely on such evenly balanced terms. Da Ponte and Boito were librettists of genius with a real poetic gift, but it is Mozart and Verdi who have immortalised them, not the other way round. For this pair of blest sirens is by nature very unevenly matched. However little we know of the music of the Greeks, we can safely say that since their day, though poetry has not grown in stature, music has; it has become something incomparably richer and more profound, not only in the diversity and musicality of instruments but in the interest of voices singing in harmony. The madrigalists were sensitive to the sound-values of words and set them beautifully without too much tyranny of bar and beat, and the poems they set were by no means trivial verses, but it was delight in music-making and counterpoint, not in poetry, that kept the English gentlemen singing round their tables. In Lieder programmes, even of Wolf with his doctrine of 'poetic supremacy', it is the music and the professional skill of the singer that crowds gather to hear. In opera we are even resigned to missing half the words in a foreign language, or, still more dire, we can take them in translation. Cherubino has to give up his amorous play,

Delle belle turbando il riposo,
Narcisetto, Adoncino d'amor,

'Disturbing the slumbers of the fair, love's young Narcissus, toy Adonis'—but the words have to be singable in English rhythm to the same notes, so we get

Here's an end to the life that was gay, lad,
Here's an end to your games with the girls.

The elegance and wit are rubbed out, and the scene is transferred to the kitchen; if we put up with that, it is because all we really care about is the music.

In these unequal conditions, the kind of poetry that can be sung to music is limited. It is best singable when not too difficult in thought, nor too concentrated, nor too self-sufficient in shape, like a sonnet or an ode, nor depending too much on subtle verbal rhythm; all our poetry of this sort is essentially for speaking or reading. If nevertheless one piece or another of it has been successfully made into song, we remember the two, the poem and the song, side by side, as two different creations which do not coalesce. The cultivated art of the singer, the blending polyphony of the accompaniment, cannot but absorb most of our attention; on the other hand, the rhythmical patterns of our song, as of much of our music in general (disregarding some modern developments) are fundamentally reducible to a regular pulse-beat, organised in double or triple time. (I am told that for the freakish 5/4 movement of Tchaikovsky's sixth symphony the conductor Richter used to instruct his players to keep the time straight by repeating to themselves 'Ein Glas Bier für mich'.) In Greek lyric all is the direct opposite of this; its expression, compared with spoken verse, is characteristically taut, elliptical, concentrated, its music is the single line of its melody, its rhythm can take 5-time in its stride, but is mostly too complex for any definable bar-time at all. For the Greek lyric poet Voice and Verse were not a pair of sirens; Verse was merely the incomplete record of a single creation, Song.

Not Voice and Verse, but Song and Instrument were the two Greek sirens which could on occasion fall into discord. Instrumental music did sometimes struggle to free itself from subservience to the human voice, and we have the record of one angry protest from a poet. Pratinas of Phlius in the later sixth century brought over to Athens his own chorus of trained 'satyrs', men masked and costumed as those wild, mischievous spirits of the countryside who had long been associated with the cult of Dionysus, and whose caperings had already in Corinth and probably elsewhere been rhythmised in song and dance as a lyric performance. Pratinas became famous as the first to compose in Athens 'satyr-plays', in which his troupe, now in the guise familiar to us from so many vase-paintings, formed the chorus of rudimentary plays on the doings of heroes, such as, in a more serious vein, Thespis and his followers were already performing in Athens with one actor and a human chorus. But Pratinas was mainly reckoned a lyric poet,[1] and this 'Hyporcheme' or 'dance-song' is a self-contained performance of a satyr-chorus to the flute, in celebration of Dionysus, danced in the quick, rushing, stamping style which came from Crete and because of its vigour was necessarily short and pungent.

τίς ὁ θόρυβος ὅδε; τί τάδε τὰ χορεύματα;
τίς ὕβρις ἔμολεν ἐπὶ Διονυσιάδα πολυπάταγα θυμέλαν;
ἐμὸς ἐμὸς ὁ Βρόμιος, ἐμὲ δεῖ κελαδεῖν, ἐμὲ δεῖ παταγεῖν
ἀν' ὄρεα σύμενον μετὰ Ναϊάδων
οἷά τε κύκνον ἄγοντα ποικιλόπτερον μέλος.
τὰν ἀοιδὰν κατέστασε Πιερὶς βασίλειαν· ὁ δ' αὐλὸς
    ὕστερον χορευέτω·
καὶ γάρ ἐσθ' ὑπηρέτας.
κώμῳ μόνον θυραμάχοις τε πυγμαχίαισι νέων θέλοι παροίνων
ἔμμεναι στρατηλάτας.
παῖε τὸν φρυνεοῦ
ποικίλου πνοὰν ἔχοντα·
φλέγε τὸν ὀλοοσιαλοκάλαμον[2]
λαλοβαρύοπα παραμελο⟨μετρο⟩ρυθμοβάταν[2]
θῆτα τρυπάνῳ δέμας πεπλασμένον.
ἦν ἰδού· ἅδε σοι δεξιὰ
καὶ ποδὸς διαρριφά,
θριαμβοδιθύραμβε κισσοχαῖτ' ἄναξ,
ἄκουε ⟨τάνδε⟩[2] τὰν ἐμὰν
Δώριον χορείαν.

[1] Cf. Plut. *De Musica*, 1146c.

[2] Exempli gratia supplevi. On ὀλοοσ. see below. Wilamowitz restores the essential trochaic run of the verse, but his βραδυπαρ. gratuitously imports a new and doubtful count into the accusation. For 'hyporcheme' (a lyric poem, not an extract from a play) see *Eranos* xlviii, 14ff.

What is this clamour? What these dancings? What outrage has come to the footfall-noisy altar of Dionysus? *Mine* is the Roaring God, mine; mine to shout, mine to stamp as I rush over the mountains with the Naiads, like the swan driving the changing wing-beat of my melody. It is Song that the Muse made queen; let the flute dance second part; he is a servant. Only in the revel-rout and the fisticuffs of young door-hammering drunks let him aspire to be leader. Beat him, with his breath of a variegated toad; burn the reedy menial with his baleful screechings,[1] his chattering growling bass, his gait without rhythm, time or tune, his body hollowed on a gimlet. Now see! here is the hand and foot outflung for you, Lord of the ivied hair and stamping dithyramb; hear the Dorian sound of my dance.

This poem has been sadly misinterpreted as an extract from a play depicting a fight between rival choruses, of humans and satyrs, even of a flute-accompanied and a lyre-accompanied chorus respectively. There is only one chorus, with its flute-player, and his attempts to conduct a flute-dance on his own are brought to order in a mock-attack which leaves him obediently fluting second-fiddle, so to speak, to the singing and dancing satyr-chorus.

'It is song that the Muse made queen', and the dance of the singers was part of their song. Classical Greek needed no Wolfian doctrine of 'poetic supremacy' because song, with its dance, was a function of the words themselves when they were alive—that is, in performance. But the performance was generally one great occasion in all its bright splendour, its ἀγλαΐα, round an altar, or in the orchestra, or processionally. What survived for the record was the written word; musical scores, where they existed, seem to have been rare, and quickly lost. With the passing of the kind of society which required and supported public performances of this type, the living art of this supple polymetry soon perished; it shrank and petrified into the words on paper, so unskilfully preserved that even the proper ordering of the phrases quickly faded from memory. A new type of

[1] With Bergk's emendation ὀλεσισιαλοκ., perhaps more ingenious than probable, this would be 'spittle-wasting reed'. But Didymus in speaking (*ap.* Ath. 392 f in a discussion of a passage in Pratinas) of the bird σιαλίς must have had in mind some kind of whistling noise as the derivation of the name; and perhaps the word here should be something like ὀλοο-σιαλο-κάλαμον, referring to the screeching of the flute's treble notes before the growl of its bass.

spoken lyric poetry took its place, which chose some of the more regular and familiar metrical shapes, or even took isolated phrases and repeated them in simple patterns, adding refinements and regularisations to satisfy the ear's demand for balance and clarity in this new medium. This unsung poetry came to late bloom in Alexandria in the Hellenistic age, and afterwards in Rome, transplanted into Latin. It only remained for the medieval Church, striding on to the scene with all the ruthless incomprehension of a new rhythm of speech and new manner of music, to take up one and another of these delicately carved and tinted but fragile survivals, break them in pieces and put them together again in simpler, naïver, but stronger rhythms with equidistant stresses. The process continued down the centuries:

Ín-teger ví-tae scélerisque pú-rus.[1]

[1] Cf. O. Seel and E. Pöhlmann, 'Quantität und Wortakzent im horazischen Sapphiker', *Philologus* ciii (1959).

15

A HEROIC END

The Messenger's description of the accident that ended Lamachus' campaign against the Boeotian raiders, Aristophanes *Ach.* 1174ff., has caused much trouble and offence. He enters and calls urgently on Lamachus' servants to boil kettles and prepare bandages, since the master has stumbled on a stake while jumping a vine-trench, ricked his ankle, and cracked his skull against a stone. So far all is clear, and when at the end of the speech Lamachus appears, carried between two soldiers and lamenting (in agonisedly resolved iambics) his sufferings from the spear-wound of an enemy, we recognise both his need to dignify the misadventure and the parody of Hippolytus. But in between come lines 1181–8:

> καὶ Γοργόν' ἐξήγειρεν ἐκ τῆς ἀσπίδος·
> πτίλον δὲ τὸ μέγα κομπολακύθου πεσὸν
> πρὸς ταῖς πέτραισι δεινὸν ἐξηύδα μέλος·
> '"Ω κλεινὸν ὄμμα νῦν πανύστατόν σ' ἰδὼν
> λείπω φάος γε τοὐμόν· οὐκέτ' εἰμ' ἐγώ.'
> τοσαῦτα λέξας εἰς ὑδρορρόαν πεσὼν
> ἀνίσταταί τε καὶ ξυναντᾷ δραπέταις,
> ληστὰς ἐλαύνων καὶ κατασπέρχων δορί.

How, commentators ask peevishly, can Lamachus, already prostrate with a sprained ankle and concussion, make a dying speech, fall into a ditch, get up and pursue runaway pillagers with a spear—and then appear on stage unable to walk, with the original sprained ankle and concussion? How indeed? It is neither sense nor amusing nonsense.

The response has been either to shrug the shoulders and say Aristophanes has escaped his own notice pursuing the joke too far, or to tinker with the text and explain the residue as over-faithful paratragedy, or to struggle with far-fetched re-interpretation of the words, or to fall back on a clumsy interpolator. The first can be dismissed as unaristophanic. The second is exemplified by the Budé text, which boldly substitutes κλάσας 'having broken' for πεσὸν in 1182 and rewrites 1185 as λείπω φάος τόδ'· οὐκέτ' οὐδέν εἰμ' ἐγώ, but unable even so to make sense of the incident translates it into a patch of high-flown verse to indicate a generalised 'parody of the Messenger-speech of tragedy'—a singularly pointless procedure, one would think. The third method was begun by the ancient scholiasts: one explains πτίλον πεσὸν as πτίλου πεσόντος, or alternatively 'falling on the rocks he mourned the great feather', another makes πτίλον μέγα stand for the whole helmet, 'since the feather could not ring against the rocks as it fell, only the helmet which was made of bronze'. Clearly they were all at sea. Of modern interpreters none has tried harder than H. Erbse, 'Zu Aristophanes', *Eranos* lii (1954). πτίλον πεσόν he regards as a nominative absolute supported by many parallels and 'hinreichend gesichert'. D. L. Page, on the other hand, in 'Some Emendations in Ar. *Ach.*', *W.S.* lxix (1956), says on this: 'We may say that πτίλον πεσόν is a "nominativus pendens" or even an "accusative absolute", and make the wearer of the helmet the subject of ἐξηύδα; we may say such things, but does anybody believe them?' (I confess to more sympathy with this view.) The feather, says Erbse, falls and is lost—where it falls is of no interest, and πρὸς ταῖς πέτραισι goes with Lamachus' despairing cry. ὦ κλεινὸν ὄμμα refers neither to the Eye of Day (the sun), as some would have it, nor to the feather ('O glorious treasure'), since Lamachus has no thought of dying, and as he lies there cannot 'behold' the feather fallen somewhere behind his head. Both these objections seem well founded. But when Erbse goes on to explain ὄμμα as Lamachus' own reflection in his shield, and φάος as his own salvation which he now loses in the shield he is about to abandon, still more when he takes εἰς ὑδρορρόαν πεσών as describing the same kind of misfortune as befell Dionysus in the *Frogs* in a moment of panic, interpretation overreaches itself. How could the audience possibly have known that they were to take the words in this extraordinary sense?

Then is there nothing for it but to assume Wilamowitz's 'wretched interpolator'? Several of the best-known commentators have agreed, none more strongly than Page in the article quoted. '"So much he spoke: having fallen into a ditch he stood up and met the runaways, driving and urging the bandits with his spear." This', thunders the Regius Professor, 'is next-door to delirium...Nowhere else in Aristophanes does parody take the form of utter confusion of thought allied to thoroughly bad writing devoid of wit...I do not see what alternative there is except to recognise wholesale interpolation by a very inferior writer.' But being honest he adds 'Such a phenomenon is...most highly abnormal. I can throw no light on its cause or source.'

Yet there *is* an alternative, so simple that I almost blush to mention it. It is to take the words straightforwardly in the grammar in which Aristophanes wrote them. 'And the Great Boastard's plume, falling on to the rocks, cried out in dreadful strain: "O Eye of glory, now having looked my last on thee I leave the light—of my life. I am no more." Thus saying it fell into a ditch, rose again and met the runaways, driving the raiders and prodding them on with its spear'—the last line a quotation from the *Telephus* of Euripides (Snell 717a). It does not much matter whether we emend the masculine participles of these last lines to the neuter form (which is easy enough) or assume that the Feather has become so assimilated to the tragic hero by this time that (assisted by the quotation) it has slipped over to the masculine. But the Feather's dying scene it is, not Lamachus's. That hero's martial spirit was all along confined to his Gorgon and his ostrich plumes; now the Gorgon has been 'roused off his shield' and the loyal Feather has taken its last farewell of Lamachus, the 'light of its life'. The words are those of a tragic hero taking leave of the upper world—until the addition of γε τοὐμόν gives an absurd twist to the meaning. It falls into a ditch but floats up again in a last defiant gesture against the enemy; ἀνίσταται is the right word for its light, wind-caught bounce, and δορί is its sharp quill. Perhaps those who saw the film *The Red Balloon* will feel more sympathy for the poor Feather's tragic end than Aristophanes' commentators have had.

16

STICHOS AND STANZA

In classical Greek poetry there is a familiar distinction between verse which repeats κατὰ στίχον, line upon line, and that which forms patterns liable to closure at intervals, in stanzas or lyric sections. This is often equated with the distinction between spoken and sung verse, but the equation is only approximate. At an earlier stage *all* verse had some musical accompaniment—so much can be deduced from a number of passages in Homer, and is in any case implicit in the nature of quantitative verse. By Hellenistic times it seems that, in new composition, the more complex lyric structures had died out, while of the simpler ones more and more were being taken over as spoken verse. In the fifth century—and this can probably be extended to at least the late sixth and most of the fourth[1]—only two kinds of verse are *known* to have dispensed with music altogether in performance: the heroic hexameter and the iambic trimeter.[2]

If we ask what these two metres have in common which distinguishes them from others, even from stichic, the most obvious answer lies in their use: they are required to sustain a far *longer* flow, of narrative or dialogue or rhetoric. The two cases are of course by no means parallel; the epic narrative metre absorbs song and speech into its own uninterrupted continuity, while in drama there are interludes of song. And the hexameter was created, and practised for generations, before any other metre had been evolved for high poetry; the iambic trimeter prevailed over other metres in its own chosen fields because it was found uniquely suitable as a formal representation of human speech.

[1] In the *Dyskolos* (879) Menander still has a flute-player for his iambic tetrameters catalectic.

[2] Doubtless the delivery of other forms of stichic verse fell short of what could properly be called singing; we usually conceal our ignorance of what it really sounded like by using the term 'recitative', a rough translation of Plutarch's παρακαταλογή, but this certainly implies some sort of instrumental accompaniment.

We cannot penetrate behind the hexameter, but everything in the Homeric line as we possess it indicates a single, master-metrical concept, not an evolution from something different nor an amalgamation of smaller entities. It is a line consciously shaped for its function as an indefinitely repeatable poetic stichos, rooted in the prosodic nature of Greek[1] yet keeping a stately distance from speech-rhythms, and by subtle observances of word-end in mid-verse keeping the movement afloat to the end of the long line. Its emancipation from music may be connected with the long performances of major epic, when perhaps the lyre-accompaniment might come to be felt an encumbrance, a hint of monotony, in the expressive declamation.

The origins of the other spoken stichos, the trimeter, are within reasonable conjecture. Plutarch in his *De Mus.* 28. 1141a, a work which contains much sound ancient tradition, some of it from Aristoxenus, attributes the invention of the trimeter, and also (among much else) of the trochaic tetrameter, to Archilochus; and since this means that for him—or rather for his source—as for us the earliest extant[2] examples of both were from that supremely inventive

[1] For instance, the ease with which Greek syllables, aided by the absence of stress-accent, lend themselves to precise conventional distinction of long and short, the abundance of short syllables, especially in the earlier stages of the language, the flexibility conferred by its many inflected forms and rich choice of particles. The device of contraction (⏑⏑ to –) is essential to the concept, for rhythmical variation and much more for word-coverage. (Imagine an epic unable to speak of ἄνθρωποι or ψυχήν!) The various licences through which it enabled itself, always under strict convention, to enlarge its vocabulary further, or adapted its formulae to linguistic change, have been strangely used as an argument for foreign derivation, but that is to pick up the problem from the wrong end altogether.

[2] I find myself quite unable to take seriously the claim that the *Margites* is older than Archilochus. Bergk's brilliant conjecture (Iambog. 153, on which see Rzach–Radermacher *s.v.* Margites in *R.E.*) Ἀρχιλόχοις Κρατῖνος disposes of the one apparent piece of evidence. Certainly the perpetrator of that farrago was himself no metrical inventor—the whole joke assumes familiarity with the iambic line and its normal uses—and we should be driven to postulate a considerable body of iambic poetry already in existence before the seventh century and a creative genius whose poetry and whose name have vanished without trace.

genius we may be content with the attribution. One thing seems certain: both verse-forms are due to the same poet.

– ∪ – ⏒͡– ∪ – ⏒ | – ∪ – ⏒͡– ∪ –
⏒ – ∪ – ⏒ ⋮ – ∪ ⋮ – ⏒͡– ∪ –

Other observances common to both in the iambographers are the ban on simultaneous word-end at | ⏒ – | ∪ – in the final metron and at – ∪ | – ∪ | – ∪ – at the end of the line.

If we ask, looking at the above pattern, which of the two came first, the answer comes readily: the tetrameter. In it, the reason for the two zeugmata is immediately obvious. The conception is of two dimeters, one complete, the second, following in response to it, catalectic. The whole is in fact a simple, short stanza-form—stanza used κατὰ στίχον—whose rhythm depends on the separate audibility of its two components. Thus there must be word-end between them, but internally each dimeter is held together as a whole, prevented from breaking up further into recurring metra; so the heavier cut, after long anceps – ∪ – – |, is forbidden within the dimeter, though the less noticeable – ∪ – ∪ | is allowed.[1] Porson's Law in the trimeter, on the other hand, is not easily accounted for in isolation, and all attempts at a theoretical explanation have been little more than a rationalisation of our acquired feeling that this rhythm is right. If Archilochus had composed a sufficient number of his tetrameters first, his ear would reject any other treatment of the end of the line.

[1] I do not feel that the explanation given by Snell, *Gr. Met.*[3], p. 11, of a time-count in iambic and trochaic is quite sufficient here. He thinks the fractional pause at word-end added to a long syllable would distort the time-relation too much; but if, as I believe, long anceps was in any case perceptibly shorter than true long, no such distortion would be felt. It is also noteworthy that Alcman in the trochaics of his Parthenion, both dimeters catalectic and acatalectic and trimeters, avoids – ∪ – ∪ | as carefully as – ∪ – – | except where the anceps, long or short, is a monosyllable (enclitic, proclitic, or neither), which suggests again that it was the rhythmic effect rather than the time-relation to which he was sensitive. (Snell does himself also speak (*ibid.* p. 6, n. 1) of the 'rhythmische Bedeutung' of Porson's Law.)

No distinction of tone or subject-matter between trimeter-verse and tetrameter-verse is traceable in our fragments of Archilochus, and until the publication of *P. Oxy.* xxii (1951), 2310 nothing could be said about their probable length, but it is significant that when an (incomplete) piece of at least 40 lines turns up it should be in trimeters. The tetrameter does not lend itself to long-continued repetition precisely because it is really a rudimentary stanza repeated κατὰ στίχον, and in the long run the paired rhythm, with its effect of 'setting to partners' in a sort of dance, could hardly escape monotony. The trochaic trimeter catalectic quoted by Hephaestion (29 D–B) might be fancied as the poet's first attempt to break up the dance, but the triumphant answer came when he discarded the opening cretic and began his line in rising movement. Here at last was a true stichos, with the necessary variety and asymmetry for the long-distance run and for the stylised representation of human speech.

It is not known whether Archilochus spoke, or sang, or half-sang his trimeters,[1] but it is very unlikely that the long, near-satirical disquisitions of Semonides and the other iambographers who were the next to grasp one use of this new medium were anything but spoken. For the earliest stages of tragedy we have no evidence, unless we are prepared to take Aristotle's statement—that the first tragedians used only tetrameters—as an account of the actual texts of those earliest plays rather than as a part of his general theory of tragedy as a kind of organism with its own laws of growth.[2] It is at

[1] Plut. *De Mus.* 1141, in referring to Ar.'s 'part song, part accompanied speech, in which he was followed by the tragedians', is anything but clear.

[2] Aristotelian fundamentalists in the 'history of Greek drama' should pause to reflect what our 'histories of Greek metric' would look like if we had no external evidence by which to check his *obiter dicta*. For him Greek drama was a thing of long, long slow growth (indeed there seems no obvious reason why on his theories tragedy did not gradually develop over the whole of literate Greece, instead of springing suddenly to life in sixth-century Attica), and the 'coming of speech' into it, which prompted 'nature herself' to invent the appropriate metre, only makes sense if dramatic dialogue antedated all other uses of the trimeter (εὗρε

least conceivable that Thespis, or whatever genius first brought together solo speech and choral song, chose the well-proved trimeter for his ῥήσεις, and that sporadic tetrameter-scenes for actors such as occurred in Phrynichus and Aeschylus were a later experiment.[1]

That Archilochus invented the tetrameter and trimeter does not of course necessarily mean that he invented the iambo-trochaic metre. We know far too little of the speed, methods, and facility of communication in these matters in the ancient world, and indeed of the relative dates of the early lyric poets and the biographical sequence of the works of each, to be able to assess priorities where neither internal evidence nor tradition gives us a lead. The very high degree of metrical conformity from end to end of the Greek world, the shortness and richness of the whole 'age of lyric', must surely mean two things: that communication *was* speedy, and effective, and that the poets whose skill and creativeness could impose themselves with authority were manageably few. The term 'iambo-trochaic', rather than iambic and trochaic, is here used deliberately, since there is early evidence of a good deal of lyric involvement of these two which in their stichic forms were to become so clearly polarised. We have been taught by Hephaestion to number off in fours, so that we label × – ∪ – × – ∪ – ∪ – – in Archilochus' epodic stanzas (112, etc.) or Alcman 10, 50, 55 'iambic trimeter catalectic', but we should beware of taking this to imply the pre-existence of the trimeter. It may quite well have been simply a hendecasyllable of

cannot mean 'discovered which was' the appropriate metre). The fact that he has shortly before been speaking of an era in which poets were either writers of heroic hexameters or of iambic lampoons (for which the trimeter duly made its appropriate appearance), this being apparently antecedent to tragedy and comedy, only shows how mistaken it is to try to reduce his various 'constructions' to a single homogeneous and logical, or historical, line of development. The organic growth he is immediately concerned with here is that of drama itself, from a capering, satyric, trochaic-singing to a dignified, human, iambic-speaking performance. The incompatibility of these two 'constructions' so close together within this one chapter raises doubts about the shape of this part of our extant *Poetics* which are another matter again.

[1] This might account for the Suda's statement that Phrynichus was the 'inventor' of the tetrameter.

iambo-trochaic movement; certainly the word-division of Alcman 55. 2 μακωνιᾶν[1] ἄρτων ἐπιστέφοισαι does not suggest a trimeter. So, similarly, Alcm. 13. 1 and 4, and 117 are iambo-trochaic enneasyllables, and it explains nothing to call them iambic dimeters hypercatalectic.[2] A still more arresting example of 'ametric' composition in Alcman is preserved by Priscian, *G.L.K.* iii. 428. 10, who tells us on the authority of Heliodorus that the poet wrote catalectic trimeters in which the 'fourth foot could be either an iambic or a spondee':

νεοχμὸν ἄρχε παρθένοις ἀείδην.
καὶ ναὸς ἁγνὸς[3] εὔπυργω Θεράπνας
χερσόνδε κωφὸν ἐν φύκεσσι πιτνεῖ

(The lines were probably in responsion; in any case they are clearly meant to be the 'same' rhythm.) Here the poet modulates in mid-verse from iambic to trochaic by way of the short anceps; the words ἄρχε, ἁγνὸς, κωφὸν overlap between the iambic penthemimer and the trochaic dimeter.

A history of Greek Metric is limited to recording the appearance of a great variety of metres, each sprung perfect like Athena in full panoply from the head of Zeus, and to tracing certain modifications of these in the practice of later poets. It is often assumed that each of these rhythmic patterns had also a long prehistory, in the loose, irregular versions of folk-poetry. If this is pressed to mean a long process of gradualness, in which this particular line slowly becomes more shapely and regular and acquires subtler nuances of rhythm, till it finally emerges in the form known to us, such a theory not only lacks all evidence but seems to be a misconception of the nature of

[1] For the form cf. Chantraine–Irigoin, *R.É.G.* lxiv (1951), 1.

[2] Nor should the three-line stanza (or part-stanza) be run together as an 'iambic hexameter'. Alcman composes in cola, and οὐδ' Ἐρυσιχαῖος οὐδὲ ποιμήν, with its long anceps and rhetorical pause, is an unmistakable colon. The smoothness of the follow-through from one line to the next is characteristic—as throughout in the Parthenion.

[3] Hermann's emendation is essential, *pace* Wilamowitz and others, not only for the improved sense but because with ἁγνᾶς the line is not only ametric but non-metrical.

Greek quantitative rhythm. Precision and regulation are its very essence, and the career of each of its metrical types starts with the first poet of genius who gave precise definition to a syllabic sequence of that particular kind. Of its popular circumambience we know next to nothing, and often the surviving fragments of folk-song and the jingles of folk-wisdom are more easily explained as a doggerel approximation to existing literary metres than as the unpolished predecessors of these. The freer, looser iambic trimeter which comedy required for its own purposes was a subsequent development, as finely calculated as Callimachus' modifications of the Homeric hexameter. Of course each new invention in the creative age of Greek poetry was conditioned by the nature of Greek words and speech-rhythm, and doubtless often suggested by existing phrases in song and dance. But all Greek quantitative verse is a matter of complex structure, in which the factor of individual invention was necessarily very high, and therefore the number of inventors very limited—limited in fact to highly gifted poets. It may be that our recorded 'first occurrences', in the fragments of poets great enough to have left a name to posterity, were often literally the first.

17

NOTE ON EURIPIDES: *HELENA* 1441–50

ΜΕ. ὦ Ζεῦ, πατήρ τε καὶ σοφὸς κλῄζῃ θεός,
βλέψον πρὸς ἡμᾶς καὶ μετάστησον κακῶν.
ἕλκουσι δ' ἡμῖν πρὸς λέπας τὰς συμφορὰς
σπουδῇ σύναψαι· κἂν ἄκρᾳ θίγῃς χερί,
ἥξομεν ἵν' ἐλθεῖν βουλόμεσθα τῆς τύχης.
ἅλις δὲ μόχθων οὓς ἐμοχθοῦμεν πάρος·
κέκλησθέ μοι, θεοί, πολλὰ χρήστ' ἐμοῦ κλύειν,
καὶ λύπρ'· ὀφείλω δ' οὐκ ἀεὶ πράσσειν κακῶς,
ὀρθῷ δὲ βῆναι ποδί· μίαν δέ μοι χάριν
δόντες τὸ λοιπὸν εὐτυχῆ με θήσετε.

So LP, except for Musgrave's palmary λέπας for λύπας in 43 and the removal of the unmetrical 'correction' λυπρά γ' in 48. Nothing more (except appropriate punctuation) is needed.

Menelaus, left with Helen upon the stage after Theoclymenus has taken the bait, prays to Zeus and the gods before going off for decisive action. The first five lines are straightforward: 'Zeus, you are called "father" and "wise god": look on us and grant a change from troubles. And as we drag our fortunes up this steep slope lend a willing hand: with just a finger's touch from you we shall reach that point in our human lot where we desire to be.' The asyndeton in the compound sentence 41–2 is idiomatic, and Kirchhoff's γὰρ for τε a fussy piece of pedantry. It is the same kind of idiom as ἀλλὰ for ἀλλὰ...γὰρ (cf. *I.T.* 65 with Platnauer's note, adding to his examples Aesch. *Pers.* 150–2; *Alc.* 136–7 with my note), and here too the main clause is in the imperative. The next three lines contain another asyndeton, κἂν ἄκρᾳ for κἂν γὰρ ἄκρᾳ (καὶ of course= 'even'). And in the last five lines is a third asyndeton 46–7 κέκλησθε [γάρ] μοι, which carries through to the end of the speech. The text of the *Helena* is difficult and corrupt enough, but we should not try to re-write one of the most carefully composed passages of this ποιητὴς σοφός.

The root of the trouble in these much-vexed lines is the sense of κέκλησθε in 47. It is only too easy, since the gods are in question, to fall straight into the notion of 'invoking', 'appealing to', and prompted by Hermann to relate κέκλησθέ μοι πολλά to *H.F.* 501 καίτοι κέκλησαι πολλάκις—'you have often been invoked by me'. The ways then divide: some make κλύειν dependent on κέκλησθε 'you have often been invoked by me to hear good things and painful from me' (=my joys and sorrows), but as Pearson justly says 'the next clause shows that Menelaus is complaining of fortune being always against him; he cannot in the same breath refer to his chequered past' (L's correction λυπρά γ' suggests that he was doing his best for this interpretation). Terzaghi tries to evade this by translating 'già molto siete invocati da me, affinché ascoltiate le cose buone che ho compiuto e le dolorose che ho sofferto', which is pushing the Greek pretty far and also sounds perilously near to taking χρήστ' ἐμοῦ together (possessive) as='my good deeds'. Several more or less elaborate emendations, none persuasive, from Hermann downwards seek to bring the statement into line with what follows. Others put a comma after πολλά and take χρηστὰ καὶ λυπρά as in apposition to it, with κλύειν in epexegetic dependence; 'good and painful to hear'; most of these, as in the Oxford text, adopt Nauck's ὁμοῦ (a not uncommon confusion) for the somewhat redundant ἐμοῦ. But apart from Pearson's still unanswered difficulty, the objection to ὁμοῦ is that it would not mean simply *both* good and painful, but *both at once*, cf. *H.F.* 950 of the servants' mixed reactions to the mad Herakles: γέλως φόβος θ' ὁμοῦ.

But if we stop 'invoking the gods' and remember Theonoe's address to her father 1029 οὔποτε κεκλήσῃ δυσσεβὴς ἀντ' εὐσεβοῦς, or *I.T.* 570 οὐδ' οἱ σοφοί γε δαίμονες κεκλημένοι, or even 1441 above (with the equivalent κλῄζῃ), the sense becomes much clearer if less respectful. 'You have been called by me many names good to hear from me and also offensive' (=agreeable and disagreeable). ἐμοῦ κλύειν: the form of the pronoun now has its point even after μοι (=from me, a mortal—or from me, Menelaus). Even if the name-calling was mainly in the process of invocation, the basic construction 'to call somebody something' must be kept firmly in view. In effect, 'I may sometimes have been less than polite, but I have had great provocation in your unending persecution'.

Menelaus, then, begins by challenging Zeus to deserve two of the χρηστὰ κλύειν, 'father' and 'wise god', by breaking their run of ill luck, an easy task for the god. The address then tactfully changes to the general θεοί: 'The troubles we have had in the past are enough: gods, you have been called many agreeable names by me in my time—and disagreeable ones, but I do not deserve unending ill-fortune; I need to walk upright. Grant me this one favour and you will make me happy for life.'

The tone of this address to a god from a mortal—what might be called the 'challenging-nouthetetic'—at the close of a scene, just before going off at a climax of the action, is typical of Euripides' latest plays. The passage which comes at once to mind, *Ion* 436–51 in which the temple-boy reads Phoebus a sharp lecture, with Zeus and Poseidon thrown in for good measure, is not of quite the same type, since it is not a prayer, nor a prelude to action; the nouthetesis is itself a high point in the development of the central theme. Euripides was ready at any period to make a character utter or imply, in prayer or any other form of address, a stinging commentary on the divinity whose machinations and interests appear to be directing the main stream of events, as in *Hipp.* 114–20 (the Servant to Aphrodite), *H.F.* 339–47 (Amphitryon to Zeus) and 847 ff. (Lyssa to Iris and Hera). But in the latest group (post 415 B.C.) there is a cluster of these prayers of minor moment, which serve mainly as a sort of conspicuous punctuation to the action of the play. Helen herself at a similar earlier point 1093–1106, before going in to make her preparations to set the trap, had appealed first to Hera by their common wifehood, then less respectfully to Cypris, 'Dione's daughter, who won the prize of beauty on the bargain of my marriage, do not destroy me; that stain was enough with which you defiled me before, when you made—not my body but my name available among the barbarians. Let me die, if you want to kill me, in my own country. Oh why are you so insatiate of mischief, dealing in passions, treacheries, underhand schemes, love-charms to bring death to the house? If you were only temperate, in all else you are found sweetest of gods to men. I mean just what I say.'

Of the two similar points in the action of *I.T.*, the later one (1230–3) is only a veiled hint, since Thoas is on the stage listening, and Iphigeneia has already made her nouthetesis to Artemis at 1082–8 when left alone after the laying of the plot. But here the tone is gentler, as befits the character and her relation to the goddess. Save me as once at Aulis, she says, and this time Orestes and Pylades too; 'otherwise through your doing Loxias will cease to be a voice of truth for men. Be graciously pleased to leave this barbarian country, which indeed is no fit place for you to live in when you could have a happy city like Athens.'

We can thus assume that in the *Andromeda*, produced with the *Helena* in 412, frag. 136 N^2 was spoken by Perseus just before leaving at a moment of decision: 'O Eros, tyrant of gods and men, either cease teaching us to recognise the beautiful when we see it or else help lovers to surmount successfully the troubles you bring upon them.' The rest of the text is slightly garbled, but the sense is clear: only by complying with these conditions will you be worthy of honour; failing that, you must expect to lose our favours. Eros, of course, is a minor deity who can be admonished with this freedom.

In *Phoen.* 84–7 Jocasta ends her opening monologue with a prayer which echoes briefly the sentiment of Menelaus. 'Zeus, dwelling in the radiant folds of heaven, deliver us, and grant that my sons may be reconciled. If you are a wise god it is your duty not to let the same mortal suffer perpetual misfortune'; then she departs to await the decisive confrontation which she has arranged.[1]

Finally, the *Cyclops* contains two brief end-of-scene prayers in the same nouthetetic manner; which suggests once more[2] that this play belongs to the latest group. Ushered into the cave with his companions to undergo the hospitality of the Cyclops, Odysseus prays for help to Athena and then (354–6) reminds Zeus Xenios of his duties: 'And you whose abode is among the radiant stars, Zeus

[1] Cf. also *Antiope* exodus 11–16. [Marginal note by author.]

[2] Cf. *Wiener Studien*, lxix (1956), 106 [= above, p. 129].

Protector of the Guest, look down on this; for if you fail to see it you are not the Zeus in whom men believe but a worthless cipher of a god.' And at 599 as he leaves for the blinding of the drunken monster he appeals to Hephaestus and Hypnos, Fire and Sleep, for their especial help, and then addresses both together: 'After the noble labours at Troy do not destroy Odysseus and his sailors at the hands of a man who cares nothing for gods or mortals, or we shall have to think Τύχη a divinity (δαίμων) and the divinities less mighty than Τύχη.'

With the exception of the *Phoenissae*, where the nouthetesis occurs very early in the action, these plays are of the 'happy-ending' group; the gods are not shown defaulting on the duties to which men have recalled them.

18

OBSERVATIONS ON DACTYLIC

I

In Greek verse[1] the metrical pattern determines each syllable as long, short or anceps. The question whether in sung lyric some longs can be protracted to extra length may be left for the moment; what concerns me in this introduction is the objective reality of the quantity called 'anceps' (ἀδιάφορον), 'indifferent'.

The term is used to cover disparate phenomena, which must be carefully distinguished.[2] First there is the prosodically ambiguous syllable, such as is formed by short vowel followed by mute+liquid; this, which in a given context could be adapted to the required length by modifying the pronunciation, may be called prosodic anceps (Greek κοινή). It needs no special symbol, and is here irrelevant. Next there is the phenomenon known as 'final anceps', by which the last syllable of a metrical period can be (in the actual word) of any length indifferently, since period-end means Pause or break (i.e. severing metrical connection with what follows), so that a short syllable is admitted here even where the metrical pattern requires a long: brevis in longo, i.e. syllaba brevis in elemento longo. Thus for instance τυραννίδα at the end of a trimeter may be correctly given the notation ⏑ – ⏑ –, but if precision is necessary in a complex context it could be written ⏑ – ⏑ ⏑̲. Finally there is anceps proper, which is an integral part of the metrical pattern itself, as in iambo-trochaic sequences or in dactylo-epitrite. This is a peculiar and important phenomenon in Greek metric, often neglected or inadequately defined by both ancient and modern metricians. For an

[1] For lyric poets other than Sappho and Alcaeus the references (e.g. Ibyc. 386 P) are to *Poetae Melici Graeci*, ed. Denys Page, Oxford University Press 1962, cited by the running number.

[2] The interesting article by L. E. Rossi, 'Anceps: vocale, sillaba, elemento' (*Riv. Fil.* xci (1963), 52–71) appeared after this was written. With much of it I am in agreement, but differ in one or two important points.

anceps syllable is never simply a 'long' or a 'short'; it is a 'long for which short can be substituted', or a 'short for which long can be substituted', and its use is limited accordingly. As the first it can never be resolved into two shorts,[1] and both anceps iuxta anceps (except in 'aeolic base' *in the Lesbian poets*) and anceps iuxta breve (not iuxta brevia) are forbidden within a period. That it had in delivery a special time-value which made it immediately recognisable can never be proved, but the existence of this anomalous factor as an essential ingredient in several metrical types strongly suggests that it had. Since in mid-verse anceps always falls between two longs (though either or both of these may be resolved), a distinction between short anceps and true short would be difficult to realise and perhaps of no practical importance, but long anceps must have been distinguishable from the neighbouring longs, or the clarity of the rhythm would suffer. It has long been assumed that the ἄλογον, the 'irrational' quantity between short and long mentioned by Aristides, refers to long anceps, and the fact that he describes it as 'in arsis' makes the assumption more probable. Whether the arsis was literal or metaphorical, the 'long for which short can be substituted' was not a syllable on which the foot would be set down in the dance.

It should be noted that in all the *basic* rhythms of Greek metric the number of consecutive longs or shorts is limited to two. A sequence of more than two shorts indicates resolution; thus for instance a 'paeon' ⏖ ⏑ – or – ⏑ ⏖ is a resolved cretic. A sequence of more than two longs *either* indicates contraction (as in dactyls or anapaests) *or*, of three apparent longs, one is not long but anceps.[2] A precise analysis by notation should therefore always

[1] The *spoken* trimeter of comedy, which allows substitution of two shorts for one short or for anceps, is a law to itself, like the special licence for the initial syllable of the tragic trimeter. This non-musical phenomenon does not apply to any form of sung verse.

[2] A possible exception might be upheld in syncopated iambic or trochaic; thus in Διὸς πλαγὰν ἔχουσιν εἰπεῖν the second, third and fourth syllables are all long, but I am inclined to regard this apparent abnormality as an argument for protraction of syllables in the bacchiac and cretic, as suggested for instance by Koster, *Traité*, p. 87: ⏑ – ⏗ ⏗ ⏑ – ⏑ – –.

mark the incidence of anceps, and I propose here to use e.g. × – ∪ – × – ∪ ∪ – ∪ ∪ – as a general statement of form for an iambelegus, ⩡ – ∪ – ⩡ – ∪ ∪ – ∪ ∪ – to indicate that in a given ode responsion shows both short and long forms of anceps, and ⨯̄ – ∪ – ⨯̄ – ∪ ∪ – ∪ ∪ – to scan such a given line as χώραν καταπνεῦσαι μετρίας ἀνέμων.

2

Dactylic rhythm is based on the alternation of single long and double short, the latter being allowed sometimes to coalesce into contracted long, but not so often as to obscure the basic rhythm. Dionysius (*De comp. verb.* 17. 109) tells us that according to 'rhythmicians' the long of a dactyl was shorter by an indeterminate amount than the value of two shorts; if this was a firm characteristic, not a mere empirical effect of the take-off from long to short, contracted rhythm could still be made to sound audibly dactylic.

The heroic hexameter is the oldest form of dactylic, and its sixth metron is always disyllabic. How should one describe this clausula? At first sight it seems enough to say that any metron can be contracted, and the sixth always is, since (by observation) *no period ends in true short*; then the last syllable may be brevis in longo by the rule of 'final anceps'. But this is not quite right, since the last syllable is clearly *not* contracted long (which by definition may resume its two shorts), so that the sixth metron is unlike the remaining five. Hephaestion indeed gives quite a different account. He says that in dactylic of any length each metron is – ⏖ except the last, which may take any of three forms: (1) acatalectic, – ∪ ∪ dactylic, or in virtue of final anceps – ∪ – cretic, (2) catalectic εἰς συλλαβήν, as in the hemiepes – ∪ ∪ – ∪ ∪ – ∧ ∧, (3) catalectic εἰς δισύλλαβον, as in the hexameter-ending – ∪ ∧ or in virtue of final anceps – – ∧.

But this account, though sometimes accepted, is not quite satisfactory either. The doctrine implied in (1) and (3) is that here a final element is true short, but because of Pause may be lengthened. This is contrary to the formulation proposed earlier, that no final *element* is true short, though a final short *syllable* may be explicable as brevis in longo (as in iambic) or short anceps (as in trochaic). If the formulation is to be saved, Hephaestion's account of the dactylic clausula must be modified, especially in (3), which affects the oldest, and all the commonest, forms of dactylic verse.

In all stichic verse each stichos is a separate period, with Pause. In lyric stanzas Pause in mid-stanza is certain only where synaphea is clearly broken by anceps/anceps, by hiatus, or by brevis in longo (though a strong presumption of its presence is also given by catalexis following on acatalectic cola, or rhetorical pause in responding stanzas, or some changes of metre).[1] Here it is important to grasp the limits of brevis in longo. It is unmistakable where the verse ends blunt, . . . ⏑ – |; and I would say also where the verse is an undifferentiated series of metra containing two adjacent longs, as at the end of a row of bacchiacs . . . ⏑ – – or of ionics . . . ⏑ ⏑ – –; and probably in syncopation, as in final ⏑ – – in syncopated iambics (assuming that in synaphea this becomes ⏑ – ⏗). But in any other colon or verse with penultimate long ('pendant' close) the final syllable is anceps; so in aeolics, paroemiacs, dactyls . . . ⏑ – ×. Where there is Pause this may become the equivalent of long; but a short anceps is not brevis in longo and therefore does not *necessarily* break synaphea. In practice the great majority of such cola in lyric end in long anceps, this giving a steadier definition to the phrase than short anceps; further, there are a great many cases where short anceps at the end of these cola does as a matter of fact register a break in synaphea (e.g. in a pherecratean following glyconic), but it does so only on the same footing as long anceps, not as brevis in longo. The point argued here is that it *need* not mean break, and that, though the rhythm – × has a natural clausular effect, yet if, exceptionally, synaphea is required at the end of such a colon, the short anceps makes a smoother carry-through than long anceps.

Aesch. *Ag.* 717–26=727–36 illustrates all these points.

[1] The significance of Pause in lyric is sometimes denied, and it is true that we understand very little of the principles of strophic construction; but Pause clearly does matter, since it is never overridden in responsion, i.e. Pause never corresponds to synaphea.

	ἔθρεψεν δὲ λέοντος ἶ-		χρονισθεὶς δ' ἀπέδειξεν ἦ-
	-νιν δόμοις ἀγάλακτον οὕ-		-θος τὸ πρὸς τοκέων· χάριν
719	-τως ἀνὴρ φιλόμαστον,	‖	γὰρ τροφεῦσιν ἀμείβων
	ἐν βιότου προτελείοις		μηλοφόνοισιν ἐν ἄταις
	ἅμερον, εὐφιλόπαιδα		δαῖτ' ἀκέλευστος ἔτευξεν,
722	καὶ γεραροῖς ἐπίχαρτον.	‖	αἵματι δ' οἶκος ἐφύρθη,
	πολέα δ' ἔσχεν ἀγκάλαις		ἄμαχον ἄλγος οἰκέταις,
724	νεοτρόφου τέκνου δίκαν	‖	μέγα σίνος πολυκτόνον.
	φαιδρωπὸν ποτὶ χεῖρα σαί-		ἐκ θεοῦ δ' ἱερεύς τις ἄ-
	-νοντα γαστρὸς ἀνάγκαις.		-τας δόμοις προσεθρέφθη.

Glyc.+glyc.+pher. – ∪ – ∪ ∪ – ⏓‖. The period-close is obvious. The next 3 lines are pendant hemiepe – ∪ ∪ – ∪ ∪ – × followed by 2 lecythia ∪ ∪ ∪ – ∪ – ∪ – and glyc.+pher. clausula. Pause is clear at 719 (catalexis, change of metre), 722 (hiatus ant.), 724 (brevis in longo ant.). The question must be left open for the hemiepe 720–2, which may be all isolated or all in synaphea, or the short anceps in both str. and ant. 721 may emphasise synaphea with the following line to the exclusion of the preceding one. (723 is also uncertain.)

The ambiguity of the phenomena, shorn of performance, and our limited understanding of strophic structure, mean that certainty is usually unattainable; in fact the effect of the above argument is to add to the uncertainties. But this extra fluidity, patiently observed, may be useful in helping to defend our slender knowledge of strophic composition against premature attempts to classify these structures in preconceived moulds of our own manufacture. There can be no doubt that, outside the most complex forms of choral lyric—of Pindar, Simonides, Bacchylides—the basic structural unit of song in all poets is the colon. The art of building cola into a strophe is one of infinite variety, suppleness and finesse, especially in the dramatists, and often all we can do is to note certain characteristic habits of each poet and certain special effects that appear, on careful observation, to be intended in a given stanza. One of the nicest points to judge is where, and how far, the metrical shape is underlining the rhetorical.

For the dactylic clausula, the parodos of the *Agamemnon* (104–59) is of unique interest, with the – × close marking off all lengths from dimeter to octameter. The majority of these are most naturally interpreted as period-ends, taking their cue, as it were, from the conventional opening hexameter. But the last 9 lines of the 'mesode', 150–9, deserve special attention:

μή τινας ἀντιπνόους Δαναοῖς χρονίας ἐχενῇδας ἀπλοίας
τεύξῃ, σπευδομένα θυσίαν ἑτέραν, ἄνομόν τιν', ἄδαιτον,
νεικέων τέκτονα σύμφυτον, οὐ δεισήνορα.
μίμνει γὰρ φοβερὰ παλίνορτος
  οἰκονόμος δολία μνάμων μῆνις τεκνόποινος.
τοιάδε Κάλχας[1] ξὺν μεγάλοις ἀγαθοῖς ἀπέκλαγξεν
μόρσιμ' ἀπ' ὀρνίθων ὁδίων οἴκοις βασιλείοις·
τοῖς δ' ὁμόφωνον
  αἴλινον αἴλινον εἰπέ, τὸ δ' εὖ νικάτω.

The two majestic heptameters coincide throughout in word-end, each after the first word cutting across the metron-pattern. The next line swerves sharply (cf. 106=125) into a rhythm which outlines the metra: νεικέων | τέκτονα | σύμφυτον | οὐ δεισήνορα. | The strong rhetorical pause and the resumption of metron-cutting in the next line make colon-end certain here; indeed so strong is the effect of a change of rhythm that one is tempted to make this an exception to normal classical usage and suppose a period-close in an open dactyl.[2] In any case the next two lines should be left in synaphea, since παλίνορτος with its short anceps ⏑ ⏑ – ⏓ though obligatory colon-end is not brevis in longo, and the advantage of keeping synaphea instead of Pause in this ominous roll of epithets need not be laboured. Similarly at the end of the stanza τοῖς δ' ὁμόφωνον is in synaphea with αἴλινον, and the refrain which in strophe and antistrophe stood in grammatical and metrical detachment is the third time rhetorically and metrically linked with the preceding phrase.[3]

Thus when the epigrammatists quoted by Hephaestion (4. 16) ingeniously fit the names Ἀριστο-|-γείτων and Ἀπολλό-|-δωρος

[1] The hexameter should be left intact with the proper name breaking conventional rhythm.

[2] See below, p. 200.

[3] Did the penultimate long in such a case perhaps assume the full value of two shorts, unlike other dactylic longs (according to Dion. Hal.)?

into the elegiac couplet by dividing them between hexameter and pentameter, the licence consists solely in the splitting of a word where there should be period-close, not in the use of short anceps in synaphea.

Hephaestion's description of the close of dactyls catalectic εἰς δισύλλαβον can thus be accepted as indicating an incomplete final metron, which however is not – ∪ but – × (anceps proper). His 'catalectic εἰς συλλαβήν' is straightforward. What of his acatalectic close – ∪ ∪, which can become – ∪ – by 'final anceps'?

Hephaestion makes no clear distinction between colon-end in synaphea and period-end with Pause; a 'line' to him is a line, and in his exposition of typical lines he does not distinguish between what is possible in the one kind or the other. His notion of 'final anceps' as accommodating either brevis in longo or (so to speak) longa in brevi made the point immaterial for him, though he might note the occurrence of such a final longa. Thus in illustrating the acatalectic tetrameter he says Alcman composed whole strophes in this metre and quotes one:

Μῶσ' ἄγε Καλλιόπα θύγατερ Διός,
ἄρχ' ἐρατῶν ϝεπέων, ἐπὶ δ' ἵμερον
ὕμνῳ καὶ χαρίεντα τίθει χορόν.

All these lines end in the acatalectic metron – ∪ ∪,[1] and Hephaestion shows no concern that the first two are in synaphea with the

[1] Neither Hephaestion nor any other Greek recognises the doctrine now fashionable among modern theorists (deriving I think from linguistics) that any 'closed' final syllable, even with a short vowel, is long unless the final consonants can be transferred to a following word. To a Greek, any syllable with a short vowel was short unless at least two consonants (mute + liquid apart) intervened before a following vowel, or, in words like ἔξ, φλέψ, Τίρυνς, intervened before silence fell. That the same principle applied in Latin is proved with exemplary clarity by Seneca, *Oed.* 449–66 (acatalectic dactyls written κατὰ στίχον). What the Greek *ear* actually measured, of course, was not 'the syllable', as we in our print-and-paper-limited fashion take it, but, in a sequence of syllables in synaphea, the time taken to move from the beginning of one vowel-sound to the beginning of the next. Metric was to the Greeks essentially a musical phenomenon, and singing-tone is a matter of vowel-sounds.

following, while the third, as ending the strophe, gives period-close and Pause; whereas we, accustomed to the practice of later poets, are sufficiently startled. (This point will be taken up below.) But most of his illustrations of acatalectic final metron are concerned with so-called 'aeolic dactyls', which he defines as dactylic lines of length varying from 4 to 6 metra, with the first metron any kind of disyllable, the middle ones dactyls, the last either acatalectic (dactyl or cretic) or catalectic εἰς δισύλλαβον (or εἰς συλλαβήν, he says, but gives no examples, nor have any survived). Thus he quotes Sappho (130 and 131 as a continuous sequence):

ἔρος δηὖτέ μ' ὀ λυσιμέλης δόνει, — ∪ —
γλυκύπικρον ἀμάχανον ὄρπετον. — ∪ ∪
Ἄτθι, σοὶ δ' ἔμεθεν μὲν ἀπήχθετο — ∪ ∪
φροντίσδην, ἐπὶ δ' Ἀνδρομέδαν πόται — ∪ —

The lines, unlike the Alcman above, are composed κατὰ στίχον, each a self-contained period. We should tend to think of the end of the second and third as brevis in longo, but for Hephaestion the second and third are the norm, while the first and fourth by licence of final anceps end in a cretic. He is committed to this interpretation because for him the lines are dactyls, their only abnormality being the 'first metron'. Similarly 110

θυρώρῳ πόδες ἐπτορόγυιοι

is an aeolic tetrameter catalectic εἰς δισύλλαβον. But looking at Lesbian metres as a whole we find that he has omitted the smallest size in this series of rhythms, the glyconic × × — ∪ ∪ — ∪ — χαίροισ' ἔρχεο κἄμεθεν, which to him instead of being an aeolic trimeter acatalectic × × — ∪ ∪ — ∪ ∪ is an 'antispastic dimeter' × × — ∪ ∪ — ∪ —; yet the principle of construction could be represented as the same as that of 'aeolic dactyls', and he could have found a form catalectic εἰς δισύλλαβον in the pherecratean (111) × × — ∪ ∪ — —.

3

The glyconic however is the smallest size in another colon-series also, the asclepiads, × × – ⏑ ⏑ – – ⏑ ⏑ – ⏑ – (antispastic trimeter to Hephaestion) etc. which begin and end like the former 'dactylic' series, but expand on a different principle in the middle. The Lesbians associate the glyconic in stanzas with both 'aeolic dactyls' (Sapph. 94) and asclepiads (Alc. 5, 67); should not a logical analysis then give the same account of the close – ⏑ ⏑ – ⏑ – of both types of rhythm, of whatever length, making the final syllable long, with possible brevis in longo like any other?

It is hardly possible to give a categorical answer to this question. Certainly Hephaestion's formulation of 'final anceps' would not hold for the generality of Greek metric, where in all cases where it is not anceps proper it takes the form of brevis in longo. But Lesbian poetry is to some extent a closed enclave with its own particular laws, which suffered some modification when its phrases were assimilated into later polymetry. ('Aeolic dactyls' as such were not assimilated at all.) Since 'aeolic dactyls' are stichoi, each a period followed by Pause, there is no proof available of the nature of the last syllable. Only the glyconic, which can appear (Sapph. 96) in such close synaphea with what follows that it ends in the middle of a word, demonstrates firmly that its last syllable is true long, and the glyconic, as we have seen, has ambiguous connections. The neater solution is undoubtedly to keep in line with the rest of Greek metric and formulate the end of 'aeolic dactyls' as – ⏑ ⏑ – ⏑ –, with allowance for the normal brevis in longo. But the surprisingly high proportion of these verses which do as a matter of fact end in a short syllable leaves a certain uneasiness; perhaps they really were intended to slide softly to a close in – ⏑ ×,[1]

ἠράμαν μὲν ἔγω σέθεν Ἄτθι πάλαι ποτά,

the frequent short anceps emphasising their inclusion within the uncontracted dactylic rhythm.

In examining the metres of early lyric, it is important not to lose sight of this danger of trying to make it conform prematurely to

[1] See below, pp. 202 ff.

later, ‘classical’ usage. The regional peculiarity of Lesbian metric is a unique phenomenon, but perhaps we ought to be more ready to recognise occasional individual non-conformity to what we have come to regard as the fundamental habits of Greek metric. The early lyric poets created an astonishing variety of metres and in general set the norm for later practice, but acceptance among later poets was not quite wholesale. ‘Aeolic base’, for instance, was no longer allowed to break the rule against anceps iuxta anceps; it survived only in the forms – × (where it was allowed resolution) or by inversion × –,[1] and only[2] in the context of the second of its two alternative series mentioned above: glyconic, pherecratean, hipponactean, phalaecean, asclepiad. Alcman, a poet of singular originality, seems to have invented a prolonged form of dactylic close . . . – ∪ ∪] – ∪ – – which he uses as the final clausula of a stanza to give extra definition after earlier – × :

πολλάκι δ’ ἐν κορυφαῖς ὀρέων, ὅκα — – ∪ ∪
  θεοῖσι ϝάδῃ πολύφανος ἑορτά, — – –
χρύσιον ἄγγος ἔχοισα, μέγαν σκύφον, — – ∪ ∪
  οἷά τε ποιμένες ἄνδρες ἔχουσιν, — – –
χερσὶ λεόντεον ἐν γάλα θεῖσα — – ×̆
  τυρὸν ἐτύρησας μέγαν ἄτρυφον ἀργιφόνταν.[3] — – ∪ – –

(The construction is clearly triadic.) In the Louvre Parthenion he startlingly uses a colon with the same final clausula in responsion (repeatedly) to a tetrameter catalectic εἰς συλλαβήν:

[1] The only non-Lesbian instance of ∪ ∪ appears to be in the scolion (903 P) ὑπὸ παντὶ λίθῳ σκορπίος ὦ ἑταῖρ’ ὑποδύεται (cf. Praxilla 750 P), a special licence in order to accommodate the proverb ὑπὸ παντὶ λίθῳ σκορπίος.

[2] Ibycus uses the form – ∪ to start off dactyls in the penultimate line of the stanza of his Polycrates-poem. For Soph. *Ant.* 966 f. see below.

[3] Alcm. 56 P, adopting Hermann’s and Welcker’s emendations and (in his important article ‘Lyrische Dactylen’, *RhM* lxxii, 1917) Fraenkel’s interpretation of the clausula. It must be admitted however that the text is uncertain, and much disputed. Alcm. 91 P χρύσιον ὅρμον ἔχων ῥαδινᾶν πετάλοισι καλχᾶν has the same rhythm; as it is an isolated line we cannot be certain that it was a final clausula.

πaγὸν ἀεθλοφόρον καναχάποδα — ⏑ ⏑
τῶν ὑποπετριδίων ὀνείρων. — ⏑ — —

ἐξ ʽΑγησιχόρας δὲ νεάνιδες — ⏑ ⏑
εἰρήνας ἐρατᾶς ἐπέβαν. — ⏑ ⏑ —

This odd case of 'approximate responsion' took no root in later practice[1] but remains as an isolated reminder of the length to which experiment could go in early lyric. The 'prolonged' clausula itself had little subsequent history, so far as we can trace. Ibycus uses it in his Polycrates-poem (quoted below, p. 201), a triadic construction in which strophe and antistrophe consist (all in synaphea) of 2 dactylic tetrameters acatalectic followed by the same line as Alcman 56. 6 and 91 quoted above: – ⏖ – ⏖ – | ⏑ ⏑ – ⏑ ⏑ – ⏑ – –.[2] The shape of this line in both poets might suggest that it was felt as a hexameter-equivalent, but for the disturbing responsion of Alcman's tetrameter-clausulae in the Parthenion. In his most famous fragment 286 P Ibycus uses this shorter closing line (l. 7) οὐδεμίαν κατάκοιτος ὥραν like Alcman's rhythm to end off a dactylic series of open tetrameters in synaphea and also perhaps (l. 12) as a separate final clausula:[3]

9 Θρηίκιος βορέας ἀίσ-
-σων παρὰ Κύπριδος ἀζαλέαις μανί-
-αισιν ἐρεμνὸς ἀθαμβὴς
12 ἐγκρατέως πάιθεν φυλάσσει || H

The relation of this line to conventional dactyls is however complicated here by its more obvious relation to the 'ibycean' ἦρι μὲν

[1] The 'tetrasyllabic scansion' of Pindar which claimed many such responsions anywhere in the verse was given its death-blow by Maas, *Die neuen Respfr.* 1913 and 1921. This would in any case have been a totally unrelated phenomenon.

[2] That this is one line is evident from l. 42; elsewhere the word-end is simply a caesura, as in the two Alcman instances. The second part of the line would be inexplicable in isolation.

[3] The shape of the whole poem is bafflingly uncertain. Snell's reconstruction, making ἦρι μὲν . . . ὥραν epode, and ll. 8–12 the following strophe, has much in its favour—except for the stubbornly resurgent impression that ἦρι μὲν αἵ τε Κυδώνιαι (with introductory μέν) was the opening line of the poem. Possibly 8–12 are lacunose, and should correspond to 1–7.

αἵ τε Κυδώνιαι – ⏑ ⏑ – ⏑ ⏑ – ⏑ – which, three times repeated, opens the stanza. Snell (GM³, p. 20) would take this as a dactylic trimeter acatalectic with final anceps in Hephaestion's sense. If text and colometry of ll. 9–12 were to be accepted as in the version above (both are highly uncertain), this would be ruled out, since the cut in ἀίσ/σων would show beyond any doubt that the last syllable of the colon was long, not final anceps. But even without this confirmation the three strong final syllables in the opening lines Κυδώνιαι, ῥοᾶν, Παρθένων and the relation to the clausular – ⏑ ⏑ – ⏑ ⏑ – ⏑ – – make it very unnatural to take the ibycean as anything but a line with four long syllables, passing from double-short to single-short, and the clausular colon as the same with added anceps ('pendant' close). If Ibycus adopted the latter from Alcman he may have interpreted it differently. Whether he regarded this line and its blunt form the ibycean as a dactylic variation is a question impossible to answer. He *may* have been familiar with it in its Lesbian context, as the 'alcaic decasyllable'.

To judge by the contexts in which they appear in the lyrics of drama, both ibycean and its pendant form have settled down as forms of 'aeolic' colon moving from double- to single-short:

Ἅλιε καὶ φάος ἁμέρας	– ⏑ ⏑ – ⏑ ⏑ – ⏑ –
οὐράνιαί τε δῖναι νεφέλας δρομαίου	– ⏑ ⏑ – ⏑ – – ⏑ ⏑ – ⏑ – –

(Eur. *Alc.* 244). The relation of the ibycean to the shorter cola **d s** and **d s** × is obvious; it is essentially the same as in the alcaic stanza, where the first two lines each combine iambo-trochaic × – ⏑ – × with – ⏑ ⏑ – ⏑ – (**d s**) while the last two, taken together in synaphea, lengthen both the iambo-trochaic (to an enneasyllable) and the **d s** segment (to **dd s** × or 'alcaic decasyllable'). There is no dactylic connection. Indeed there seems no reason to characterise these rhythms in the lyric of drama as cola displaying 'Daktylenschlüsse' of Alcman's type (so Fraenkel and many others, following him). Of the list of passages in tragedy quoted by Fraenkel in these terms the great majority are alcaic decasyllables (in Aeschylus sometimes with initial anceps added), which are clearly lifted as wholes from their familiar aeolic context as sonorous clausular rhythms, more substantial than the related short 'aristophanean' **d s** ×. Only rarely, *P.V.* 166, Eur. *Or.* 1391,[1] does this hinge on to open dactyls. Of course in the typical manner of tragic polymetry dactylic cola of various kinds (hemiepe, trimeters or tetrameters ending – ×) may appear in the context, as in the noble stanzas Aesch. *Supp.* 524–55, but even where they follow such cola that does not make the aristophaneans or alcaic decasyllables into 'lyric dactyls'; they do not here merge into the dactylic movement, and their other affinities (e.g. with iambo-choriambic) are equally apparent from the context.

There are two passages in tragedy which seem to be generally accepted as dactylic with 'lesbian' ending – ᴗ –, but each has a very weak and implausible case. Soph. *Ant.* 966–7=979–80 is metrically ambiguous as well as textually insoluble. Starting, as one must, from the antistrophe,

κατὰ δὲ τακόμενοι μέλεοι μελέαν πάθαν
κλαῖον, ματρὸς ἔχοντες ἀνύμφευτον γονάν

we are invited[2] to see 'aeolic dactyls'

ᴗ ᴗ ᴗ – ᴗ ᴗ – ᴗ ᴗ – ᴗ ᴗ – ᴗ –
– – – ᴗ ᴗ – ᴗ ᴗ – – – – ᴗ –

with resolution admitted in the base and contraction (-φευ-) in one dactyl. Such a hybrid is scarcely recognisable; contraction in an early dactyl might be conceivable, but not at such a sensitive point near the end of the rhythm. The second line must be taken for what it appears to be, an elegiambus set on aeolic base (tragic style)—a kind of long and daring extension of the glyconic type of colon:

– $\overline{\times}$ – ᴗ ᴗ – ᴗ ᴗ – $\overline{\times}$ – ᴗ –

This sends us back for another look at the first line, which can easily (with μελέαν πάθαν, -έαν in synizesis) be given the same pattern:

ᴗ ᴗ ᴗ – ᴗ ᴗ – ᴗ ᴗ – $\overset{\smile}{\times}$ – ᴗ –

[1] Fraenkel may be right in claiming Eur. *Or.* 1300 as a 'praxillean' (**d d d s** ×) Daktylenschluss, but it depends precariously on the form ἐμοῖσι, since with ἐμοῖς it becomes an ordinary elegiambus.

[2] E.g. by W. Kraus, *Strophengestaltung in der gr. Tr.* p. 129.

With this in mind, my reconstruction of 966

παρὰ δὲ κυανέων πελαγέων πετρῶν διδύμας ἁλὸς

would be, not to throw out πετρῶν as a gloss, but with Triclinius to dismiss πελαγέων as an unwanted doublet:

παρὰ δὲ κυανέων διδύμας ἁλὸς πετρῶν
⏑ ⏑ ⏑ – ⏑ ⏑ – ⏑ ⏑ – ⏓ – ⏑ –

supplying the dative for παρά in the next line ἀκτᾷ Βοσπορίᾳ,[1] the rest of it being beyond restoration. The strong ending πετρῶν is more appropriate than the final anceps of ἁλὸς for the long glyconic-substitute colon.

The other passage is the parodos of *Medea*, 131 ff., a stanza with no antistrophe. Here, after some anapaests which make a straightforward start but then proceed unaccountably to shuffle and drag their feet, we are given two unparalleled pentameters of 'lyric dactyls' (ending, that is, in cretics – ⏑ – though without the excuse of aeolic base) and a syncopated iambic trimeter:

ἔκλυον φωνάν, ἔκλυον δὲ βοὰν
τᾶς δυστάνου Κολχίδος, οὐδέ πω
ἤπιος· ἀλλ' ὦ γηραιά,
λέξον. ἐπ' ἀμφιπύλου γὰρ ἔσω μελάθρου βοὰν
ἔκλυον· οὐδὲ συνήδομαι ὦ γύναι ἄλγεσιν
δώματος, ἐπεί μοι φίλον κέκρανται.

The whole of this construction is balanced precariously on the one word βοὰν (since ἄλγεσι[ν] is obviously neither here nor there), and Elmsley, not unnaturally taking this as a copyist's careless repetition from above, substituted γόον, which in some editions has won deserved recognition. Hermann saw that the anapaests must end with the monometer τᾶς δυστάνου (before change of metre, cf. 150), leaving the correption οὐδέ πω ἤπιος for dactyls, and chose to read ἀλλὰ γεραιά (one might perhaps prefer to risk ἀλλ' ὦ γραῖα) rather than the γηραιά (for which V has a penchant, cf. *Hec.* 143) which scrapes together so awkward a paroemiac. We then have three dactylic pentameters followed by iambics:

[1] H. Lloyd Jones, in *C.Q.* n.s. vii (1957), 23.

ἔκλυον φωνάν, ἔκλυον δὲ βοὰν
τᾶς δυστάνου
Κολχίδος, οὐδέ πω ἤπιος· ἀλλ' ὦ γραῖα,
λέξον· ἀπ'[1] ἀμφιπύλου γὰρ ἐγὼ μελάθρου γόον
ἔκλυον, οὐδὲ συνήδομαι ὦ γύναι ἄλγεσι
δώματος, ἐπεί μοι φίλον κέκρανται.

It is true that this turn of clausula is characteristic of Sophocles[2] rather than Euripides, but there is probably another *Alc.* 464=474.

4

'Aeolic dactyls', then, whatever their nature, vanish from later lyric, which confines itself to the shorter set phrases **d s** and **d d s**, always in the strong ibycean form in which the last syllable is true long. Similarly, the dactylic *final* clausula – ⏑ – – used by Alcman survives in extant lyric only in Ibycus' Polycrates-song, without the strange responsion of the Parthenion; in drama we have again a series of set types, from aristophanean **d s** × to 'alcaic decasyllable' **d d s** × and 'praxillean' **d d d s** × (Aesch. *Ag.* 1548, *Eum.* 996, Soph. *Ant.* 134–5), not as dactylic cola nor as final clausulae. The dramatic poets, in fact, while developing an unexampled polymetric richness of strophic construction, keep to a much more conventional metrical grammar, so to speak, within the colon.

The result is that we are badly placed for judging abnormalities in the early lyric poets, being continually uncertain in the fragmentary state of the tradition whether the problem we are investigating is a

[1] Paley, Vitelli. The usual text (see above) seems to me untranslatable. Even supposing that ἀμφιπύλου could be a noun meaning 'doorway' (which looks like an invention *ad hoc* by one Σ), is this really Greek for 'I at my doorway heard a cry within her hall'? Elmsley's explanation—that the Chorus had heard her through the back door and now comes to call at the front—is undoubtedly right; ἀμφιπύλου in its natural sense 'with a door at each end' makes this another case where the σκηνή is imagined as concealing a through-passage from back to front, as with ἀμφιτρῆτος Soph. *Phil.* 19 and Eur. *Cyc.* 706. Cf. 'Seen and Unseen on the Greek Stage', *Wiener Studien* lxix (1956), 105 [=above, p. 128].

[2] See below, pp. 205 ff.

real one or would disappear with a better text, whether it was properly understood by an ancient authority reporting on it, whether it genuinely illustrates an early experiment which failed to get canonised. Dactyls, which naturally play a large part in the development of early lyric, present us with some peculiarly awkward examples of this.

It is unfortunate that the early poet who makes greatest use of dactyls, Stesichorus, has survived in such scanty and unreliable quotations (to which P. Oxy. 2359 and 2360 can add nothing helpful) that close metrical analysis would be a waste of time. All we can deduce is that his lines take off in rising (⏖ –) as well as in falling rhythm, and that his long periods sometimes appear to be composed of cola with link-anceps and some admixture of single-short (trochaic?) which suggest a beginning of something like dactylo-epitrite.[1] But where even a slight modification of literary dialect in this word or that can quite change the metrical aspect of a passage we can get no further than vague generalities.

We have already noticed the isolation, in all lyric known to us, of Alcman's anomalous responsion of final clausulae in the Louvre Parthenion. There repetition puts the phenomenon beyond doubt. The strophe of three acatalectic tetrameters quoted by Hephaestion (above, p. 191) is devoid of such confirmation, and we are left wondering whether in Alcman a final clausula can really end in the double-short of an open dactyl – ⏑ ⏑ ||. This is no brevis in longo, which would give a line out of balance – ⏑ ⏑ – ⏑ ⏑ – ⏑ ⏑ – ⏑ –, in no rhythmical relation to the other two[2] and unknown in Greek lyric of any period. The only possible alternative would be – ⏑ ×, and for this again the evidence elsewhere is slight and very difficult to assess.

Even if we possessed a dozen strophes of Alcman 67, all ending in a short syllable, this would not be conclusive proof, since theoreti-

[1] P. Oxy. 2387, Alcm. 3P, gives Alcman also a hitherto unexampled 'elegiambus' – ⏑ ⏑ – ⏑ ⏑ – ⏓ – ⏑ – – as a final clausula to open-ended tetrameters.

[2] Unlike the ibycean – ⏑ ⏑ – ⏑ ⏑ – ⏑ – which the ear readily accepts among tetrameters.

cally a thirteenth might still show long anceps. All we could establish would be that for Alcman the double-short was the norm, and since in all other metres ending in anceps the long form heavily predominates because of its greater steadying power we could say that the possibility of – ⏑ × could be discounted until an example actually appeared. It should be noted that in the 'metrical grammar' of the classical age – ⏑ × whether clausular or not is quite unsupported, since nowhere is an anceps iuxta breve permitted, while of – ⏑ ⏑‖ there are faint and inconclusive traces, as in Aesch. *Ag.* 153 (p. 190 above), Soph. *Phil.* 1205, Ar. *Peace* 116 (tetrameters with hiatus before the next line), and possibly Eur. *Supp.* 277 in a hexameter.

Casting around in early lyric for any straws that might seem to support one or the other of these alternatives, we find a curious clausula in the Polycrates-poem of Ibycus:[1]

νῦν δέ μοι οὔτε ξειναπάταν Πάριν   str.
ἔστ' ἐπιθύμιον οὔτε τανίσφυρον
ὑμνῆν Κασσάνδραν Πριάμοιό τε παῖδας ἄλλους
Τροίας θ' ὑψιπύλοιο ἁλώσιμον   ant.
ἆμαρ ἀνώνυμον· οὐδ' ἐπελεύσομαι
ἡρώων ἀρετὰν ὑπεράφανον οὕς τε κοίλαι
νᾶες πολυγόμφοι ἐλεύσαν   ep.
Τροίᾳ κακὸν ἥρωας ἐσθλούς·
τῶν μὲν κρείων Ἀγαμέμνων
ἄρχε Πλεισθενίδας βασιλεὺς ἀγὸς ἀνδρῶν
Ἀτρέος ἐσθλοῦ πάις ἐκ πατρός.

This is clearly a dactylic stanza in triadic structure. The little strophe and antistrophe are each a period of two tetrameters in synaphea with a line showing the 'prolonged' clausula in single-short of Alcman's Cheese-poem (above, p. 194). The three following are the Πηληιάδεω Ἀχιλῆος section of the hexameter, used freely by Stesichorus as one of his 'rising dactyls' (οὐκ ἔστ' ἔτυμος λόγος οὗτος); then comes a pentameter – ⏑ – ⏑ ⏑ – ⏑ ⏑ – ⏑ ⏑ – –

[1] Text as in D². Nothing turns on the particular small supplements adopted.

starting off in single-short rhythm, then the clausula – ⏑ ⏑ – – ⏑ ⏑ – ⏑ ⏑. The other decipherable epodic clausulae in the text are χρυσοέθειραν διὰ Κύπριδα, . . . ἄρ]γυρος, ὡς κατ' ἀοιδὰν καὶ ἐμὸν κλέος. Compared with the great preponderance of long anceps at all other period-closes in the poem this 100% showing of – ⏑ ⏑ seems unlikely to be accidental. The line seems to be in form a dactylic tetrameter with inner syncopation – ⏑ ⏑ – ‸ – ⏑ ⏑ – ⏑ ⏑ instead of catalexis; in principle like the trochaics of Soph. *O.C.* 1734–6, which are obviously all in synaphea, so that the clausula αἰῶνα τλάμον' ἔξω must be – ‸ – ⏑ – ⏑ – –.[1]

So far then, there is a slight bias in favour of the possibility of clausular – ⏑ ⏑|| in early lyric. But on the other side arises the spectre which has always troubled serious metricians, the notorious 'Solvitur' asynarteton of Archilochus which Hephaestion quotes to show that the poet treated the last syllable of the dactylic tetrameter as anceps:

καὶ βήσσας ὀρέων δυσπαιπάλους, οἷος ἦν ἐφ' ἥβης

Our ear registers this as a bump which disturbs the flow of the rhythm, and it is hard to believe that a Greek ear was not affected too. Punctuation is found in other examples between the tetrameter and the ithyphallic, though at the other extreme there is a barely minimum diaeresis in

τοῖος γὰρ φιλότητος ἔρως ὑπὸ καρδίην ἐλυσθείς

The principle of all Archilochus' asynarteta is that two metrically distinct cola are juxtaposed, leaving word-end between them, to form a single Verse (in the German sense); the two segments are always so chosen that they *can* form a new single line; thus not only is there no anceps iuxta anceps or iuxta breve at the join but if the type of movement changes it is always (in the genuine Archilochian cases) from double-short to single-short—the smoothest kind of continuous flow, as if the initial impulse were slowly fading out. Moreover, his other asynartete segments are portions detached from existent verses,[2] and one would naturally look, for this open dactylic

[1] It cannot be ia. dim. cat., since with preceding ἄπορος it would leave anceps iuxta anceps. Cf. Soph. *Ant.* 881–2.

[2] Snell, *Gr. Met.*^{3}, 31 ff.

tetrameter, to the hexameter cut off at bucolic diaeresis; where would he have got the notion of a colon ending – ◡ × ?

Though one longs to be rid of this anomaly, neither tinkering with the dialect (why should Archilochus suddenly affect the accusative plural δυσπαιπάλος?) nor emendation of so awkwardly incomprehensible a fragment (δυσπαίπαλος, οἷος would give syntactical improvement but no easily imaginable sense) can offer any solution likely to be acceptable. Unfortunately the only verses that might be adduced as a parallel fall just short of cogency themselves. Hellenistic poets took up the epode form again, and used some of the asynarteta of Archilochus as ingredients in various combinations. Hephaestion tells us that the 'Solvitur' was a favourite with later poets, and we find some half-dozen instances of it in Callimachus and Theocritus. All of these are normal except for one in Theocritus, *Ep.* 20, where it alternates with phalaeceans:

ὁ μικκὸς τόδ' ἔτευξε τᾷ Θραΐσσᾳ	phal.
Μήδειος τὸ μνᾶμ' ἐπὶ τᾷ ὁδῷ κἠπέγραψε Κλείτας.	solv.
ἕξει τὰν χάριν ἁ γυνὰ ἀντὶ τήνων	phal.
ὧν τὸν κῶρον ἔθρεψε· τί μάν; ἔτι χρησίμα καλεῖται.	solv.

The second line of this is generally taken to be a deliberate echo of the δυσπαιπάλους rhythm, and it is true that Theocritus does occasionally leave the article in hiatus in the hexameter (ταὶ ὄιες, etc.). If so, this still does not imply that Archilochus used the licence often; there is nothing in Hephaestion's statement inconsistent with its being an isolated instance, and he probably took over the datum from Alexandrian scholarship. But the Theocritean line is itself not unambiguous; if he used 'prodelision' or synizesis to scan τᾷ ὁδῷ as two long syllables it would be no stranger than the same device in the phalaecean just below; Hephaestion (15. 51) tells us that Cratinus used the 'Solvitur' in the form – ◡ ◡ – ◡ ◡ – ◡ ◡ – – | – ◡ – ◡ – – (probably κατὰ στίχον):

χαίρετε πάντες ὅσοι πολύβωτον   ποντίαν Σέριφον,

and Theocritus might for all we know have regarded the contraction as a legitimate if rare variation on the usual rhythm.

The other possible instance of – ⏑× is in the Polycrates-poem. One strophe (ll. 23 ff.) reads

> καὶ τὰ μὲν ἂν Μοίσαι σεσοφισμέναι
> εὖ ῾Ελικωνίδες ἐμβαίεν λογ̣[
> θνατὸς δ᾽ οὔ κεν ἀνὴρ διερὸς τὰ ἕκαστα εἴποι.

The γ is doubtful and the rest is missing, but what word other than λόγῳ can be supplied? Yet all the other tetrameters end – ⏑ ⏑ in synaphea with the following line; then, since obviously no one could believe in a chance brevis in longo in all corresponding tetrameters, we should have to assume here again a colon-end – ⏑× like δυσπαιπάλους.

We are left with a row of indecisive phenomena. A cautious guess might follow the principle of economy in attempting to explain all of them taken together: that in early lyric there was a notion of a dactylic phrase ending in open double-short – ⏑ ⏑, which was usable not only as a colon in a longer period but could itself end a period. Exceptionally, this acquired a slight *rallentando* at the close by treating the last metron as – ⏑ ×, and, as it happens, our surviving examples are not at period-close but in synaphea within a period, where the effect is to our ear at least more disconcerting. It is one more piece of evidence that long anceps was in delivery very clearly distinct from true long. If 'aeolic dactyls' are accepted as also ending in – ⏑×, this is a somewhat different usage, confined to period-close, admitting long anceps more freely, and extending to a longer verse. Outside Lesbian only the dactylic tetrameter, complete or syncopated, appears to be susceptible of this treatment. In later lyric the unorthodox anceps disappears (apart from one possible imitation in Theocritus), but there are faint signs of the double-short of the dactyl being accepted before Pause.

5

In no metre is the practice of the three tragic poets more clearly distinct than in dactylic.[1] Aeschylus' long rolling periods and his

[1] Dactylo-epitrite is left out of account here, as a special development proceeding somewhat apart from other dactylic.

iambo-dactylic are spread over the fifteen years which cover the plays known to us, and were at the time of the *Frogs* regarded as his most easily recognisable metrical manner, perhaps to some extent inherited from Phrynichus (*Av.* 749, *Ran.* 1299). Sophocles' favourite colon is the open tetrameter, which in him shows a strong tendency to assimilate itself to the 'dimeter' length—four longs with their accompanying shorts, in various metres—which on the whole tends to predominate in the polymetry of drama. (The line is indeed often, rather confusingly, called 'dactylic dimeter'.) Euripides uses dactylic less frequently but more concentratedly than the other two. *Hcld.* 608 ff., *Andr.* 1173 ff., *Hel.* 375 ff., and above all the long triad of the complete ode *Phoen.* 784–832 are all homogeneous or nearly so, in cola of varied length.

The Sophoclean dactylic tetrameter appears, at least within the limits of our extant material, to be a lineal descendant of the colon of Alcman and Ibycus, capable of running in a series in synaphea and usually requiring a change of rhythm at the close. Its nature and its habits have often received cursory mention, but never, so far as I know, in chronological terms; yet when we come to examine it from this point of view, the development of a characteristically Sophoclean manner seems too intimately connected with other, unmistakable changes in his lyric to be merely an accidental product of survival.

Tr. is the only play which contains no dactylic tetrameters. In *Aj.* there is only the first line of the strophe of the parodos (172=182), which introduces a dactylo-epitrite stanza:

ἦ ῥά σε Ταυροπόλα Διὸς Ἄρτεμις,
ὢ μεγάλα φάτις, ὢ μᾶτερ αἰσχύνας ἐμᾶς

The transition to **d d** in the second colon is of the smoothest possible kind.

Ant. 332 ff. (πολλὰ τὰ δεινὰ) starts in aeolo-choriambic, moves over to iambic, ending in catalexis and Pause, then has a final period of two tetrameters and clausula

ἄφθιτον, ἀκαμάταν ἀποτρύεται,
ἰλλομένων ἀρότρων ἔτος εἰς ἔτος,
ἱππείῳ γένει πολεύων

all in synaphea. The last line (οὔρειόν τ' ἀκμῆτα ταῦρον in the antistrophe) has been very variously interpreted. 'Spondee + ithyphallic'—but what is 'spondee'? The most obvious way to take it is as doubly syncopated iambic: – · – · – ∪ – ∪ – –, and this may be right. Wilamowitz (*GV* 516) rather unattractively makes the line a trochaic dimeter, with ἱππίῳ and οὔρεον. Friedländer, followed by Kraus, *Stropheng.* 124, assimilates it to the rare clausula Aesch. *Pers.* 575=583, found also Eur. *Supp.* 804=810, ∪ – – ∪ – ∪ – –,

βοᾶτιν τάλαιναν αὐδάν (τὸ πᾶν δὴ κλύουσιν ἄλγος).
προσαυδῶ σε τὸν θανόντα (ἐν ἀγκῶσι τέκνα θῶμαι).

The first syllable of the *Ant.* clausula would then be long anceps, and this would be an isolated early example of what later became almost an obsessive habit with the poet, of checking the headlong falling movement of a dactylic tetrameter with a rising initial anceps. But the four[1] cases of initial short in the clausulae quoted above argue strongly against this identification, and though the matter is not susceptible of proof I find myself in reading those passages quite unable to accept anything but a short in either metrical context. How the colon is to be analysed is uncertain: perhaps it is a syncopated iambic line ∪ – – ∪ – ∪ – with a pendant extra syllable—as it were iambo-trochaic—at the end for clausular effect. In syncopated iambic the 'bacchiac' retains a short syllable.

For *Ant.* 341 I would personally prefer initial – (∪∪), whether with contraction or with diaeresis of the diphthong ἱππεΐῳ, οὐρέϊον, making the line an aeolo-choriambic – (∪∪) – ∪ – ∪ – – harking back to the style of the opening colon. In any case the first syllable is true long, so that here again Sophocles is making the obvious smooth transition from tetrameter to following colon.

In the earliest group[2] of plays, then, the open tetrameter is rare, and there is nothing, except perhaps its penultimate position in *Ant.*

[1] There appear to be three more in the fragments of Eur. *Andromeda* 117–18–19, all with initial short.

[2] It would of course be naïve to suppose that the mainly negative evidence of this colon could help to determine their order within the group, or that its absence in *Tr.* could be pressed in any way to contribute to the dating of that play, which rests on quite other evidence.

332 ff., specially characteristic in its use. In the parodos of *O.T.* there are the first signs of a change. The first strophe (151 ff.: Pearson's arrangement, with separate tetrameters and dimeters, consorts better with the whole ode than running them together where possible into hexameters) is mostly dactylic throughout and gives nothing new to report. But the second, after an opening period of two iambic dimeters and a paroemiac, continues (171):

	ᾧ τις ἀλέξεται· οὔτε γὰρ ἔκγονα		tetram.
×	κλυτᾶς χθονὸς αὔξεται οὔτε τόκοισιν	‖	expanded paroem.
	ἰηίων καμάτων ἀνέχουσι γυναῖκες·	‖	ia.+paroem.
	ἄλλον δ' ἂν ἄλλῳ προσίδοις ἅπερ εὔπτερον ὄρνιν	‖	iambo-dact. (cf. Aesch.)
	κρεῖσσον ἀμαιμακέτου πυρὸς ὄρμενον		tetram.
×	ἀκτὰν πρὸς ἑσπέρου θεοῦ.		ia. dim. cat.

Twice here the tetrameter forms a period with a colon opening in anceps, and the second of these is the final clausula. It may be noted[1] that in the meantime Euripides seems to have made the same transition in *Alc.* 463 and *Med.* 136, but with all the gaps in our available material this cannot be pressed. Aristophanes has the same dactyl/anceps once, in the final period of the stanza of the parodos of *Nub.* 288–90:

ἀλλ' ἀποσεισάμεναι νέφος ὄμβριον	tetram.
ἀθανάτας ἰδέας ἐπιδώμεθα	tetram.
τηλεσκόπῳ ὄμματι γαῖαν[2]	paroem.

The really important development, however, comes only in the last three plays.[3] Here the open tetrameter is used only occasionally

[1] See above, p. 198. Possibly there is a third instance in *Hipp.* 1109 = 1116 ἄλλα γὰρ ἄλλοθεν | ἀμείβεται, μετὰ δ' ἵσταται ἀνδράσιν αἰών dact. dim. followed by the same colon as *O.T.* 173 quoted above, ἰηίων καμάτων ἀνέχουσι γυναῖκες, but the metrical interpretation is here uncertain.

[2] Cf. *Av.* 1753–4. [Marginal note by author.]

[3] The evidence is enough to add a little further support to the strong case for a late dating of the Sophoclean *Electra*. Eur. also has such series of tetrams. in his (late) *Hypsipyle*, but without the characteristic Sophoclean clausula.

in choral stasima[1] but frequently in monody and kommos, often in a series of three or more cola, in contexts of passionate despair or urgent pleading or vehement rejection ('never, never, never...'). The parodos of *Electra* (121–250) has the form of a kommos between Electra and the Chorus, in the course of which the tetrameter occurs 28 times, singly or in groups of 2 or 4, and in every case except the last (236–8), where the movement sands up in contractions, it passes out into the anceps of an iambic colon. In the kommos of *Phil.* 1081–1218, the first part, which is strophic, contains ten instances, all single lines in synaphea with a following anceps (at 1092=1113 in a dochmiac); in the final ἀπολελυμένα 1169 ff. we seem all set for a long series at 1196, but there is an unexpected variation:

	– βᾶθί νυν ὦ τάλαν ὥς σε κελεύομεν.	– ∪ ∪
	– οὐδέποτ' οὐδέποτ', ἴσθι τόδ' ἔμπεδον,	– ∪ ∪
1198	οὐδ' εἰ πυρφόρος ἀστεροπητὴς	– –
	βροντᾶς αὐγαῖς μ' εἶσι φλογίζων.	– –
	ἐρρέτω Ἴλιον οἵ θ' ὑπ' ἐκείνῳ	– –
	πάντες ὅσοι τόδ' ἔτλασαν ἐμοῦ ποδὸς	– ∪ ∪
	ἄρθρον ἀπῶσαι. ἀλλ'	dim. – –
	ὦ ξένοι ἕν γέ μοι εὖχος ὀρέξατε.	– ∪ ∪
	– ποῖον ἐρεῖς τόδ' ἔπος; – ξίφος, εἴ ποθεν,	– ∪ ∪
	ἢ γένυν ἢ βελέων τι προπέμψατε.	– ∪ ∪ H
	– ὡς τίνα δὴ ῥέξῃς παλάμαν ποτέ;	– ∪ ∪
	– κρᾶτα καὶ ἄρθρ' ἀπὸ πάντα τέμω	
	χερί·	– ∪ ∪
	φονᾷ φονᾷ νόος ἤδη.	$\overset{\cup}{\times}$ – ∪ – ∪ ∪ – –

The final syllables in 1198–1200 do not make these into tetrameters catalectic εἰς δισύλλαβον; they are real contractions of the double-short, just like those earlier in the line in 1198 and 1199. The dimeter (adonean), if the text is to be trusted, gives an awkward synizesis across rhetorical pause; Jackson, *Marg. Scaen.* 103, may be right in deleting ἀλλ' as a later addition, and if so there is Pause here before

[1] As *Phil.* 861, in an epode; *O.C.* 676=689, each time followed as if through habit by anceps.

the agitated exchange which follows.[1] The aeolo-choriambic clausula 1209 opens as usual in anceps.

In *O.C.* the kommos of the parodos again ends in a long passage of ἀπολελυμένα, with more variations on the tetrameter-motif. 229 ff. is a πνῖγος of 6 tetrameters, of which the second, third and fourth each break the last word and leave one syllable to the beginning of the next line; this is the climax of the Chorus's agitation, when it has learnt the fearful identity of the blind stranger who has invaded its sanctuary. The πνῖγος ends with a dimeter and an iambic colon:

μή τι πέρα χρέος — ∪ ∪ — ∪ ∪
ἐμᾷ πόλει προσάψῃς. ⏑̽ — ∪ — ∪ — —

Antigone now pleads desperately against the sentence of dismissal; after an aeolic opening the pattern is (241 ff.) tetrameter, the nameless colon — ∪ ∪ — — ∪ —, 6 tetrameters, — ∪ ∪ — — ∪ —, 3 tetrameters, iambic monometer ⏓ ∪͡∪ ∪ — separated by hiatus from the final ithyphallic. The next kommos contains only two tetrameters, 540 = 547, each penultimate to the final clausula ia. trim. cat. The last kommos of the play has four, 1674–5 = 1701–2, before ia. dim. cat.

It has often been suggested that the great expansion, in Sophocles' late plays, of monody and lyric exchanges between actor and Chorus in place of reflective choral stasima is influenced by Euripides and the new music. This may well be so, though the preceding years are a long blank in our knowledge of Sophocles; but it should be noted that the metrical technique is wholly Sophocles' own, nowhere more so than in this development of the dactylic tetrameter.

[1] For the doubtful significance of the hiatus 1205–6 see above, p. 201. It may be no more than an empirical break at change of speaker, excused by the general agitation.

19

THE CHORUS IN THE ACTION OF GREEK TRAGEDY

Greek tragedy was born in Attica in the sixth century B.C. when some poet of genius, perhaps one called Thespis, set into a choral lyric performance insertions of recited solo speech, in a form of verse descended ultimately from Archilochus. The history of Greek tragedy, so far as we can follow it, is to an important extent made by the adjustment of the relation between these two elements, a fluctuating relation, sometimes close, sometimes looser. The spoken element quickly became dominant, since it was the chief vehicle of the forward movement of the action. The Chorus always impersonated a definite group of people; it was 'in' the story, not an impersonal Voice, but its anonymous collectivity tended to push it away from the centre, where things happened. This was emphasised by its physical separation from the speaking actors, in the orchestra where it had room to dance, and from which it had often to watch in silence long sequences of dramatic, even agonising intensity. Yet it always remained within speaking and listening contact with the actors. Thus half-in, half-out of the action, the Chorus had some curious and even illogical effects on the mechanics of staging—and incidentally proves itself the greatest stumbling-block in modern productions of these plays. But what I want to do here is to consider some effects of the presence of a Chorus upon the progress of the spoken action itself, as composed by the poet; for in this interaction of individuals and anonymous collective lies something of the distinctive character of Greek drama.

Obviously the degree of such interaction varies widely from one play to another. At one extreme, it might seem, are a few plays in which the fortunes of the Chorus itself are the subject of the play. The notion that this was in the earliest dramas universal or even usual is probably false, one of the sweeping conclusions drawn from our former belief in the early date of the *Supplices* of Aeschylus. We have Aristotle's word for it that Aeschylus cut down the proportion of lyric and made the spoken dialogue the most important thing in the play, but that is a different matter. Twice in Aeschylus, in *Supplices* and *Eumenides*, and again in the *Supplices* of Euripides the Chorus itself is a party to the main conflict. But this is not enough in itself to determine the relation of the Chorus to the action; there is no resemblance in this respect between the Aeschylean plays and the Euripidean. In the latter the Chorus (the mothers of the dead Seven against Thebes) is a passive body of sufferers and leaves its cause to be pleaded by actor-characters, Aethra and Adrastus and later Theseus; its own interventions in the dialogue are as scanty as in any play. In sharp contrast to this both Danaids and Eumenides assert their will and dominate the action. Is this simply because the intervening forty or so years had seen such a diminution of the role of the Chorus that a change of this sort was inevitable? That is partly the reason, of course, but there is more to it than that. The *Supplices* of Euripides, for all the edifying morality of its ideas, is dramatically not among the most successful plays, and all its characters are rather pallid and unmemorable. But more important is the growth of the rhetorical element in tragedy. If the bereaved Argive women have a cause to plead to Theseus it is unthinkable that at this date it should not be argued in detail, and opposed, in set speeches; and that is something a Chorus cannot do. For it is an unbroken law, all through the history of Greek tragedy, that though a Chorus may join in the dialogue to a limited extent it must never make a set speech, a 'rhesis', never marshal arguments, try to prove or refute a contention, or speak a descriptive set piece. The whole province of what Aristotle calls 'dianoia', the art of developing at length all that can appropriately be said on a given subject, is closed to the Chorus. In this union of speech and lyric which is Attic tragedy, while the actor's solo-lyric from the stage came in course of time to encroach upon the sphere of the Chorus, the Chorus never trespass upon the actor's ground; the Chorus-leader may *speak to* the actors but he makes no speeches.

Let us now return to Aeschylus' *Supplices* and *Eumenides*. In the former the Danaids have to *explain* their coming to the King of

Argos and *persuade* him to grant them asylum. They do not use their father Danaus as an intermediary but speak for themselves. How are they to convey all this complex information? and what 'persuasion' is possible without a rhetorical speech? Surely Peitho is the essence of rhetoric? Aeschylus' solution is interesting. The King enters (234) and comments wonderingly upon the strangeness of this suppliant-band, and the Chorus ask if he is the person in authority. He replies in a speech of 25 lines and asks them to explain *briefly* who they are, since his city disapproves of long speeches. The Chorus obediently state in 3 lines their claim to be Argives themselves, which provokes him to 14 lines of disbelief. The necessary information, or proof, is conveyed in a long interchange of short questions and answers, often line for line; sometimes the Chorus asks the questions (leading questions, these), sometimes the King, and it is established that their views of past history agree. Now they must *persuade*, and they do so in a pattern of lyric appeal alternating with his spoken expressions of doubt, unwillingness and indecision. He argues, but they do not—argument and lyric utterance are in Greek an uneasy association; they implore, they warn, they passionately reject his alternative suggestions. Finally (438 ff.) he sets out his agonising dilemma in a longer speech and seems on the point of refusing. Stronger pressure is necessary, and the Chorus force a decision in line-for-line spoken interchange—not the kind of stichomythia which answers point with point, thrusting and parrying in rhetorical debate, but something like this: 'You see these girdles?'—'Yes.' 'There *is* a way...' 'What do you mean?' 'If you do not do what I ask —' 'What will you do?' 'Hang myself on the images of your gods.' 'Oh horrible!' 'Now you know.' The Chorus have won their point, but by choral methods, not by the rhetoric of reason.

In the *Eumenides* the same technique is even more striking since the action culminates in a court-trial. Athena, arriving in response to Orestes' appeal, first (415 ff.) takes a deposition from each party, from the Chorus in line-for-line interchange, from Orestes in a set speech. When the trial opens (582) Athena calls upon the prosecution to speak first. The Chorus challenge Orestes to admit the deed in a series of questions and answers designed to elicit the facts. Commentators have so often called attention to the echoes in this scene of actual trials in Athenian public life that the remarkable departure from real life tends to be obscured: neither plaintiff nor defendant makes a set speech. The Furies cannot because they are a Chorus; therefore, lest the scales should be too obviously weighted against them, Orestes also refrains, but calls upon Apollo to bear witness for him. The case for Orestes is then argued by Apollo, with short objections interpolated by the Chorus: the command to slay Clytaemnestra was given by Apollo, who always speaks the will of Zeus; she had murdered her husband, a sceptred king, which was a far worse crime than killing a woman. Than killing a parent? The real parent is the father, not the mother; witness Athena born of Zeus. The description of the murder of Agamemnon heaps odium on the character of Clytaemnestra (there is no corresponding description of the piteous murder of Clytaemnestra), and Apollo adds a *captatio benevolentiae* by a promise, if his side wins, of glory for Athens and a faithful Argive ally. Against this the Furies have succeeded in establishing only the bare fact—the murder of Clytaemnestra by Orestes; they are a Chorus and in forensic oratory cannot do more, without an advocate to speak for them. No wonder they lose the case! In the following scene Athena sets to work to persuade them to give up their designs of vengeance upon the city and to accept a new and honourable office there. Her persuasion naturally takes the form of speeches, and the suddenness of their capitulation has often been noted. So long as they remain obdurate they sing, and twice over the repetition of the same stanza underlines their deafness to the voice of reason. The line-for-line exchange in which they yield (892 ff.) is no reasoned debate, but a mere request for information and for guarantees. There is a similar pattern in the *Septem*, 180 ff., where in the scene between Eteocles and the Chorus of Theban women Eteocles' angry but rational exhortations to self-control and obedience meet with reiterated lyric cries of fear and convulsive clinging to the images of the gods, till at the end of the following line-for-line exchange the Chorus abruptly give way. When later in the play (677 ff.) they endeavour to dissuade Eteocles from fighting his brother the formal pattern is the same, lyric against speech and then line against line, but this time neither party is attempting to reason. The Chorus warn and implore, and Eteocles reiterates that it is too late to draw back, since fate and his father's curse and the gods all will it. Neither side can influence or reach the other.

So far, then, we have seen that even when the Chorus takes a large part in the action, whether in its own cause or as the main interlocutor confronting the chief character, its contribution is lyric or emotional in tone, never rhetorical, and its interventions in the spoken dialogue are kept short. This is naturally easiest to see in Aeschylus where the Chorus is more prominent than it later became. But if we turn to the end of the century, we see that though the Chorus has long become fixed in a subordinate role it may still have to use similar devices to avoid a set speech. In the *Oedipus at Colonus* the first confrontation of the blind old man and the Chorus is so charged with emotions, anger, fear, horror and pity, that a Kommos, a lyric interchange, is the only possible medium; but later, at l. 461, we find them in a calmer mood advising him to make a propitiatory sacrifice to the Eumenides. Such a sacrifice is indeed in harmony with the theme of the play, but the *necessity* of it at this particular moment is dramaturgical: all three actors—Oedipus and his two daughters—are on the stage, so one of them (Ismene volunteers) must be got off it in order to reappear as Theseus. A mere perfunctory reference to a sacrifice would risk exposing this motive too nakedly; the ritual must be given a circumstantial solemnity. But since the Chorus must not make a speech the description has to be conveyed in short question and answer, even at the cost of some artificiality. 'Wreaths of what?' asks Oedipus. 'Libations of what?', and (several times) 'And then what?' Only the final description of the prayer is allowed to run on a little longer. 'Ah!' says Oedipus, 'this sounds important', and gets seven lines of instruction.

In contrast to this, when in the *Oedipus Tyrannus* we are to be shown the confidence of the citizens of Thebes in their king, though citizens constitute the Chorus the poet has to introduce a special delegation *in the prologue*, so that one of them may make the stirring speech of description and appeal which is debarred to the Chorus. Since the Chorus already represent the ordinary citizens, the delegation has to be composed of boys and old men.

It is interesting to note that the longest continuous speech ever given to a Chorus in our texts of the tragedians is *Agamemnon*, 489 ff., which runs to 14 lines—and in the MS tradition is spoken *not* by the Chorus but by Clytaemnestra, except for the last two lines, which as we read them stand in awkward detachment from the rest, and are by the MSS given to the Chorus. The passage was restored to its right shape by the latest edition of the play, that of Denniston–Page. Apart from the more technical points of interpretation of the text and of staging well argued by the editors, it would be altogether abnormal for a Chorus to speak at such length, or indeed in such highly wrought metaphors. No Chorus ever *said*, though it might have *sung*: 'My witness is mud's sister and next-door neighbour, thirsty dust', whereas Clytaemnestra constantly speaks in that style.

Leaving now plays in which the Chorus is itself a party to the main conflict or at least has much to say to the protagonist, what of the much larger area of tragedy in which its role is subordinate and its spoken interventions slight? This is in some aspects a well-worn theme; we need not go into the effect of this collective presence on the unities of time and place, nor do I want to make a list of those passages where the Chorus helps a 'sympathetic' character by keeping watch, or calling for help, or misdirecting his enemies, or where it is embarrassed by its own failure to intervene in the action. My present concern is with the different degrees of penetration of the action by the choral presence; setting aside the choral odes, where has the poet composed a play, or a scene, to achieve an effect which would be impossible in a chorusless form of drama? It is clear, for instance, that the Chorus of Theban Elders make the whole of the *Antigone* after the prologue a *public* action; proclamations, reports, prophecies, defiance, repentance, all concern the community and make an impact on public opinion. This continuous publicity is simply and economically attained by the choice of chorus and by Creon's didactic insistence on the identity of his will and the interests of the state. The Persians, and the citizens of Colonus, have in their very different ways the same kind of effect on the scope and reference of the action in their plays. There is nothing like it in later drama, where any audience effects have to be specially contrived each time—crowd-scenes, courtiers, soldiers and the like, much as the Greek poets do on occasion in their prologues, as in the *Oedipus Tyrannus*, or the *Septem* where Eteocles addresses the citizen-soldiers. Contrast with this a play like the *Trachiniae*, where apart from the lyrics the Chorus simply plays the part of a confidante to Deianeira and thus in the later part of the play, between Heracles and his son, has no particular function at all and is almost silent. The 'agon' again, the set debate between antagonists, is sometimes played to a choral audience involved or passionately interested in the outcome, as in the second half of the *Ajax* or the *Trojan Women* (Hecuba *v.* Helen), as well as to the great surrounding audience; but sometimes, as in the disputes in the *Andromache* or the scene between Admetus and Pheres in the *Alcestis*, the agon seems in this relation little more than a quarrel before the servants. This is not to criticise the dramatic effect of such scenes in themselves, but simply to show how the Chorus as a factor in the action can either keep us aware of its presence or recede so far into the background as to be all but invisible.

It has often been pointed out how the growing elaboration of plots and the development of intrigue and deception as tragic motifs make the Chorus at times something of an encumbrance to the movement of the action. So long as the Chorus is sufficiently devoted to the interests of one of the participants there is no difficulty; in the *Philoctetes* for instance there is an admirably effective contrast between the eager support they give to their young master's deception of the castaway and their troubled incomprehension in face of his later scruples, which they leave him to resolve alone. But the number of Euripidean plays in which the Chorus has to be sworn to secrecy indicates a certain stereotyping and loss of vitality in the choral function. There is, however, a considerable difference between one play and another in the use of this device. Medea sets herself at her first appearance to win the sympathy of the

Corinthian women and asks them to keep her secret if she can devise some scheme of revenge. The whole of the action is thus played against this complicity, and at each stage of it Medea takes them into her confidence as fellow women; we are made to feel their approval of her first moves, their acquiescence in the earlier murders and horrified rejection of the later. When she extracts a day's grace from Creon and fools Jason into thinking she has had a change of heart her dissimulations acquire an extra zest from being *played at* this appreciative audience. In the *Hippolytus* there is some superficial similarity, but Phaedra, in extracting the oath of silence just before she leaves the stage, tells the Chorus nothing of her plan except her resolve to die. They wish no ill to either Hippolytus or Theseus, but though they know the message left by Phaedra to be a lie, and beg Theseus to unsay his curse, they show no particular trouble or uneasiness, when left alone, at their failure to act and save an innocent life. Hippolytus ought to be able to call them as witnesses of his innocence, but he appears, now as earlier, unaware of their existence, and only wishes that the walls of the house could acquire a voice and speak for him. The *Hippolytus* is a profounder play than the *Medea*, but in it Euripides has left the Chorus with little more than its lyric function; for most of the spoken dialogue he wishes us to be scarcely conscious of its presence.

The famous 'irony' with which Sophocles achieves such tremendous tragic effect in the *Oedipus Tyrannus* and which Euripides tends to use in plays of lighter calibre, like the *Iphigeneia in Tauris*, and *Helen*, and *Ion*, is in its most characteristic form directed over the heads of actors and Chorus alike at the audience, whose fuller knowledge hears in the words of the ignorant speakers an unconscious significance which is either ominous or piquant, according to the type of play. But irony can take another form, in which only one actor-character is ignorant, while his antagonist deliberately leads him on to collaborate, in deed and in fateful word, in his own undoing. In such a scene the Chorus always shares the knowledge of the superior party, and the irony reaches the audience, as it were, through the medium of the Chorus. In such a scene as the deception of Theoclymenus by Helen the long string of *doubles ententes* make her seem to be continually winking at the Chorus; but the effect can in a different setting be of the grimmest. At the end of the Sophoclean *Electra* when Clytaemnestra has already been killed, the conspirators are waiting to waylay Aegisthus. The Chorus warns them of his arrival, and urges them to speak him fair and falsely, so that he may rush into the trap which justice has set. Every line uttered by the brother and sister and by the wretched victim is pregnant with double meaning. Aegisthus calls triumphantly for a public exhibition of the body (Orestes, as he thinks), and thus ensures his own public discomfiture. The veiled corpse is thrust before him, Orestes standing by. 'Uncover the face; family mourning is a tribute due even from me.' 'Lift the veil yourself; this is a sight for your eyes, your greeting, not mine.' 'I will; call Clytaemnestra if she is at home.' 'She is close by you, no need to look further.' Aegisthus' enemies, actors and Chorus, press around him, savouring every mocking word.

The scene is short, and Aegisthus is not a character to win our sympathy, so we are not too disturbed by it. One reason why the *Bacchae* is such a terrible play is that some degree of mutual understanding of this kind links Dionysus with the Chorus all through. It is not so complete as in the *Electra*; that would impair the dramatic effect. The god appears to them in the guise of his own prophet, endowed with strange powers, and there is in this an additional layer of irony directed over their heads at the audience, who learned the truth in the prologue. But he is in continual rapport with them, and when he begins to assert his power over his victim he demands their admiring attention; all the scene in which Pentheus is robbed of his will and reason and made the unconscious instrument and mouthpiece of his own doom is played against their excited complicity. Even when Dionysus is no longer on the stage his presence and his power are felt, and the Bacchae egging on the demented Agave, brandishing her son's head, to further flights of horrid exultation are still responding to him. When the revulsion comes the Chorus fade from the picture and we are allowed to forget them. The technique gives to the theme a peculiar gloating cruelty which for us further blackens the character of the god himself.

Whether it was so intended by Euripides is perhaps not so clear; what is certain is that the problem of keeping the Chorus within its own sphere and yet a vital force in the action of the drama has never been more brilliantly solved.

It is evident even from this scattered treatment of the subject that the significance of the Chorus for the action follows no straight line of chronological development. The *Philoctetes*, the *Oedipus at Colonus* and the *Bacchae*, which exemplify three quite different kinds of significance, are among our latest plays; while the *Iphigeneia at Aulis*, in the same posthumous group as the *Bacchae*, has a Chorus whose function is as nugatory as any; when Agamemnon (542) adds a line commanding them to keep silence about what has happened it seems a perfunctory salute to a worn-out convention. Nor is the excellence or interest of a play to be measured in these terms; the poet sometimes sacrifices this consideration to other aspects which are more important for his immediate purpose. But those plays which make the fullest use of the forms and conventions peculiar to their tradition do attain thereby a kind of characteristic harmony and balance of structure. Let us end by considering for a moment one use of the Chorus in the *Agamemnon*, a small point to set beside the splendour of the lyrics but telling in its own way. At this period in Attic drama no free interchange of dialogue between three speakers is possible: if the Chorus first engages the Herald in conversation, Clytaemnestra must wait till that exchange is finished. But when she in turn (587) addresses the Herald the whole of her speech is directed *at* the Chorus. '*I* raised the cry of triumph long ago when the fire-messenger came, and there were some who spoke sharply to me for being a woman and credulous...You need not tell me more now, for my husband will be here. Tell him to come quickly, and how we long for him, and how well I have looked after everything and given no cause for gossip to link my name with any other man's.' It is an act of public defiance, repeated even more recklessly on Agamemnon's arrival (855). She confronts king and Chorus, and the air is cold with undeclared distrust and hostility. The manner of her address would be scarcely possible outside the accepted Greek stage convention that the Chorus is a proper recipient of reports. Instead of greeting Agamemnon 'Dear husband, how I have longed for your return', she makes a public proclamation of her love and suffering: 'My lords of Argos, I will so far forget my modesty as to describe to you what a loving wife I have been.' For the first part of the description Agamemnon is 'this man'; then she slides into the second person in explaining, with an insinuation of popular disloyalty, the absence of Orestes; then again in a burst of flaunting hyperbole she declares the joy and relief of 'this man's' arrival; finally comes a direct endearment, with the invitation to walk the purple. The Chorus is held within the action in order to point the relation of one character to another.

20

THE 'ELECTRA' OF SOPHOCLES

'The atmosphere of this powerful play is as tragic as that of any ancient drama, and apart from the opening lines with their occasional reference to the sights and sounds of dawn, the grimness of the *Electra* is both continuous and unrelieved.' Letters, *Sophocles*, p. 244.

'The *Electra* is not a great tragedy, is not even (in a deep way) a tragedy.' Waldock, *Sophocles the Dramatist*, p. 195.

Having once seen a great performance of the play (in modern Greek), I would unhesitatingly support the former of these two judgments. Admittedly, Mme Paxinou might be capable of overlaying the proper significance of the drama by the sheer power of her acting. And Waldock is a subtle and brilliant critic whose little book is packed with insight into the way a dramatist works; time and again he yanks us out of our brooding scholarly concentration and restores scenes and characters to their real proportions in the theatre, and what he says of that opening scene of the *Electra* must be taken seriously: 'The first seventy-six verses set the scene. They perform the all-important office of *stationing* us, of giving us a certain angle of vision. Opening passages in this way are always crucial. They set our faces in a certain direction, impose an orientation hard to break.' Nevertheless, in his feeling for the play as a whole, Letters, who is an Australian poet, has seen deeper than the literary critic.

This somewhat paradoxical contrast, of the hope, the steady untroubled resolve of the opening scene, together with its unmistakable echo at the end of the play, where hope is fulfilled and there appears the prospect of a happy life ahead for this troubled house, and on the other hand of heavy and terrible passions implacably at work, even in the final triumph—this contrast is only an extreme case of the single-mindedness with which Sophocles pursues the *action* of each of his plays to its conclusion. There is no dichotomy of 'action' and 'character'; 'character' is an essential part of the action, which spends itself in service to the whole and withdraws from the foreground of our attention where it is no longer required. No play of Sophocles can be defined as a 'character-study', though the realisation of one or more characters can fill out a greater or a lesser part of the whole action. This is not the same thing as saying that one, or more than one, of the dramatis personae may be most prominent in the action; the two Oedipus plays are certainly 'about' the fate, and ultimately the death, of Oedipus, but the amount of their meaning, and interest, that is contained in the 'character' (in the sense which the word usually bears) of Oedipus is by no means proportionately large; indeed, Jocasta in the *Oedipus Tyrannus* is a more completely realised character, though of subordinate importance. Philoctetes, Odysseus and Neoptolemus are three characters who between them determine the action of the *Philoctetes*, and of the three Neoptolemus is most crucial *as a character* and is most lovingly filled out as such, but he is not therefore the protagonist.

In every play the action is strongly dramatic, with unpredictable vicissitudes which cheat the expectations of the personages involved, of the Chorus, and of the audience when it comes new to the drama; yet at the close all survivors are left conscious that the end was implicit in the beginning and that something which was set in motion has run its full course to completion. Only in the process the characters are liable to change their focus, to light up strongly and then fade, sometimes with a completeness which to a modern reader, or even spectator, may seem disconcerting. What has become of Deianeira by the end of the *Trachiniae*, or even Antigone by the end of the play named after her? It is not their physical extinction that is decisive, but rather the forward movement of the action that seems to have closed over their heads and passed on to further issues with obliterating effect. So does the tragic Electra who has filled so much of our consciousness during the dramatic events of the play vanish in the closing lines behind the triumphant culmination of the conspiracy launched in that hopeful dawn at the beginning of the play.

Perhaps it is not simply chance that in our extant plays of Sophocles this kind of eclipse should be peculiarly the lot of women.

The exquisite line-drawing that gives us a Tecmessa, Jocasta, Deianeira is matched only by the ruthlessness with which they are subordinated to the main tenor of the action, which concerns Ajax, Oedipus, Heracles.

Tecmessa's most moving appeal to Ajax wins only rough words, instructions for their son's safety, and a demand for her unquestioning obedience: let her now close up the house, stop her woman's crying and not be so foolish as to think that anything she can say will influence him. So must it have been, we all recognise; and when after a choral ode Ajax reappears and says the pity stirred in him by this woman's pleading has unmanned him and made him change his mind, the falseness of the pretence should be so strikingly apparent as to warn us against believing the rest of the speech. Tecmessa (now a mute, not an actor) seated with the child by the dummy corpse as a tableau for the last 300 lines of the play is a symbol of her loss of significance in the whole issue.

Jocasta's life is as broken and devastated as Oedipus' by the revelation of the truth. Her death, as we see from other versions, was not a canonical part of the legend, but in Sophocles it is inevitable. For her there is *nothing left*, no strange, unearthly radiance of awe and suffering such as sets Oedipus apart from the rest of humankind, only an intolerable, choking horror which calls for her immediate annihilation. And at the last all she can think of is blindly, hopelessly to try to spare Oedipus the knowledge that has dawned on her: 'In god's name, if your life means anything to you, do not pursue this matter further. Leave to me the suffering'—ἅλις νοσοῦσ' ἐγώ, the most heartbreaking half-line in all Sophocles.

But Tecmessa and Jocasta are defined in clear terms by the course of the developing action as subsidiary characters; Deianeira in the *Trachiniae* is at the centre of the action for three-quarters of the play, a figure of gentle dignity, kind and pitying even to her young supplanter, patient all these years with the infidelities of the husband she deeply loves and so rarely sees, but now at a crisis, conscious of her fading attractions and fearing to lose him and suffer the indignity of being spurned in her own house. She decides to use the supposed love-charm, and becomes aware just too late of what she now sees as her own culpable readiness to let herself be deceived. Convicted of murder by her son's impetuous reproaches, she turns away into the house without a word of self-excuse, and the death-scene described by the Nurse (shorn of its grotesque interpolation)[1] shines with the same restraint and dignity. The reactions of other characters further refine her portrait—Lichas' consideration for her, and Hyllus' overmastering remorse and the courage with which he forces his raging father to hear the truth about her grievous mistake. But after all this the course of the action follows Heracles' lead: he wastes no word of pity or reconcilement upon her; she simply becomes irrelevant and unimportant in the great blaze of understanding which breaks upon him when he realises that this was the final act of his life's drama, to which all portents had been leading up.

There are moments when one almost feels provoked to the foolishness of protesting against the austerity with which their creator rubs out his characters from the action and from our attention, as if he were too heartless to realise how infinitely to be pitied his own creations were! Yet it may be that this same austere refusal to comment or to let them linger contributes to the peculiar distinctness and solidity with which they invade our imagination. Perhaps it is because Sophocles for once half breaks this rule at Antigone's last appearance, in her conventionally decorative threnody for her own fate and her strange piece of rhetorical self-justification, that so many scholars have felt offended as by the intrusion of something un-Sophoclean in this otherwise perfectly characteristic play. Most Sophoclean, certainly, is the way retribution for his wrongdoing catches up with Creon in the later part of the play while Antigone recedes into the background. Even Haemon appears to kill himself more for shame at having drawn sword upon his own father than for love of Antigone, and in the closing scene no one harks back with so much as a word to her deed and her fate.

[1] Lines 904–11 (or possibly 912) are an obvious intrusion from another play, senseless in their context and totally at variance with the rest of the account. Unfortunately they have been joined up with the grammatical construction and have ousted some of the genuine text, so that they cannot be neatly excised.

To come back to the *Electra*: here one could almost speak of two parallel lines of interest running through the play were it not that the action is so intricately blended of both. The conspiracy is treated externally, as an exciting and dangerous enterprise cleverly carried through to success with no broodings upon its justification or the involvement of Apollo or any other superhuman powers. The main brunt of its execution falls upon Orestes and the Paedagogus, and they too are seen from the outside—except where, in the involutions of the plot, they encounter Electra; then, they begin to glow with the inner warmth of her emotional fires. For Electra is an intensely realised *character*, full of love and burning hatred, and the desire for revenge, and these passions give her an infinite capacity for suffering. Orestes is determined to right an injustice, to step into his own inheritance and restore his disgraced and fallen house. His visible duel is mainly with Aegisthus, with whom there can be no complicated emotional relationship; he is the young Prince coming from another land, full of clear-eyed purpose, not a doom-laden figure driven to avenge one sin by taking upon himself worse guilt. The opening scene is his, and what our faces are set towards, in Waldock's metaphor, is the conspirators' aspect of the situation. But there are *two* scenes in the Prologue. They leave the stage; and we are turned round, made to face in another direction, towards a shapeless dark figure and a voice laden with passion, calling upon the nether gods and the Furies. For Electra the whole meaning of her existence is the grief and hatred which took possession of her the night of Agamemnon's murder those many years ago and have now swelled into an overmastering need for revenge and for more and more demonstrative expression of unappeasable enmity. Her passion brings to life those who cross her path: Chrysothemis is revealed as a lightweight, timid and shallow but amenable to the stronger will so long as nothing too difficult is demanded of her; Clytaemnestra (a hateful figure) is defied and rejected with a biting scorn that brings out the worst in her; Orestes is wakened to a realisation of what his sister's life has been all these years, and for very shame he casts aside the conspirator's cloak and reveals the truth. He is all but overwhelmed by the sudden uprush of her joyful love; even the Paedagogus is momentarily softened by her loving recognition of him: 'never was man so hated and so loved by me on one and the same day'. The brother and sister go in to kill their mother, Orestes without a tremor, Electra uplifted by emotion: 'Do not be afraid that she will read my delight on my face; the old hatred is burnt too deep into me, and since I have seen you I cannot stop weeping for joy.' The Chorus sing briefly in highly charged dochmiacs of the approach of retribution, and Electra emerges, to watch for the coming of Aegisthus, and reports that the scene is set within and the deed about to be done. The cries of Clytaemnestra in the house are savagely answered by Electra in the audience's sight and hearing; the physical deed is Orestes' but the exultation which makes it real to us is Electra's: 'Strike again, if you have the strength', and to her mother's last cry 'If only that were for Aegisthus too'. (It is cruelly disappointing that there is a lacuna in the text, shown unmistakably by the careful antistrophic pattern, just where Electra makes her final comment on her mother's death. Did she perhaps cry to her father's appeased ghost?)

In the final scene, the trapping of Aegisthus with Clytaemnestra's corpse as the bait, the conspiracy takes charge, with brother and sister playing into each other's hand and the dupe with misguided complacency inviting retribution. Electra has only one more characteristic utterance, of impatience for the final act of vengeance: 'Do not let him talk; kill him and throw his body out to the dogs, away from our sight. For me only this can wipe out our afflictions.' The deed is for Orestes to perform, and the last dialogue, spun out as if for the purpose of withdrawing Electra from our attention, is between him and his beaten enemy, with the Chorus to pronounce final deliverance for the house of Atreus.

The *Electra* has formally speaking a 'happy ending'; it is a tragedy because Electra is a tragic figure, tragic in the suffering which mounts in intensity through the first two-thirds of the play, and hardly less so in the exultation which follows her deliverance. We must not let ourselves be mesmerised by the labels 'recognition', 'peripety', 'stratagem', 'deliverance' into thinking this play has anything in common with those others of the same decade which can be analysed under these motifs. There is a sense in which the sufferings of Iphigeneia, Helen, Creusa are real, but we watch with a certain detachment the troubles of these figures of a fairy-tale world whose stories we know to be of the 'happy ending' type. Electra's sufferings and her deliverance from them belong to another world altogether. That neither she herself nor any of the plotters seems aware of anything but a triumphant outcome does not mean that such an interpretation is illegitimate. Nor is this a case of trying to pursue the story and the characters beyond the author's own limit; it is not for events imagined after the end of the play but for what we see during its course that we are made to feel pity and fear. Sophocles after his usual manner has made no explicit comment, and has withdrawn the 'character', though not her physical presence, before the end.

It is always hazardous to try to explain a play by Sophocles or Euripides too closely in terms of a reaction to the other's version or to Aeschylus (except where reminiscence is unmistakable, as in the recognition scene of Euripides' *Electra*, which deliberately makes fun of Aeschylus). There were other dramatists writing, and the large gaps in our knowledge inevitably cause us to concentrate too myopically on what we possess. But in this legend of the Atridae we can at least have more assurance now of getting the sequence of events right. So long as the dogma held that the Euripidean *Electra* was firmly anchored in the year 413 by the speech *ex machina* of the Dioscuri, with what was taken to be a reference to the Athenian ships off Syracuse, plus a programmatic advertisement of the subject of the *Helena* next year, it was possible to argue either that the Sophoclean or that the Euripidean play came first; and many people did, with roughly equal cogency, or lack of it, on each side. The fact that the *Electra*, *alone* among Euripidean plays, thus fell right out of line in the metrical chronology of Euripides was recognised, but either shrugged off ('it shows that metrical criteria won't always work', or 'all you can show by metrical criteria is that it doesn't belong either to the earliest or to the latest group but somewhere in the middle') or explained on the theory of a gap of some years between composition and production; then when the poet took his draft out of the top drawer and polished it up he added a few topical touches to bring it up to date. Even Zieliński, whose great work it was to formulate the metrical criteria in detail and show how what mattered was not merely the sum-total of resolutions but careful statistics about the shapes of words in different parts of the trimeter, lacked the courage to trust his own demonstration and was so hypnotised by the 413 dating that he fell back on the top-drawer theory. It was Zuntz, in a carefully argued chapter of *The Political Plays of Euripides* (1955), who showed the flimsiness of the arguments for 413 and restored the *Electra* to the period 420–418 where its metrical style would place it. But this means the priority of the Euripidean to the Sophoclean play, since the latter has been shown, by Reinhardt, Lesky and others, to be closely linked in attitudes and spirit with the last two plays, the *Philoctetes* and the *Oedipus Coloneus*, and since it also shares with them some significant formal characteristics, it is extremely difficult to see how it could be pushed back to 421–419.

There is moreover a significant echo from Sophocles' *Electra* 56–64 to Euripides' *Helen* 1050–6. Orestes, bringing his own funeral urn as a present to Clytaemnestra, indulges in some careful bravado about the ill-omened device of 'dying in word'—λόγῳ θανών. To die in word, he says, need not worry you if it gives you life and glory *in deed*, since no mere word is evil if you do well out of it—οὐδὲν ῥῆμα σὺν κέρδει κακόν: in fact he has often heard of sages falsely given out in word as dead—λόγῳ μάτην θνῄσκοντας—who then turned up again in their usual haunts and made a profitable sensation out of it. So we find Helen, when plotting their escape out of Egypt, urging Menelaus to report his own death at sea to the king, and Menelaus says that in spite of the bad omen he is willing, if there is any profit in it (κέρδος again), to λόγῳ θανεῖν. Yes, says Helen, and then I could put on mourning and do a typical female lamentation. But how does all this help us? asks Menelaus. 'The idea isn't a very original one', παλαιότης γὰρ τῷ λόγῳ γ' ἔνεστί τις. This of course is less Menelaus than Euripides being naughty. But if the audience was to catch the point the exact phrasing must be fresh in their minds. The *Helen* was in 412—yes, of course last year there was that man 'dead in word' and his sister did a tremendous feminine lament over his urn. Bruhn pointed this out long ago, in his Introduction to the *Electra*, but because he thought the date 413 was pre-empted for the Euripidean *Electra* he had to do some awkward juggling with dates, and his arguments failed to carry the conviction they deserved. Now, thanks to Zuntz, the year 413 is clear and we can peacefully put the Sophoclean *Electra* there, just near enough to the *Philoctetes* and the *Oedipus Coloneus* to account for its stylistic affinities. Thus if Euripides in writing his *Electra* was stimulated by a predecessor in the field it must have been by a revival of Aeschylus' *Oresteia*, and the only play of his own that could have been provoked by the Sophoclean *Electra* is the *Orestes* in 408. Then how much was Sophocles reacting to the Euripidean *Electra*? We can only guess, perhaps unprofitably. The whole question, of such fierce urgency in Euripides, of the sort of god, and the sort of religion, which could enjoin the duty of matricide is left completely untouched by Sophocles; but that masterly brittle, hag-ridden figure of Electra cannot easily have been altogether absent from his mind when he created so different a character. It was in *her* nature to love, and one of the things for which she cannot forgive Clytaemnestra (616 ff.) is that such vileness has made her turn her whole life into one long expression of unnatural hatred. Electra is a tragic figure—perhaps one might concede just so much to Waldock as to say that she is a figure whom a Mme Paxinou *can* legitimately make the centre of a grim tragedy, since her creator, as his manner is, has left us to judge without his help how much she is to be pitied.

21

SPEECH-RHYTHM, VERSE-RHYTHM[1] AND SONG

At a meeting of the Classical Association during the war, I listened to a scholar propounding the thesis that our theories about Greek lyric metres were hopelessly astray because we never remembered that these verses were sung, and that music transforms the spoken rhythms of words. He illustrated this by reminding us of 'Daisy, Daisy, give me your answer do', and then showed how by judicious prolongations of syllables, pauses and various adjustments, we could make good rhythmical sense of some at first sight shapeless Greek passages. He urged us to remember the distinction made by an ancient critic, and instead of being metricians mechanically measuring only long and short syllables, to cultivate a sensitive ear and become rhythmicians, launching out boldly under the guidance of the unchanging and self-evident laws of rhythm. In this way even Pindar could be made an intelligible poet.

His argument ignored so many questions and begged so many others that it makes a convenient starting-point for this paper and one to which it can return at the close. It is true that a comparative study of verse-rhythms in different languages and at different periods would find the same demands recurring everywhere: stress, quantity, pitch, syllable-counting, pause, word-end, assonance (including rhyme), alliteration, anaphora. But that is not to say that what is rhythmical to one people and generation will necessarily naturally appear so to another. And if it does, the reason may sometimes be that it has been falsified in some degree; the written word cannot defend itself, and the wrong elements may easily be pulled into prominence while others are lost to sight. For what counts is not the presence, but the use made of these several elements, their proportions, and their disposal in relation to each

[1] Lecture given to the Federation of University Women in Christchurch, New Zealand, June 1959.

other. Such adjustment, on which depends the development of verse-rhythm in a given language, is determined in the main by three factors; the rhythm of ordinary speech, the workings of historical tradition, and the relation to music.

Nowhere perhaps are these complexities reducible to such simple terms as in medieval Latin poetry. Latin long remained a spoken as well as a written language, but it was not in its later days subject to the relentless pressures that mould popular speech, and the natural conversation of poetry kept this international idiom relatively static and free from local influences. The main changes from classical pronunciation which have to be presupposed in this type of Latin versification were already an accomplished fact before the fall of Rome. The determining principle of this verse is an alternation of stress and unstress, most commonly in alternating syllables. Such a principle is only realisable in a language which has well-marked stresses in its ordinary speech rhythm, and in fact in medieval Latin these can be reduced to an unusually simple formula.

A word carries a stress on its penultimate syllable, except that in words of three or more syllables the stress shifts back to the antepenultimate if the penultimate is short (*capit*, *recipit*). Words of three or more syllables often have a slight secondary accent next but one to the syllable with main stress, the intervening syllable being a single short vowel (*dissonantia*, *grandiores*, *cubiculo*, *sanctissimas*, *considerabit*); hence the prevalence in verse of the simple alternate stress-rhythms—in the loose modern application of the terms, iambic or trochaic lines. Now it is clear that where the relation of stress to word-shape is so regular, lines of a corresponding verse pattern will tend to show a high degree of regularity in the incidence of word-end. This little picture of winter, for instance, is typical:

De ramis cadunt folia,	1 2 2 3
nam viror totus periit;	1 2 2 3
iam calor liquit omnia	1 2 2 3
et abiit;	1 3
nam signa caeli ultima	1 2 2 3
sol petiit.	1 3

The author *could* of course have introduced more variety, but it should be noted that a disyllable is impossible at the end of a line in this 'iambic' metre, and that if a four-syllabled word such as 'miserrimo' ended a line it could not be preceded by a disyllable without dislocation of the stress, and so on. The number of possible variations is strictly limited, and in fact poets undoubtedly make deliberate use of these recurring word-patterns as part of their rhythmical stock-in-trade. Consider next a familiar 'trochaic' poem in octosyllables, the *Dies Irae*. In 18 three-lined stanzas the author only thrice fails to divide the line midway, and the resulting groups of four syllables are so disposed as to give a judicious degree of repetition in word-lengths within each stanza—often a balance of two identical lines out of three. Thus recurring word-pattern reinforces the strong double rhymes and the anaphora of words or syllables:

Dies irae, dies illa
solvet saeclum in favilla,
teste David cum Sibylla.

Quantus tremor est futurus,
quando iudex est venturus
cuncta stricte discussurus.

The division into 4+4 syllables with the frequent further division of one half or the other into 2+2, keeps the deep throbbing note characteristic of this poem, though the formula 2+2+2+2, giving 4 maximum stresses in the line, would if too much repeated be exaggerated and over-restrictive, and after the opening crash is sparingly used. The changes are mostly played on 1+3, 1+1+2, 4 in one word, the *end* of the group thus tending to be intact at the expense of the beginning.

In both the examples I have quoted the words are so arranged that their natural spoken stress always falls within the ideally regular alternate stress which the prevailing rhythm of the verse leads the ear to expect. Such an ideally regular *beat* in a stress-rhythm is often called the metrical ictus, and the name implies an analogy with musical rhythm where the music has bars: the ictus syllable is as it were the first note of the bar. This absolute regularity is never attained in spoken verse except as a *tour de force*, but the words may be so disposed that the departures are purely negative (*recordare, Jesu pie*), while actual *conflict* of word-stress and ictus is avoided. In medieval Latin this is most easily and frequently achieved in 'trochaic' verse. 'Iambic' verse on the other hand leads much more naturally to conflict, because of the great numbers of disyllabic words, some of which are sure to be required at the beginning of lines, especially in a language which lacks the article. (*Timor mortis conturbat me.*) The resulting cross-pull between word-stress and ictus comes then in its turn to be deliberately used, often giving a tension to the beginning of a line which is loosened off at the close; so this account of the creation:

Excelsus mundi machinam
praevidens et harmoniam
caelum et terram fecerat,
mare, aquas condiderat,
herbarum quoque germina,
virgultorum arbuscula,
solem, lunam ac sidera,
ignem ac necessaria,
aves, pisces et pecora,
bestias, animalia,
hominem demum regere
protoplastum praesegmine.

(*Early Irish, sixth century*)

Syllable-counting is clearly essential to such rhythms, since the word-groupings, whether precise echoes or deftly ordered variations, can only be realised in a constant number of syllables. There is no difference as far as rhythms are concerned between Latin sacred and profane poetry, and undoubtedly much of the surviving poetry of both kinds was intended to be sung. There is however no answer to the all-important question here: did the poet in any given instance write his verses with a knowledge of the tune they were to be sung to, either because he composed the music himself or because the general type of tune to which that size and shape of poem was likely to be sung was fairly well fixed by traditional practice? Let me make this clear. The words of the ditty with which this essay began—'Daisy, Daisy'—were obviously written for the tune which accompanies them, whether one man wrote both or there was close collaboration. But types of tune for certain rhythms of verse may be available in stock fittings like gloves. Robert Bridges, in an essay on the rules of English stress-rhythms, points out very truly that the effective stress-units into which a line of English verse divides are often not the regular metrical units descended from classical theory, and he illustrates this at one point by a verse of Bishop Heber's hymn beginning

Brightest and best of the sons of the morning.

This, he says, was no doubt intended by its author for an accentual dactylic line, and would have been scanned by him thus:

– ∪ ∪ – ∪ ∪ – ∪ ∪ – ∪

whereas its right division into stress-units would be

– ∪ ∪ – ∪ ∪ – ∪ ∪ – ∪

But for once the good bishop was right. He was writing it not as spoken verse but to fit a hymn-tune, and even if he did not yet know the melody he knew—or at least could take a heavy bet—that hymn-lines written with those stresses would get an 'accentual dactylic' tune, i.e. one in 3/4 time, with an accented first beat, or possibly in common time with a double note to each stressed word (like Abelard's dactylic *O quanta qualia sunt illa sabbata*). In either case his scansion was right and Bridges' wrong. Music imposes its own regularity upon the spoken word.

We do not know enough of the attendant circumstances of these medieval Latin poems to be able to determine their relation to music. Their metrical form does not provide any certain criterion for deciding which of them were composed for singing. It does however give us the right to say that *either* they were meant for a music which followed their metrical outline closely or they were composed as spoken verse without regard for a possible accompaniment. Their careful patterning, their observance of word-end within the line, is enough proof of this.

In the history of European verse-rhythm medieval Latin stands at a uniquely important turning-point. All mature literature which survives from the previous ages—that is, Greek and Latin literature—has *metrical* verse in the strict sense of the word, verse whose rhythm is based on quantity, the *measurement* of syllables which are either long or short. Both Greek and Latin verse eventually changed their nature, and appear in the early Middle Ages as rhythm based on stress. Of the two, the change in Latin was the more important for the history of European literature, since from the Romance languages, which assimilated and transformed, each into its own currency, the Latin which was actually undergoing this modification, later influences reached to other languages also and coalesced with indigenous elements to produce over the greater part of Europe verse-rhythms which for all their differences are recognisably akin.

Poetry and common speech use the same raw material and there is always a near relation between the rhythms of the two. A nation's poetry is often our best evidence for a change in its speech-rhythm, but a process of this kind is not always easy to disentangle from the effect of purely literary influences, especially from a foreign source, which may also be a powerful modifying factor. Such foreign influences, however first manifested, in the long run always present a history of assimilation with the native genius of the language. The nature of the change from quantitative to stress-rhythm in Latin is a vexed and controversial subject because of the uncertainty prevailing about the earlier change when in the third century B.C., largely as the work of one poet, Ennius, Latin verse adopted wholly Greek metres and Greek principles of scansion, abandoning its older Saturnian measures. What this change meant is difficult to assess, since no one has yet elucidated from the scanty fragments a really satisfactory account of how Saturnian metre worked or how far if at all it had come under Greek influence. Those who think that it was based on stress speak of the reforms of Ennius and his predecessors as a violent wresting of Latin away from its natural trend of development, and the change to medieval versification as a re-emergence of natural and popular rhythms, like a stream whose currents had long run underground. Those who think the Saturnian in the main quantitative naturally see the medieval change as a transformation rather than a reversion to popular forms. But in this school of thought too there is a cleavage, since some believe that it was the whole speech-rhythm of Latin that changed from quantitative to accentual, and in so doing carried the verse-rhythm with it; while others think there was stress-accent as well as quantity audible in ancient Latin speech-rhythm, but that whereas quantity at first determined verse-rhythm and word-stress was audible through it, stress determination gradually got the upper hand and quantitative distinctions in stressed vowels gradually disappeared, having meanwhile weakened in speech-rhythm too.

Since the case cannot be argued here, I can only state categorically what I believe, at the risk of falsifying through over-simplification. Latin and Greek speech-rhythms had a considerable degree of likeness; otherwise the transplantation by Ennius and others could not have been effected with such extraordinary success. The two languages both underwent the same sort of evolution, in that from having a word-accent that was at first one of pitch, not stress (cf. the Latin word *accentus* from *cantus*, 'singing') and a speech rhythm that was mainly quantitative, they evolved a verse-rhythm also based on quantity. But the Greeks achieved this much earlier (their civilisation had several centuries' start) and with far greater thoroughness, diversity and suppleness because they took music to help them. Music holds, steadies, and determines the more approximate quantities of speech; *more* than this, for all the *great* generations of Greek poetry, it was not asked to do; that is to say, the rhythm of Greek music was not autonomous, as in modern music, but itself limited by speech-quantities long or short, with the long in general twice the length of the short. Later, some kinds of metre emancipated themselves wholly or partly from music and became spoken verse, or in some cases were spoken through music in a kind of recitative, but without changing their character in the process; lyric verse all through the classical period retained its music. Word-accent, rising or falling in pitch, was audible through the quantitative rhythm, though quite independent of it, in spoken and recitative verse, and possibly sometimes in the melody of sung verse, though never in responding strophe and antistrophe, where it had to be ignored (and this covers the greater part of lyric). Latin poetry, being with few exceptions spoken verse, lacked this musical discipline, and its quantitative system down to the third century B.C. was in consequence much less fully developed, and more adulterated with other elements, such as the practice of leaving indifferent the quantity of syllables before certain mid-line pauses. Too little Saturnian has survived for us to elucidate its proper formula. In the third century B.C. Ennius and his fellows borrowed the fully quantitative system of Greek verse and grafted it (with some modifications) with extraordinary skill upon their own language. As in Greek, the pitch-accent of the words (placed as already described for stress in medieval Latin) was audible through the rhythm, but with the important difference that in Latin this rise in pitch, owing to the rules of its application and to the general preponderance of long syllables in Latin as compared with Greek, much more often coincided with a long quantity. This combination of pitch and long quantity gave to such syllables a greater prominence in the verse-line than the pitch-accented syllables of Greek, and made them felt more as a structural element. Hence when Plautus adapts the Greek comic iambics and trochaics for his dialogue, and finds a lack of short vowels, instead of restricting the flow of words available he is able to substitute, over much of the line, – – for – ⏑, so that a line such as

Qui falsas litis falsis testimoniis

is felt as rhythmical, whereas such a line of 10 long syllables and 2 short would be shapeless in Greek. Hence too the care with which Latin poets regulated the length of words towards the end of the line in hexameters and pentameters, the end of the line or of the rhythmical phrase being, as we saw in the medieval poems, the most sensitive point for the ear. The notion so long prevalent, especially among German and English scholars, of a conflict followed by a coincidence between word-accent and metrical ictus in hexameters, is I think untenable and indeed is hard to reconcile with Ovid's regulations for the pentameter. Metrical ictus I believe to be wholly a product of stress-rhythm; it plays no part in classical Greek or Latin verse. The period in which word-accent changed in either language from pitch to stress is impossible to determine closely; perhaps for Greek at least it was beginning before the Christian era, but all we can say with certainty is that by A.D 400 the change is already apparent in both Greek and Latin poetry and that therefore the process must have been going on for a long time previously. With this change the distinction between long and short vowels in stress position disappeared in both languages (in Latin *sonum* comes to rhyme with *regionum*, *mali* with *tali*), and the quantitative rhythm that vanished with it has never since reappeared in any European language.

With quantity went also the principle of 'metrical equivalence', by which two short syllables can stand in the place of one long, just as in music 2 quavers = 1 crotchet. I have said already that the most characteristic medieval Latin rhythm is of alternate stressed syllables; in spite of transitory attempts to substitute accentual for quantitative hexameters and therefore to write lines where – ◡ – was interchangeable with – ◡ ◡ –, this attempt to mould an existing traditional form to new rhythmical tendencies never took firm root; the most successful remodellings were of the old iambic and trochaic verses, though *pure* accentual dactyls also are not uncommon. The interchangeability of – ◡ – and – ◡ ◡ – is a common principle of English, German and Scandinavian stress-rhythms, but on quite different grounds, namely the frequency of slurred syllables and unvoiced vowels in the speech-rhythm of each, which makes it easy to slip in an extra one without great disturbances of the regularity of the stress-incidence. Romance languages, like Latin itself, are too clearly articulated syllabically to do this, and all adopt the principle of syllable-counting. Stress in Romance languages has fared differently according to the speech-rhythm of each. Italian for instance slightly drawls its word-stress and thereby produces a markedly uneven effect in a line of verse, a continual tautening and slackening of pace. These drawled syllables coincide with an alternate stress, especially at the all-important ends of lines, just often enough to leave an echo of underlying regularity, a ghost of ictus, upon the ear, but often pull strongly against it earlier in the line, so that strict syllabism is essential if the rhythm is not to dissipate itself. Italian word-stress, while in many respects inherited directly from Latin, gains considerably in variety through the final stresses of certain classes of word (*trovò*, *pietà*, *fuorchè*) and the optional omission of the final *-e* of infinitives; and the addition of the articles to the language gives a wider range to its line-openings in rising rhythm and a lightening of the whole by the sprinkling of unemphatic monosyllables throughout the line. It also reaches back to classical Latin for those elisions and half-elisions which Virgil used to enrich the rhythmic possibilities of his line.

The subject of stress in French rhythm is a thorny one, and I may perhaps be allowed to get by with the lightest of grazes by saying that it is entirely subordinate to syllable-counting as a determining principle of rhythm. It plays a somewhat weak and fluctuating part in speech-rhythm where, though it tends to settle lightly on the final syllable of a word, it is heard more as the culminating points of the whole sentence than as the inalienable property of separate words, and this has diminished its regulative function in verse; in particular it lacks the predominantly alternating character which the ear seizes on in Germanic verse-rhythms. The falling rhythm at the ends of words, so characteristic of Latin and Italian and so productive in itself of alternate stress, is in French either truncated or flattened out to a long vowel with a following silent or much-muted final *-e*: *diurnus*, *giorno*, *jour*; *mater*, *madre*, *mère*. No longer a recurrent, underlying beat, stress now serves to support the balanced groupings of syllables, both whole lines and parts of lines, by emphasising the ends of these and often also by giving them an earlier culminating point, the placing of which is deliberately varied. With the weakening of stress, rhyme and pause achieve a greater prominence. To enable the ear to apprehend and distinguish the succeeding phrases, all lines except those which are too short to need it divide into two or occasionally three or four parts by the ending of a word of some rhetorical importance, which entails a slight pause and stress; the stronger pause at the end of the line is reinforced by rhyme, very often a 'rime riche'. A closing *e* mute, instead of forming part of the syllabic structure of the line like the falling rhythms of Latin and Italian, is left as a sort of overhang, admitted (with its rhyming response) at will at the end of the line; while in mid-line this half-muted syllable, with the prolongation it throws back upon the preceding syllable, is productive of some of the most delicate and characteristic modulation of French verse.

The mid-line break is a widespread metrical device, and it is often hard to distinguish what is traditional here and what is a natural development repeating itself in different languages. Such a break is a characteristic common to most spoken verse that moves in even, homogeneous lines. It serves the same general purpose in all cases—to keep the phrasing in lengths that the ear can hold, by balancing the first part of a line against the second, but its more precise function differs according to the type of metre in which it is used. It appears in the earliest Greek metres which emerge from music into speech or recitative, either in the form of caesura or as diaeresis; the former causes a break by word-end in the middle of a metrical unit, the latter at the end of such a unit. The main effect of the *caesura* is by breaking against the grain, as it were, to prevent the line from disintegrating into its own component units; often it ensures that the two divisions shall open and close in contrary rhythm—rising, falling; falling, rising:

θεοὺς μὲν αἰτῶ | τῶνδ' ἀπαλλαγὴν πόνων

or the reverse:

μῆνιν ἄειδε, θεά, | Πηληϊάδεω 'Αχιλῆος,

and often it is only part of a more elaborate control of word-end extending to other parts of the verse. But where there is diaeresis, as for instance in anapaests, the line may break into two equal halves:

τάδε μὲν Περσῶν τῶν οἰχομένων.

Latin poetry used a middle break of some kind in Saturnians, and when it adopted Greek metres built up its own modifications of Greek rules. Medieval Latin retained the commonest classical caesura in position when it adapted a classical metre to stress-rhythm:

Pro universis | immolatus dominus

but when it used less traditional forms, as in trochaics:

Dies irae | dies illa

or dactyls:

O quanta qualia | sunt illa sabbata

it tended to adopt the simpler diaeresis, leaving the verse in two equal halves, of which only the second was reinforced by rhyme. Italian, in so far as it uses the device, prefers a mobile break shifting slightly but somewhere near the middle of the line. The French *césure*, structurally more important in the absence of a metrical ictus, varies between the fixed and the shifting. English verse, in spite of the case of some practitioners intent upon foreign models, tends to reject formal rules and to distribute its pauses on more empirical considerations. Its most characteristic five-stressed line will of course not carry an exact half-way break. It is noteworthy that in the freer, more irregular style of versification called by Gerard Manley Hopkins 'sprung rhythm' the mid-line break can be made to play a much more important part, as in Meredith's *Love in the Valley*; the subordinate half-line groupings help to keep the more elusive rhythm clear. But even a brief consideration of the more modern developments of sprung rhythm and free verse in various languages would need a paper to itself, and I am concerned here only with the great body of traditional verse in each language.

English verse, having evolved its own method of exploiting the strong stresses of its ancient Anglo-Saxon speech-rhythm, in irregularly spaced hammer-blows driven home by alliteration, was lifted completely out of that line of development and set down in another. This was Chaucer's forceful act of genius, comparable to that of Ennius and equally decisive for the future. Other poets besides Chaucer and Ennius had experimented with the new medium, but in each case it was the completeness of the achievement in one great poem of genius that made inevitable the triumph of the new and the obliteration of the old. Modelled on French syllabism, Chaucer's decasyllabic line assimilated the natural alternate stresses of English rhythm; and the great mass of English verse, rhymed and blank, in various lengths of line and patterns of stanza, has gone that way ever since. The great variety of stressed positions among the syllables of its words, the frequency of monosyllables (whole stanzas have been written in monosyllables without artificiality), and the ease with which extra syllables in the unstressed area will either disappear or keep their value as required (*following*, *different*, *heaven*, *meteor*, *memory*, *cruelly*, *mysterious*), give an enormously greater range and flexibility to alternate-stressed verse in English as compared with the stiff word-patterns of its forerunner, medieval Latin; while at the same time it shares with Latin, especially in words derived thence, the secondary stresses on alternate syllables in numerous longer words (like *renunciation*, *acquiescent*, *incarnadine*, *dissatisfaction*). The attraction of alternate stress will affect even groupings of words in common speech; we say chúrchyard, but St Paúl's Churchyárd.

By far the greater part of this verse is 'iambic'—in rising rhythm, doubtless partly through the influence of tradition, partly because of the convenience of starting lines with an article, conjunction, preposition or similar low-toned monosyllable. So strongly is the notion of 'beat' present in our stressed verse that the interweaving of 'trochaic' and 'iambic' openings passes almost unnoticed, the first syllable slipping in like an introductory 'up-beat' or overhang from the concluding word of the preceding line:

Rose-leaves, when the rose is dead,
are heaped on the beloved's bed;
and so thy thoughts, when thou art gone,
Love itself shall slumber on.

This I take to be one of the many echoes from contemporary music traceable in English lyric; the likeness of these regular stress-rhythms to simple song music with bar and beat cannot have failed to give rise to some half-unconscious adaptations of musical practice. 'Iambic' verse itself can easily be made to accommodate the opposite type of line-opening, where the first word starts with a stress, by the process of inversion, the substitution of – ∪ ∪ – for ∪ – ∪ –

Season of mists and mellow fruitfulness.

The beginning of the line is accepted by the ear as the most natural place for such inversion, and sometimes it is retained almost throughout a stanza or poem in order to isolate the opening word of each line, as in Masefield's *By a Bierside*:

This is a sacred city built of marvellous earth.
Life was lived nobly here to give such beauty birth.
Beauty was in this brain and in this eager hand.
Death is so blind and dumb, Death does not understand.
Death drifts the brain with dust and soils the young limb's glory.
Death makes justice a dream, and strength a traveller's story.
Death drives the lovely soul to wander under the sky.
Death opens unknown doors. It is most grand to die.

The double inversion of 'Death makes justice a dream', – ∪ – ∪ ∪ – for ∪ – ∪ – ∪ – (on the principle of 'solem, lunam ac sidera') is a kind of dislocation which though common enough in dramatic blank verse is used much more sparingly in traditional English lyric than for instance in Italian, and inversions later in the line:

O gentle child, beautiful as thou wert...

are also much restricted in comparison with the common initial sort.

'Dactylic' or 'anapaestic' rhythms—a triple-spaced stress—meet with much more opposition from the natural prose-rhythm of English words; obstructing groups of consonants and heavy monosyllables are apt to drag at the skirts of the Muse. Shelley clearly uses this rhythm with an intention of speed in 'My coursers are fed with the lightning', but even he cannot wing English monosyllables:

I desire; and their speed makes night kindle...
That their flight must be swifter than fire...

The quantitative double-short of Greek verse, which grew so lightly from that language's rhythm of abounding short syllables,

οὔ μ' ἔτι, παρθενικαὶ μελιγάρυες ἱμερόφωνοι,

bequeathed to posterity an abiding memory which stress-rhythm has striven manfully to recapture, from Abelard's

si quantum sentiunt possint exprimere

to the German epigrammatist on Perugia:

du reichest
Malern und Dichtern zugleich den unerschöpflichsten Stoff,

but the speech struggles against this unnatural bondage. The more natural use of these trisyllabic units is to combine them with alternate stresses in mixed rhythms, the most characteristic mixture being lines which move from triple to double time:

Oh, I am the cook and the captain bold,
And the mate of the *Nancy* brig

It need not be doggerel:

A sensitive plant in a garden grew

Most of the types of stress-rhythm found in English poetry are at home in German too, where the strong accent on the root-syllable of all native words leads naturally into verse with predominantly stress-rhythm. The main difference between the two languages lies in the much greater proportion of 'trochaic' ends to German words, produced mainly by inflected terminations, which English has lost or taken up (in pronunciation) into the preceding syllable—*ich denke, ich dachte, ich habe gesungen, eine rote Rose, sie liessen die Köpfe hangen*. The result is a far greater proportion of lines ending in falling rhythm, with double rhyme—*gefangen, hangen*—so that for instance in a type of verse subject to strict rules of form like the sonnet, the English version tends to keep to plain 'iambic', whereas the characteristic German types have either this rhythmic overhang all through on the Italian model, or an ordered distribution of 'masculine' and 'feminine' rhyme, while in continuous blank verse or rhymed pentameters where admixture of feminine endings is admitted at will ('I come to bury Caesar, not to praise him') the proportion in German is like that in our own Chaucer who adopted this licence from French at a time when our language still needed accommodation for its final terminations:

Whan that Aprille with his shoures sote
The droghte of Marche hath perced to the rote

Here the disyllabic 'sote' and 'rote' would now, with 'sweet' and 'root', be plain 'iambic'.

Of Scandinavian poetry before it was drawn into the main stream of Europeanised literature in the eighteenth century, I am not qualified to speak. Its later rhythms are naturally of the Germanic stress-type, but the main point of interest to a student of Greek is that Swedish alone, of modern languages known to me, has a pitch-accent attached to the pronunciation of separate words and modified but never lost in the rhythm of the whole sentence. This is of two alternative types, and affects the syllable following the stress-accent, being in fact (here of course quite unlike the old Greek pitch-accent) a sort of delayed reaction to stress. But though the Swedish poet is always sensitive to its effects, it remains an arbitrary and empirical factor in the verse like assonance or alliteration, and never acquires any structural significance for the rhythm. Stress carries the whole structure just as quantity did in Greek.

French, German and English influences, roughly in that order, prevailed in Russian poetry also in the eighteenth century. The decisive factor was French, and indeed the strict syllabism which this entailed is peculiarly well adapted to Russian speech-rhythm. The stress-accent upon one syllable (which varies from the final to the sixth from the end) is so heavy that the other vowel-sounds in the word become greatly modified according to their position before or after the stressed syllable, and according to their distance from it. A faint secondary accent is sometimes audible in the longer words, but not on any principle of alternation. As the vocabulary even of poetry tends to be more polysyllabic than in Italian or English or German, the number of natural stresses available is often not enough to carry the rhythm without the help of strict syllabic equivalence in corresponding lines. But the importance of stress for the structure of the line is seen in that if a metrical ictus be imagined operating in the line in a series of equidistant beats, the actual stressed syllables will almost invariably fall within that series; the occasional dislocations which pull away from the beat in English are found to a negligible extent in Russian, at most in a rare opening inversion. No two consecutive ictus-beats are left unaccented. The ictus is usually 'iambic' (occasionally 'trochaic') with optional feminine ending, though 3/4 time rhythms are not uncommon; the verse will not carry the mixed 2/4–3/4 type of English and German. The contrast with the French use of stress can be seen in

Golenishchev-Kutuzov's adaptation of the alexandrine, in twelve-syllabled lines with a regular break after the sixth. The ictus is 'iambic', but there is no attempt to make an accent fall regularly on the sixth syllable, which may equally well be the tail of a word accented from the fourth syllable. It will be seen that the encouragement offered to the unfortunate beginner (accents are not printed in Russian) to learn his accents by reading poetry is a somewhat elusive carrot.

In this distortingly brief summary of what I conceive to be the main principles of traditional verse-rhythm in such languages as I happen to be able to read, I have tried to show how in spite of the modifications introduced by the characteristic speech-rhythm in each case there is a considerable similarity of underlying structure from the beginnings of medieval Latin onwards. This is in part the product of a common European tradition; syllabism, patterns of stanza, habits of rhyme, blunt or falling line-endings can be handed on and passed from one language to another by eye, can even be formulated in an *Ars Poetica* and given the prestige of cultural precepts. The relation of all these to stress-rhythm runs deeper in the currents of national speech, and is often so little conscious that contemporary theory (as in the case of the English critics of the seventeenth and eighteenth centuries who assumed that English verse was quantitative) can remain quite in the dark as to its real nature, and theoretical agreement is even today quite unobtainable. Yet in practice no cultivated ear finds insuperable difficulty in passing from one modern European verse-rhythm to another and apprehending at least something of each, and one contributory reason for this degree of common understanding is the existence of a common heritage of song-music. From the seventeenth century at least the alliance in this of regular stress with bar and phrase has provided a musical analogy to the rhythms of spoken verse and accustomed the ear to metrical ictus, though how far this is simply a parallel development or whether music and poetry have interacted on each other would be difficult to determine in detail. The Frenchman who has sung *Au clair de la lune* to 2/4 time can make the transition from French to German spoken rhythm; though perhaps the German on the contrary is encouraged in a slight falsification of

French spoken verse. But the link between musical and metrical stress has been made at the expense of the link between musical and metrical quantity. The ancient Greeks, lacking any clear-cut stress in their pronunciation of words, harnessed music to verse through quantitative determination of the syllables, so their musical rhythm developed in subordination to word-rhythm, and (so far as we can tell from the miserably scanty fragments) lacked most of what to our ear constitutes purely musical form, since it lacked not only bar and beat but the capacity to develop in freedom its own pure quantitative relations. Today the quantities of spoken rhythm are as indeterminate as stress was in ancient Greek, so that if verse is now 'set to music' as we significantly call it, the musician is (within reasonable limits) given *carte blanche* to define these quantities in his own terms. So he can take two straightforward lines like

> Orpheus with his lute made trees
> And the mountain-tops that freeze

and give the syllables quantities varying from $\frac{1}{2}$ to 4 units of time, in a pattern which, without doing violence to any of the stresses, has a purely arbitrary relation to the rhythm of the words. The only revolution in the history of European verse-rhythms took place in the centuries round about the Christian era, when stress ousted quantity, and syllabism in consequence changed its principles. Accompanying that revolution and deeply involved in it is the emancipation of music from attendance upon the spoken word. The spoken word, thus deserted, evolved its own verse-systems, with intricacies which depended no longer on the formal patternings of music but on the imprecise and infinitely varying modulations of the human voice; structurally simpler, it added infinite complexities of small adjustments often in close relation to the meaning in each case as they occurred. Music, thus released, acquired and organised its own vast domain; and henceforward when music and poetry enter into an alliance the poetry must divest itself of all its own rhythmical subtleties and submit even what formal structure it has to the elaborations of its stronger partner.

22

EXPRESSIVE RHYTHM IN THE LYRICS OF GREEK DRAMA

We read lyric poetry; the Greeks watched and listened to it. It is easy for us to forget this simple yet profound difference. The Greek poet composed his songs for performances; children learned at school to perform the works of old masters, for to do so required some skill and knowledge, and short of performance the poetry lacked complete expression. The modern opera and concert hall afford no parallel; we attend them to listen to music, not poetry, and their lyrics are either a mere libretto or were composed by a poet as spoken verse and subsequently set to music by a musician. Wagner himself wrote the words of the *Ring*, but 'Nothung, Nothung, neidiges Schwert' and the rest of it is not poetry, scarcely even verse. 'Now sleeps the crimson petal, now the white' has been set to appropriate music, but not by Tennyson; here are two works of art, the poem, and the song which uses the same words. Even where words and music seem to us fused into one and inseparable, as in the *Marseillaise*, the words can be detached and will then read, metrically correct but unfamiliar, as spoken French verse. 'Spoken' verse, it may be said, implies recitation and therefore listening, and in reading an ode of Keats to ourselves we silently recite. But our recitation, and even Keats' composition, are not arts which have to be *learnt* in the sense in which music must be learnt by musician and virtuoso; there is a 'grammar' of music (notes, scales, keys, intervals, chords) but not of English prosody. An ode of Alcaeus or Aeschylus or Pindar was composed as song, and perhaps one reason why it is so easy for us to forget or ignore this is that the thought and its expression are so far from facile. English lyric did not become what the Greeks called σπουδαῖον, poetry to be taken seriously for its own sake, until in the seventeenth century it shook itself free from music and began an independent tradition of spoken verse. Till then it was just words written for music. The words of Greek lyric were written, not *for* but *in* music; and in addition, an Aeschylean or Pindaric ode was communicated with the help of dance—that is of expressive movement. The poet, before weaving his new patterns of verse, had to learn the elements of verse-writing—not because, as at a later day, music and dance were elaborate technical accomplishments in a sense in which bare verse-making was not, but because ποιητική itself involved the complex technical craft of ῥυθμική, or, as a more analytical generation expressed it, of μετρική. In lyric verse μετρική required music, or music and movement, for its clear expression just because it was more varied and complicated than the μετρική of intoned or spoken verse such as epic or iambic. No modern poetry, English or other, has a formal 'metric' in this sense and there is no body of verse known to us in any language which can show a complexity of structural rhythm approaching that of classical Greek.

The music and dance of Greek lyric have vanished unrecorded, and we are left the naked words for our silent reading; how far is it possible to re-create these as poetry for our ear? There was of course a reading public too in Greece, but even for contemporary readers choral lyric, addressed to the eye and ear of the spectator, must have been difficult, if not impossible, to recover in its entirety from the written roll. The great Alexandrians were already uncertain of much of its metrical interpretation, and later metricians whose works have survived appear lost in an analytical wilderness in the outskirts of which we, more than 2,000 years later, still find ourselves wandering. Only a continuous tradition of performance could ensure full understanding; where this continuity was broken the poetry itself became partly unintelligible. Thus one of the most intricate and beautiful creations of Greek poetry, its lyric ῥυθμική, was early lost to comprehension and can never be fully recovered. We, at this distance of time, with our alien speech and alien musical conventions, can only deceive ourselves if we rush into the attempt trusting to ear alone, arguing from some imagined 'natural sense of what is rhythmical'. Our ear has first to unlearn some of its prejudices and be trained afresh by study of the texts, and to some extent the perception of Greek verse-rhythm will always remain for us an act of intellectual rather than sensuous apprehension.

Among any people, indigenous verse will bear some relation to the rhythms of ordinary speech. English, like German, is spoken in stressed and unstressed syllables, and its verse-rhythms are based on equidistant stresses, partly according with, part subtly countering, the normal accent of words. French words have no marked inherent stress, and the structure of most French verse is based on syllable-numbering and pause. In classical Greek, pitch and quantity, interrelated to some extent, were properties of words taken by themselves, while stress only gradually replaced tonic pitch at a later date. The tonic accent must of course have been audible in spoken verse; how far it was preserved in recitative or song it is impossible to say, but certainly it bore no relation in any kind of delivery to the structural principles of poetic rhythm. These were based on quantity alone—syllables were either long or short. Dynamic stress, though it may sometimes have been thrust upon recurrent long syllables by the stamp of the dancers' feet in lively, simple comic rhythm, is not to be imagined as an ictus determining the metrical scheme of any form of verse. This at once creates grave difficulties for us. We are accustomed to pronounce Greek words either with an English form of syllable-stress or in the modern Greek way with the stress on the old pitch-accented syllable (Διονῦσος or Διόνυσος). And to an English ear a complex verse-rhythm divorced from stress is not easy to pronounce or even to hear.

ὦ παῖ παῖ δυστανοτάτας

We tend in speaking this choriambic dimeter to convert it into a line of four stresses, reinforcing some of the long syllables by ictus and slightly falsifying the quantities to satisfy our craving for regular beat—assimilating it in fact to the familiar rhythm of

Fear no more the heat o' the sun

It is an almost impossible task to emancipate our pronunciation from this ingrained habit of stress, nor does it greatly matter so long as we are aware of using this un-Greek device simply to keep distinct the phrases of quantitative rhythm for our imperfectly trained ear. But any system of Greek metric reared on ictus-theories is built in the void. Ictus is a notion born of a musical tradition which in song uses bar and beat to regularise the rhythms of spoken verse, or to break them up and superimpose its own different rhythm. The syllables of English verse when sung do acquire fixed quantities, but these are a property of the musical notes arranged in bars, not of the syllables themselves—a short light syllable of spoken verse may become a crotchet or minim when sung. The bars carry a regular beat, which is substituted for the spoken stresses and may stifle them completely. (The hymn 'Sun of my soul' was written in alternate stress but set to music in 3/4 time.) Greek singing music had no such independent convention, no bar and beat; hence it is misguided to attempt to simplify such metres as Pindar's dactylo-epitrite by setting them to a musical beat which imposes a falsely monotonous unity on their rhythmical variety. The mingling of two contrasted rhythms—dactyl with double-short and epitrite with single—in intricately balanced patterns, is of the essence of this metre.

Σάμερον μὲν χρή σε παρ' ἀνδρὶ φίλῳ
στᾶμεν, εὐίππου βασιλῆι Κυράνας,
ὄφρα κωμάζοντι σὺν Ἀρκεσίλᾳ,
Μοῖσα, Λατοίδαισιν ὀφειλόμενον Πυ-
-θῶνί τ' αὔξῃς οὖρον ὕμνων,...

Trochee is not to be equated to dactyl by prolonging the long syllables, nor dactyl to trochee by a scrambling correption of the shorts. The changes from one rhythm to the other keep the component phrases distinct and make it possible for the ear to retain the rhythmical shape of the longer periods. Music steadies the natural quantities to a precision not attained in speech, the most general equation being 1 long = 2 shorts, and the dancers' movements perhaps (we know nothing about it really) made visible the response of strophe to antistrophe and the echo of each epode in the next.

The truth is that quantity as a formal principle of song-rhythm allows of a far greater diversity within the same poem than does stress. Modern music has trained our ear to the appreciation of incomparably richer effects of harmony and melodic line than the Greeks ever dreamed of, but has blunted it to the perception of complex rhythm. As a result, when we meet an ode of Sophocles in which the rhythm changes from stanza to stanza, from period to period within the stanza, and in the phrases which form the component parts of a single period, we are apt to feel at a loss.

> πολυώνυμε, Καδμείας ἄγαλμα νύμφας
> καὶ Διὸς βαρυβρεμέτα
> γένος, κλυτὰν ὃς ἀμφέπεις
> Ἰταλίαν, μέδεις δὲ
> παγκοίνοις Ἐλευσινίας
> Δηοῦς ἐν κόλποις, ὦ βακχεῦ,
> βακχᾶν ματρόπολιν Θήβαν
> ναίων παρ' ὑγροῖς
> Ἰσμηνοῦ ῥείθροις, ἀγρίου τ'
> ἐπὶ σπορᾷ δράκοντος.

In our ἀπορία over this sort of thing we tend either to say that the vanished music must by this or that 'hold' and pause have ordered it into something more recognisable as a 'tempo' or to content ourselves by affixing labels: 'this is a glyconic followed by two telesilleans plus a reizianum—pause—iambic dimeter with two extra syllables tacked on...' and so on. If that is all, we can only shrug our shoulders at the end of it, and Greek metric will remain an incomprehensible and unattractive subject to the student of Greek. But these labels, if the periods and component phrases are correctly distinguished, are chiefly convenient for purposes of reference; the essential is to recognise the rhythmical shape of the whole by observing the units of phrasing or cola, the manner in which they combine in a particular context, and their habits of association in general, for the technical art of the Greek lyric poet is primarily one of combination. He selects cola bequeathed him from this or that source of metrical tradition, with occasional inventions or modifications of his own, and builds them into a rhythmical structure which has balance but rarely uniformity. The movement may be homogeneous, like the syncopated iambic odes of the *Agamemnon*; or predominantly of one type (dactylic, ionic, dochmiac); or just mixed (polymetric). In every case it is the rhythmical context and the shape of the whole which make sense of this diversity; and if we read patiently and often, studying similar cola in different contexts and combinations, we begin to absorb some notion of what the Greeks meant by ῥυθμική. Music and dance have faded and life and colour with them, but in the written words the rhythmic line of the original survives, faint and a little broken, but true.

Solo lyric and commemorative choral ode were single, self-contained performances. The lyrics of a tragedy or comedy are related to the larger whole of the play, and each song as it intervenes is part of the situation or emotional mood at the point reached. We might expect some more particular significance in the choice of rhythm in such a lyric, some relevance to its larger context. Metrically no two lyrics follow the same pattern; can we ask, then, why *this* particular metre and pattern is in this given place? Ultimately, doubtless, the only answer is that the theme presented itself in this form to the poet, but in some cases a more definite rhythmical propriety seems to have guided his choice. The question would be easier if we were less ignorant of the origins of different types of metre, of the precise manner of their delivery, and of the emotional response of the Greek spectator to rhythmical sound and movement.

The broadest distinction might be that between comic and tragic verse. The lyrics of comedy were in general more homogeneous metrically than those of tragedy, and the effect of this in certain metres was to make the song go with a swing. This of course does not apply to metres delivered in recitative—anapaests, some of the more regular iambics and trochaics, and possibly dactylic hexameter—which naturally had a recurrent rhythm and were used in tragedy and comedy alike. But in song-metres proper when comedy uses the same metres as tragedy the phrases tend to repeat far more, so that the rhythmical construction is simpler to grasp. Further, in its search for the sort of metre which could be expressed in vigorous dance, perhaps with stamping and high kicks, comedy evolved certain kinds of patter-rhythm with quick resolutions; such are the cretic-paeonic:

ἐκπέφευγ', οἴχεται
φροῦδος· οἴμοι τάλας

τῶν ἐτῶν τῶν ἐμῶν.
οὐκ ἂν ἐπ' ἐμῆς γε νεότητος ὅτ' ἐγὼ φέρων
ἀνθράκων φορτίον
ἠκολούθουν Φαΰλλῳ τρέχων, ὧδε φαύλως ἂν ὁ
σπονδοφόρος οὗτος ὑπ' ἐμοῦ τότε διωκόμενος
ἐξέφυγεν οὐδ' ἂν ἐλαφρῶς ἂν ἀπεπλίξατο.

Aeschylus in his earlier manner has short stanzas of cretic-paeonic, but after that it almost disappears from tragedy; evidently a developed taste discarded it as too φορτικόν. Another very similar metre only found in comedy is a sort of anapaestic which resolves into runs of short syllables and is not constructed like recitative anapaest in dipodies:

τόδε τοι τὸ πάθος μετ' ἐμοῦ
ὅ τι βουλόμεναί ποτε τὴν
Κραναὰν κατέλαβον ἐφ' ὅ τί τε
μεγαλόπετρον ἄβατον ἀκρόπολιν
ἱερὸν τέμενος.

These are lyric versions of the breathless πνῖγος or 'choke' which was a regular *tour de force* at the end of comic recitative anapaests or iambics.

Conversely, there are types of metre which are the peculiar province of tragedy, borrowed by comedians only for barefaced parody. Such are the dochmiac—δοχμιακός 'running askew'—in its short broken line, and the related shorter and longer phrases found in association with it and like it sometimes dragging into irregular long syllables at their close—the cretic-molossus and the prosodiacs. These dochmiac and kindred types are I think the only lyric rhythms which carry an inherent emotional expression—namely passionate feeling of some kind: Theseus' grief over the dead Phaedra, the extravagant joy of Iphigeneia recognising Orestes, Io gnat-goaded, the howls of tortured Polymestor, the awful excitement at the approaching death or translation of Oedipus. Here then is a clear lead into Greek rhythmic sensibility; strong emotion is expressed in phrases of short compass and multifarious form, with a telling contrast between mourning *rallentando* closes and excited resolution into short syllables. If ⏑ – – ⏑ –, 'The wise kangaroos' (a happy mnemonic I owe to Professor Gilbert Murray), be taken as the norm for a dochmiac, this may modify, for instance into

τάλας. φεῦ μόχθων.

breaking into

ἄδικος ἄδικα τότ' ἄρ' ἔλακεν ἔλακεν ἀπό-
φονον ὅτ' ἐπὶ τρίποδι Θέμιδος ἄρ' ἐδίκασε.

The same vehemence of contrast appears in the melic anapaests sung by Euripidean soloists (Creusa in the *Ion*, for instance), anapaests frequently contracted into a series of longs and then breaking into a string of shorts, and indeed dochmiacs are often found intermixed in such contexts. Passion on this scale is more often the prerogative of actors than of chorus; it is noteworthy that a play which has almost the whole of its lyric in dochmiac or iambo-dochmiac is the *Septem*, where the chorus is still a leading character. In the solo arias, the ἀπολελυμένα, of Euripides the dochmiac and prosodiac with their irregular forms play much part; such rhythm evidently found congenial expression in the new music then being developed by Timotheus. For in the closing decades of the fifth century the tendency for music to become interesting at the expense of words is reflected in some Euripidean lyric; repetitions and flourishes begin to appear which are part of the musical motif rather than of the sense of the passage—they are song *rather* than poetry. The song of Electra by the sleeping Orestes is pure opera:

κάταγε κάταγε πρόσιθ', ἀτρέμας ἀτρέμας ἴθι...

Aristophanes enjoyed himself in this vein; listen to the ἀναγνωρισμός of the pseudo-Helen and Menelaus:

ὦ χρόνιος ἐλθὼν σῆς δάμαρτος ἐσχάρας
λαβέ με λαβέ με πόσι, περίβαλε δὲ χέρας.
φέρε σε κύσω. ἄπαγέ μ' ἄπαγ' ἄπαγ' ἄπαγέ με.

And in the *Frogs* Glyke's 'Rape of the Cock' parodies, not only fancy forms of dochmiac metre, but the general tendency to use this passionate rhythm incongruously for the expression of homely sentiments; after all, Electra in the ode I quoted is only saying to the Chorus in effect: 'Sh! don't make a noise and wake him.'

Rhythm then might be φορτικός or τραγικός by its inherent properties; a more external kind of significance might sometimes be lent it by emotional association. It is probable, for instance, that the sequence of metres used by the Mystae in the *Frogs* occurred at actual stages of the religious processions in Attica on festival days, and so struck the ear and eye of spectators who would be calling to mind the familiar scenes while listening to the new words. But in this whole question we are on rather uncertain ground, and the metricians' occasional notes on origins do not help much. The short iambo-trochaic colon called the ithyphallic—χρῆμά τοι γελοῖον, οὐκ ἄνολβος ἔσται—may indeed as its name implies have been used in ritual processions, but that means nothing for the lyrics of drama, where it is simply a very common phrase, usually a clausula, in all kinds of metrical contexts, and comes trailing no cloud of associations. In tragedy perhaps the only clear case is the ionic metres, in their straightforward and anaclastic forms:

ἴτε βάκχαι ἴτε βάκχαι
φέρ' ὕδωρ, φέρ' οἶνον ὦ παῖ.

These were sung in the orgiastic cults of Cybele and Dionysus introduced from Asia Minor, and the lyrics of the *Bacchae* are appropriately full of their characteristic measures:

τά τε ματρὸς μεγάλας ὄρ-
  -για Κυβέλας θεμιτεύων,
ἀνὰ θύρσον τε τινάσσων
κισσῷ τε στεφανωθεὶς
Διόνυσον θεραπεύει.

Probably the ἴτε βάκχαι ἴτε βάκχαι is an echo of the actual cry of the frenzied hierophants. The Persian chorus of Aeschylus also sings its first lyric in ionic metre, describing the pomp and splendours of the royal army's advance over land and water into Greece:

πεπέρακεν μὲν ὁ περσέπτολις ἤδη...

Perhaps this rhythm, which some of the audience might actually have seen and heard performed by leaping priests to the clash of cymbals, conveyed here indirectly a suggestion of Oriental ἁβρότης and gave a warning of something unstable and illusory in the martial display which the words evoked. It is difficult for us to appreciate this aspect of ionic rhythm, and still more the notion of something dissolute and effeminate, which was alleged to inhere in the ἀνακλώμενοι or 'broken' ionics of the anacreontic variety. This may be a somewhat theoretical pronouncement of a later date based on the *de facto* association with Phrygian eunuchs and the traditional version of Anacreon's character. At least where this metre appears in extant dramas—in the earlier choruses of the *Prometheus*, for instance—no suggestion of the kind can be intended:

> πρόπασα δ' ἤδη στονόεν λέλακε χώρα,
> μεγαλοσχήμονά τ' ἀρχαιοπρεπῆ στένουσι τὰν σὰν
> ξυνομαιμόνων τε τιμάν.
> ὁπόσοι τ' ἔποικον ἁγνᾶς
> 'Ασίας ἕδος νέμονται,
> μεγαλοστόνοισι σοῖς πήμασι συγκάμνουσι θνατοί.

'All the tribes of men in all the lands round about, the seas and rivers and the dark concerns of the underworld, all bemoan your harsh fate, Prometheus, even I bemoan it.' That is the theme of the whole of this chorus, which passes from ionic into trochaic and iambic and other metres; the ionic-anacreontic is not in any way signalised.

When all this is said, much the greater part of the ῥυθμική of the lyrics of Greek drama remains outside these categories, not susceptible, at least with the knowledge at our disposal, of any definite analysis in terms of emotional suggestion. In general, one and the same metre can in different contexts and with different words be used to convey the most diverse effects. Moreover, one metrical type frequently shades off into another with a large imperfectly defined neutral zone between the clear-cut extremes; thus iambic melts into trochaic, dactylic into anapaestic, ionic into choriambic or other aeolic types. It is sometimes asserted that Greek verse must have had some form of ictus in order to keep these ambiguous metres distinct. But need they have been in every case so carefully distinguished?

The nature of their rhythm was relevant only to the immediate context; and either the ambiguous colon took its tempo from that, *or* the distinction is a mere matter of terminology, *or* some slight adjustment and manipulation of long and short quantity now untraceable by us made clear the characteristic movement intended. Further, a great number of the lyrics of tragedy are polymetric in character, even within the same stanza, and it is only where one rhythmical theme predominates that there can be any question of the metre itself conveying or reinforcing some significant meaning on its own account. One swallow does not make a summer, nor one dochmiac even a spasm of emotion. In English verse, with its simple structural form and arbitrary subtleties of rhythmic variation, the slightest change in tempo *may* be used with significant effect in collaboration with the sense of the words. In these lines of A. E. Housman:

Crossing alone the nighted ferry
  with the one coin for fee,
whom, on the wharf of Lethe waiting,
  count you to find? Not me.
The brisk fond lackey to fetch and carry,
  the true, sick-hearted slave,
expect him not in the just city
  and free land of the grave.

Raymond Mortimer justly calls attention to 'the fifth line so quick and busy, the end so slow and spacious and serene'. Greek lyric ῥυθμική, an art of great structural complexity, is much more rarely concerned with this transitory irradiation of the words. It stands on its own formal interest and beauty.

23

INTERIOR SCENES AND ILLUSION IN GREEK DRAMA

In an age and climate which encourage private life within four walls, our theatres look for most of their drama in an enclosed box with the fourth wall missing. The stage itself is shaped like that. The Athenians started drama in the open air, their tragic themes are mainly from public life, and incorporate a mostly passive group of twelve or fifteen people as a sounding-board for the action. So they naturally developed a quite different set of scenic conventions. The scene was in the open air in front of some solid structure, and it was divided into two planes, that of actors on the stage and that of Chorus in the orchestra. The actors were often at a slightly higher level, but one important thing was the physical separation of Chorus and actors, their distinct modes of utterance and movement, and the fact that the one was collective, the others individual. Moreover, with the open sky above their heads, the Greek poets were tempted to make their Olympian gods, with their interest in the affairs of men, into visible presences, sometimes overhead, sometimes even visibly descending. In the orchestra there was movement in depth; on the stage the lines were mainly lateral like a sculptured frieze, occasionally vertical. Scenery was rudimentary; what there was served the barest needs of clarity and convenience, not illusion. Dress was formal and splendid; grouping, movement and sound were the essentials.

Comings and goings were either along the parodoi or through the door in the rear structure; the needs of the drama determined which, without any ambiguity. Since the same actor had often to make his exit by the one and return in another character by the other, he must have been able to get round behind unseen. Either therefore the rear structure extended along the whole line of the stage as far as the parodoi, or there must have been a screening fence of some kind; we do not know which, or if the one changed in course of time to the other.

The massive simplicity of this setting was enough for most requirements, and in general the poets constructed their dramas for this scene. But occasionally they conceived an action which demanded more, and refused to mutilate their conception by bringing it into line with the conventional setting. Such exceptional demands were mainly two: for change of scene and for the view of an interior. Here, and here alone, the resources of our modern theatre have some advantage for the staging of Greek plays. We have lost the sense of space, the double plane, the gift of significant movement and audible choral song, but we have a curtain and scene-shifters (at the heavy price of a break in the performance), and with depth of stage, interior lighting and frontal seating we can open up an interior scene.

These two special demands remained exceptional. To some limited extent the history of fifth-century tragedy is one of slightly increasing complexity and slight concessions to something like realism. But as far as staging was concerned *all* the essential problems were posed and solved by Aeschylus. Or rather, all we can say with certainty is that they were solved within his lifetime and the solutions used in his plays; personally I find it almost inconceivable that it was not his own masterful originality that was chiefly responsible.

Let us start with the *Persae*, the oldest extant Greek tragedy. (Now that we have got rid of the fallacy that the *Supplices* represents an older and more primitive form of drama, for which some specially simple kind of staging must be imagined, it is easier to get the whole picture, and to see that there is not much question of development, but simply of the different requirements of different plays.) In this play all exits and entrances are from a distance, except for the appearance of Darius on his own tomb, which clearly occupies the central position. The Queen comes from the palace, the Messenger and Xerxes from the army (the latter on his way to the palace)—obviously from opposite sides, therefore. The Queen, like Agamemnon and Cassandra after her, makes her first appearance in a chariot (since at her next appearance she says she has come without one this time), perhaps drawn by mules as fairly reliable, quiet beasts (they were presumably led by attendants). This device gives her height and dignity to respond seated to the obsequious Chorus;

next time, of course, when she is to confront Darius, such a posture would be out of place. How are we to picture the tomb of Darius? The Elders summon him to 'the topmost summit of the mound'—ἔλθ' ἐπ' ἄκρον κόρυμβον ὄχθου. But a 'mound' in the sense of a bank or hill is pure Wilamowitz, who is always wanting one thrown up on his 'primitive' scene, an unhandy thing to fix up on a stage with no scene-painting, and surely we are not meant to imagine the Great King buried in a kind of tumulus? He ought to have an outsize in tombs, and the tomb itself is an 'eminence'. The word ὄχθος is vague, and when Orestes later τύμβου ἐπ' ὄχθῳ τῷδε calls to his (dead) father he is presumably standing upon the steps of a tomb with a stele in the Athenian manner. But Darius is to appear ἐπ' ἄκρον κόρυμβον ὄχθου, stepping up in his royal saffron slippers—κροκόβαπτον ποδὸς εὔμαριν ἀείρων—i.e. surely he is to stand on the top of the tomb, a majestic towering figure, perhaps with visibly yellow slippers, perhaps not, if the building had a pediment, gazing down upon his salaaming, awestruck courtiers. What in fact would the tomb be but the central building, the σκηνή or booth which must have been there from the beginning of drama, where Thespis in the Agora kept his disguises and came out as actor in one mask and another to address the Chorus? So essential a building, for changes of costume, for exits and entrances, for background framing, for acoustics, can never have been given up, whether or not it was permanently there between festivals.

Since the rear structure is needed as a tomb, its doors cannot be used for exits and entrances, and the palace is therefore at a distance—in any case Aeschylus wants to send off Xerxes in a lamenting exodos with the Chorus. But it has in the early part of the play another function. The Chorus has to *sit down*. People argue a good deal about the amount of realism required by an Athenian audience and the amount that is simply taken on suggestion or description. In some passages it is clear that description is being used instead of representation, as when the sight-seeing women in the parodos of the *Ion* describe the wonderful metopes that they see on the temple when clearly the audience sees nothing of the sort. Sometimes, too, description is used because the audience is being informed of the lay-out of an interior scene; this has caused a good deal of misunderstanding, as we shall see. But in general when a speaker says 'Here am I, doing so-and-so', or 'having come on a winged car', or the like, I take it that he must in some way suit the action or the appearance to the word. And I am very doubtful of symbolic dances, as when G. Thomson's Oceanids execute a dance which is known to the audience to symbolise nymphs on sea-horses. So here, when the Chorus says 'Come let us sit down and debate', and proceeds to debate, I believe they sat down, not performed a dance indicative of sitting down to debate. So they must have had somewhere to sit; obviously a tragic Chorus does not squat on the ground. What they say is τόδ' ἐνεζόμενοι στέγος ἀρχαῖον, a deliberately vague phrase—'this ancient building'—and ἐνεζόμενοι can mean either 'sitting in' or 'sitting on'. There is only one building there, and only one place where they could sit—the steps surrounding it, which naturally they sit *on*. But of course they are meant to be *in* a council chamber; this in fact is Aeschylus' simple way here of getting over the 'interior' problem—by ignoring it. The Chorus is of Persian elders whose function is to debate and take counsel, so Aeschylus gives them in these brief anapaests a token debate—φροντίδα κεδνὴν καὶ βαθύβουλον θώμεθα, and they start off. How is Xerxes getting on? has the bow or the spear proved victorious? Perhaps it is an echo of that council meeting for which a few years previously Phrynichus' Eunuch had arranged the seats, only his counsellors were not a Chorus but supers, who could continue sitting. Aeschylus' counsellors are interrupted next minute by the arrival of the Queen, whereupon they arise, or perhaps fall prostrate (προσπίτνω). Pickard-Cambridge objects that it is unlikely that they would describe the fairly recent tomb of Darius as a στέγος ἀρχαῖον, or sit on it to debate, but of course the answer is that it is not the tomb of Darius, but a council chamber. At this stage the audience has no thought of Darius, or his tomb; all it sees is a nondescript 'ancient building' which is the scene of brief and abortive deliberations, and is obviously understood to be containing the counsellors who sit upon its steps.

A similar use of the rear building was made in the *Niobe*, with the grief-stricken mother sitting silent and veiled by her children's tomb for a large part of the play—a Greek tomb this time, but as there were fourteen children, quite reasonably a large one. In the *Supplices* it is an altar to all the gods

222 πάντων δ' ἀνάκτων τῶνδε κοινοβωμίαν σέβεσθε

—abstract for concrete, implying a κοινὸς βωμός like that of the twelve gods in the agora. Again the Chorus are told by Danaus to sit, on the πάγου ἀγωνίων θεῶν, and there is also room by it for the βρέτη, the images to which they cling, and for Danaus to stand there as at a look-out post and see the approaching ship—clearly the steps are roomy and would give plenty of space for the movement of actors when not cluttered up with seated Chorus. The same kind of tableau is found in the *Septem* on the acropolis of Thebes with the Chorus clinging to a number of βρέτη δαιμόνων until bullied by Eteocles into retiring to a little distance (the orchestra). No rear building seems to be required at all in this play, and perhaps the βρέτη arranged in a row in front were meant to obscure the view of it so that the audience could ignore it—or perhaps it served as a κοινὸς βωμός here too; in the *Laius* and *Oedipus*, earlier in the trilogy, it had probably served as a palace-front. In the *Agamemnon* and *Choephoroe* it is a palace, in the *Eumenides* a temple. Probably it was built with pilasters anyway, and if in a satyr-play it had to represent a cave you ignored the pilasters or curtained them over, but of course Sophocles may by this time have introduced some form of scene-painting, perhaps in the form of canvas screens drawn in front when necessary. Certainly it must have been solidly built, with a roof that was safe for several people to walk on, and of course with a back staircase, not a mere ladder, which could be negotiated in full dress. The *Prometheus Vinctus* presents problems too long to be discussed here; briefly, I assume that Aeschylus did write this play, though possibly (like the *Septem*) not quite in the form we now have it in, that it was intended for production in Athens whether actually produced in the poet's lifetime or not, that the Oceanids were not swung on by a gigantic crane in an aerial bus weighing over a ton but arrived in separate winged cars on the roof out of sight of Prometheus (perhaps they walked on holding wings before them, perhaps they were pushed seated on a little trolley) and in response to his request (272) made their way down the back staircase to reassemble in the orchestra during the Oceanus scene. Possibly only three or four appeared on the roof while the rest sang off-stage. Oceanus on his griffin probably was swung on by the μηχανή. The machine was used, according to Pollux, in the *Psychostasia* for Eos to flutter to earth, pick up her dead son Memnon (as on the lovely Duris cup) and fly away with him. This play was full of daring experiment; apparently the scene for part of the time (perhaps the prologue) was laid in Heaven, i.e. on the roof of the σκηνή, which had to support Zeus with a large pair of scales weighing the souls of Achilles and Memnon (one would give a lot to know what the souls looked like, or were they perhaps invisible in the scale-pans?) flanked by Thetis and Eos.

The most vexed problems of all, however, are raised by the trilogy; how were the interior scenes represented, by some form of eccyclema or just inside a wide-opened doorway? The use of the eccyclema used to be taken for granted, but recently a powerful movement has been launched against the idea, and Pickard-Cambridge, following Bethe and Reisch, discards it altogether for the fifth century. I would however point out a grave difficulty in the way of the exposed-threshold theory. Greek doors normally opened inwards; were the doors of the theatre-building an exception to this rule, and if so how were they secured back? were there always two mute door-holders in action? And if, as one would naturally assume, these doors behaved like any others and opened inwards how did they manage to clear the corpses or the seated Ajax or the sleeping Furies, especially as the opening would need to be wide, so that the door-leaves must have been of considerable breadth? Corpses *could* of course be dumped outside by attendants, though at ruinous cost to the tableau-effect (Clytaemnestra with two corpses at the end of the *Agamemnon*, Orestes with two corpses at the end of the *Choephoroe*), but Ajax and his grisly trophies could not, nor could Heracles lashed to his broken pillar in *Hercules Furens*, nor the contents of Apollo's temple in the *Eumenides*. I suppose one could get round it by assuming that in plays where interior scenes were impending movable screens were substituted for doors, but this seems unlikely when the doors are used for ordinary purposes at other parts of the play.

However it is true that as Pickard-Cambridge says Pollux and our other ancient authorities classify or refer to stage machinery and other properties all in the lump without reference to chronology or development, and they use language which seems to refer to two different sorts of device for the ἐκκύκλημα or ἐξώστρα, one a platform pushed forward on wheels, one a pivoting arrangement, and tend to muddle the two. I think the pivoting arrangement and anything requiring heavy or complicated machinery can be left out of account for the fifth century, when there was only one pair of doors available, which had for the rest of the time to behave normally. The word itself—ἐκκύκλημα—is not attested before the second century A.D. but may come from earlier commentators. Apart from inferences from the texts of the plays themselves our only contemporary evidence is two scenes in Aristophanes, from the *Acharnians* and the *Thesmophoriazusae*. Euripides in the one, Agathon in the other is wheeled out—the verb ἐκκυκλέω is used in both—and wheeled in again. Euripides orders κλῇε πηκτὰ δωμάτων which is a bit of Euripidean diction, Agathon uses εἰσκυκλέω, εἴσω τις ὡς τάχιστά μ' εἰσκυκλησάτω. The supporters of the eccyclema claim that this is a skit on the use of the eccyclema in tragedy, its opponents that the word ἐκκυκλέω has no particular significance and is used quite untechnically for wheeling out someone on a wheeled couch.

I am not sure that the word ἐκκυκλέω would be quite such an obvious choice for the process, and were wheeled couches a commonplace article of furniture? If the answer is 'no, but they would be needed to bring a bedridden person out on the stage' then we are back at the question 'was apparatus for bringing out heavy things fairly often wanted on the stage anyway?' If so, the simplest way of bringing out a person on a couch was surely to dump an ordinary couch on the wheeled platform or truck used for such operations and trundle it in. And in these two scenes there is strong evidence that this did in fact happen, since both poets hand over a whole series of articles for which they are asked, Euripides rags and a beggar's outfit, Agathon female paraphernalia. These would naturally be lying to hand on the platform, not extracted like a conjuring trick from under the pillow.

Perhaps not much can be made of the point that since these are both tragic poets this is getting at the use of the eccyclema in tragedy. The one scene is obviously reminiscent of the other; Aristophanes is using once more in the *Thesmophoriazusae* a motif that had gone over well in the *Acharnians*, but the main point of the parody lies in the handing over of the equipment of tragic inspiration. In any case the purpose of the eccyclema is different in each case; Agathon is coming out to sun himself, because he composes better in the open air, and so his use of an eccyclema would be parallel to that of Phaedra's in the *Hippolytus*; Euripides however is using it to save time—he has no leisure to come out and talk to Dicaeopolis. He is composing, we are told, 'with his feet up'—ἀναβάδην (the ordinary meaning of the word; the Scholiast's alternative explanation, that it may mean 'in an upstairs room', is a mistaken inference from καταβαίνειν δ' οὐ σχολή, which picks up this scene comically—'I haven't time to get down'). But here the inference that the representation of an interior scene is intended is surely irresistible, for the simple reason that it would be a good joke, whereas the alternative would not be funny at all. 'Euripides, listen to me,' says Dicaeopolis. 'No time. Busy' says Euripides from within. ἀλλ' ἐκκυκλήθητι—'Get yourself wheeled out' doesn't answer the objection at all; 'Use the eccycle then' would bring a roar from the theatre. 'Can't.' 'Oh, *do*.' 'Very well, I'll eccycle. But I've no time to get down.' Aristophanes is having fun with the device of eccyclema, though not necessarily in tragedy; he uses it too often in his own comedies for that. In the *Thesmophoriazusae* there is a stage direction at the end of the prologue saying that the 'shrine is pushed (ὠθεῖται) forward'; this indicates the change of scene from before the house of Agathon to the precinct of the two goddesses. It would be the obvious vehicle for the transport of the two cages in which, according to the Scholiast, the Just and Unjust Arguments are shut up like fighting-cocks, for the colossal statue of Peace which the Chorus drag up from the hole (i.e. out of the doorway), for the beds of Strepsiades and Pheidippides and doubtless much more. Some of these are *simply* a question of transport, sometimes an interior scene is conveyed. In the *Clouds* the interior of the Reflectory is undoubtedly shown by these means, with pupils crouched in various grotesque attitudes hard at work. Pickard-Cambridge objects that they must be meant to run outside the door because the Disciple presently orders them to go in—it is against the rules for them to stay too long in the open air; but of course that is simply Aristophanes fooling again with the literal use and the conventional significance of the eccyclema. It should be noted that in all cases, tragic and comic, the objects conveyed are either inanimate, or else prostrate, seated or crouching figures.

Now let us return to Aeschylus. All three plays of the triology expose an interior scene—is this Aeschylus delighted with a new toy? If he used an eccyclema there must be room on it in the *Agamemnon* for two dummy corpses, one of them caught in a net and sprawled over a bath (1539). Clytaemnestra of course steps forward separately, takes up her position (centre, behind her victims?) and declares ἕστηκα δ' ἔνθ' ἔπαισ' ἐπ' ἐξειργασμένοις. (This tableau gives some indication of the width of the top step of the rear building.) Was this perhaps the first electrifying use of the interior scene revealed? The *Choephoroe* is even more adventurous in its staging, since it changes scene as well, by telescoping the distance between the tomb of Agamemnon and the palace. It is impossible to say whether the first part is played in the orchestra, using the altar there as a tomb, or whether, as I am more inclined to believe, the tomb was in front of the palace, perhaps on the lowest step. In any case it must have had a central position; anything else is unthinkable for the grouping of the great κομμός, the centre-piece of the whole trilogy. If the tomb was by the stage it is even possible that the palace in the background was so to speak rendered invisible by the Chorus starting its song ἰαλτὸς ἐκ δόμων ἔβαν and yet appearing by way of the parodos. Orestes having seen them coming withdraws with Pylades to the far side of the σκηνή building. After the κομμός the palace as it were comes into existence when Orestes hammers at the door.

It is often claimed that the normal number of doors in the back scene was three, the outer two being usually attributed to projecting wings or paraskenia. I am not qualified to argue about the archaeological evidence as to the date when that shape of stage-building was first adopted—whether in the fifth or fourth century. (Evidently it is far from conclusive.) But I can see no textual evidence whatever for the existence of more than one *door* in any fifth-century tragedy, and even about comedy I am doubtful. (I have no time to go into this question here; it all depends on whether you are prepared to give comic poets *carte blanche* to call the same single building now the country-house of Dicaeopolis, now the town-house of Euripides or of Lamachus; now the house of Heracles, now the palace of Pluto, and so on. Personally I find this much easier than to suppose a lot of lop-sided grouping.) For tragedy the strongest evidence is usually held to be the *Alcestis*, played 438, perhaps even before the Periclean reconstruction of the theatre. Admetus tells an attendant to show Heracles in: ἡγοῦ σὺ τῷδε δωμάτων ἐξωπίους ξενῶνας οἴξας, and this is said to indicate a side-door which the attendant is to be seen opening; but surely 'take him along and open up the guest-chambers away from the [main] palace' is meant to inform the spectators of the *inner* lay-out of the palace-buildings which they cannot see, and it goes on in the same way 'and make sure they close the doors between the courts'. The same technique is responsible for a ludicrous and widespread misunderstanding of the scene in the *Orestes* (136 ff.) where the Phrygian Eunuch says he *has* escaped [πέφευγα] in his barbarian slippers over the balconies and Dorian triglyphs of the pillared halls and is of course describing the inner courtyard scene when he scrambled out of the women's quarters before reaching the visible outer doors which he has just walked through in the ordinary way. The Chorus has just described his emergence in a normal heralding speech: 'Hush, the door is rattling—here is one of the Phrygians coming out, we shall soon know what has happened.' Unfortunately a Scholiast—one of the chattery Byzantine kind—said these lines *must* be spurious (not, observe, that they were missing in some manuscripts), inserted by actors who didn't want to risk their necks in the acrobatics described —this being of course an inference from his misunderstanding of the text. All our texts obediently bracket these lines, which are quite idiomatic normal Euripidean Greek, and if deleted leave an aching gap in which the Chorus apparently gazes in stupefied silence at the Eunuch's Rudolph Valentino act—as well they might—and without any comment on his surprising approach or any of the usual 'But soft! who comes?' leave him to introduce himself (very inadequately) and then sing a description of what they have just seen him do.

When, therefore, in the *Choephoroe* (875 ff.) the Servant bursts out of the palace crying that Aegisthus is murdered and demanding that the γυναικεῖοι πύλαι be opened and Clytaemnestra come out, it is most unlikely that we are to suppose a side-door. No actual γυναικωνῖτις was in such a position, and the audience would be most surprised at such a peculiar stage-set. The Servant might call out from within the house, but I think it more likely that he comes out, wrings his hands in desperation as he laments, then turns and calls back through the door towards the supposed interior. After Clytaemnestra has emerged, Orestes and Pylades appear, probably followed by the body of Aegisthus on the eccyclema, since all apostrophise the body as if it were present. At the end of the stichomythia it is withdrawn and Orestes drives his mother within to her death. (Afterwards, of course, there is the full tableau with both corpses and the bath-robe of Agamemnon.) The natural scene for these events in real life would be first the inner courtyard with the Servant rushing out of the ἀνδρῶνες and clamouring for the women's quarters to be opened, then in the room where Aegisthus was killed; as this is not a film Aeschylus brings it all out in front, and orientates the spectators with the careful mention of γυναικεῖοι πύλαι, whereas on Orestes' first arrival he spoke of the ἑρκεῖοι θύραι, the outer gates. It is essentially the same technique as when his Persian counsellors said they were sitting *in* this ancient hall and then later we find it turning into the tomb of Darius. The minimum of descriptive hint is given, since elaboration would only emphasise improbabilities. The use of the eccyclema is merely a convenient device for the transport from the interior of stationary objects which are like the rest supposed to be inside but cannot emerge on their own legs; it does not of itself cause the audience to register 'Interior Scene'. It was presumably used with no notion of the kind in the opening scene of the *Diktyoulkoi* when (we gather from the fragments) the fishermen haul the chest containing Danae and Perseus out of the sea in a 'hollow' between the rocks—i.e. cast their nets into the rear doorway and appear to tug out a sort of large rabbit hutch on a trolley; they presently open it and disclose Danae sitting there holding a doll (or a bundle). I expect the rock of Prometheus was set up on it, and in the final catastrophe, when this was hurled into the abyss, it was tipped backwards and so could be withdrawn through the door. The eccyclema is a simple and indispensable all-purposes bit of stage machinery.

In the final play of the trilogy Aeschylus makes the most daring change of scene in Greek tragedy. Since this is not merely a question of telescoping distance in the same neighbourhood but of moving from Delphi to Athens, the Chorus has to be sent off, and make a second entry. So far as we know, only Sophocles in the *Ajax* attempted anything similar. Of course, not only the change of scene is in question; Aeschylus wishes to convey also the flight and pursuit of Orestes. The eccyclema neatly reinforces the change. In the Prologue the Pythia walks up a parodos (why should she be supposed to emerge from a side-door?), arriving in the early morning at her duties in Apollo's temple. Fleeing precipitately on hands and knees from the sight within she describes this in detail, so that the audience will be able to interpret the rather sketchy selection from it which they will presently see on the eccyclema. After her departure perhaps Hermes comes out first, then the eccyclema with Orestes crouching by the omphalos with wreath and sword, and a token Fury or two, perhaps the Chorus-leader and one other, huddled in sleep in front of him. Apollo steps up behind and speaks comforting words. Then he sends off Orestes with Hermes, and retires into his temple. The ghost of Clytaemnestra appears from the shadows behind to take his place, and reproaches the leader, who answers in her sleep. The ghost disappears, the leader wakes, calls to her companions and steps off the eccyclema, which is withdrawn, and the rest of the Chorus come out in twos and threes, singing in baffled rage. Apollo shoos out the last, and drives them down the steps off the precinct into the orchestra. After their quarrel Apollo withdraws into his temple, the doors shut, the Chorus hurl themselves in pursuit down the parodos by which Orestes left. The stage is empty. The doors open again, the eccyclema appears with the statue of Athena in her temple on the Acropolis of Athens. The audience know, of course, that it would really be inside, but this is of no importance. Orestes enters and takes up a suppliant attitude by it; then the Chorus follow snuffing like hounds, and presently catch sight of him. Whether later, in the trial scene, the scene is supposed to change to the Areopagus, is not clear, and doubtless Aeschylus deliberately left the answer vague. The final procession closed in a burst of splendour what must have been an incomparable morning's experience in the life of the world's theatre.

24

THE CREATION OF DRAMATIC CHARACTERS

The Greeks invented drama, and whatever we may be told about the inadequacy of the Aristotelian notion μίμησις for the act of artistic creation, there is an obvious straightforward sense in which the theatre does 'imitate' the activity of living people. A king, a soldier, a young girl and a group of old men speak and move about the stage; the actors, got up to look these parts, impersonate them in flesh and blood, and the spectators watch and listen. It is a remarkable invention and the writer who chooses this medium, whether his object is to thrill or amuse his audience or to interpret life, has to attain it within certain restrictions, which in turn carry certain compensating advantages. First, the subject must be something which happens to people, or as Aristotle would put it, it is the representation of an action; and secondly, it must be made intelligible by the words people say to each other. Sometimes the conventions allow partial exceptions to this latter rule; the Greek Chorus may utter comments half in and half out of the action; at the beginning of a play a personage may address the audience directly: 'I am the god Dionysus, the situation is thus, and my intentions are as follows'; or he may speak his own thoughts aloud, unheard except by the audience, as in 'To be or not to be', or in a modern Expressionist play like *The Adding Machine*. But in general it is what people say to each other that carries the meaning, and the writer's communication to his audience is therefore oblique throughout. Yet in so far as human conversation conveys the writer's meaning, the drama's is the direct method as opposed to the indirect of recited epic or read novel in which conversations occur. The mimetic performance presents the action to two senses simultaneously, and even when we read a play the cutting-out of everything except direct speech (with an occasional stage-direction) prevents the dissipation of our attention away from the imagined speakers.

The speakers, then, and their words, are in the forefront of drama more than in any other form of literary creation. The audience has to make the acquaintance of the speakers mainly *through* their words. In the modern theatre we may be helped by the programme of the cast, but in any good play this should not be indispensable. The dress, the make-up or mask, provide a start but do not take us far. The actors, who have studied their parts, have some conception of the sort of people they are impersonating. It is the business of the dramatist to convey to actors and audience, by the words he puts into the mouths of his personages, what kind of people he intended them to be, if the actors and the audience are to interpret this correctly. In other words, the dramatist has to 'create characters' not by description, but by letting them speak for themselves. His personages, that is, have to speak 'in character'.

Now this notion of the 'creation of character' is so familiar to us that we are liable to assume that all dramatists at all periods are concerned with it in the same sort of way, and even that it is an end in itself. Aristotle warns us that 'the characters exist for the sake of the action', not *vice versa*; but the truth is, of course, that in separating 'characters' and 'action' at all we are to some extent making an unreal abstraction. The characters only exist in the action, and the action is what it is because these characters take part in it. Henceforward I shall use the word 'action' only in this wider sense, and call 'plot' the sequence of incidents in so far as these can be referred to in abstraction from the whole. Assuming, then, that one of the functions of the words the dramatist writes is to 'create characters', it is clear that the *extent* to which this function applies in any given play will be determined by the action of the play, by how far this turns on the participators being persons of a very particularised sort; and it will also to some extent depend upon the theatrical convention of the time and the idiosyncrasies of the dramatist. I am arguing about this because there is a widespread tendency in modern literary criticism to overpress this notion of 'character-drawing' in appraising a Greek play. You all know the subsection entitled 'The characters' in our annotated editions. The editor tries to think of as many of the dramatis personae as possible, and squeezes the speeches hard in an effort to do this, rather on the model of the Verity Shakespeares he dimly remembers reading at school. 'Anything a person says may be used against him' is the motto, and even good scholars are not immune. Page finds 'inconstancy of temperament' the 'keynote' of Medea's character, and illustrates this by her changes of mood: 'At the beginning of the play her voice is heard within uplifted in passionate lamentation. Then she enters the scene, not convulsed with grief as we had expected, but self-possessed, pleading for sympathy with sly, deceitful arguments', etc. Now it is true that in the course of the play Medea is depicted a prey to fierce passions of jealousy, pride, indignation and hatred, that these sometimes boil over in paroxysms, sometimes simmer beneath a false pretence of submission and reconciliation, sometimes struggle for victory over her love for her children. But all this has nothing to do with inconstancy of temperament; and the contrast which makes Page adopt this 'keynote' between her passionate lamentations within and her reasoned speech on her first appearance, is the contrast between lyric utterance and formal speech, especially the first speech of a leading personage, which convention requires to be pitched in a moderately low key. As for the reasoned arguments, any speaker in a Greek play who is labouring under great stress of emotion is liable to speak in this manner because it is part of the rhetorical tradition of Greek drama, and especially of Euripidean drama, that they do so analyse and expound their case; but this does not mean that the poet intended us to conceive any of them as the sort of person whom passion tends to make eloquently analytical. The influence of the set speech in the law-courts, even to its formal pattern and subdivisions, also became increasingly strong in Greek drama, and produced a kind of stage-speech quite alien to our notions of theatre. Denniston, again, trying to enumerate for Orestes (in Eur. *El.*) as long a list of characteristics as possible, says 'he is cynically distrustful of the Farmer's motives (260)—and rude to the Old Man (553–4)'. Both these passages occur in quick dialogue, one in stichomythia, the other near it, and in both Orestes has not yet disclosed his identity to his sister, who is still addressing him as ξένε. In stichomyth you always score as many *points* as you can, and where there is a case of concealed identity these points are sure to play up the irony of the situation—one of the speakers, and the audience, knows the truth, while the other does not. So when Orestes asks Electra why her husband has never claimed his rights over her as his wife and gets the answer 'he does not regard Aegisthus as lawfully able to dispose of my hand, stranger', he nods: 'I see, he might one day have to answer for it *to Orestes*.' Electra says 'yes, that was his fear, but also he is a decent man'—πρὸς δὲ καὶ σώφρων ἔφυ. This draws from Orestes an admiring φεῦ—'this is a noble spirit, who should be rewarded'. In the other passage the Old Man who had been παιδαγωγός to Agamemnon and had saved the infant Orestes from Aegisthus comes in to ask the strangers (Orestes and Pylades) if they have any news of Orestes. He is inclined to be suspicious of the newcomers—says they look like gentlemen, but many a cad is well-born; still he bids them welcome. Orestes returns the greeting, then turning to Electra asks which of her friends this aged relic of a man might be—παλαιὸν ἀνδρὸς λείψανον. This is not rudeness; it emphasises the oldness and feebleness of the man who, as Electra says in her reply, brought up Agamemnon himself, and therefore, as Orestes next wonderingly realises, snatched the baby Orestes from his enemies. So old and frail is their one link with the past, with the ancient house now under an alien master.

Here then are some ways in which distortion is achieved by making the words spoken reflect back in detail upon the character of the speaker when they were never meant to be looked at from that angle. Another aberration of that subsection 'The characters' is to pursue inquiries about them which are not within the scope of the play itself: 'Would Othello have been really happy with Desdemona in the long run?' 'How many children had Lady Macbeth?' (L. C. Knights). So in the *Ion*: Xuthus is left supposing Ion to be his own illegitimate son by a Delphian girl, and not told that (as the boy and his mother and the Chorus and the spectators learn) Ion was the son of his wife and Apollo; he is lightly guyed by Euripides, but without much malice. A. S. Owen reflects on coming events:

We are bound to feel sorry at what is in store for him. On his return from Parnassus he would find his wife and 'son' gone without him. The advantage of having divine escort had made them hurry away without leaving any message or apparently giving him a thought. Nor can we believe that it would be long before he knew the unpleasant truth about Ion, for the slaves who had disclosed his secret to Creusa when threatened with death would not be likely to be more reticent when they found him treating his stepson as though he were really his own son.

Now if coming events outside the plot are of any significance for the action of a Greek play they cast a very black and definite shadow before. If there is no shadow, then gratuitous supplements of this kind ought not to be allowed to colour our impressions of the characters of Xuthus, Ion and Creusa. Xuthus drops out of the story because he is not relevant to the action any more, and no one who was not trying to think what could be squeezed out of the 'character' of Xuthus would notice that a message was not left for him. The case is quite different in the *Tr.*, where Deianeira has gone silently away to kill herself and Heracles on hearing of her death and its motive has not a word or a thought more for her. *That* silence means something for the character of Deianeira and Heracles within the action. The plea that the characters are so 'real' to us that they persist in living outside the story may be flattering to the author but has nothing to do with the work he has created. Such additions to the action would in fact alter the characters, so far from helping us to understand them. It is true that Shaw in his preface to *Pygmalion* informs us testily that Eliza Doolittle did *not* marry the Professor; she married Freddie Hill, who was unsuccessful in business, and they were constantly hard up for money. But this is the Shavian way of objecting to a stage-interpretation of the play itself which is concerned to show the Professor and Eliza falling in love, and sentimentalised the acting accordingly.

This brings me to another point: the influence of the actor on the interpretation of the play, particularly in the modern stage-tradition. This tradition is predominantly realistic, so that almost any actor in in any part tends to fill in some of the—from his point of view—unfinished portrait of the character he is acting; he tries to integrate it more into a personality from which the words he has to speak may proceed, as they would in actual life. So when Greek plays are acted on the modern stage we get a host of nuances added to the plain text. The actor perhaps feels embarrassed at the long declamatory speeches of poetic drama, or its artificial stichomyth, and tries to touch up the part where possible to give it a rounder character-content; thus the just perceptibly comic flavour of some of the minor parts may be exaggerated, or a rustic surliness or a Messenger's affectations be laid on a good deal thicker. Orestes may find it a relief to throw in a rude or cynical tone; Medea may smoulder a little too transparently under her somewhat sophistically thorough rationalisations of her position, as though she were hinting that this was just *pour épater le bourgeois* and irrelevant to her real feelings. This is inevitable on a stage and before a public steeped in the naturalistic tradition of dramatic writing and acting, without masks, unrhetorical, and often a little ill at ease with poetry. Only the Expressionist theatre in modern days has been able to liberate actors and audience from this naturalistic tradition; such ballets as the *Green Table* have helped to accustom us to the Expressionist idiom of *The Insect Play* or the second act of Sean O'Casey's *The Silver Tassie*. Here it is easier to resist the temptation to interpret each utterance as exposing a new facet of the speaker's character.

The concentration of a single actor upon a single part, which is nowadays almost universal, also conduces to the effort to make that part as interesting a personality as possible. The Greek actor who had to put on in turn the masks of the Watchman, the Herald, Agamemnon, Cassandra and Aegisthus, all in the same play, was naturally less concerned to work up subtle interpretations of all these as 'character-parts'. I am not suggesting that the Greek notion of acting was superior to ours, or inferior, but simply that the dramatist would count on a different style of ὑπόκρισις, and a less ambitious one. A slow and sonorous delivery, somewhat stylised gestures, the mask and dress, and a clear and exact understanding of the meaning—the dramatist would expect no more interpretation than this. The broad lines of a character would appear in the words; subtleties of light and shade varying from actor to actor as Gielgud's Lear differs from Olivier's Lear—these would not and could not be realised. The great tableaux—Clytaemnestra haranguing a silent and immovable Cassandra, Deianeira turning silently into the palace, the dying Hippolytus gasping his half-reproachful farewell to the serenely aloof Artemis—would remain eloquent enough interpretation of the poet's characters in action.

It will be said that surely these different interpretations in performance show the inherent vitality and 'truth' of the characters created by the dramatist, that they wear a different guise in different productions and before different audiences just as historical personages might, and emerge triumphantly 'real'. Yet if we want to understand the play properly we should realise how much is given by the words of the dramatist and how much is adventitious. Not only stage conventions but attitudes of mind, religious and moral beliefs, the prevailing notions of what is admirable or pitiable or funny, will vary from one generation to another and inevitably affect our reaction to drama that survives from a past age. If we get the impression of feeling more sympathy for Clytaemnestra or Jocasta or Tecmessa, or Shylock or Falstaff, than their creators did, we should look carefully at the play and try to discover whether we are starting from different premises, or being influenced by an actor's performance, or whether perhaps after all our justification lies in the dramatist's words and their implications.

The historical development of Greek drama and its formal separation of tragedy and comedy are important for this question of character-creation. Ancient (post-Aristotelian) critics used to claim that ἦθος was the proper concern of comedy, πάθος of tragedy. This is of course one of those antitheses so dear to Greek theory, but the distinction is more applicable than might at first appear. All Greek audiences liked to proceed from a large solid basis of the familiar to the new and unfamiliar.

In tragedy the familiar was the particular legend with its particular participating figures; in the New Comedy (I leave the Old out of count because it is so clearly not interested in producing 'characters' except as vehicles for the illustration of comic ideas) the familiar was the traditional kind of plot and the typical characters, clarified by conventional masks. The personages of tragedy—Agamemnon,

Oedipus, Pentheus—had a strange eventful history of a highly individual kind which had to be incorporated into the action, and the poet interpreted this in the light of his views upon the nature of sin and suffering, or the relation of men to gods, or the hideousness of war, or the shortcomings of accepted conventional beliefs. Into this larger theme which lies behind the plot the conception of individual characters enters as one factor, of varying importance and prominence. It is more important in the *Medea* than in the *Troades*, in the *Philoctetes* than in the *O.T.* Euripides sometimes, as in the *Orestes*, takes a more than twice-told tale and gives it an entirely new twist by a more realistic psychological treatment of the main characters. But besides the main, the 'historical' characters as we might call them, who bear the well-known individual names, there are the anonymous ones, a Watchman, a Messenger, a Herald, a Nurse, a Paidagogos, a Servant. These are brought in to help the action along, to elicit or give information, in exchanges with the chief personages or the Chorus (i.e. the audience). They are usually of the poet's own invention, and while they may be ethically neutral, almost impersonal, like most Messengers for instance, they may also be given a free rein to indulge in a little ethos, so to speak, with touches of realism, sometimes almost of comedy, which is fleetingly an anticipation of the ἠθοποιΐα of the νέα κωμῳδία and which is sternly denied to the historical characters; so the φύλαξ of the *Antigone*, the nurse in the *Oresteia*, the Phoenician slave in the *Orestes*. But it was left to the authors of New Comedy, especially Menander, to evolve consistently a new function of dramatic speech which is much closer to that of our modern stage. Just because the plots and the masks were so stereotyped the emphasis was thrown on to detail of character interpretation; this made one play different from another, and gave its interest and originality to the action. For the first time in the history of drama characters are so portrayed that it is possible to refer each speech to the author's conception of the character of the speaker. *All* the characters, even subordinate ones, are on the same plane in this, the minor turns given to the action arise directly out of their idiosyncrasies, and some of the central characters—the Flatterer, the Miser, the Braggart Soldier, become themselves, as 'character-studies', the main theme behind the action. They become proverbial, like a Tartuffe, or a Sairey Gamp, though they are remembered not under their individual name but under their type-name.

I have purposely said little in this short essay of the trend of Greek literary criticism on this subject, because the Greek ἦθος is a term with fluctuating content, sometimes approaching in scope what we mean by 'character', sometimes much narrower than this. Its sense is coloured on the one hand by the need to distinguish it from διάνοια, as roughly the moral aspects of a person's utterances as distinct from their intellectual aspects, on the other by an antithesis to πάθος, as when Aristotle contrasts the action of the Iliad which is simple and παθητική with that of the Odyssey which is complex and ἠθική. This later hardened into the antithesis I have already referred to, allotting πάθος to tragedy and ἦθος to comedy, and Longinus developed it in a characteristic and interesting way when he represented the Iliad as the work of Homer's maturity and the Odyssey, the 'comedy of manners' (κωμῳδία τις ἠθολογουμένη), as a kind of sunset of creation, the product of an old age in calm of mind, all passion spent. Allowing for the distortions which the use of antithetical concepts always produces, there is an underlying assumption all through this that ἦθος is something which comes to expression through a process of *elaboration* which is not strictly compatible with an action which reflects high and serious tragic events. It is something which the audience must be able to sit back and contemplate at leisure, unmoved by the emotional winds that shake them at the tragic spectacle. 'Comedy of manners'—the word 'manners' of course has not its modern meaning (it is more like *mores*), but it emphasises the everydayness of the action, and reminds us that drawing-room *tragedy* was invented by Ibsen. ἦθος is not our 'dramatic character', it excludes the great tragic personality; and one reason why it excludes it is the actual practice of Greek dramatists in the relation of dramatic speech to a conception of dramatic character.

25

OLD COMEDY: THE 'ACHARNIANS' OF ARISTOPHANES[1]

Old Comedy is a unique form. It existed in fifth-century Athens, and nothing like it has ever been known or could be imagined elsewhere. It is composed within stranger and more elaborate conventions than any other surviving form of Greek poetry—composed within them? perhaps it would be truer to say rolls loosely round among them—and it also contains a larger element of pure untrammelled invention. We possess nine specimens of it, all from its closing phase, the two decades 425–405 B.C., and all by the same author. The *Acharnians* was the earliest of these, the work of a young man of twenty, an age at which even a genius composes within the inherited tradition. I cannot here speculate upon the growth of that tradition during the sixty years since Old Comedy was officially adopted by the State, nor upon its rudimentary beginnings before that; I am simply going to talk about the *Acharnians* as a typical play of this latest phase, particularly about what it looked like on the stage, a controversial subject on which the most diverse views are held. If some of mine seem heretical I must ask your indulgence; they are soberly held conclusions adopted after many years of doubt and much careful consideration of the evidence.

What are the general characteristics of an Aristophanic Old Comedy? The time is the present; the scene may be anywhere on earth or above it or under it and may at any time be changed with a word; the actors' masks and costumes are mostly grotesque; the characters may be few or many; there is a vigorous Chorus of twenty-four which in the middle of the play breaks the action to 'come forward and address' the spectators direct (parabasis); the dialogue, in various metres, is mostly spoken but sometimes half-chanted, or even sung now and again; and the solos of the actors and

[1] Delivered as a lecture at Bryn Mawr College, Pennsylvania, in March 1959.

songs of the Chorus are usually simpler in form than those of tragedy. The object is chiefly to entertain, but also to make a satirical attack on some aspect of Athenian life, which often meant on some Athenian public figures under their real names; the basis of the play is a comic idea which can be given concrete shape: this idea is quite simple and quite mad, and is put into execution with an air of sober conviction and logical consequence. For instance in the three plays the *Acharnians*, *Pax*, *Lysistrata*, which attack the continuation of the Peloponnesian War: Let the hero make a private, one-man truce with the enemy (truce-libation—σπονδαί, preserved in a bottle) and proceed at once to live in all the comforts and abundance of peace to the envy of his warring fellow-citizens. Or send the hero up to heaven on a giant dung-beetle (a cheaper version of Pegasus, easier to feed) to recover the fair lady Peace from the gods. Or get the women to stop the war by a sex-strike. This idea has to be conveyed to the audience, and therefore all Old Comedies start with a long preliminary (prologos), 200–300 spoken lines to explain (often very directly) to the spectators and get the action going, often quite a long way, before the Chorus appears. Then the Chorus arrives, to oppose, or to back up, or to watch with ironical comments. Scenes follow in which opposition or other difficulties are overcome, usually in a set debate of peculiar form (agon) and it is often after this, at the point of success, that the parabasis occurs, leaving little for the later part of the play but a demonstration of the idea in practice; the close is usually a triumphal exodos in a dance of revelry—the κῶμος from which comedy took its name.

This is a pattern open to many kinds of far-reaching modification, but often the variations themselves fall into similar shapes, pattern within pattern traced after some old traditional formula of action and song familiar to the audience. *Acharnians* is fairly typical except that the dialogue is nearly all spoken: there is no formal, half-chanted agon in which opposition is refuted, because here the Chorus itself is the chief opponent, and an agon needs two opposing actors with the Chorus to hold the sidelines as spectators and judges. For the comic Chorus is a much more *active* body than the tragic; in most plays it is a central collective character, turbulently behaved, passionately interested and involved in the issue which forms the theme of the play (least so, as it happens, in *Nubes* and *Ranae* which are in many formal ways the least typical of our surviving comedies). In a play like *Acharnians*, where the poet is putting across a case likely to go against popular feeling, the Chorus may represent views to be expected in the theatre-audience; the indignation and near-violence of its reaction is a kind of safety-valve for the poet. Contrast *Pax*, at a date when all the Greeks were ready for peace and there is no opposition from the Chorus, only a little bickering among themselves. The exception is *Aves*, where the same pattern is followed for a non-controversial issue, not necessarily as the survival of an ancient formula, but perhaps just as a sort of convenient habit. Here in *Acharnians* the hero succeeds in winning over only half the Chorus at first, then the other half. This opposition between the two halves of the Chorus is found again in *Lysistrata*, where half the Chorus is male and half female, and it is a manifestation of one of the basic characteristics of comedy. The number, 24, is twice the 12 of early tragedy, and it is a constant tendency of comic structure to pair, to set to partners as it were, to divide into semi-choruses, to run scenes in dual correspondence, to expand a play by series of insertions symmetrically constructed. The same kind of dual correspondence is found in the parabasis: the first part of this is an address to the public by the Chorus-leader, speaking for the poet ('Our poet says he has always given you the best advice...') (this is known as the anapaests, ending in the choke, in double-quick time), then follows a 'song-speech pair' ('epirrhematic syzygy')—song *A*, speech *A*, song *B*, speech *B* in strict responsion, with the length of the speeches always a multiple of four lines. Here unmistakably is some ancient traditional survival; what it means and how it was performed is one of our many unanswerable questions. After the parabasis, in the second part of *Acharnians* as of several other comedies, the Chorus dwindles to a spectator making comments, or even singing interludes without much reference to the play, lampooning some person or persons from actual life. Yet even in these loosely strung-together 'demonstration-scenes'—demonstrating the comic idea in practice—there are many symmetries of form or content or both; the riotous, earthy, irreverent invention of the poet spreads foaming along these channels of inherited formalism.

Acharnians starts with Dicaeopolis sitting alone on the Pnyx, much bored, waiting for the ecclesia to assemble. Much of the play's success will depend upon him. It was the actors of tragedy who became famous and were highly regarded by connoisseurs, but in terms of *our* notion of 'acting' the real talent was needed for comedy. The tragic actor must study rhetorical declamation, beautiful elocution; he must know how to speak poetry and have the power to move his audience to tears. But these comic leads like Dicaeopolis needed salty characterisation, wonderful timing to put across the jokes, the greatest subtlety of delivery. For every Aristophanic comedy was full of 'paratragoedia' which had to be made audible in every speech, everything from sustained quotation or parody to a faint risible echo, in words or metre: the sudden drop from tragic diction, tragic stateliness of rhythm with its regulated word-end in the line, to comic bathos, a vulgar or commonplace word, a little hop or a little bump in the rhythm never heard in tragedy. Yet even at its loosest, comic verse was far removed from prose and was composed with a rhythmic subtlety for which modern stage-speech neither has nor ever had any kind of parallel.

Where did Dicaeopolis sit, and what was the scene? On the comic stage at this period there were certain scenic conventions but no scenery: comedy did without. There was simply the ordinary stage-building in the background, the σκηνή, with a double door opening inwards and side-extensions forming covered passages to conceal actors' movements behind the stage; somewhere in these, on one side or on both, there must have been an emergency exit for actors to make their way off without having to go inside—for instance, if they needed (ostensibly) to run round to the back of the house as in *Vespes*. This was not often used, and was not a door, since it was never used to go *in* or to come *out*; possibly it was a gap covered by a curtain (some such arrangement was perhaps needed for Hermes in *Ion*). The audience remained unconscious of the background in any local sense until told by the poet what it had to be in any particular scene, or even what change was required from one speech to another. It is difficult for us to throw off our natural expectation of stability in a scene: since Dicaeopolis, Euripides and Lamachus all have to 'come out' we assume they must have three visibly separate houses; once Euripides has emerged from a door we think that must be 'Euripides' house' even though Euripides has vanished from the play. But the Greek comic stage at this period only distinguishes 'inside' and 'outside', and though the action takes place in front of the σκηνή that does not mean that it is as in New Comedy *in the street outside the house or houses of X*, *Y* or *Z*; it is simply unlocalised except when we are told where it is. In *Acharnians* the scene is simply 'Attica', town or country as required, starting on the Pnyx; in *Pax* it is earth–heaven–earth; in *Ranae* it is earth (or wherever Heracles is suppose to live)–Styx–Elysian Fields–underworld in general. But certain conventions are always kept: the interior of the σκηνή always represents 'inside'; entry by a parodos means arrival from a certain distance; if a character reappears it must always be from where he last went off; if an interior has to be shown the eccyclema-platform is rolled out.

Dicaeopolis then, as he informs us in l. 20, is sitting on the Pnyx thinking aloud—sitting, that is, on the step or steps projecting in front of the σκηνή leaving a platform slightly elevated above orchestra-level. He starts with a few jokes to warm up the public, and then we find he is sick at heart for the country life from which the war cuts him off and determined to keep peace as a subject of discussion before the assembly. Enter from the side-parodos a straggle of citizens marshalled by the Herald, to represent the ecclesia (where they sit). A certain Amphitheos, who claims to be an immortal (the inwardness of the joke escapes us now) declares that the gods have entrusted to 'me alone' (ἐμοὶ...μόνῳ) the making of peace with Sparta, but the officials won't give him journey-money. The Herald calls for the police to put him out, as being out of order. There follows a parody of assembly-business: ambassadors to the Great King have returned after four years bringing the Royal Eye back with them. The Royal Eye talks in unintelligible barbarisms until with startling clearness a near-Greek sentence (104) emerges suggesting that the Great King will see them further before giving them any money. The ambassadors try to cover up, and in disgust Dicaeopolis resolves on his great scheme, for which Amphitheos's phrase has given him the idea; he summons Amphitheos to him, gives him 8 drachmae, and sends him to Sparta to make peace for 'me alone' (ἐμοὶ...μόνῳ) (130–1)—with wife and children. Exit Amphitheos. Now the ambassador to the King of Thrace brings along some scarecrows of Thracian mercenaries, one of whom snatches the garlic from Dicaeopolis's luncheon-packet. He makes an outcry, declares he felt a drop of rain and gets the assembly postponed and broken up. Amphitheos comes back from Sparta with samples of peace in bottles, Dicaeopolis chooses the 30-year sample, and Amphitheos runs off to escape the fury of the Acharnians who are in hot pursuit. Dicaeopolis, whose war is now happily over, *goes in*—to the house in his country-deme—to celebrate the Rural Dionysia. The comic idea is launched, and now it is going to run into fierce opposition.

Enter from a side-parodos the Chorus of elderly charcoal-burners, running around the orchestra to quick stamping cretic-paeonic metre, angry at letting their prey escape from their stiff old limbs, this man who has made peace with the hated enemy, the destroyers of their vineyards. Dicaeopolis is heard calling from within for holy silence, the Chorus assume he is their man: hush, draw off to the side and see what happens; he is coming out for sacrifice. The offender marshals his household for a small-scale domestic version of the Rural Dionysia procession, and sings the Phales-song in rollicking iambics. (This throws no light on Aristotle's claim that comedy began from τῶν ἐξαρχόντων τὰ φαλλικά.) The Chorus pounces with a shower of stones, and Dicaeopolis finds he must convince them that he has done right. He offers to argue his case, proving that others nearer home are just as much responsible as the Spartans for these troubles, and he will speak with his head over a chopping-block (318). This seems an eccentric thing to do, but it is just Aristophanes taking literally a remark made by one of Euripides' heroes many years before—by Telephus, who when beset by an angry and threatening mob cried out 'I will not keep silence on my just case even if there were an axe raised to come down on my neck.' Dicaeopolis will go one better and have an actual kitchen chopping-block of the kind used by Athenian citizens to chop up their joints on; *that* will show them his confidence in the justice of his cause. When the Chorus refuse to listen he stages another *Telephus* parody, Telephus having (in a Messenger-speech) snatched up the baby Orestes and threatened to kill him unless given a hearing. There is no baby available, but there are charcoal-burners and he knows what will harrow their feelings. He runs into the house and fetches out a charcoal-scuttle and a sword. They beg him to spare its life, and a truce is made; the chopping-block is put ready, and all seems set to begin the hearing.

Here is where the agon would normally come, but in this play there is no antagonist except the Chorus which is also judge and jury, and no attendant buffoon (as in *Aves*) to punctuate the argument with his comments. So there is just the single oration of Dicaeopolis, and the scene is filled out, first with a ludicrous parody of Euripides' tragic characters, and then with a short demonstration and counter-demonstration—it cannot be called a debate—between Dicaeopolis and an Athenian senior officer Lamachus as representing the war-party.

Since Dicaeopolis' head is at stake, he must make the maximum appeal to the pity of his audience (384, the Chorus sing excited dochmiacs). In these straits he remembers his tragic performances: Euripides had a whole crowd of tragic heroes who looked woefully pathetic in rags, lame, or blind. He will beg Euripides to lend him some of his tragic clothes and properties. He knocks at the door (the same door). The Servant says Euripides is at home but not at home; his mind is out gathering phraselets, his person is in, composing a tragedy with his feet up. *Dicaeopolis*: Admirably put; call him out. *Servant* (402): Impossible (ἀλλ' ἀδύνατον). *Dicaeopolis*: ἀλλ' ὅμως. But all the same...The Servant slams the door, and Dicaeopolis knocks and calls wheedling: 'Euripides, Euripidion, do hear what I have to say.' *Euripides* (from within): Too busy. *Dicaeopolis*: Then do an indoor-roll-out. *Euripides*: An impossibility (406) (ἀλλ' ἀδύνατον). *Dicaeopolis*: Yes, but all the same...(ἀλλ' ὅμως). *Euripides*: Well, I'll do a roll-out, but I've no time to get down.

This scene by itself *proves* the use of the eccyclema on the fifth-century Greek stage, which so many scholars refuse to accept. Without it there would be no joke. The notion (of, for example, Pickard-Cambridge, following Bethe) that ἐκκυκλέω simply means wheel out in a bath-chair or on a sofa is not only not funny, it presupposes furniture running on castors as so ordinary that the audience would immediately understand the strange passive imperative ἐκκυκλήθητι ('be wheeled out'); and it is also no answer to Euripides' objection that he is *too busy*. The point of the eccyclema is that he can come out to talk while remaining indoors undisturbed. 'An impossibility', says Euripides, not unreasonably. 'Yes, of course,' says Dicaeopolis, 'but do it all the same'. The whole effect of the repetition of the earlier ἀλλ' ἀδύνατον...ἀλλ' ὅμως is lost unless the pregnantly literal sense comes out at the second go.

In a scene full of absurd Euripidean parody Dicaeopolis borrows a ragged cloak and other properties of beggary one by one (Euripides' study and its furniture having rolled out with him, cf. Agathon's properties in the *Thesmophoriazusae*), the poet protesting that he will have no tragedy left. Finally his patience is exhausted (470): 'The fellow's rude: shut fast th'impenetrable halls', back goes the eccyclema, and Dicaeopolis is left addressing a Euripidean monologue to his soul on his inadequate equipment and the ordeal before him: 'My Soul, unparsley'd must we now fare forth...' ὦ θύμ' ἄνευ σκάνδικος ἐμπορευτέα.

At last we have the promised speech defending his conduct—and behind, or rather in front of, Dicaeopolis the peasant addressing the Acharnians we find Aristophanes the comic poet addressing the audience, with echoes from Telephus the tragic hero disguised as beggar addressing the Greek chieftains: 'Friends and spectators, do not resent it if I, a beggar, venture to address you about the city, though this is a comedy; for even comedy can speak the truth. This is only the Lenaea, and there are no foreigners present.' It is not a very closely argued speech, nor will it bear historical examination; one might by denuding it of all life extract a serious message on these lines: 'The war arose from a series of trivial incidents, heated up by considerations of prestige and disproportionately violent retaliations, and there you were. You blame the Spartans, but put yourselves in their place for a moment.' It is all very indirectly hinted, sheering off into comic metaphor and comic exaggeration whenever it might seem to be getting near the bone, and ending on a note of parody again: 'Of course that's how you would have reacted; then why not—the Spartans? No?—then why not Telephus? sense you have none.' This was about as far as a comic poet could go, in the middle of a war, with feelings running high. Only half the Chorus is convinced, and comes to blows with the other half; these call in Lamachus, who largely because of the form of his name is made, no doubt quite unfairly, into a figure of fun as the swash-buckling *miles gloriosus*. There is no *argument* here, only a hint that war suits the book of officers on high pay, and of ambassadors, not of ordinary people. The point is really to make fun of Lamachus' crested and plumed helmet and Gorgon-shield, in preparation for the final scene.

The Chorus—it is not clear why—now declares itself convinced, the actors go off, and it turns to address the spectators in the parabasis with the words (627) ἀλλ' ἀποδύντες τοῖς ἀναπαίστοις ἐπίωμεν—'let us strip and attack the Anapaests'. The meaning of this is much disputed; is it literal or metaphorical? It would take too long to argue the point here properly; I will only say that it seems to me impossible to interpret the words in the sense that the Chorus discard their cloaks (assuming they wear any) and appear in tunics alone because they need to be unencumbered for energetic dancing. They might have needed such freedom at their first appearance, chasing the peacemonger, but the notion of wildly flung capers accompanying the anapaests spoken by the Chorus-leader is grotesque; the parabasis was meant to be *listened to*, and any discreet flute-music such as probably accompanied an anapaestic chant seems singularly ill-suited to the timing of high kicks and twirls. It is often suggested that the 'stripping' happened regularly at this point, and was meant to illustrate the putting-off of their stage-personality in order to speak for the poet direct to the public (here in the third person, but in some plays in the first person singular). But stage-personality was visible in the mask rather than the cloak, and the word ἀποδύω is properly used for clothes, not masks. And if they took off masks they would have to go through the business of tying them on again for the second part of the parabasis where they are back as old Acharnians. The word then seems likely to be a metaphor, like our 'roll up our sleeves and get down to it', as in the compound ἐπαποδύομαι elsewhere (*Lysistrata* 615). It is conceivable that the *choice* of the metaphor at this particular point is significant—that it is a 'vestigial' survival of some actual procedure in one of those ancient choral performances from which Old Comedy originally sprang, but this is guesswork which receives no support from the other plays. (Cf. θαἰμάτια βαλόντες (so B) *Vespes* 408 to παιδία, who never wore them. 'Strip, men.')

The Anapaests provide no very 'serious message' from the poet. He has never 'come forward', they declare, to praise himself to the audience, but since Cleon has seen fit to slander him as one who offends the State by his comic jibes he must reply that his satire is always salutary: he prevents the Athenians from lapping up the fulsome flatteries of some foreigners—poets with their fancy epithets for Athens, quoted by ambassadors who *want* to get something out of her—and he shows how the subject-cities are governed by an imperial democracy (this is an allusion to his play of the previous year, the *Babylonians*), so that their citizens flock to Athens with their tribute to see this brave and candid poet; even the Great King asked a Spartan embassy, first which side had control of the sea, secondly which side had this poet for its satirist, since they must surely win...and so on. The symmetrical 'song-speech pair' which follows has nothing to do with the action of the play either; it is a plea for fair treatment for the elderly who can't keep up with the smart tricks of the young in the law-courts.

The remaining 500 lines of the play are mostly uproarious farce, demonstrating the comic idea in its triumphant realisation. The scenes fall into roughly symmetrical groups, the first of these being the free-trade group. Dicaeopolis declares a private free-trade market, to be kept in order by market-inspectors (three leather straps duly elected by lot). To this come first a Megarian from the south-west, talking broad Megarian, who barters his two hungry small daughters disguised as piglets for a head of garlic and a peck of salt, then a Theban from the north-west, talking broad Boeotian, offering game and fish, particularly a fine Copaic eel. (Humours of non-Attic dialects and foreigners' Greek.) Each of these scenes is interrupted by an informer, the first of whom is chased off by the market-inspectors, while the second is trussed up and handed over to the Theban as a genuine unique Athenian product in exchange for his eel; each scene is rounded off by a choral song about the advantages of peace. There follow some small skirmishes over various claimants to the bartered articles of trade or to a few drops of peace from the bottle.

In the midst of this (1000) a Herald has proclaimed the Feast of Pitchers, with a drinking competition for the prize of a skin of wine. Since Dicaeopolis' household is now living in an oasis of peace and plenty in a war-skimped economy, he makes preparations for the festival on a lavish scale, with a cooking-scene which makes the Chorus's mouth water. Now a cooking-scene implies a domestic interior, which means the eccyclema again. Our stage directions usually require slaves to carry out a brazier from the house, but to cook outside the house-door instead of in the kitchen where all the equipment was would be an eccentric procedure. At 1003 ὦ παῖδες ὦ γυναῖκες οὐκ ἠκούσατε; the roll-out appears again, with brazier and utensils and food and one or two of the household crouched by it, ready to mime cooking-motions when the master calls out his directions. So since Dicaeopolis' household is outside, it is easier for the inside to belong to Lamachus for the time being. For in the following symmetry (let us call the chunk of balancing, paired-off action by this name, for want of a better) Messenger *A* comes to fetch Lamachus to repel a Boeotian raid in wintry weather, while from the opposite side Messenger *B* summons Dicaeopolis to dine with the priest of Dionysus (the kind of dinner where the guests brought the more solid food with them and the host provided the extras—sweetmeats, perfumes, dancing-girls and other attractions). Stage-directions can be deduced from the dialogue; thus at 1096 Dicaeopolis orders: 'Shut up the house, and pack the dinner.' This has caused editors much worry; they complain it is a hysteron proteron. So it would be, of course, but the point is that the eccyclema has first to be rolled in again to clear the stage. Now the peace-champion and the war-champion stand one each side of the stage, and call in turn for their items of baggage to be 'brought out' —παῖ παῖ φέρ' ἔξω δεῦρο. Their respective slaves simply bring the things 'from within'; there is no need for visibly separate houses. There is much ridiculous 'capping' of phraseology and actions—a round shield this side, a round cheese-cake that, Slave *A* holds the spear-case while his master pulls out the spear, Slave *B* holds the spit while his master pulls off the long sausage. Again Lamachus' Gorgon and feathers are conspicuous. Exeunt in opposite directions; an irrelevant little lampoon is sung by the Chorus to mark the passage of time.

The final symmetry is prepared by a messenger-speech—a tragic device, hence a mixture of high-flown description and sudden descents to the commonplace. Lamachus' servant reports his master's wounding—not in heroic action against the enemy, but on a stake as he tried to leap a trench, so that he sprained an ankle and cracked his pate, and startled the Gorgon off his shield, and his beautiful ostrich-plume fell on to the rocks and made a dying speech in the best tragic style. (An odd point here: the failure to observe that the speech is made by the Feather, not by Lamachus, has caused endless trouble; editors struggle vainly with grammar and sense, finding a strange accusative absolute which our grammar-books would not recognise, and a pointless anticlimax: the three lines 1186–8 they often delete in despair, shaking their heads reproachfully at Aristophanes for making Lamachus, who has already a sprained ankle and concussion, first fall into a ditch and then get up and chase people with a spear. Then he appears on the scene—with the original sprained ankle and concussion. Such unfunny nonsense is not in the poet's manner; it is the *Feather* which, heroic to the last, falls into a ditch, bounces up again and bobs after the runaways, prodding them with its quill. All that is necessary is to emend the masculine participles to the neuter—πεσών to πεσόν, etc.) 'Boil a kettle' calls the Servant to Lamachus' house-slaves (the house has reverted to him), 'have ready cotton-wool and splints; here he comes—have the door open ready.' Enter from the one side Lamachus hopping and staggering between two attendants and bemoaning his fate; enter from the other side Dicaeopolis, also staggering (he has won the competition), between two attendant courtesans. The two rivals exchange compliments in pungent but untranslatable style, Lamachus vanishes indoors, and the Chorus swing into line behind Dicaeopolis singing the Victor's Song—τήνελλα καλλίνικος—in the low comic metre, the iambic tetrameter, going off in a κῶμος with the emptied wineskin to claim the prize from the judge.

Old Comedy, as I said at the beginning, is a unique form. It was *political* comedy (using 'political' in the Greek sense), and perhaps the man chiefly responsible for that was Aristophanes' great predecessor Cratinus. But only in that kind of πολιτεία which was an ancient democratic city-state, with its limited size, its un-remote, unbureaucratic forms of government, its concentrated, intensely personal, universally familiar public life, could a primitive type of performance which included the mockery and lampooning of individuals by name have grown into a State-festival performance which included the mockery of powerful figures of State as well as of social and literary public figures, and derided decisions of war and peace and alliances as well as the functioning of law-courts, education, philosophy, modern tragedy and modern music. It mocked good things as well as bad, small pathetic unfortunates as well as the important and the self-important, but its laughter wears better than any other laughter from the past. It could not continue after the fifth century, not only because the Athens that had brought it into being had declined from her precariously held summit of glory, but because its own form was not tough and simple enough for self-renewal. It was too particularised and peculiar, blown up and expanded by a sort of ramshackle multiplication of a structure meant for a smaller, less ambitious and comprehensive type of performance. And it was constantly exposed to the pull of its more august sister, tragedy, in which the actor's part was now absorbing all interest and the Chorus was in rapid decline. Aristophanes' last two surviving plays, *Ecclesiazusae* and *Plutus*, are from the fourth century; they have no parabasis, and *Plutus* has almost no choral interest. They belong already to Middle Comedy, the period of transition to New, whose ancestry is as much tragedy as Old Comedy; it has acquired a coherent plot, character-types, homogeneous structure, and lost the passionate interest in the present, the madness, and the gales of laughter which blew through Aristophanic comedy.

BIBLIOGRAPHY OF THE WRITINGS OF A. M. DALE

BOOKS AND PAPERS

A Junior Ancient History, Methuen, London 1928.

Lyrical clausulae in Sophocles, from *Greek Poetry and Life*, essays presented to Gilbert Murray, Oxford at the University Press (1936), pp. 181–205.

Metrical Observations on Aesch. *Pers.* 922–1001, from *C.Q.* XXXI (1937), 106–10.

The Lyric Metres of Greek Drama, Cambridge at the University Press, 1948.

Stasimon and Hyporcheme, from *Eranos* XLVIII (1950), 14–20.

The Metrical Units of Greek Lyric Verse, I, from *C.Q.* XLIV (1950), 138–48.

The Metrical Units of Greek Lyric Verse, II, from *C.Q.* I (1951), 20–30.

The Metrical Units of Greek Lyric Verse, III, from *C.Q.* I (1951), 119–29.

Κισσύβιον, from *C.R.* II (1952), 129–32.

Euripides: *Alcestis*, Oxford at the University Press, 1954.

An interpretation of Aristophanes, *Vesp.* 136–210 and its consequences for the stage of Aristophanes, from *J.H.S.* LXXVII (1957), 205–11.

Seen and Unseen on the Greek Stage, from *W.S.* LXIX (1956), 95–106.

Resolutions in the Trochaic Tetrameter, from *Glotta* XXXVII (1958), 102–5.

The Hoopoe's Song, from *C.R.* IX (1959), 199–200.

The Transformation of Io, *Ox. Pap.* XXIII, 2369, from *C.R.* X (1960), 194–5.

Ethos and Dianoia: 'Character' and 'Thought' in Aristotle's *Poetics*, from *AUMLA* XI (1959), 3–16.

Words, Music, and Dance, Inaugural Lecture, 1960.

A Heroic End, from *B.I.C.S.* VIII (1961), 47–8.

Stichos and Stanza, from *C.Q.* XIII (1963), 46–50.

Note on Euripides: *Helena* 1441–50, from *Maia* XV (1963), 310–13.

Observations on Dactylic, from *W.S.* LXXVII (1964), 15–36.

'The Chorus in the Action of Greek Tragedy', from *Classical Drama and its Influence*, essays presented to H. D. F. Kitto, ed. M. J. Anderson, Methuen, London (1965), pp. 17–27.

The *Electra* of Sophocles, from *For Service to Classical Studies* (1966), pp. 71–7.

Euripides: *Helen*, Oxford at the University Press, 1967.

The Lyric Metres of Greek Drama (Second Edition), Cambridge at the University Press, 1968.

REVIEW ARTICLE AND REVIEWS

Greek Metric 1936–1957, *Lustrum* II (1957), 5–51.

C.R.

XLVI (1932), 176 Howe and Harrer, *Handbook of Classical Mythology.*
233 Lavedan, *Dictionnaire de la Mythologie.*
XLVIII (1934), 196 Rose, *Hygini fabulae.*
L (1936), 16 Tucker, Translations of Aeschylus *Agamemnon* and *Prometheus Bound.*
68 Untersteiner, *Sofocle.*
171 Tucker, Translation of Aeschylus *Persae.*
LI (1937), 64 Méautis, *Eschyle et la Tragédie.*
79 Koster, *Traité de la métrique grecque.*
169 Moeller, *Untersuchungen zum Desmotes des Aischylos.*
Stoessl, *Die Trilogie des Aischylos.*
LXI (1947), 15 Opstelten, *Sophocles en het Grieksche Pessimisme.*
LXII (1948), 122 Kolar, *De Re Metrica.*
IV (1954), 290 Opstelten, *Sophocles and Greek Pessimism.*
V (1955), 37 Irigoin, *Recherches sur les mètres de la lyrique chorale grecque.*
39 Letters, *The Life and Work of Sophocles.*
204 Koster, *Traité de la métrique grecque.*
VI (1956), 105 Dain–Mazon, *Sophocle* i.
X (1960), 16 Dain–Mazon, *Sophocle* ii.
XII (1962), 21 Dain–Mazon, *Sophocle* iii.
157 del Grande, *La Metrica Greca.*
XVI (1966), 204 Dain, *Traité de métrique grecque.*

Gnomon

(1952), 234 Höhl, *Responsionsfreiheiten bei Pindar.*
(1953), 442 Martin, *Essai sur les rythmes de la chanson grecque antique.*
(1956), 192 Snell, *Griechische Metrik.*

J.H.S.

LXIII (1943), 135 Little, *Myth and Society in Attic Drama.*
LXX (1950), 86 Van Lennep, *Euripides: the Alkestis.*
LXXVI (1956), 115 Jackson, *Marginalia Scaenica.*
LXXVII (1957), 325 *Symbolae Osloenses*, 31, 1955.
LXXIX (1959), 165 Strohm, *Euripides*, *Zetemata* 15.
LXXXI (1961), 163 Srebrny, *Studia scaenica.*
LXXXII (1962), 161 Fondation Hardt. Entretiens VI. *Euripide.*
171 Thomson, *Greek Lyric Metre.*
LXXXIV (1964), 166 Bond, *Euripides Hypsipyle.*
LXXXV (1965), 188 Rossi, *Metrica e critica stilistica.*

INDEX LOCORUM

TRAGEDY

AESCHYLUS

Agamemnon
104–59: 189 f.
121: 10
153: 201
225–6: 11
355 ff.: 3
452–5: 2
471–4: 2
489 ff.: 215
587: 219
681 ff.: 5, 11
717–36: 188 f.
855: 219
1539: 267
1548: 199
also pp. 122, 123, 144, 147, 219–20, 252, 264, 267, 277–8

Choephori
469–70: 8
639 ff.: 12
653: 119
712: 120
875: 120
875 ff.: 269
also pp. 146, 264, 267, 279

Eumenides
47: 123
140 ff.: 123, 124
179: 124
582: 212
685 ff.: 120
892 ff.: 213
996: 199
also pp. 123, 211, 213, 264, 270 f., 415 ff., 212

Persae
107: 21
125 ff.: 12
140–9: 119
150–2: 180
171: 133
556–7: 8
566–7: 8
575–83: 206
720: 133
922–1001: 25 ff.
also pp. 36, 216, 256, 260 ff., 269

Prometheus
128: 33
132: 11, 17
133: 33
135: 11, 17
166: 197
272: 264
400: 33
406: 33
408: 33
526–44: 59
588: 10, 12
also pp. 121, 254, 257, 262, 263, 270

Septem
89: 33
180 ff.: 213
185: 119
265: 119
677 ff.: 213
also pp. 211, 216, 255, 263

Supplices
96: 20
165: 10, 14
189: 119
222: 263
234: 212
438 ff.: 212
524 ff.: 5, 197
625 ff.: 3
also pp. 210, 211

Fragments
pp. 117, 121, 124, 262, 264, 270

SOPHOCLES

Ajax
172 ff.: 60, 205
181: 9
192 ff.: 9, 13
193: 6
199–200: 7
224: 5
226: 16
232: 5
329: 123
344 f.: 123
400: 8
420: 8
457 ff.: 153–4
582: 21
596 ff.: 8
597: 8
604: 8
629: 21
634: 21
646 ff.: 154
667: 155
693 ff.: 13, 39
701: 10, 17
713: 4
718: 4
1191: 8, 16
1199 ff.: 6
1201: 6
also pp. 120–2, 125, 146, 216, 222, 264, 270, 278

Antigone
140: 16
154: 16
332 ff.: 205, 207
341: 206
353 ff.: 8
361: 20
362: 8
364: 20
610: 13
613: 13
614: 5, 13, 14

Antigone (cont.)
624–5: 14
781–2: 16
789–90: 16
857 ff.: 15
867–8: 15
881–2: 202
904 ff.: 153
966 ff.: 194, 197, 198
976: 5
1115 ff.: 252
1132: 31
1186: 104
1293: 122
also pp. 146, 215, 222, 224, 279

Electra
56–64: 228
121–250: 3, 208
127: 4
135: 13, 199
152: 13
172: 3
233–5: 48
249–50: 4
479: 9
486–7: 9
504 ff.: 8
505: 6
515: 6
616 ff.: 229
853: 21
1058 ff.: 16
1062: 17
1066–8: 21
1069: 5
1074: 17
1390: 5
1427 f.: 226
also pp. 207, 218, 221 ff.

Oedipus Coloneus
9–10: 125
19: 126
59: 125
84–110: 126
117: 112
118 ff.: 15
129: 10, 15, 17
132–3: 15
165: 15
192–206: 3, 126
229 ff.: 209
241 ff.: 209
461: 214
513: 14
518: 14
520: 14
540–7: 209
668 ff.: 36
676–89: 208
679–80: 15
700–3: 22, 24
702: 6
703–6: 21, 23
716–19: 21
717: 21
888: 133
1074 ff.: 15
1140: 23
1239 ff.: 9
1248: 16
1455–6: 12
1536: 23
1674–1702: 209
1734–6: 202
also pp. 214, 216, 219, 228, 254

Oedipus Tyrannus
151 ff.: 5, 6, 207
158: 5
171–3: 207
202: 5
463 ff.: 15
469–70: 14
511: 5
863 ff.: 13
871: 14
872: 8, 14
881–2: 14
900: 9
902: 9
910: 9
1061: 223
1086 ff.: 15, 20, 39
1096–7: 8
1187: 18
1189: 9
1196: 9, 31
1197: 18
also pp. 214–17, 222, 223, 278, 279

Philoctetes
19: 199
145 ff.: 128
169 ff.: 3
179: 5
206–8: 17
209–18: 18, 20
211: 128
687–9: 17
814: 127
827 ff.: 9
861: 208
1000: 127
1081–1100: 3
1081–1218: 208, 209
1176–7: 20
1180: 19, 20
1205: 201
1405: 133
also pp. 127, 129, 216, 219, 222, 228, 279

Trachiniae
216: 38
223–4: 7
848–9: 13
860: 13
879 ff.: 7
890: 7
892: 7
904–11: 224
1259: 33
also pp. 205, 206, 216, 222 ff., 276, 278

Fragments
pp. 10, 16, 137 f.

EURIPIDES
Alcestis
136–7: 180
244: 196
463: 207
464–74: 199
546 ff.: 126
576–7: 12
756: 101
also pp. 146, 216, 268

Andromache
125: 4
501 ff.: 3

Andromache (*cant.*)
1173 ff.: 205
also p. 216

Bacchae
72: 21
509: 126
591: 124
613: 132
862–911: 3
881: 10
also pp. 125, 218, 219, 256

Cyclops
151: 101
222: 105
354–6: 183
388 ff.: 101
390 f.: 99
426–7: 129
599: 184
701 ff.: 129
706: 199

Electra
112–212: 3
260: 274 f.
553–4: 274 f.
859 ff.: 39
also pp. 227 ff., 274 f.

Hecuba
97: 30
143: 198
905 ff.: 8, 23

Helen
375–80: 138, 205
1050–6: 228
1093–1106: 182
1180: 126
1441–50: 180 ff.
1635: 133
also pp. 217, 227

Heraclidae
608 ff.: 205

Hercules Furens
339–47: 182
348–441: 3
501: 181
570: 181
847 ff.: 182
863: 132
905–9: 124
998–1000: 124
1029: 123
also pp. 152, 264

Hippolytus
114–20: 182
141 ff.: 8
170–1: 121
741: 12, 18
751: 18
808: 122
905: 122
1109–16: 207
1110: 5
1130: 5
also pp. 170, 217, 254, 266, 278

Ion
436–51: 182
453–509: 4
468–9: 23
1059–60: 12
1254: 132
also pp. 125, 217, 227, 255, 261, 275 f., 284

Iphigeneia Aulidensis
164 ff.: 3
356: 133
394: 131
542: 219
799–800: 12
859: 132
869: 133
884: 132
886: 132
911: 131
1322: 30
1349: 132
1354: 132
also p. 219

Iphigeneia Taurica
65: 180
113: 112
570: 181
1082–8: 183
1205: 133
1230–3: 183
1232: 131
also pp. 8, 112, 125, 217, 227, 254

Medea
96 ff.: 112
131 ff.: 198
136: 207
410–30: 59
419–20: 15
824 ff.: 59
1081 ff.: 35
also pp. 216–17, 274, 279

Orestes
140: 37
149–50: 48
738: 132
740: 133
790: 133
797: 131
962: 20
966: 20
970: 20
1300: 197
1366 ff.: 126–7, 268 f.
1391: 197
1524: 131
1561–2: 104
also pp. 229, 255, 279

Phoenissae
84–7: 183
202 ff.: 3, 37–8
248–9: 12
607: 131
636: 133
784–832: 205
1018–66: 4
1294–5: 12
also p. 184

Supplices
277: 201
372–4, 376: 20
606: 5
625: 5
804–10: 206
990 ff.: 3

Supplices (*cont.*)
1123 ff.: 4
also p. 211

Troades
1312: 136
also pp. 8, 152, 216, 279

Fragments

Andromeda
pp. 101, 183, 206

Hypsipyle
p. 207

Telephus
pp. 172, 286 f., 288

Incert.
p. 133

COMEDY

ARISTOPHANES
Acharnenses
20: 285
104: 285
130: 286
204: 35
262: 112
318: 286
384: 287
402–6: 287
407 ff.: 124
470: 288
627: 289
740–5: 138
1000: 291
1003: 291
1096: 109, 291
1174–88: 170 ff., 292
also pp. 107, 108, 111 f., 121, 265 f., 281 ff.

Aves
227 ff.: 135–6
328: 136
749: 205
1753–4: 207
also pp. 283, 287

Ecclesiazusae
33–4: 111
199: 111
327: 111, 113
729: 110
877 ff.: 111, 112
879: 112
884: 112
924: 112
934–76: 112
989–90: 113
also pp. 107, 110–11, 293

Equites
488: 115
565: 134

Lysistrata
615: 290
also pp. 107–9, 282–3

Nubes
1–132: 114 ff.
132–255: 115
181–99: 124
183 ff.: 114
288–90: 207
508: 115
801–3: 115
812: 23
843–89: 116
1105–1212: 116
1212–1485: 114
1485: 116
also pp. 107, 110–11, 113–16, 267, 283

Pax
82–172: 117
116: 201
223: 117
232: 115
427: 117
663: 118
720: 117
also pp. 57, 113, 116–18, 266, 282–3, 285

Plutus
pp. 107, 111, 293

Ranae
323: 33
330: 32
350: 33
1058–9: 147
1281: 38
1299: 205
also pp. 107–8, 171, 255–6, 283, 285

Thesmophoriazusae
96 ff.: 124
276: 114
797: 112
also pp. 110, 114, 265 f., 288

Vespae
130 ff.: 104
136–210: 103 ff.
270: 37
367 ff.: 104
408: 290
1482–4: 105, 106
also p. 284

MENANDER
Dyskolos
879: 173

Perikeiromene
50: 131
148: 134

LYRIC ETC.

ALCAEUS
L–P
5 (118 D^2): 96, 193
10 (123 D^2): 94
67: 193
70 (43 D^2): 92, 94
73 (46B D^2): 95
354 (14 D^2): 70, 91
357 (54 D^2): 91, 93
368 (99 D^2): 92
376 (34 D^2): 90, 91
380 (68 D^2): 94
383 (40 D^2): 58, 93
384 (63 D^2): 93
387 (15 D^2): 92
93 D^2: 91
new frag. 24 C: 96

ALCMAN
PMG
1: 84 ff., 175, 178, 194 f., 199 f.
3: 200
14 (7 D^2): 178
16 (13 D^2): 178
19 (55 D^2): 177 f.
26 (94 D^2): 243
27 (67 D^2): 191 f., 200
30 (10 D^2): 177
56 (37 D^2): 85, 194 f., 201
57 (43 D^2): 84
89 (58 D^2): 84
91 (105 D^2): 194 f.
96 (50 D^2): 177
adespota 974 (117 D^2): 178

ANACREON
PMG
358 (5 D^2): 88
388 (54 D^2): 87–8
408 (39 D^2): 32, 88

ANONYMOUS SCOLIA
PMG
884–90 (1–7 D^2): 96
892 (9 D^2): 96
893 (10 D^2): 96
897 (14 D^2): 96
902–5 (19–22 D^2): 96, 194
35 D^2: 97

ARCHILOCHUS
60: 134
64: 134
74: 132, 134
112: 177
P. Oxy. xxii (1951), 2310: 176
also p. 202

BACCHYLIDES
Epinician
3: 63
Snell
16: 72
17: 69, 70, 77
18: 71, 72, 76
19: 71, 82
20*b*: 58, 83
21: 58

CALLIMACHUS
Aetia
frag. 178 Pf.: 100

CORINNA
PMG
654: 88

HOMER
Iliad
xviii. 478 ff.: 158

Odyssey
viii. 378–82: 158
ix. 346: 100
xvi. 52: 100

IBYCUS
PMG
282 (3 D^2): 85, 194, 195, 199, 201, 204
286 (6 D^2): 85, 195

PINDAR
Ol.
1: 64 ff., 68, 69, 73, 77
2: 62, 77 f.
4: 73, 75
6: 56
7: 56, 63, 67
9: 46, 72
10: 66, 68, 73, 75, 76, 77
13: 63, 64
14: 75

Pyth.
1: 59
2: 74
3: 56, 58
5: 66, 74 f.
8: 70–4
9: 59, 63, 73
10: 69
12: 54

Nem.
1: 55, 75
3: 67, 70
4: 73
6: 75 ff.
7: 47, 70, 71, 73
8: 55, 59, 73
10: 63
11: 63

Isth.
3–4: 74
8: 72

Paean
2: 70
6: 75

Fragments
97: 39

PRATINAS
Hyporcheme
39, 167–8

PRAXILLA
PMG
750: 194

SAPPHO
L–P
1: 93
49: 92
53 (57 D^2): 93

SAPPHO (*cont.*)
81: 93
82 (63 D²): 95
94 (96 D²): 96, 193
95 (97 D²): 90, 91, 94, 96
96 (98 D²): 90, 91, 94, 96, 193
100 (85 D²): 94
102 (114 D²): 94
110 (124 D²): 92, 192
112+116 (128 D²): 94
113 (130 D²): 94
127 (154 D²): 94
128 (90 D²): 93
130: 192
131 (137 D²): 91, 192
132 (152 D²): 94
133 (144*a* and *b* D²): 91
135 (86 D²): 94
136 (121 D²): 92
140 (107 D²): 92
141 (135–6 D²): 90
151 (106 D²): 92
154 (88 D²): 90
158 (126 D²): 93, 94
inc. 13 (93 D²): 92, 95
inc. 21 (148 D²): 93
156 D²: 93

PMG
976 (94 D²): 90

SIMONIDES
PMG
509 (23 D²): 80
521 (6 D²): 83
531 (5 D²): 81
542 (4 D²): 80
543 (13 D²): 44, 80
555 (30 D²): 81
564 (32 D²): 82
571 (28 D²): 58
579 (37 D²): 82
581 (48 D²): 80
584 (57 D²): 80
595 (40 D²): 58
76 D²: 97

STESICHORUS
Oresteia
57

PMG
187 (10 D²): 57
223 (17 D²): 57
232 (22 D²): 57
P. Oxy.
2359–60: 200

THEOCRITUS
i. 27: 98 ff.

Ep.
20: 203

GENERAL INDEX

Abelard, 234, 243
Actor, 276 ff., 284, 293
Adding Machine, The, 272
Adonean, 5, 6 7, 16, 62, 90, 208
Aeolic, 60, 62 f., 80–97, 188, 192, 196 f., 209, 257
Aeolic base, 67 f., 70, 84, 90, 186, 194, 197 f.
Aeolo-choriambic, 87, 205 f., 209
Aeschylus, 1–33, 66, 147, 177, 204, 207, 210 ff., 227, 253, 260, 263, 267 ff. *et passim*
Agon, 151 f., 216, 282, 287
Alcaeus, 52, 84, 86, 89–96, 163
Alcaic, 5, 10 f., 16, 85, 93, 95 f., 196 f., 199
Alcman, 52, 84–9, 174 ff., 194, 196, 201, 205
Aly, 37
Anaclasis, 20 f., 23 f., 43, 50, 88, 256
Anacreon, 43, 52, 87 ff., 91, 94, 257
Anacreontic, 33, 44, 56, 94, 257
Anacrusis, 6
Ananius, 134
Anapaestic, 8, 14 f., 25–32, 35, 47, 56, 62, 85, 117, 130 ff., 136, 198, 240, 243, 254 f., 283, 289 f.
Anceps, 13 f., 29, 32, 43, 49 ff., 53–9, 61–79, 82, 84, 86 f., 89 ff., 94 ff., 130, 175, 179, 185–209; different types of, 50, 185 ff.; *see also* Duration of syllables
Anouilh, 147
Antispast, 22, 43, 192 f.
Archilochian, 9, 15, 32
Archilochus, 86 f., 91, 94, 174–7, 202 f., 210
Ariphron, 45, 59
Aristarchus, 159
Aristides, 186
Aristophanean, 197, 199
Aristophanes, 57, 103–18, 135–6, 207, 255, 265 ff., 281–94
Aristophanes of Byzantium, 121
Aristotle, 34 ff., 45, 139–55, 176, 211, 272
Aristoxenus, 174
Arne, Thomas, 164
Arnott, W. G., 130
Arsis and thesis, 41, 49, 186
Asclepiad, 8, 22, 84, 92, 94 ff., 192 ff.
Asynarteton, 202 f.
Athenaeus, 39, 98, 100 ff., 134, 158 f., 168

Bacchiac, 6, 7, 66, 77, 95, 186, 188, 206
Bacchylides 45, 52, 54, 57 ff., 63, 80 ff., 89, 91, 189
Beare, W., 104 f., 122
Beggar's Opera, The, 164
Bergk, 72, 91, 168, 174
Bethe, 264, 288
Blaydes, 26
Blomfield, 27 f., 32
Boeckh, 45
Boito, 165
Brachycatalexis, 6, 9, 59
Brevis in longo, 45, 56, 59, 67, 71, 75, 85, 95 f., 185–209 *passim*
Bridges, Robert, 234
Browning, Robert, 153
Bruhn, 4, 16, 229
Brunck, 27, 32
Budé editors, 106, 113, 117, 170
Bulle, 107
Burney, 29

Caesura, 17, 19, 88, 106, 130 f., 195, 240; of colon, 88, 91; of metron, 190
Callimachus, 179, 203
Campbell, 18, 22
Catalexis, 3, 6, 21, 23, 32, 43, 45 f., 87, 95, 135 f., 175, 187 ff., 202, 205, 208
Cato, 102
Chantraine–Irigoin, 178
Chatzidakis, 99
Chaucer, 241, 244
Choral lyric, non-dramatic, 41–97, 160, 163, 253
Choriambic, 1–24 *passim*, 27, 31, 42, 88, 91–4, 250, 257
Chorodidaskalos, 34, 41
Chorus, 210–20, 259, 272, 281 ff., 287, 293
Clausula, 1–24, 59, 79, 84 f., 87 f., 184–209, 256
Cobet, 114 f.
Cola, 1, 13, 16, 19, 31 ff., 43 ff., 54, 58 f., 80–97, 178, 189 ff., 199, 202, 204, 252 f., 258 *et passim*

Comedy, 1, 35, 37, 44 f., 52 f., 84, 88, 103–18, 133, 153, 163, 179, 186, 237, 250, 253 f., 268, 278 ff., 281–94
Compound rhythm, 49, 89, 92 f.
Contraction, 43, 50 f., 55, 68, 73, 75, 77, 163, 174, 186 f., 197, 206, 208, 255
Corinna, 52, 88 f.
Correption, 33, 198, 251
Coryphaeus, 28, 35
Cratinus, 203, 293
Cretic, 7, 10, 12, 16, 95, 131, 133 f., 176, 186 f., 192, 198
Cretic-molossus, 254
Cretic-paeonic, 36, 39, 66, 253 f., 286
Crowfoot, 137

Da Ponte, 165
Dactylic, 5 f., 10, 12 f., 19, 30, 43, 51, 56 f., 75, 84 ff., 130 ff., 185–209; dactylic dimeter, 205; *see also* Final syllable
Dactylo-anapaest, 57 f.
Dactylo-epitrite, 9 f., 15, 32, 53–60, 61–97, 185, 200, 204 f., 251
Dactylo-iambic, 82
Dactyls, accentual, 234, 238, 241, 243; aeolic, 43, 192 f., 197, 199, 204; cyclic, 43; lyric, 198
Dance, 34–40, 53, 68, 77, 136, 156–69, 176, 179, 186, 249, 251, 253, 262, 289
Denniston, 215, 274
Diaeresis, 2, 13 f., 21, 31, 33, 54, 72, 75, 78, 82, 85, 134, 202 f., 206, 240 f.
Dianoia, 139–55, 211, 280
Didymus, 168
Diehl, 91
Dindorf, 8, 18, 21, 33
Dionysius of Halicarnassus, 187, 190
Dionysius of Samos, 100
Dithyramb, 39, 57, 82, 140
Dochmiac, 5, 8, 10–13, 25–33, 48, 50, 61, 66, 68, 77, 135 f., 208, 226, 254 f., 258, 287
Double-short unit, 49 ff., 53 ff., 63 ff., 73, 77, 87, 89 ff., 202 *et passim*
Dowland, 162
Drag, 8, 16, 51, 59, 63 f., 67 f., 70–3, 75, 77, 81, 84, 91
Duration of syllables, 66, 77, 162, 175, 185 ff., 188, 191, 204, 258; *see also* Anceps

Eccyclema, 109, 113–18, 120–7, 259–71, 285, 287 f., 291 f.
Elegiac, 97, 191, 237
Elegiambus, 197, 200
Elmsley, 15, 26, 198 f.
Encomia, 57
Encomiologus, 54, 58, 93
English verse, 234, 238, 241 f., 244 ff., 248 ff., 258
Enneasyllable, 15 ff., 21, 60, 93, 178
Ennius, 235 ff., 241
Enoplius, 9, 17, 84
Epicharmus, 100, 133
Epinicians, 57, 83
ἐπιπλοκή, 49, 50, 95
Epirrhematic syzygy, 283, 290
Epitrite, 20, 53, 58
Epode, 5, 6, 9, 56, 63, 79, 177, 202 f., 251
Erbse, H., 171
Ethos, 139–55, 221 ff., 272–80
Euripides, 1–24, 108 f., 132 f., 146, 151 f., 205, 209, 211, 216 ff., 227 ff., 255, 274, 287 f., *et passim*

Favorinus, 83
Final syllable, whether 'true short', 187, 190 ff., 200–9; *see also* Anceps
Flute, 39, 159, 163, 167 f., 173, 289
Folk-art, 157 f., 178 f.
Fraenkel, 110 ff., 135 f., 194, 196 f.
French verse, 239 ff., 244 ff., 248, 250
Friedländer, 206
Fritzsche, 99

German verse, 238 f., 243–6
Gielgud, 277
Gilbert and Sullivan, 156, 163, 165
Glyconic, 2, 3, 6, 8, 12, 16–18, 21 f., 24, 44, 47, 66, 70, 76, 87 f., 90 f., 93, 96, 188 f., 192 ff., 197, 252
Golenishchev-Kutuzov, 246
Gow, A. S. F., 98, 101
Green Table, The, 277
Gudeman, 35

Headless unit, 56, 62 f., 66, 68 f., 77, 97
Heber, Bishop, 234
Heliodorus, 178
Hellenistic verse, 173, 203
Hemiepes, 10, 12, 15, 187, 189, 197
Hephaestion, 32, 39, 43, 86, 90, 93 f., 176 f., 185–209

Hermann, 6, 22, 23, 26, 27, 28, 31, 32, 33, 34, 76, 103, 178, 181, 194, 198
Hermippus, 134
Herodotus, 98, 154
Hesiod, 160
Hexameter, 43, 86, 89, 163, 173 f., 179, 187, 201, 237 f., 253
Hiatus, 15, 28, 33, 45 f., 59, 72, 75, 78, 85, 95 f., 136, 188 f., 201, 203, 209
Hipponactean, 3, 8, 15, 16, 60, 90, 194
Hipponax, 134
Hopkins, Gerard Manley, 241
Housman, A. E., 258
Hymn to Apollo, 159, 164
Hypercatalexis, 6, 178
Hyporcheme, 34–40, 167

Iambelegus, 60, 93, 136, 187
Iambic, 1–24, 36, 44, 62, 163, 173 f., 188, 232 f., 238, 242, 245, 252, 293 *et passim*
Iambo-choriambic, 87 f., 197
Iambo-dactylic, 205, 207
Iambo-dochmiac, 66, 255
Iambo-trochaic, 67, 177 f., 185, 196, 206
Ibsen, 144, 147, 280
Ibycean, 85, 195 f., 199 f.
Ibycus, 52, 84 f., 88 f., 196, 205
Ictus, 232 f., 237 f., 241, 245 ff., 250 f., 257
Initial syllable, in Pindar, 77; in trimeter, 186; *see also* Aeolic base, Anceps
Insect Play, The, 277
Inversion, 242 f., 245
Ionic, 2, 5 f., 11, 19–24, 26 f., 32 f., 36 f., 43 f., 55 f., 75, 86, 88, 90, 93 f., 136, 188, 256 f.
Iono-anacreontic, 87 f.
Irony, 154, 217 f., 275
Italian verse, 238 f., 241, 243 ff.
Ithyphallic, 4 f., 9, 11 ff., 15, 20, 29, 59, 94, 202, 206, 209, 256

Jackson, 208
Jebb, 6 f., 18, 22, 104, 128
Junction of metrical units, 50, 63, 65 *et passim*; *see also* Anceps

Kaibel, 91, 100
Keats, 248
Kirchhoff, 180
Knights, L. C., 275
Kommos, 3, 7, 13, 34 ff., 208 f., 214, 267
Koster, 186
Kranz, 36
Kraus, W., 197, 206
κῶμος, 41, 282, 293

Lachmann, 18, 27, 32
Latin verse, 169, 235–40
Lawes, Henry, 164
Lecythion, 9, 12, 20, 27, 66, 94, 189
Lesbian lyric, 58, 66, 70, 83, 86 f., 89, 94 ff., 193 f., 197, 204
Lesky, 228
Letters, 221
Lloyd-Jones, 137, 198
Lobel, 93, 137
Logaoedic, 9 f.
Longinus, 280
Longus, 101
Lucian, 38, 99, 101
Lyre, 86, 97, 158 ff., 163, 174

Maas, P., 7, 41, 53, 60, 67, 75, 77, 83 f., 195
Mair, 70
Margites, 174
Mariandynian, 31
Masefield, 161, 242 f.
Matthiae, 133
Mazon, 27
μηχανή, 115 f., 263 f.
Medieval Latin verse, 231, 233 ff., 240 f., 246
Meineke, 22, 25, 28
Melos, 35
Menander, 108, 146, 279
Meredith, 241
Metra, 42 ff., 58, 82, 86, 130–4 *et passim*
Milton, 164
Molossus, 14
Mommsen, 78
Monosyllables, 31, 133, 162, 175, 239, 241 ff.
Moore, Thomas, 164
Mortimer, Raymond, 258
Mozart, 156, 165
Murray, Gilbert, 68, 110, 255
Musgrave, 180
Music, 2, 41 f., 68, 136, 140 f., 156–69, 173 f., 191, 209, 230–47, 248, 255, 293

Nauck, 7, 16, 19, 22, 30, 133, 181

O'Casey, Sean, 277
Olivier, 277

Orchestra, 34, 210, 259, 264, 267
Ovid, 237
Owen, A. S., 275 f.

Paean, 39
Paeon, 186
Page, D. L., 171 f., 185, 215, 274
Paley, 199
Palimbacchiac, 75
Parabasis, 109, 111, 115 f., 118, 281 ff., 289 f., 293
Paraceleusmatic, 29
Paraskenia, 107 f., 259, 268, 284
Parodoi, 108, 118, 128, 259, 267, 270 f., 285 f.
Parodos, 34
Paroemiac, 2, 25 ff., 30, 32 f., 48, 55, 85 f., 136, 188, 198, 207
Pause, 2, 10, 12–14, 17, 19, 21, 185–209, 239, 241, 252
Paxinou, Mme, 221, 229
Pearson, 6 f., 9, 16, 18, 22, 181, 207
Penthemimer, 29, 33, 178
Period, 14 f., 41–97, 185, 207 *et passim*; major and minor periods, 86
Pfeiffer, 137
Phalaecean, 4, 15, 21, 71, 91, 96, 194, 203
Phales-song, 286
Pherecratean, 1–24, 47, 70, 87 f., 188 f., 192, 194
Philemon, 100
Phrynichus, 177, 205, 262
Pickard-Cambridge, 107, 109, 262, 264 f., 267, 288
Pindar, 39, 41–79, 80, 82, 89, 91, 156, 162, 163, 189, 195, 230, 251
Pitch accent, 48, 162, 230, 236 ff., 245, 250
Platnauer, 180
Plato, 38, 118, 139 f., 147
Plautus, 108, 237
Pliny, 102
Plot, 139–55, 221 f., 273, 276, 279, 294
Plutarch, 36, 39, 167, 173 f., 176
Pnigos, 5, 16 f., 209, 254, 283
Pohlenz, 39
Pollux, 264 f.
Porson's law, 175
Powell and Barber, 68
Praxis, 143
Priapean, 2, 5, 11, 21, 22, 23, 24, 44, 47
Primary rhythmic units, 49 *et passim*; *see also* Double-short *and* Single-short
Priscian, 178
Prolongation, 49, 50, 63, 65, 67, 89 ff., 94 f., 240, 251
Prosodiac, 44, 55, 254 f.
Prosodion, 39, 57
Protraction, 185 f.
Pseudo-Arion, 45
Pyrrhic, 55

Quantitative verse, 49, 52, 161, 173, 179, 230–47, 250 f.

Radermacher, 6 f., 9, 19, 22 f., 174
Recitative, 35, 51, 86 f., 163, 173, 210, 236, 253
Red Balloon, The, 172
Refrain, 10 f., 13, 190
Reinhardt, 228
Reisch, 264
Reizianum, 4, 9 ff., 13, 15 f., 32, 47, 61, 70, 252
Repetition, *see* Compound rhythm
Resolution, 23, 43, 50 f., 55, 63 f., 68 f., 73 ff., 77 f., 89, 130–4, 163, 170, 186, 194, 197, 255
Responsion, 1, 5, 8, 17 f., 29 f., 30, 32 f., 37, 39, 43, 47 f., 52, 68, 75, 80, 82, 84, 88, 90, 161, 164, 178, 187 f., 194 f., 200, 236, 283 *et passim*
Rhyme, 135, 238 ff., 241, 244, 246
Rhythm, 2, 12, 19 f., 23 f., 36, 43, 45 f., 48 f., 57, 59, 81, 86, 88, 136, 160, 162, 164, 166, 178, 186, 205, 230–58, 284 *et passim*
Robertson, Donald, 41
Roebuck, 158
Rossi, L. E., 185
Rupprecht, 130
Russian verse, 245 f.

Sapphic, 44, 93, 95; *see also* Lesbian lyric
Sappho, 52, 84, 86, 89–96, 163
Saturnian metre, 235, 237, 240
Satyr-play, 39, 101, 167, 263
Scandinavian verse, 238, 244 f.
Scenery, 105 ff., 119, 125, 259, 284
Schmid-Stählin, 36 f., 39
Schneidewin, 16, 19, 22
Schoenborn, 114
Schroeder, 4, 7, 9, 19, 23, 28 f., 31, 33, 70, 73 f., 76, 135 f.

Scolia, 52, 87, 89, 90, 96 f., 164
Seel and Pöhlmann, 169
Semonides, 176
Seneca, 191
Shaw, Bernard, 147, 276
Shelley, 243
Silenus, 100
Simonides, 45, 52, 57, 80 ff., 89, 97, 189
Single-short unit, 49 ff., 53 ff., 63 ff., 73, 77, 87, 89 ff., 93, 200 ff. *et passim*
Skene, 107, 112, 116 f., 124 f., 199, 259, 261 ff., 264, 284 f.
Skene steps, 108, 111, 118, 119, 125 f., 262 f., 267 f., 271, 285
Snell, Bruno, 41, 174, 195 f., 202
Solo lyric, 34, 45, 52, 53, 58, 86 f., 163, 208 f., 211, 253, 255
Sonnet, 244
Sophocles, 1–24, 41, 47, 51, 152, 154 f., 199, 205, 217, 221–9, 263 *et passim*
Speech-rhythm, 48, 230–47 *et passim*
Spondaic, 8 f., 13 f., 18, 28, 68, 72, 81, 85, 178, 206; *see also* Drag
Stage-door, 104, 107, 111 ff., 120 ff., 126 f., 259, 264 ff., 284, 287
Staircase, backstage, 103, 112, 263 f.
Stanza, 173–9 *et passim*
Stasimon, 34–40
Stephanus, 90
Stesichorean, 53 f.
Stesichorus, 45, 52, 57, 89, 200 f.
Stichic verse, 51, 57, 86 f., 89 f., 92 ff., 173–9, 188, 192 f., 203, 240
Stichomythia, 212, 274 f., 277
Stobaeus, 84
Stress, 48, 162 f., 174, 230–47, 250
Suda, Suidas, 38, 177
Syllable-counting, 84, 89, 163, 230, 233, 238 f., 241, 245 ff.
Symmetry, in verse, 17, 45, 49, 89, 176; on stage, 114, 119, 126, 128, 267 f.; in comedy, 283, 290 ff.
Synaphea, 33, 85 f., 89, 188 ff., 190 f., 193, 195 f., 201 f., 204 ff., 208
Synartete, 31
Syncopation, 15, 20, 43, 50, 186, 188, 198, 202, 204, 206, 252
Systems, 85–8

Tchaikovsky, 166
Telesillean, 8, 9, 13 ff., 23, 70, 252
Tennyson, 248
Terence, 108
Terzaghi, 181
Theatre of Dionysus, 108 f.
Theocritus, 98–102, 203 f.
Thespis, 167, 177, 210, 261
Thomson, G., 262
Thomson, James, 164
Threnos, 25, 35, 57, 83, 224
Timocreon, 53, 87
Timotheus, 101 f., 255
Trendall, 100
Triadic, 11, 28 f., 45, 52, 73, 82 f., 87, 194 f., 201, 205
Triclinius, 15, 19, 22, 33, 198
Trochaic, 2, 4, 7, 11 f., 19, 35 f., 58, 62, 84, 130–4, 167, 174 f., 202, 232 f., 238, 240, 242, 244 f. *et passim*
Turyn, 70, 74, 75
Tzetzes, 36, 38, 40

Unity of space, 109 ff., 119 ff., 124, 215, 262, 268 ff., 281, 285

Van Leeuwen, 105 f., 113
Verdi, 165
Virgil, 239
Vitelli, 198 f.
Von Blumenthal, 146

Wagner, 248
Waldock, 221, 225, 229
Webster, T. B. L., 158
Wecklein, 26
Weil, 27, 30
Welcker, 194
Westphal, 35
Wilamowitz, 2, 6 f., 9 f., 14, 16, 18 ff., 23, 25–33, 59, 70, 76, 81, 109, 124, 167, 171, 178, 206, 261
Winnington-Ingram, R. P., 125
Wolf, G., 6
Wolf, Hugo, 165, 168
Women in Sophocles, 222 ff.
Word, beginning, middle, end, in metre, 130 f., 135, 174 f., 190, 202, 209, 230 ff., 234, 240 *et passim*
Wunder, 18, 21

Xenodamus, 39

Zeugmata, 175
Zieliński, 228
Zuntz, 228 f.